Strategic Market Management

'The truism that business is becoming more global is perceived as an opportunity for many business leaders, but as a painful reality for others.

The first edition of Professor McLoughlin's book addressed the necessity for leaders to understand how to prepare for their future while this much-anticipated edition addresses these issues from a more global perspective. It contains a balance of analysis and case studies, supporting business leaders' understanding of future competitive space, along with the greatest opportunities for profitability.

I would highly recommend Professor McLoughlin's book to anyone who cares about the future of their business.'

Aidan Connolly, Vice President of Alltech.

'Any manager seeking to develop a market driving strategy or any student wanting to learn about best practice in strategic marketing needs to read this book. The Global edition of Strategic Market Management offers readers a real opportunity to get to grips with the issues facing firms wishing to have an effective market driving strategy in the new global environment.'

Sarah Everitt, Google Marketing Academy (EMEA)

CONTENTS

PREFACE

Developing and implementing strategies is now very different to only a few decades ago, when the business environments were more stable and simpler. Every market can now be described as dynamic. As a result, firms need to be able to adapt strategies in order to stay relevant. It is a challenging but exciting time, full of opportunities as well as threats.

This edition of *Strategic Market Management: Global Perspectives* is motivated by the strategic challenges created by the dynamic nature of markets. The premise is that all traditional strategic management tools either do not apply or need to be adapted to a more dynamic context.

The unique aspects of the book are its inclusion of:

- A business strategy definition that includes product/market scope, value proposition, and assets and competences. Too often the business strategy concept is vague and ill-defined, leading to a diffused focus and weak communication.
- A structured strategic analysis, including a detailed customer, competitor, market, and environmental analysis, leading to an understanding of market dynamics that is supported by a summary flow diagram, a set of agendas to help start the process, and a set of planning forms.
- Concepts of strategic commitment, opportunism, and adaptability and how they can and should be blended together.
- Growing the business by energizing the business, leveraging the business, creating new business, and going global. Each option has its own risks and rewards, and all should be on the table.
- Bases of a value proposition and strong brands. A strategy without a compelling value proposition will not be market driven or successful. Brand assets that will support a business strategy need to be developed.
- Creating synergetic marketing with silo organizations defined by products or countries. All organizations have multiple products and markets, and creating cooperation and communication instead of competition and isolation is becoming an imperative.

Coping with a dynamic market requires customer-driven strategies and creativity. The book will emphasize a customer perspective and the fact that every strategy should have a value proposition that is meaningful to customers. It will also identify paths to break out of the momentum of the past to generate creative strategies and offerings.

GLOBAL PERSPECTIVES

This edition, which is again compact, offers a radically different chapter structure to the previous European edition. There are also a host of updated material and fresh examples. In terms of chapter structure, the number of chapters has been reduced to 15, with a tighter introduction and overview. The first five chapters on strategic analysis remain the same, but the second half of the book has been completely reorganized and substantially rewritten.

Chapter 7 considers the challenge of creating advantage. The first section considers the nature of sustainable competitive advantage, the second the role of synergy, and the third strategy styles. Chapter 8 raises the issue of value propositions and explores a number of alternatives. Quality and value are explored in detail. Chapter 9 is a new chapter on brand equity. Each of the four major components of brand equity – awareness, loyalty, associations, and identify – are explored.

Chapter 10 on energizing the business is also a new chapter and has three sections. The first is on innovating the offering by improving the product or experience and branding that improvement through the use of branded differentiators. The second covers energizing the brand by involving the customer, promotions, and the use of branded energizers. The third covers increasing the usage of existing customers. Chapter 11 considers leveraging the business and covers brand extensions, how to expand the scope of an offering, and entering new markets. Chapter 12 on creating new business is an entirely new chapter that taps into the innovation literature. Chapter 13 examines the issues involved in developing global strategy. Chapter 14 considers the process of setting priorities for businesses and brands.

Chapter 15, the organization chapter, has been completely recast. It still presents the basic organizational levers of structure, systems, people, and culture. However, the context is now how to overcome the barriers that powerful organizational silos create to inhibit cooperation and communication across silos. The silo problems are analysed, and how the four levers of the organization can be employed to promote cooperation and communication is discussed in the context of the CMO team attempting to create great brands and marketing.

There are also six new cases, with the other two updated to take into account contemporary events. The first new case explores the future of the newspaper industry, considering how a changing environment is leading to radically new business models. The second case is on Spotify – how will their business model shape up against the Apple iTunes giant? The third case examines Alltech, a high-growth global company that is using its sponsorship of the world equestrian games in 2010 to communicate its achievements as a global leader. Fourth is the case of HTC, the Taiwanese mobile phone manufacturer, and its move to add a branded offering to its world-class contract manufacturing business. The fifth case is based in India and the launch of the Tata Nano car. Can this innovation live up to its promise? Finally, the area of social innovation is covered in a sixth case that considers a range of corporate social initiatives and asks about their value to firm and recipients.

In addition, the reader will notice the following changes and additions:

- The role of corporate social responsibility (CSR) has been expanded. The role of being green is considered in detail under external analysis, and the potential of social programmes, especially branded social programmes to supply a value proposition, is covered in more detail.

- The problem of creating strategy in tough economic times is considered in some detail.
- Using the Internet to engage customers and get ideas is highlighted.
- The three strategic philosophies are retained, but now a blended philosophy has been added.
- The Nintendo case study illustrates the power of competitive analyses in leading to strategies.
- Communicating value without harming the brand.
- Dimensions of fit for extensions.
- Extended discussion of contexts in which country customization of strategy is needed.
- Evaluating transformational innovations after their newness wears off and competitors emerge.
- Marketing in China.

AN OVERVIEW

This book begins with an introduction that defines a business strategy, followed by an overview of the book and a discussion of the CMO and strategy. Part I of the book, Chapters 2 to 6, covers strategic analysis, with individual chapters on customer, competitor, market, environmental, and internal analysis. Part II of the book, Chapters 7 to 15, covers the development and implementation of strategy. Chapter 7 discusses the concept of a sustainable competitive advantage (SCA) and introduces four strategy styles: strategic commitment, strategic opportunism, strategic adaptability, and strategic intent.

Chapter 8 provides an overview of the scope of strategic choices by describing several value propositions. Chapter 9 shows how brand equity can be created and leveraged. The next four chapters discuss growth options: Chapter 10 covers energizing the business, Chapter 11 leveraging the business, Chapter 12 creating new businesses, and Chapter 13 global strategies. Chapter 14 discusses setting priorities and the disinvestment option. Finally, Chapter 15 introduces organizational dimensions and their role in supporting strategy and moving silo organization towards cooperation and communication.

THE AUDIENCE

This book is suitable for any course in a school of management or business that focuses on the management of strategies. In particular, it is aimed at:

- the marketing strategy course, which could be titled strategic market management, strategic market planning, strategic marketing, or marketing strategy;

- the policy or entrepreneur course, which could be titled strategic management, strategic planning, business policy, entrepreneurship, or policy administration;
- executive or short programmes with a similar focus, which will also benefi from the breadth of coverage and the accessible style.

The book is also designed to be used by managers who need to develop strategies in dynamic markets – those who have recently moved into general management positions or who run a small business and want to improve their strategy development and planning processes. Another intended audience are those general managers, top executives, and planning specialists who would like an overview of recent issues and methods in strategic market management.

A WORD TO INSTRUCTORS

For instructors, a fully revised instructor's resource guide is available on request. The resource guide has a PowerPoint presentation organized by chapter, a test bank, and a list of cases to consider

To request, please write a mail to acadmktg@wiley.com

ACKNOWLEDGEMENTS

This book could not have been created without help from my friends, students, reviewers, and colleagues at the UCD Michael Smurfit Graduate Business School. I am particularly grateful to Dean Tom Begley, who provided strong support. I benefited from the input of all of my colleagues in the Marketing group at Smurfit School, but the views of Prof. Frank Bradley and Dr Andrew Keating were particularly formative. I am also grateful to my colleagues on the Marketing Development Programme, Antoinette, Nicola, and David. Yansong Hu, now of Warwick Business School, and Yvonne McNamara both played an important role in the previous edition of this text.

My good friend and colleague, Simon Bradley, was similarly important on this occasion and prepared the instructor's materials.

I have been lucky again to work with good friends at John Wiley & Sons. On this occasion Steve Hardman, a good friend and supporter since the start of my career, played the leading role. I was also supported this time by Mark Styles and Anneli Mockett, and previously by Sarah Booth and Emma Cooper.

Above all, I must acknowledge the great love and support provided to me by my daughters, Dearbhla and Bebhinn, and my wonderful wife and friend, Brenda. This edition required a good deal more patience than the last, and they gave it willingly.

This book is dedicated to Alan Sattell, a good friend, an inspiration, and a role model for me in the past and today.

Damien McLoughlin
October 2009

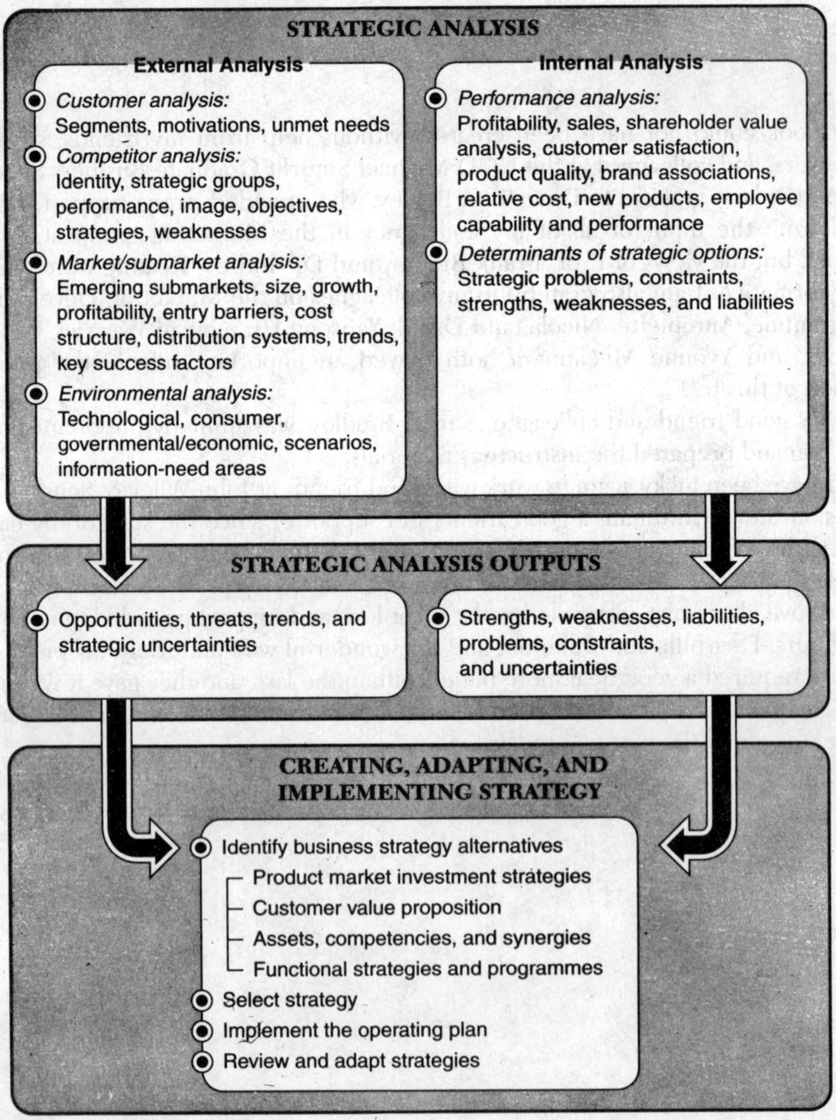
STRATEGIC ANALYSIS
External Analysis
Customer analysis:
Segments, motivations, unmet needs
Competitor analysis:
Identity, strategic groups, performance, image, objectives, strategies, weaknesses
Market/submarket analysis:
Emerging submarkets, size, growth, profitability, entry barriers, cost structure, distribution systems, trends, key success factors
Environmental analysis:
Technological, consumer, governmental/economic, scenarios, information-need areas
Internal Analysis
Performance analysis:
Profitability, sales, shareholder value analysis, customer satisfaction, product quality, brand associations, relative cost, new products, employee capability and performance
Determinants of strategic options:
Strategic problems, constraints, strengths, weaknesses, and liabilities
STRATEGIC ANALYSIS OUTPUTS
Opportunities, threats, trends, and strategic uncertainties
Strengths, weaknesses, liabilities, problems, constraints, and uncertainties
CREATING, ADAPTING, AND IMPLEMENTING STRATEGY
Identify business strategy alternatives
Product market investment strategies
Customer value proposition
Assets, competencies, and synergies
Functional strategies and programmes
Select strategy
Implement the operating plan
Review and adapt strategies

CHAPTER ONE

Strategic Market Management: An Introduction and Overview

We don't know where our first impressions come from or precisely what they mean, so we don't always appreciate their fragility.
—Malcolm Gladwell

Even if you are on the right track, you'll get run over if you just sit there.
—Will Rodgers

If you don't know where you're going, you might end up somewhere else.
—Casey Stengel

All markets today are dynamic. Change is in the air everywhere, and change affects strategy. A winning strategy today may not prevail tomorrow. It might not even be relevant tomorrow.

There was a time, not too many decades ago, when the world held still long enough for strategies to be put into place and refined with patience and discipline. The annual strategic plan guided the firm. That simply is no longer the case. New products, product modifications, subcategories, technologies, applications, market niches, segments, media, channels, and so on and so forth, are emerging faster than ever in nearly all industries – from food to pharmaceuticals to cars to financial services to software. Multiple forces feed these changes, including Internet technologies, the rise of China and India, trends in healthy living, energy crises, political instability, and more. This results in markets that are not only dynamic but risky, complex, and cluttered.

Such convoluted markets make strategy creation and implementation far more challenging. Strategy has to win not only in today's marketplace but in tomorrow's, when the customer, the competitor set, and the market context may all be different. In environments shaped by this new reality, some firms are driving change. Others are adapting to it. Still others are fading in the face of change. How do you develop successful strategies in dynamic markets? How do you stay ahead of competition? How do you stay relevant?

The task is challenging. Strategists need new and refined perspectives, tools, and concepts. In particular, they need to develop competencies around five management tasks – strategic analysis, innovation, getting control of multiple business units, developing sustainable advantages, and developing growth platforms:

- *Strategic analysis.* The need for information about customers, competitors, and trends affecting the market is now higher than ever. Furthermore, the information needs to be on-line, because a timely detection of threats, opportunities, strategic problems, or emerging weaknesses can be crucial to getting the response right. There is an enhanced premium on the ability to predict trends, project their impact, and distinguish them from mere fads. That means resources need to be invested and competencies created in terms of getting information, filtering it, and converting it into actionable analysis.
- *Innovation.* The ability to innovate is one key to successfully winning in dynamic markets, as numerous empirical studies have shown. Innovation, however, turns out to have a host of dimensions. There is the organizational challenge of creating a context that supports innovation. There is the brand portfolio challenge of making sure that the innovation is owned and not a short-lived market blip. There is the strategic challenge of developing the right mix of innovations that ranges from incremental to transformational. There is the execution challenge; it is necessary to turn innovations into offerings in the marketplace. There are too many examples of firms that owned an innovation and let others bring it to market.
- *Multiple businesses.* It is the rare firm now that does not operate multiple business units defined by channels and countries in addition to product categories and subcategories. Decentralization is a century-old organizational form that provides for accountability, a deep understanding of the product or service, being close to the customer, and fast response, all of which are good things. However, in its extreme form, autonomous business units can lead to the misallocation of resources, redundancies, a failure to capture cross-business potential synergies, and confused brands. A challenge, explored in Chapter 15, is to adapt the decentralization model so that it no longer inhibits strategy adaptation in dynamic markets.
- *Creating sustainable competitive advantages (SCAs).* Creating strategic advantages that are truly sustainable in the context of dynamic markets and dispersed business units is challenging. Competitors all too quickly copy product and service improvements that are valued by customers. What leads

to SCAs in dynamic markets? One possible cornerstone is the development of assets (such as brands, distribution channels, or a customer base), competencies (such as social technology skills), or sponsorship expertise. Another is the leveraging of the organizational synergy created by multiple business units, which is much more difficult to copy than a new product or service.

- *Developing growth platforms.* Growth is imperative for the vitality and health of any organization. In a dynamic environment, stretching the organization in creative ways becomes an essential element of seizing opportunities and adapting to changing circumstances. Growth can come from revitalizing core businesses, making them growth platforms, as well as by creating new business platforms.

This book is concerned with helping managers identify, select, implement, and adapt market-driven business strategies that will enjoy a sustainable advantage in dynamic markets, as well as create synergy and set priorities among business units. The intent is to provide concepts, methods, and procedures that will lead to competencies in these five crucial management tasks – and, ultimately, to high-quality strategic decision-making and profitable growth.

The book emphasizes the customer because in a dynamic market it is a customer orientation that is likely to be successful. The current, emerging, and latent motivations and unmet needs of customers need to influence strategies. Because of this, every strategy needs to have a value proposition that is meaningful and relevant to customers.

This first chapter starts with a very basic but central concept, that of a business strategy. The goal is to lend structure and clarity to a term that is widely employed but seldom defined. It continues with an overview of the balance of the book, introducing and positioning many of the subjects, concepts, and tools to be covered. Finally, the role of marketing in business strategy will be discussed. There is a significant trend for marketing to have a seat at the strategy table and to see the chief marketing officer (CMO) be empowered to create growth initiatives.

WHAT IS A BUSINESS STRATEGY?

Before discussing the process of developing sound business strategies, it is fair to address two questions. What is a business? What is a business strategy? Having groups of managers provide answers to these basic questions shows that there is little consensus as to what these basic terms mean. Clarifying these concepts is a necessary start towards a winning, adaptable strategy.

A Business

A business is generally an organizational unit that has (or should have) a defined strategy and a manager with sales and profit responsibility. They can be defined by a variety of dimensions including product line, country, channels, or segments. An organization will thus have many business units that relate to each other horizontally and vertically. For example, the Tata Group is an Indian conglomerate with interests in information systems, engineering, materials, energy, services, consumer products, and chemicals. Each of these business units requires planning. Within the services division, the Indian hotels business requires planning, as does the financial services business. A strategy will be developed for Taj hotels in India, with a separate plan for the international development of the chain.

There is an organizational and strategic trade-off in deciding how many businesses should be operated. On the one hand, it can be compelling to have many units, because then each business will be close to its market and potentially capable of developing an optimal strategy. Thus, a strategy for each country or each region or each major segment may have some benefits. Too many business units become inefficient, however, and result in programmes that lack scale economies and fail to leverage the strategic skills of the best managers. As a result, there is pressure to aggregate businesses into larger entities.

Business units can be aggregated to create a critical mass, to recognize similarities in markets and strategies, and to gain synergies. Businesses that are too small to justify a strategy will need to be aggregated so that the management structure can be supportable. (Of course, two business units can share some elements of operations, such as a sales force or a facility, to gain economies without merging.) Businesses that have similar market contexts and business strategies will be candidates for aggregation to leverage shared knowledge. Another aggregation motivation is to encourage synergies among business units when the combination is more likely to realize savings in cost or investment or create a superior value proposition.

There was a time when firms developed business strategies for decentralized business units defined by product, countries, or whatever. These business strategies were then packaged or aggregated to create a firm strategy. That time has passed. There now needs to be a firm strategy that identifies macro trends and strategy responses to time, allocates resources among business units, and recognizes synergy potentials. So there needs to be a strategy for the Volkswagen company, for each of its brands including Volkswagen, Audi, Bentley, SEAT, and Skoda, as well as for the VW Touareg.

A Business Strategy

Four dimensions define a business strategy: the product market investment strategy, the customer value proposition, the assets and competencies, and the functional strategies and programmes. The first specifies where to compete, and the remaining three indicate how to compete to win, as suggested by Figure 1.1.

The Product Market Investment Strategy: Where to Compete

The scope of the business and the dynamics within that scope represent a very basic strategy dimension. Which sectors should receive investments in resources and management attention? Which should have resources withdrawn or withheld? Even for a small organization, the allocation decision is key to strategy.

The scope of a business is defined by the products it offers and chooses not to offer, by the markets it seeks to serve and not to serve, by the competitors it chooses

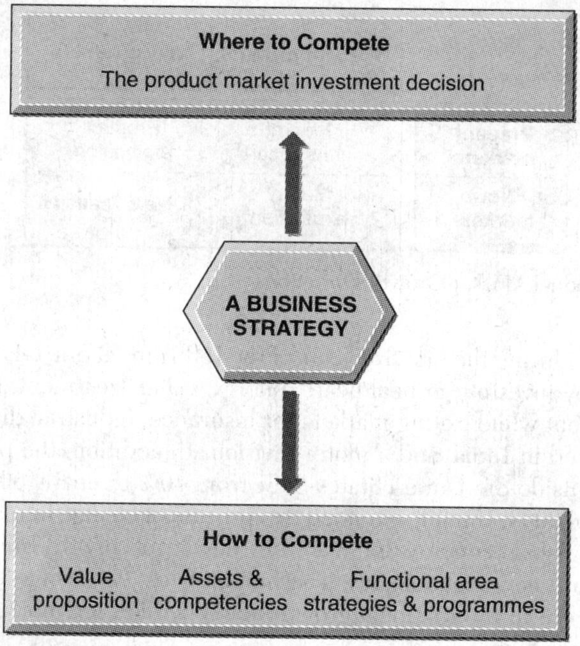

Figure 1.1 A Business Strategy

to compete with and to avoid, and by its level of vertical integration. Sometimes the most important business scope decision is what products or segments to avoid, because such a decision, if followed by discipline, can conserve resources needed to compete successfully elsewhere. Peter Drucker, the management guru, challenged executives to specify: 'What is our business and what should it be? What is not our business and what should it not be?' Such a judgement can sometimes involve painful choices to divest or liquidate a business or avoid an apparently attractive opportunity. Chapter 14 discusses disinvestment judgements and why they are hard to make and easy to avoid.

Many organizations have demonstrated the advantages of having a well-defined business scope. IKEA offers functional, well-designed furniture at low prices. Danone has defined its business as developing and marketing food products that promote good health in order to take advantage of changes in global demographics and food consumption. Henkel and Hindustan Lever (HUL) provide a broad spectrum of consumer packaged goods. Australia's Woolworths and Carrefour have a wide scope that generates both scale economies and a one-stop shopping value proposition.

More important than the scope is the scope dynamics. What product markets will be entered or exited in the coming years? As Figure 1.2 suggests, growth can be generated by bringing existing products to new markets (market expansion), by bringing new products to existing markets (product expansion), or by entering new product markets (diversification).

Expanding the business scope can help the organization achieve growth and vitality and can be a lever to cope with the changing marketplace by seizing opportunities

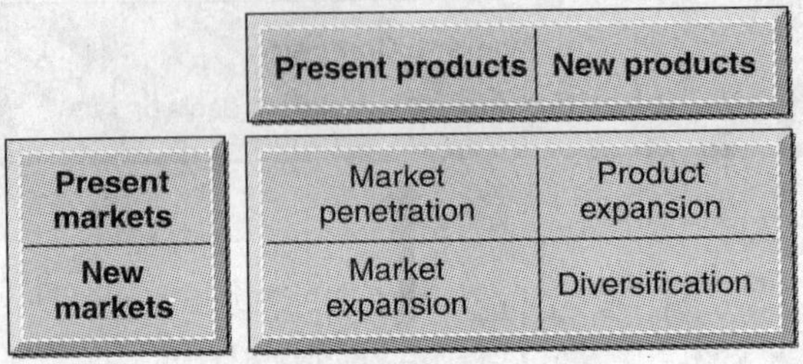

Figure 1.2 Product Market Growth Directions

as they emerge. During the first five years of the Jeff Immelt era, GE changed its focus and character by investing in healthcare, energy, water treatment, home mortgages, and entertainment while exiting markets for insurance, industrial diamonds, business outsourcing based in India, and a motor division. In addition, the percentage of revenue sources outside the United States grew from 40% to nearly 50%. Following the financial crisis of 2008, Immelt extended this process of change in response to what he saw as a 'reset' global economy dominated by new levels of government intervention, new markets, and new technologies. The emphasis of the change for GE will be on further investment in international growth markets, high technology manufacturing, and social responsibility.[1]

However, expanding the business scope poses risks as well. As the scope expansion ventures further from the core business, there will be increased risk that the firm's offering will not be distinctive, there will be problems in operations, or the firm's brands will not support the expansion. Bausch & Lomb's attempt to move from eye care to mouthwash was a product and brand failure. An effort by a manufacturing equipment company to go into robots failed when it could not create or acquire the needed technology. Attention and resources may also be diverted from the core business, causing it to weaken.

The investment pattern will determine the future direction of the firm. Although there are obvious variations and refinements, it is useful to conceptualize the alternatives as follows:

- invest to grow (or enter the product market);
- invest only to maintain the existing position;
- milk the business by minimizing investment;
- recover as many of the assets as possible by liquidating or divesting the business.

P&G had lost half its stock value in the six months before A.G. Lafley took over as CEO in 2000, in part because the firm invested considerable resources behind new business initiatives that disappointed or failed.[2] Two years later it had recovered most of that decline, even though the overall stock market dropped over a third of its value during that time. A key to the turnaround was a strategy of focusing on its twelve largest brands, each contributing over a billion dollars in sales, and reducing investment in its other eighty or so brands, and brands with low strategic fit were disposed of. A similar strategy was also pursued by a number of the major consumer goods firms such as Nestlé, Kraft, Danone, Diageo, and Unilever. In each case, organic growth and acquisition of product groups and brands in high growth areas became the drivers. The need for such an approach to investment was driven by the growing strength of international retailers in global consumer markets and the realization that the developing world has strong long-term growth potential.

The Customer Value Proposition

Ultimately, the offering needs to appeal to new and existing customers. There needs to be a value proposition that is relevant and meaningful to the customer and is reflected in the positioning of the product or service. To support a successful strategy, it should be sustainable over time and be differentiated from competitors. The customer value proposition can involve elements such as providing to customers:

- good value (Aldi);
- excellence on an important product or service attribute such as getting clothes clean (El Bulli restaurant in Spain);
- the best overall quality (Krug Grande Cuvée);
- product line breadth (Tesco);
- innovative offerings (Logitech);
- a shared passion for an activity or a product (Ducati);
- global connections and prestige (HSBC).

Assets and Competencies

The strategic assets or competencies that underlie the strategy often provide a sustainable competitive advantage (SCA). A *strategic competency* is what a business unit does exceptionally well – such as a customer relationship programme, manufacturing, or promotion – that has strategic importance to that business. It is usually based on knowledge or a process. A *strategic asset* is a resource, such as a brand name or installed customer base, that is strong relative to that of competitors. Strategy formulation must consider the cost and feasibility of generating or maintaining assets or competencies that will provide the basis for a sustainable competitive advantage.

Assets and competencies can involve a wide spectrum, from buildings and locations to R&D expertise to a symbol such as the Michelin Man. For P&G it is consumer understanding, brand building, innovation, go-to-market capability, and global scale.[3] Although a strong asset or competency is often difficult to build, it can result in an advantage that is significant and enduring.

The synergies obtained from operating a business that spans product markets can be an important asset and SCA source. Synergies, which are significant because they are based on organizational characteristics that are not easily duplicated, can come in many forms. Two businesses can reduce costs by sharing a distribution system, sales force, or logistics system, as when P&G acquired Gillette. Synergy can also be based on sharing the same asset, as with the Tata brand shared by the dozens of business units, or a competence such as Toyota's ability to manage manufacturing plants across brands and countries. Another source of synergy is the sharing of functional area strategies across business units. Atos Origin, the international IT service provider, is a sponsor of the 2012 Olympic Games. While the global parent has the ability to support and benefit from this investment, it is unlikely that the Argentinian division alone could. Still another synergy source is the sharing of R&D. P&G aggregates brands such as Head & Shoulders, Aussie, Infusion, and Pantene into a hair care category not just to provide shelf-space guidance to retailers and to create promotions more easily, but also to manage the use of product innovations. Finally, a combination of products can provide a value proposition. Some software firms have aggregated products in order to provide a systems solution to customers; Microsoft Office is one example.

The ability of assets and competencies to support a strategy will in part depend on their power relative to competitors. To what extent are the assets and competencies strong and in place? To what extent are they ownable because of a symbol trademark or long-standing investment in a capability? To what extent are they based on organizational synergy that others cannot duplicate?

Assets and competencies can also provide points of parity. For dimensions such as perceived quality, distribution strength, or manufacturing cost, the goal may be not to create an advantage but to avoid a disadvantage. When an asset or competency is close enough to that of a competitor to neutralize the latter's strength, then a point of parity has been achieved. Such parity can be a key to success; if the perceived quality of a Lidl offering is regarded as adequate, its price perception will then win the day.

Functional Strategies and Programmes

A target value proposition, or a set of assets and competencies, should mandate some strategy imperatives in the form of a supportive set of functional strategies or programmes. These strategies and programmes, in turn, will be implemented with a host of tactical programmes with a short-term perspective.

The functional strategies or programmes that could drive the business strategy might include:

- a customer relationship programme;
- a brand-building strategy;
- a social technology strategy;
- a communication strategy;
- an information technology strategy;
- a distribution strategy;
- a global strategy;
- a quality programme;
- a sourcing strategy;

- a logistical strategy;
- a manufacturing strategy.

The need for functional strategies and programmes can be determined by asking a few questions. What must happen for the firm to be able to deliver on the value proposition? Are the assets and competencies needed in place? Do they need to be created, strengthened, or supported? How?

Criteria to Select Business Strategies

The principal criteria useful for selecting alternatives can be grouped around six general questions:

- *Is the ROI attractive?* Creating a value proposition that is appealing to customers may not be worthwhile if the investment or operating cost is excessive. Starbucks opened in Japan in 1996 in the Ginza district and grew to over 400 units, many of which were in the highest-rent areas. The result was a trendy brand but one that was vulnerable to competitors, who matched or exceeded Starbucks' product offerings and were not handicapped with such high overheads because they developed less costly sites.

EXPANDING THE BUSINESS SCOPE

In his classic article 'Marketing Myopia', Theodore Levitt explained how firms that define their business myopically in product terms can stagnate, even though the basic customer need they serve is enjoying healthy growth.[4] Because of a myopic product focus, others gain the benefits of growth. In contrast, firms that regard themselves as being in the transportation rather than the railroad business, the energy instead of the petroleum business, or the communication rather than the telephone business are more likely to exploit opportunities.

The concept is simple. Define the business in terms of the basic customer need rather than the product. Visa has defined itself as being in the business of enabling a customer to exchange value (any asset, including cash on deposit, the cash value of life insurance, or the equity in a home) for virtually anything anywhere in the world. As the business is redefined, both the set of competitors and the range of opportunities are often radically expanded. After redefining its business, Visa estimated that it had reached only 5% of its potential, given the new definition.

Defining a business in terms of generic need can be extremely useful for fostering creativity, in generating strategic options, and in avoiding an internally oriented product focus.

- *Is there a sustainable competitive advantage?* Unless the business unit has or can develop a real competitive advantage that is sustainable over time in the face of competitor reaction, an attractive long-term return will be unlikely. To achieve a sustainable competitive advantage, a strategy should exploit organizational assets and competencies and neutralize weaknesses.

- *Will the strategy have success in the future?* A strategy needs to be able to survive the dynamics of the market, with its emerging threats and opportunities. Either the strategy components should be expected to have a long life or the strategy should be capable of adapting to changing conditions. In that context, future scenarios (described in Chapter 5) might be used to test the robustness of the strategy with respect to future uncertainties.
- *Is the strategy feasible?* The strategy should be within both the financial and human resources of the organization. It also should be internally consistent with other organizational characteristics, such as the firm's structure, systems, people, and culture. These organizational considerations will be covered in Chapter 15.
- *Does the strategy fit with the other strategies of the firm?* Are the sources and uses of cash flow in balance? Is organizational flexibility reduced by an investment in financial or human resources? Is potential synergy captured by the strategy?

STRATEGIC MARKET MANAGEMENT

Strategic market management is a system designed to help management create, change, or retain a business strategy and to create strategic visions. A *strategic vision* is a projection of a future strategy or sets of strategies. The realization of an optimal strategy may involve a delay because the firm is not ready or because the emerging conditions are not yet in place. A vision will provide direction and purpose for interim strategies and activities and can inspire those in the organization by providing a purpose that is worthwhile and ennobling.

Strategic market management involves decisions with a significant long-term impact on the organization. The resulting business strategies can be costly in terms of time and resources to reverse or change. In fact, emerging strategic decisions can mean the difference between success, mediocrity, failure, or even survival.

Developing the right business strategies is a basic goal, but it is not the end of the story. With a business strategy in hand, the task is to:

- continuously challenge the strategy in order to make sure that it remains relevant to the changing marketplace and responsive to emerging opportunities;
- ensure that the organization develops and retains the necessary skills and competencies to make the strategy succeed;
- implement the strategy with energy and focus; the best strategy badly implemented will be a failure (or worse, jeopardize the firm).

Figure 1.3 provides a structure for strategic market management and for this book. A brief overview of its principal elements and an introduction to the key concepts will be presented in this chapter.

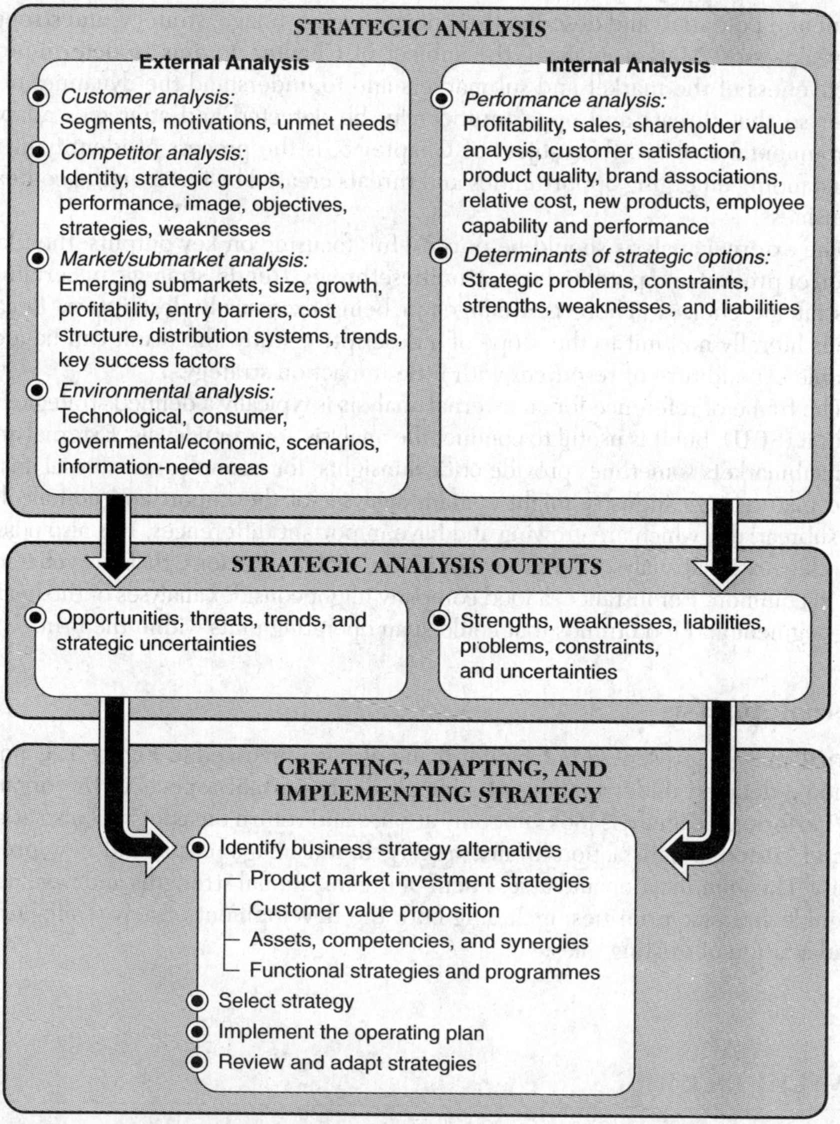

Figure 1.3 Overview of Strategic Market Development

External Analysis

External analysis, summarized in Figure 1.3, involves an examination of the relevant elements external to an organization – customers, competitors, markets and submarkets, and the environment or context outside the market. Customer analysis, the first step of external analysis and a focus of Chapter 2, involves identifying the organization's customer segments and each segment's motivations and unmet needs. Competitor analysis, covered in Chapter 3, attempts to identify competitors (both current and potential) and describe their performance, image, strategy, and strengths and weaknesses. Market analysis, the subject of Chapter 4, aims to determine the attractiveness of the market and submarkets and to understand the dynamics of the market so that threats and opportunities can be detected and strategies adapted. Environmental analysis, the subject of Chapter 5, is the process of identifying and understanding emerging opportunities and threats created by forces in the context of the business.

The external analysis should be purposeful, focusing on key outputs: the identification of present and potential opportunities, threats, trends, strategic uncertainties, and strategic choices. There is a danger in being excessively descriptive. Because there is literally no limit to the scope of a descriptive study, the result can be a considerable expenditure of resources with little impact on strategy.

The frame of reference for an external analysis is typically a defined strategic business unit (SBU), but it is useful to conduct the analysis at several levels. External analyses of submarkets sometimes provide critical insights; for example, an external analysis of the mature beer industry might contain analyses of the import and non-alcoholic beer submarkets, which are growing and have important differences. It is also possible to conduct external analyses for groups of SBUs, such as divisions, that have characteristics in common. For instance, a food company might consider analyses of the healthy-living segment and food trends that could span operating units within the firm.

Internal Analysis

Internal analysis, presented in Chapter 6 and also summarized in Figure 1.3, aims to provide a detailed understanding of strategically important aspects of the organization. Performance analysis looks not only at sales and return on assets but also at measures of customer satisfaction/loyalty, quality, brand image, costs, and new product activity. The identification and assessment of organizational strengths and weaknesses will guide strategic priorities, including both the development of new strategies and the adaptation of existing ones.

WALKERS CRISPS

Founded in 1947, Golden Wonder was the first company to sell crisps in packets. They were also first to make and sell flavoured crisps, and by 1964 they operated the largest crisp factory in the world. Its best-known brands have included the iconic Golden Wonder, Wotsits, Golden Lights, and Wheat Crunchies. In addition, they supplied large retailers with own-label crisps. In 2006 they went into receivership, and were subsequently sold to a competitor. Much of the blame for the demise of Golden Wonder was directed towards the relentless competition of Walkers Crisps, owned by PepsiCo since 1989. While Walkers had a similar long history in the British market and enjoyed much of the same nostalgic halo, it also had a long history of consistent investment in its brands, product innovation, and response to market trends. It started an advertising campaign with Gary Lineker, an English football legend, and a man famous for being nice, in the early 1990s. More than 10 years later, Lineker was the brand spokesman, and Walkers had a library of outstanding commercials featuring the footballer to their credit. Golden Wonder's response was to launch an advertising campaign with the slogan 'Employ celebrities to sell crisps ... we'd rather use newsagents'. In 2002, Walkers launched its Sensations range of crisps, designed to take advantage of the trend towards adult crisps and to counterweight the decline in the crisps market. Golden Wonder's response was to mock the trend and employ the slogan 'Where a crisp is a crisp' to indicate its unwillingness to change. As part of a corporate restructuring in 2002, Golden Wonder sold a prized asset, Wotsits, to Walkers. In the mid-2000s the issues of salt and fat content of food and obesity began to impact on consumer attitudes and behaviours towards the snack foods business. Walkers' response was a radical one – it did not simply launch a new product, it changed the way it manufactured all of its crisps to reduce the amount of saturated fat in its products by 70% and the level of salt to 8% of the recommended daily allowance. This change was supported by an advertising campaign featuring Mr Lineker. Golden Wonder's response to this emerging trend was to launch a subbrand, Golden Lights. Finally, Walkers refused to supply crisps on an own-label basis, preferring to keep the focus on developing its own products and brands. Where did the blame for the demise of Golden Wonder truly lie?[5]

Creating, Adapting, and Implementing Strategy

After describing strategic analysis, the book turns to the creation, adaptation, and implementation of strategy. How do you decide on the business scope? What are the alternative value propositions, and how do they guide strategy development? What assets and competencies will provide points of advantage, and which will aim for points of parity? What functional strategies and programmes will lead to strategic success? What growth options will receive investment? Is the core business to be the source of growth, or is there a need to move beyond the core? What is to be the global strategy? How should the business units be prioritized? Should there be disinvestment in the business portfolio? How can the organization be adapted so that it supports rather than constrains strategy?

Chapter 7 discusses the concept of an SCA and the slippery concept of synergy before introducing four strategic philosophies: strategic commitment, strategic opportunism, strategic adaptability, and strategic intent. These strategy styles provide a good overview of alternative ways to manage strategy in the face of dynamic markets. Chapter 8 provides an overview of the scope of strategic choices by describing over a dozen possible value propositions, each of which provides an umbrella over a business strategy. Chapter 9 shows how brand equity, a key asset and adaptability lever, can be created and used. The next four chapters discuss growth options: Chapter 10 covers energizing the business, Chapter 11 leveraging the business, Chapter 12 creating new businesses, and Chapter 13 global strategies. Chapter 14 discusses the disinvestment option, an important and often overlooked dimension of the investment decision. Finally, Chapter 15 introduces organizational dimensions and their role in strategy choice and implementation.

Strategic Market Management – the Objectives

Strategic market management is intended to:

- *Precipitate the consideration of strategic choices.* What external events are creating opportunities and threats to which a timely and appropriate reaction should be generated? What strategic issues face the firm? What strategic options should be considered? The alternative to strategic market management is usually to drift strategically, becoming absorbed in day-to-day problems. Nothing is more tragic than an organization that fails because a strategic decision was not addressed until it was too late.
- *Help a business cope with change.* If a particular environment is extremely stable and the sales patterns are satisfactory, there may be little need for meaningful strategic change – either in direction or intensity. In that case, strategic market management is much less crucial. However, most organizations now exist in rapidly changing and increasingly unpredictable environments and therefore need approaches for coping strategically.
- *Force a long-range view.* The pressures to manage with a short-term focus are strong, but they frequently lead to strategic errors.
- *Make visible the resource allocation decision.* Allowing allocation of resources to be dictated by the political strengths or inertia (i.e. the same strategy as last year) is too easy. One result of this approach is that the small but promising business with 'no problems' or the unborn business may suffer from a lack of resources, whereas larger business areas may absorb an excessive amount.
- *Aid strategic analysis and decision-making.* Concepts, models, and methodologies are available to help a business collect and analyse information and address difficult strategic decisions.
- *Provide a strategic management and control system.* The focus on assets and competencies and the development of objectives and programmes associated with strategic thrusts provide the basis for managing a business strategically.
- *Provide both horizontal and vertical communication and coordination systems.* Strategic market management provides a way to communicate problems and proposed strategies within an organization; in particular, its vocabulary adds precision.

The Planning Cycle

Too often an annual planning exercise is perceived as strategy development when the output is an operating and resource budget that specifies financial targets, hiring plans, and investment authorizations but not strategy. Research at McKinsey involving a survey of over 700 executives suggests ways to make the strategy development process more effective.[6] In particular, a strategy process should:

- *Start with the issues.* CEOs say that planning should focus on anticipating big challenges and spotting important trends. Strategy choice will be well served by identifying the key associated strategic issues. One CEO asks the business leaders in his firm to imagine how a set of specific trends will affect their business. Another creates a list of 3–6 priorities for each business to form a basis for discussion.

- *Bring together the right people.* In particular, it is not enough to involve only the people who will implement the strategy, the decision-makers must also be engaged. Also, in order to foster cross-silo synergies and strategies, it is worth having relevant teams of businesses represented.
- *Adapt planning cycles to the businesses.* It is unrealistic to say that all businesses need to have planning exercises each year. Some may need it every other year or even every third year. Also, it might be useful to have trends, events, or issues that trigger a strategy review even if it is not in the annual cycle.
- *Implement a strategy performance system.* Too many businesses fail to follow up on strategy development. As a result, it becomes a rather empty exercise. Major strategic initiatives should have measurable progress goals as well as end objectives. What will be the barrier to success? What needs to happen for the strategy to be on track?

MARKETING AND ITS ROLE IN STRATEGY

Marketing has seen its strategic role growing over the years. The question for each organization is whether the chief marketing officer (CMO) and his or her team have a seat at the strategy table or are relegated to being tactical implementers of tasks such as managing the advertising programme. The view that marketing is tactical is changing; it is now more and more frequently being accepted as being part of the strategic management of the organization. Given the definition of a business strategy and the structure of strategic market management, the roles that marketing can and should play become clearer.

One marketing role is to be the primary driver of the strategic analysis. The marketing group is in the best position to understand the customers, competitors, market and submarkets, and environmental forces and trends. By managing marketing research and market data, it controls much of the information needed in the external analysis. Marketing should also take the lead in the internal analysis with respect to selected assets (such as the brand portfolio and the distribution channel) and competencies (such as new product introduction and the management of sponsorships).

A second role is to develop business strategies. The dimension of business strategy most clearly owned by marketing is the customer value proposition: What is the value that the firm will offer, now and in the future? Marketing, in fact, ought to be the voice of the customer in the strategic discussions, making sure that the value proposition is based on substance and is meaningful to the customer. Other components of a business strategy are also marketing-centric. The choice of market scope needs to draw on a segmentation strategy. Many assets and competencies, such as brand equity or customer relationship programmes, are based in marketing. Finally, marketing programmes will be among the functional area programmes that are integral to strategy.

A third role is to drive growth strategy for the firm. Growth options are either based on or dependent on customer and market insights, and marketing therefore should be a key driver. In fact, a study by Booz Allen and Hamilton of some 2000 executives found that a small (9%) but growing number of firms describe the CMO as a growth champion involved in all strategic levers relating to growth.[7]

A fourth role is to deal with the dysfunctions of product and geographic silos. Although all functional groups need to deal with this problem, marketing is often on the front line. The corporate brand and major master brands usually span silos, and a failure to exercise some central control and guidance will result in inefficiencies and inconsistencies that can be damaging to one or more business strategies. Business-spanning marketing programmes such as sponsorships or distribution channels need to be actively managed if opportunities are to be realized and waste and inefficiency are to be avoided.

KEY LEARNINGS

- Strategy needs to be developed and executed in the context of a dynamic market. To cope, it is important to develop competencies in strategic analysis, innovation, managing multiple businesses, and developing SCAs.
- A business strategy includes the determination of the product market investment strategy, the customer value proposition, assets and competencies, and the functional area strategy.
- Strategic market management is a system designed to help visions. A strategic vision is a vision of a future strategy or sets of strategies. Strategic market management includes a strategic analysis of the business to identify existing or emerging opportunities, threats, trends, strategic uncertainties, and strategic alternatives.
- The CMO role has grown over the years and is now often charged with being a partner in developing strategies and a vehicle to deal with the dysfunctions of the product market silos.

FOR DISCUSSION

1. What is a business strategy? Do you agree with the definition proposed? Illustrate your answer with examples.
2. Consider one of the following firms. Read the description of a business strategy in the text. Go to the firm's website and use it to gain an understanding of the business strategy. Look at elements such as the products and services offered, the history of the firm, and its values. What is the business strategy? What are the firm's product markets? What are its value

propositions? How are the value propositions delivered? What assets and competencies exist? What strategic options? Consider the scope question raised by Levitt. What would be a narrow and broad scope specification?

(a) Spotify.

(b) Haier.

(c) Santander.

(d) A firm of your choice from a continent other than your own.

3. Consider the description of Walkers Crisps' strategic marketing activity outlined in the chapter. How would you evaluate their actions? How would you compete against them?

4. Apply the marketing myopia concept to print media, magazines, and newspapers. What is the implication?

5. Which criteria to pick a strategy would you consider most important? Why? How would the context affect your answer?

6. Which quote at the front of the chapter do you find the most insightful? Why? Under what circumstances would its implications not hold?

NOTES

1. Damian Reece, 'Jeff Immelt Seeks to Map Out GE's Future beyond America', *The Daily Telegraph*, 30 June 2009; available at: http://www.telegraph.co.uk/finance/newsbysector/industry/5688366/Jeff-Immelt-seeks-to-map-out-GEs-future-beyond-America.html (accessed 6 October 2009).
2. Katrina Brooker, 'The Un-CEO', *Fortune*, 16 September 2002, pp. 68–78.
3. A.G. Laffey, 'What Only the CEO Can Do', *Harvard Business Review*, May 2009.
4. Theodore Levitt, 'Marketing Myopia', *Harvard Business Review*, July–August 1960, pp. 45–56.
5. www.GoldenWonder.com; http://walkers.corpex.com/crl15p5/index.htm.
6. Renee Dye and Olivier Sibony, 'How to Improve Strategic Planning', *McKinsey Quarterly*, 2007, (3), pp. 41–49.
7. Constantine von Hoffman, 'Armed with Intelligence', *BrandWeek*, 29 May 2006, pp. 17–20.

PART I

STRATEGIC ANALYSIS

CHAPTER TWO

External and Customer Analysis

The purpose of an enterprise is to create and keep a customer.
—Theodore Levitt

Without a specific reason for the consumer to behave, without a reward or benefit, the overwhelmed consumer will refuse.
—Seth Godin

You can't just ask customers what they want and then try to give that to them. By the time you get it built, they'll want something new.
—Steve Jobs

Developing or adapting strategy in a dynamic market logically starts with external analysis, an analysis of the factors external to a business that can affect strategy. The first four chapters of Part I present concepts and methods useful in conducting an external analysis. The final chapter of Part I turns to internal analysis: the analysis of the firm's performance, strengths, weaknesses, problems, liabilities, and constraints.

EXTERNAL ANALYSIS

A successful external analysis needs to be directed and purposeful. There is always the danger that it will become an endless process resulting in an excessively descriptive report. In any business there is no end to the material that appears to be potentially relevant. Without discipline and direction, volumes of useless descriptive material can easily be generated.

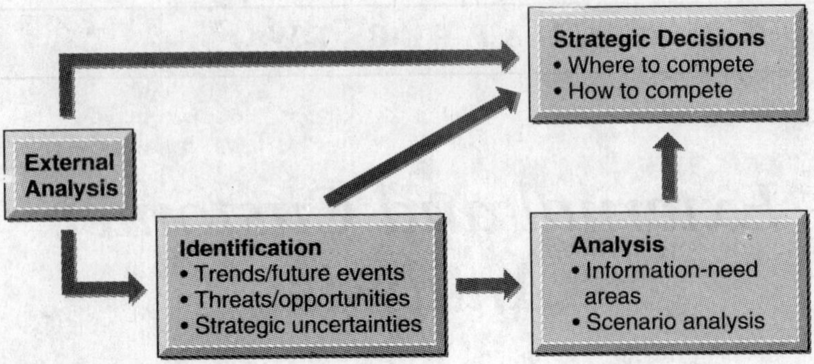

Figure 2.1 The Role of External Analysis

Affecting Strategic Decisions

The external analysis process should not be an end in itself. Rather, it should be motivated throughout by a desire to affect strategy. As Figure 2.1 shows, an external analysis can impact on strategy directly by suggesting strategic decision alternatives or influencing a choice among them. More specifically, it should address questions such as:

- Should existing business areas be liquidated, milked, maintained, or a target for investment?
- Should new business areas be entered?
- What are the value propositions? What should they be?
- What assets and competencies should be created, enhanced, or maintained?
- What strategies and programmes should be implemented in functional areas? What should be the positioning strategy, segmentation strategy, distribution strategy, brand-building strategy, manufacturing strategy, and so on?

Additional Analysis Objectives

Figure 2.1 also suggests that an external analysis can contribute to strategy indirectly by identifying:

- significant trends and future events;
- threats and opportunities;
- strategic uncertainties that could affect strategy outcomes.

A significant trend or event, such as concern about saturated fat or the emergence of a new competitor, can dramatically affect the evaluation of strategy options. A new technology, which can represent both a threat to an established firm and an opportunity to a prospective competitor, can signal new business arenas.

Strategic Uncertainties

Strategic uncertainty is a particularly useful concept in conducting an ex analysis. If you could know the answer to one question prior to making a strat gic commitment, what would that question be? If Alfa-Romeo were to consider whether to add an electric car to its line, important strategy uncertainties might include the following:

- What will the car sales profile of electric cars be in upcoming years? How many will be sold in what categories?
- How will offering an electric car impact upon Alfa-Romeo's brand equity?
- What will be the electric car strategies of Alfa-Romeo's direct competitors?
- What new technologies might emerge that will affect the performance and acceptance of electric cars?

Strategic uncertainties focus on specific unknown elements that will affect the outcome of strategic decisions. 'Should Alfa-Romeo extend its line to electric cars?' is a strategic decision, whereas 'What is the future demand for full-size electric cars?' is a strategic uncertainty. Most strategic decisions will be driven by a set of these uncertainties.

Below are some examples of strategic uncertainties and the strategic decisions to which they might relate. A strategic uncertainty can often lead to additional sources of strategic uncertainty. One common strategic uncertainty, as portrayed in the table that follows, is what the future demand for a product (such as ultrasound diagnostic equipment) will be.

Strategic Uncertainties	**Strategic Decisions**
• Will a major firm enter?	• Investment in a product market
• Will a tofu-based dessert product be accepted?	• Investment in a tofu-based product
• Will a technology be replaced?	• Investment in a technology
• Will the Euro strengthen against other currencies?	• Commitment to offshore manufacturing
• Will computer-based operations be feasible with current technology?	• Investment in a new system
• How sensitive is the market to price?	• A strategy of maintaining price parity
Strategic Uncertainties	**Second-level Strategic Uncertainties**
• What will be the future demand of an ultrasound test? ←	• Performance improvements? • Competitive technological developments? • Financial capacity of healthcare industry?

Asking 'On what does that depend?' will usually generate additional strategi uncertainties. One uncertainty might address technological improvements whereas another might consider the technological development and cost/benefit levels achieved by competitive technologies. Yet another might look into the financial capacity of the healthcare industry to continue capital improvements. Each of these strategic uncertainties can, in turn, generate yet another level of strategic uncertainties.

Analysis

There are three ways of handling uncertainty, as suggested by Figure 2.1. First, a strategic decision can be precipitated because the logic for a decision is compelling and/or because a delay would be costly or risky. Second, it may be worthwhile to attempt to reduce the uncertainty by information acquisition and analysis of an information-need area. The effort could range from a high-priority task force to a low-key monitoring effort. The level of resources expended will depend on the potential impact on strategy and its immediacy. Third, the uncertainty could be modelled by a scenario analysis.

A scenario is an alternative view of the future environment that is usually prompted by an alternative possible answer to a strategic uncertainty or by a prospective future event or trend. Is the current popularity of male grooming a fad or does it indicate a solid growth area? Such a question could be the basis for a positive and a negative scenario. Each could be associated with very different environmental profiles and strategy recommendations. In Chapter 5, information-need areas and scenario analysis will be covered in more detail.

A host of concepts and methods are introduced in this and the following three chapters. It would, of course, be unusual to employ all of them in any given context, and the strategist should resist any compulsion to do so. Rather, those that are most relevant to the situation at hand should be selected. Furthermore, some areas of analysis will be more fruitful than others and will merit more effort.

External Analysis as a Creative Exercise

In part, external analysis is an exercise in creative thinking. In fact, there is often too little effort devoted to developing new strategic options and too much effort directed to solving operational problems of the day. The essence of creative thinking is considering different perspectives, and that is exactly what an external analysis does. The strategist is challenged to look at strategy from the perspectives of customer, competitor, market, and environment, as well as from an internal perspective. Within each there are several subdimensions; in Figure 1.3, more than two dozen are identified. The hope is that, by examining strategy from different viewpoints, options will be generated that would otherwise be missed.

The Level of Analysis – Defining the Market

An external analysis of what? To conduct an external analysis, the market or submarket boundaries need to be specified. The scope of external analysis can involve an industry broadly defined (sporting goods), narrowly defined (high-performance skis), or using a scope definition that falls in between, such as:

- ski clothing and equipment;
- skis and snowboards;
- downhill skis.

The level of analysis will depend on the organizational unit and strategic decisions involved. A sporting goods company, such as Adidas, will be making resource decisions across sports and thus needs to be concerned with the whole industry. A ski equipment manufacturer, such as Salomon, may only be concerned with elements of sporting goods relating to skis, boots, and clothing. The maker of high-performance skis might be interested in only a subsegment of the ski industry. One approach to defining the market is to specify the business scope. The scope can be identified in terms of the product market and in terms of the competitors. Relevant, of course, are the future product market and competitors, as well as the present.

There is always a trade-off to be made. A narrow scope specification will inhibit a business from identifying trends and opportunities that could lead to some attractive options and directions. Thus, a maker of downhill skis may want to include snowboards and cross-country skis because they represent business options or because they will impact upon the ski equipment business. On the other hand, depth of analysis might be sacrificed when the scope is excessively broad. A more focused analysis may generate more insight.

The analysis usually needs to be conducted at several levels. The downhill ski and snowboard industry might be the major focus of the analysis. However, an analysis of sporting goods might suggest, and shed light on, some substitute product pressures and market trends. Also, an analysis may be needed at the segment level (e.g. high-performance skis) because entry, investment, and strategy decisions are often made at that level. Furthermore, the key success factors could differ for different product markets within a market or industry. One approach is a layered analysis, with the primary level receiving the most depth of analysis. Another approach could be multiple analyses, perhaps consecutively conducted. The first analysis might stimulate an opportunity that would justify a second analysis on a submarket.

WHEN SHOULD AN EXTERNAL ANALYSIS BE CONDUCTED?

There is often a tendency to relegate the external analysis to an annual exercise. Each year, of course, it may not require the same depth as the initial effort. It may be more productive to focus on a part of the analysis in the years immediately following a major effort.

The annual planning cycle can provide a healthy stimulus to review and change strategies. However, a substantial risk exists in maintaining external analysis as an annual event. The need for strategic review and change is often continuous. Information sensing and analysis therefore also need to be continuous. The framework and concepts of external analysis can still play a key role in providing structure, even when the analysis is continuous and addresses only a portion of the whole.

External analysis deliberately commences with customer and competitor analyses because they can help define the relevant industry or industries. An industry can be defined in terms of the needs of a specific group of customers – those buying ice cream in France, for instance. Such an industry definition then forms the basis for the identification of competitors and the balance of external analysis. An industry such as the ice cream industry can also be defined in terms of all its competitors.

Because customers have such a direct relationship to a firm's operation, they are usually a rich source of relevant operational opportunities, threats, and uncertainties.

THE SCOPE OF CUSTOMER ANALYSIS

In most strategic market-planning contexts, the first logical step is to analyse the customers. Customer analysis can be usefully partitioned into an understanding of how the market segments, an analysis of customer motivations, and an exploration of unmet needs. Figure 2.2 presents a basic set of questions for each area of inquiry.

SEGMENTATION

Segmentation is often the key to developing a sustainable competitive advantage. In a strategic context, *segmentation* means the identification of customer groups that respond differently from other groups to competitive offerings. A segmentation strategy couples the identified segments with a programme to deliver an offering to those

---

SEGMENTATION

- Who are the biggest customers? The most profitable? The most attractive potential customers? Do the customers fall into any logical groups based on needs, motivations, or characteristics?
- How could the market be segmented into groups that would require a unique business strategy?

CUSTOMER MOTIVATIONS

- What elements of the product/service do customers value most?
- What are the customers' objectives? What are they really buying?
- How do segments differ in their motivation priorities?
- What changes are occurring in customer motivation? In customer priorities?

UNMET NEEDS

- Why are some customers dissatisfied? Why are some changing brands or suppliers?
- What are the severity and incidence of consumer problems?
- What are unmet needs that customers can identify? Are there some of which consumers are unaware?
- Do these unmet needs represent leverage points for competitors or a new business model?

Figure 2.2 Customer Analysis

segments. Thus, the development of a successful segmentation strategy requires the conceptualization, development, and evaluation of a targeted competitive offering.

A segmentation strategy should be judged on three dimensions. First, can a competitive offering be developed and implemented that will be appealing to the target segment? Second, can the appeal of the offering and the subsequent relationship with the target segment be maintained over time, in spite of competitive responses? Third, is the resulting business from the target segment worthwhile, given the investment required to develop and market an offering tailored to it? The concept behind a successful segmentation strategy is that, within a reduced market space, it is possible to create a dominant position that competitors will be unwilling or unable to attack successfully.

How Should Segments Be Defined?

The task of identifying segments is difficult, in part, because in any given context there are literally hundreds of ways to divide up the market. Typically, the analysis will consider five, 10, or more segmentation variables. To avoid missing a useful way of defining segments, it is important to consider a wide range of variables. These variables need to be evaluated on the basis of their ability to identify segments for which different strategies are (or should be) pursued.

The most useful segment-defining variables for an offering are rarely obvious. Among the variables frequently used are those shown in Figure 2.3.

CUSTOMER CHARACTERISTICS	
• Geographic	• Small communities as markets for discount stores
• Type of organization	• Computer needs of restaurants versus manufacturing firms versus banks versus retailers
• Size of firm	• Large hospital versus medium versus small
• Lifestyle	• Jaguar buyers tend to be more adventurous, less conservative than buyers of Mercedes-Benz and BMW
• Sex	• Mothers of young children
• Age	• Cereals for children versus adults
• Occupation	• The paper copier needs of lawyers versus bankers versus dentists
PRODUCT-RELATED APPROACHES	
• User type	• Appliance buyer – home builder, remodeller, homeowner
• Usage	• Concert – season ticket holders, occasional patrons, non-users
• Benefits sought	• Dessert eaters – those who are calorie conscious versus those who are more concerned with convenience
• Price sensitivity	• Price-sensitive Hyundai buyer versus the luxury Mercedes-Benz buyer
• Competitor	• Users of competing products
• Application	• Professional users of chain saws versus homeowners
• Brand loyalty	• Those committed to Heinz Ketchup versus price buyers

Figure 2.3 Examples of Approaches to Defining Segments

The first set of variables describes segments in terms of general characteristics unrelated to the product involved. Thus, a bakery might be concerned with geographically defined segments related to communities or even neighbourhoods. A consulting company may specialize in the financial services industry. A financial services firm in Germany may target the over-65s market, as this segment is projected to be almost 25% of the population by 2020.

Demographics are particularly powerful for defining segments, in part because a person's life stage affects his or her activities, interests, and brand loyalties. Another reason is that demographic trends are predictable. The European population over 65 is expected to grow to 136 million in 2020, when more than 36 million people will be 80 or older. A British firm, Comfort Plus Products, has recognized this trend and established itself as a source of products designed for the elderly. Adjustable beds, rise-and-decline chairs, and scooters are just some of the Comfort Plus products that appeal to this often ignored segment.

Another demographic play is represented by Reckitt Benckiser,[1] who launched an on-line corporate branding campaign in order to connect with people in the 22–32 age bracket across six of its biggest markets: the United Kingdom, the United States, Brazil, India, Russia, and Germany. The objective of the campaign was twofold: to be seen by this emerging consumer group as one of the top three global FMCG brand owners, and to ensure that those considering careers in marketing will be aware of the quality of opportunities open at Reckitt Benckiser.

The second category of segment variables includes those that are related to the product. One of the most frequently employed is usage. A bakery may follow a very different strategy in serving restaurants that rely heavily on bakery products than in serving those that use fewer such products. A manufacturer of light bulbs may design a special line for a large customer such as Tesco in the United Kingdom or Woolworths in Australia, but sell through distributors using another brand name for other outlets. Four other useful segment variables are benefits, price sensitivity, loyalty, and applications.

Benefits

If there is a most useful segmentation variable, it would be benefits sought from a product, because the selection of benefits can determine a total business strategy. In the baby food market, twin (and apparently conflicting) benefits of convenience and healthy products have driven growth. German company Hipp has used these benefits to segment the baby food market and offer a range of organic ready-made meals that provide parents with both benefits. The athletic shoe industry segments into serious athletes (small in number but influential), weekend warriors, and casual wearers using athletic shoes for street wear. Recognizing that the casual wearer segment is 80% of the market and does not really need performance, several shoe firms have employed a style-focused strategy as an alternative to the performance strategy adopted by such firms as Nike.

Price Sensitivity

The benefit dimension representing the trade-off between low price and high quality is both useful and pervasive; hence, it is appropriate to consider it separately. In many product classes there is a well-defined breakdown between those customers concerned first about price and others who are willing to pay extra for higher quality and features. Food retailers operate along a well-defined hierarchy from discounters such as Aldi and Lidl, through (in the United Kingdom) ASDA and Sainsbury, to Marks & Spencer foodhalls and on to prestige food emporia. Hotels similarly operate from the inn concept, through branded chains like Accor, to luxury hotel groups such as Taj or the Four Seasons and on to the great prestige hotels such as the George V in Paris and Claridges of London. In each case the segment dictates the strategy.

THE MALE SHOPPER[2]

The male shopper has long been ignored. A segmentation scheme provides insight into how males differ and suggests strategies for appealing to very different segments.

The Metrosexual. An affluent urban sophisticate, aged 20 to 40, who loves to buy and looks for trendy, prestigious, and high-quality products. Into men's grooming, expensive haircuts. Think Polo Ralph Lauren, Beiersdorf, and Banana Republic.

The Retrosexual. Traditional male behaviour, into football and NASCAR, rejects feminism, nostalgic for the way things were, prefers below-casual clothing, not into moisturizers for men. Think Levi's, Nike, Old Spice, Burger King, and Target.

The Modern Man. Between 'metro' and 'retro', this shopper shares their interests but does not go overboard. A sophisticated consumer in his twenties or thirties, he is comfortable with women but does not shop with them. Think Gap, Macy's, and fast casual restaurants.

The Dad. Good income. Involved in the family shopping. Efficient shopper. More functional clothing. Think Nordstrom's, McDonald's, and Amazon.

The Maturiteen. More savvy, responsible, and pragmatic than earlier generations of teens. A technology master adept at on-line research and buying. Sony, Adidas, Old Navy, Circuit City, and Internet sites of all types do well.

Loyalty

Brand loyalty, an important consideration in allocating resources, can be structured using a loyalty matrix as shown in Figure 2.4. Each cell represents a very different strategic priority and can justify a very different programme. Generally, it is too easy

	Low Loyalty	Moderate Loyalty	Loyal
Customer	Medium	High	Highest
Non-customer	Low to Medium	High	Zero

Figure 2.4 The Brand Loyalty Matrix: Priorities

to take the loyal customer for granted. However, a perspective of total profits over the life of a customer makes the value of an increase in loyalty more vivid. Thus, the highest priority is to retain the existing loyal customer base and, if possible, increase their commitment intensity and perhaps encourage them to talk to others.

The key is often to reward the loyal customer by living up to expectations consistently, providing an ongoing relationship, and offering extras that surprise and delight.

The loyalty matrix suggests that the moderate loyals, including those of competitors, should also have high priority because they represent one route to increase the size of the loyal segment. Using the matrix involves estimating the size of each of the six cells, identifying the customers in each group, and designing programmes that will influence their brand choice and loyalty level. The brand loyal non-customer is a low priority because the cost to attract is usually prohibitive unless a competitor misstep provides an opportunity. The non-loyal group will have a reduced long-term value because they will be easily enticed by a price deal.

Applications

Some products and services, particularly industrial products, can best be segmented by use or application. A laptop computer may be needed by some for use while travelling, whereas others may use it at the office. One segment may use a computer for word processing, and another may be more interested in gaming. Some might use a four-wheel drive for light industrial hauling, and others may be buying primarily for recreation.

Christensen *et al.*[3] argue that an application focus is more likely to lead to successful new products and marketing programmes than other segmentation schemes. They illustrate this by telling the story of a milkshake seller who found that many consumers bought the product in the morning in order to help them kill time while driving to work and provide energy to tide them over until lunch. Being efficient to buy and capable of being consumed with only one hand was therefore critical. Such an insight leads to ideas like making the shake thicker (so it takes longer to consume), making the purchase even more efficient with buyer cards, and adding fruit to make it more interesting in the context of a boring commute. The basic concept is that ideas for products and marketing programmes are more likely to come from a deep understanding of how the product is used than from an understanding of the customer. The success of Australian firm Billabong in extending its business can be credited to a focus on equipment and accessories for board sports (skateboarding and surfing) sold under multiple brand names, including wetsuits (Xcel), surfboards (Sector 9), luggage (DaKine), watches (Nixon), and skate clothing (Element).

Multiple Segments versus a Focus Strategy

Two distinct segmentation strategies are possible. The first focuses on a single segment, which can be much smaller than the market as a whole. Wal-Mart, now the world's largest retailer, started by concentrating on American cities with populations under 25 000 in eleven south-central states – a segment totally neglected by its competition, the large discount chains. This rural geographic focus strategy was directly responsible for several significant SCAs, including an efficient and responsive warehouse supply system, a low-cost, motivated workforce, relatively inexpensive retail space, and a lean-and-mean, hands-on management style.

An alternative to a focusing strategy is to involve multiple segments. For example, L'Oreal competes in five segments with multiple brands. These are consumer (L'Oreal and Garnier), professional (Redken and Mizani), luxury (Lancôme and Cacherel), active (La Roche Posey and Skinceuticals), and the Body Shop, which L'Oreal acquired in 2006.

In many industries, aggressive firms are moving towards multiple-segment strategies. Campbell Soup, for example, has introduced different-flavour soups for different areas in Europe. For example, in countries like Ireland and the United Kingdom they have introduced Oxtail flavour. They have also developed different flavours specific to countries. Developing multiple strategies is costly and often must be justified by an enhanced aggregate impact.

There can be important synergies between segment offerings. For example, in the alpine ski industry, the image developed by high-performance skis is important to sales at the recreational-ski end of the business. Thus, a manufacturer that is weak at the high end will have difficulty at the low end. Conversely, a successful high-end firm will want to exploit that success by having entries in the other segments. A key success factor in the general aviation industry is a broad product line, ranging from fixed-gear, single-engine piston aircraft to turboprop planes, because customers tend to trade up and will switch to a different firm if the product line has major gaps.

CUSTOMER MOTIVATIONS

After identifying customer segments, the next step is to consider their motivations: What lies behind their purchase decisions? And how does that differ by segment? It is helpful to list the segments and the motivation priorities of each, as shown in Figure 2.5 for air travellers.

Internet retailers have learned that there are distinct shopper segments, and each has a very different set of driving motivations:[4]

- *Newbie shoppers* – need a simple interface, as well as a lot of hand-holding and reassurance.
- *Reluctant shoppers* – need information, reassurance, and access to live customer support.
- *Frugal shoppers* – need to be convinced that the price is good and they do not have to search elsewhere.

Segment	Motivation
Business	Reliable service, convenient schedules, easy-to-use airports, frequent-flyer programmes, and comfortable service
Vacationers	Price, feasible schedules

Figure 2.5 Customer Motivation Grid: Air Travellers

- *Strategic shoppers* – need access to the opinions of peers or experts, and choices in configuring the products they buy.
- *Enthusiastic shoppers* – need community tools to share their experiences, as well as engaging tools to view the merchandise and personalized recommendations.
- *Convenience shoppers* – (the largest group) want efficient navigation, a lot of information from customers and experts, and superior customer service.

Some motivations will help to define strategy. The Tata Nano in India has been designed and positioned with respect to price. Priced at IR 115 000 (€1700, US$ 2400, as of August 2009) the car is designed to allow an Indian family to meet its transport needs with four wheels rather than two (many buyers will previously have met their transport needs with the motorcycle). Before making such a strategic commitment, it is crucial to know where price fits in the motivation set. For the Tata Nano, price was central, and more than 200 000 vehicles were ordered in two weeks following its launch. Other motivations may not define a strategy or differentiate a business, but represent a dimension for which adequate performance must be obtained or the battle will be lost. If the prime motivation for buyers of juice drinks is health, a viable firm must be able to deliver at least acceptable health benefits.

Determining Motivations

As Figure 2.6 suggests, consumer motivation analysis starts with the task of identifying motivations for a given segment. Although a group of managers can identify motivations, a more valid list is usually obtained by getting customers to discuss the product or service in a systematic way. Why is it being used? What is the objective? What is associated with a good or bad use experience? For a motivation such as car safety, respondents might be asked why safety is important. Such probes might result in the identification of more basic motives, such as the desire to feel calm and secure rather than anxious.

Customers can be accessed with group or individual interviews. Griffin and Hauser of the MIT Quality Function Deployment (QFD) programme compared the two approaches in a study of food-carrying devices.[5] They found that individual interviews were more cost effective, and that the group processes did not generate enough extra information to warrant the added expense. They also explored the number of interviews needed to gain a complete list of motivations, and concluded that 20–30 would cover 90–95% of the motivations.

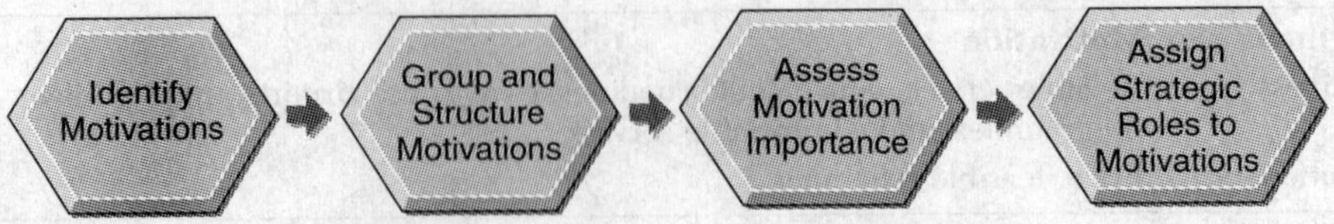

Figure 2.6 Customer Motivation Analysis

The number of motivations can be in the hundreds, so the next task is to cluster them into groups and subgroups. Affinity charts developed by a managerial team are commonly used. Each team member is given a set of motives on cards. One member puts a motive on the table or pins it to a wall, and the others add similar cards to the pile until there is a consensus that the piles represent reasonable groupings. An alternative is to use customers or groups of customers to sort the motives into piles. The customers are then asked to select one card from each pile that best represents their motives. Although managers gain buy-in and learning by going through the process themselves, Griffin and Hauser report that, in the twenty applications at one firm, the managers considered customer-based approaches better representations than their own.

BUYER HOT BUTTONS

Motivations can be categorized as important or unimportant, yet the dynamics of the market may be better captured by identifying current buyer hot buttons. Hot buttons are motivations whose salience and impact on markets are significant and growing. What are buyers talking about? What are stimulating changes in buying decisions and use patterns?

In consumer retail food products, for example, hot buttons include:

- *Freshness and naturalness.* Grocery stores have responded with salad bars, packaged precut vegetables, and efforts to upgrade the quality and selection of their fresh produce.
- *Healthy eating.* Low fat, particularly saturated and trans fat, is a prime driver, but concern about sodium, sugar, and processed foods is also growing and affecting product offerings in most food categories.
- *Ethnic eating.* A growing interest in ethnic flavours and cooking, such as Asian, Mediterranean, and Caribbean cuisines, has led to an explosion of new offerings. Brands usually start in ethnic neighbourhoods, move into natural-food and gourmet stores, and finally reach the mainstream markets.
- *Gourmet eating.* The success of Williams-Sonoma in the United States, Forman and Field in the United Kingdom, and similar retailers reflects the growth of gourmet cooking and has led to the introduction of a broader array of interesting cooking aids and devices.
- *Meal solutions.* The desire for meal solutions has led to groups of products being bundled together as a meal and to a host of take-away prepared foods offered by both grocery stores and restaurants.
- *Low-carb foods.* The influence of low-carb diets has created a demand for reduced-carb food variants in both grocery stores and restaurants.

Another task of customer motivation analysis is to determine the relative importance of the motivations. Again, the management team can address this issue. Alternatively, customers can be asked to assess the importance of the motivations directly or perhaps through trade-off questions. If an engineer had to sacrifice response time or accuracy in an oscilloscope, which would it be? Or, how would an airline passenger trade off convenient departure time with price? The trade-off question asks customers to make difficult judgements about attributes. Another approach is to see which judgements are associated with actual purchase decisions. Such an approach revealed that mothers often selected snack food based on what 'the child likes' and what was 'juicy' instead of qualities they had said were important (nourishing, easy to eat). A fourth task is to identify the motivations that will play a role in defining the value proposition of the business. The selection of motivations central to strategy will depend not only on customer motivations but also on other factors such as competitors' strategies that emerge in the competitor analysis. Another factor is how feasible and practical the resulting strategy is for the business. Internal analysis will be involved in making that determination, as will an analysis of the strategy's implementation.

Qualitative Research

Qualitative research is a powerful tool in understanding customer motivation. It can involve focus-group sessions, in-depth interviews, customer case studies, or ethnographic research (to be described shortly). The concept is to search for the real motivations that do not emerge from structured lists. For instance, buyers of active lifestyle brands, like Quiksilver, might really be expressing their rebellious or adventurous attitude. The perception that a product is too expensive might really reflect a financing gap. Getting inside the customer can provide strategic insights that do not emerge in any other way.

Although a representative cross-section of customers is usually sought, special attention to some is often merited. Very loyal customers are often best able to articulate the bonds that the firm is capable of establishing. Lost customers (those who have defected) are often particularly good at graphically communicating problems with the product or service. New customers or customers who have recently increased their usage may suggest new applications. Organizational buyers using multiple vendors may have a good perspective of the firm relative to the competition.

Changing Customer Priorities

It is particularly critical to gain insight into changes in customers' priorities. In the high-tech area, customer priorities often evolve from needing help in selecting and installing the right equipment to wanting performance to looking for low cost. In the coffee business, customer tastes and habits have evolved from buying coffee at grocery stores to drinking coffee at gourmet cafés to buying their own whole-bean gourmet coffees. Assuming that customer priorities are not changing can be risky. It is essential to ask whether a significant and growing segment has developed priorities that are different from the basic business model.

The Customer as Active Partner

Customers are increasingly becoming active partners in their relationship with the firm and brand rather than passive targets of product development and advertising.

The trend is illustrated by patients taking control of medical issues and the control of media shifting as audiences move to DVRs, and the power-enhancing access to information and fellow customers that is provided by the Internet. To harness this change, managers should:[6]

- *Encourage active dialogue.* Contact with customers must now be considered a dialogue of equals. Blogs, if managed with honesty and integrity by a firm, can be a good way to create dialogue with customers.
- *Mobilize customer communities.* The Internet facilitates stronger and more widespread on-line customer communities. The challenge is to organize and create the context for the communities so that they become an extension of the brand experience and a source of customer input into the product and its use.
- *Manage customer diversity.* Particularly in technology products, there will be a wide range of sophistication among customers, and the challenge will be to deal with multiple levels. The more sophisticated group will be the most active partners.
- *Co-creating personalized experiences.* An on-line florist might let customers design the type and arrangement of flowers and vases, rather than merely providing a menu of choices. Co-creating experiences go beyond customization in tailoring the offering to the needs of individuals.

Interacting with the customer on the Internet requires skills in listening, engaging, and leading. Each has challenges. Often there is information overload. There is a mention of McDonald's on the Internet every five seconds or so. Software to summarize content can play a role if integrated into an information system. Engaging can be difficult because it will depend on whether the firm has permission to enter the space, and there can be risks of a misstatement or inflaming an issue if it is engaged. However, clearly identified firm spokespeople can be effective. Leading usually requires getting in front of the Internet discussion with products or programmes.

UNMET NEEDS

An unmet need is a customer need that is not being met by the existing product offerings. NetJets was set up to sell a one-sixteenth interest (and greater) in corporate jets to business travellers who needed the flexibility of a private jet but were unwilling or unable to buy their own aircraft. Unmet needs are strategically important because they represent opportunities for firms to enhance existing brand relationships, increase their market share, break into a market, or create and own new markets. They can also represent threats to established firms in that they can be a lever that enables competitors to disrupt an established position. The Swiss company Ricola, manufacturer of herb drops and candy, has entered a number of international markets by offering consumers a sugar-free candy. Its path has been smoothed because of a lack of competition in this market and consumer desire to reduce their sugar intake.

Sometimes customers may not be aware of their unmet needs because they are so accustomed to the implicit limitations of existing equipment. Who could have conceived of a need for an electric light bulb or a tractor before technology made them possible? Unmet needs that are not obvious may be more difficult to identify, but they can also represent a greater opportunity for an aggressive business because there will be little pressure on established firms to be responsive. The key is to stretch the technology or apply new technologies in order to expose unmet needs.

Using Customers to Identify Unmet Needs

Customers are a prime source of unmet needs. The trick is to access them and to get customers to detect and communicate unmet needs. What product-use experience problems have emerged? What is frustrating? How does it compare with other product experiences? Are there problems with the total-use system in which the product is embedded? How can the product be improved? This kind of research helped Unilever come up with Magnum, a line of adult ice cream bars with rich ingredients that addressed the need for an adult ice cream treat.

USER-DEVELOPED PRODUCTS

The Dutch electronics firm, Philips, has used the ideas of customers in innovative ways to feed into new product development. Using a website, Live Simplicity, they invite customers to discuss six areas; including communication, Internet and technology, and wellness, and to offer their opinions on particular viewpoints. Philips has also actively used customers, in this case lead users, to explore issues such as sleep quality. Again using a website, Leadusers.nl, the company has studied lead users with the objective of understanding needs and identifying new product opportunities.

In the early 1970s, store owners and sales personnel in southern California began to notice that youngsters were fixing up their bicycles to look like motorcycles, complete with imitation exhausts and chopper-type handlebars. Sporting crash helmets and Honda motorcycle T-shirts, the youngsters raced fancy 20-inchers on dirt tracks. Obviously onto a good thing, the manufacturers came out with a whole new line of motorcross models. California users refined this concept into the mountain bike. Manufacturers were guided by the California customers to develop new refinements, including the 21-speed gear shift that doesn't require removing one's hands from the handlebars. Mountain bike firms are enjoying booming growth and are still watching their West Coast customers.

A structured approach, termed *problem research*, develops a list of potential problems with the product. The problems are then prioritized by asking a group of 100–200 respondents to rate each problem as to whether (1) the problem is important, (2) the problem occurs frequently, and (3) a solution exists. A problem score is obtained by combining these ratings. A dog-food problem research study found that buyers felt dog food smelled bad, cost too much, and was not available in different sizes for different dogs. Subsequently, products responsive to these criticisms emerged. Another study led an airline to modify its cabins to provide more leg room. Eic von Hippel, a researcher at MIT who studies customers as sources of service innovations, suggests that lead users provide a particularly fertile ground for discovering unmet needs and new product concepts.[7] Lead users can be characterized as follows:

- They face needs that will be general in the marketplace, but face them months or years before the bulk of the marketplace. A person who is very into health foods and nutrition would be a lead user with respect to health foods, if we assume that there is a trend towards health foods.
- They are positioned to benefit significantly by obtaining a solution to those needs. Lead users of office automation would be firms that today would benefit significantly from technological advancement.

An effective and efficient way to access customers is to use the Internet to engage them in a dialogue. Apple agreed to replace defective screens on its iPod Nano after receiving complaints from customers that it cracked too easily and discovering a website dedicated to complaints about the device. Other firms have sought more actively to involve customers in improving existing products and services. Starbucks, with its MyStarbucksidea.com site, is among many firms that are attempting to do something similar.

A risk with customer-driven idea sites is that there can be a surge around an idea that is impractical or unwise and the company would then be defensive. But it has the potential of leveraging many perspectives to generate ideas that can result in real energy and innovation. To actively engage with this, many firms have invited customers to enter competitions to design new products; these include the Henkel Innovation Trophy, the Nokia Concept Lounge, and the Electrolux Design Lab. The benefits for the firm include the ability to identify totally new products that those within corporate boundaries may not be able to see, or, at a minimum, to be inspired to think differently about their own innovation efforts.

Ethnographic Research

Ethnographic or anthropological research involves directly observing customers in as many contexts as possible. By accurately observing not only what is done involving the target or service but *why* it is being done, companies can achieve a deeper level of understanding of the customer's needs and motivations and generate actionable insights. For example, Motorola observed that Chinese businessmen had developed a unique system of using pagers to communicate with each other when they were in areas with no telephone service. This led the company to develop a two-way pager for the market.[8] Although this research approach has been around for nearly a century, it has taken on new life in the last few years not only in packaged goods firms like Procter & Gamble but also in business-to-business firms like Intel and GE.

Ethnographic research is particularly good at identifying breakthrough innovations. Customers usually cannot verbalize such innovations, because they are used to the current offerings. Henry Ford famously observed that, had he asked customers what they wanted, they would have said faster horses. By watching people buy and use in the context of their lives or their businesses, however, experienced and talented anthropologists (or executives, in many cases) can generate insights that go beyond what customers could talk about.

Ethnographic research works.[9] After one study observed the difficulty people had in cleaning the bathroom, P&G developed Magic Reach, a device with a long handle and swivel head. Visits to contractors and home renovators resulted in the development of the OXO hammer (with a fibreglass core to cut vibration and a rubber bumper on top to avoid leaving marks when removing nails) as part of a line of professional-grade tools. Sirius followed 45 people for a week, studying what music they listened to, which magazines they read, and which TV shows they watched, and then developed a portable satellite-radio player that could load up to 50 hours of music for later playback.[10] Black & Decker's observation that cordless drill users ran out of power led to the detachable battery pack. Intel's research in the Third World led it to develop a cheap PC that could run on truck batteries in 100 degree temperatures. GE found through ethnographic research that buyers of plastic fibre for fire-retardant jackets were more concerned with performance than price. That led to a completely different business model in GE's efforts to enter the field.

Ethnographic research can also be used to improve existing products or services. London Underground, operators of the 'Tube', found that the low brand evaluations of the service were driven not only by rational problems such as heat, crowding, and customer information but also by a more significant response to the fact of being deep underground. Using this insight, London Underground took a number of actions, including redesigning stations to be less cluttered and more spacious and welcoming, introducing a requirement for an on-train announcement within 30 seconds of a train stopping in a tunnel, and playing classical music at some stations. Combined these had the dual effect of improving the atmosphere and encouraging youth engaged in antisocial behaviour to go elsewhere.[11]

The Ideal Experience

The conceptualization of an ideal experience can also help to identify unmet needs. A major publisher of directories polled its customers, asking each to describe its ideal experience with the firm. The publisher found that its very large customers (the top 4%, who were generating 45% of its business) wanted a single contact point to resolve problems, customized products, consultation on using the service, and help in tracking results. In contrast, smaller customers wanted a simple ordering process and to be left alone. These responses provided insights into improving service while cutting costs.[12]

KEY LEARNINGS

- External analysis should influence strategy by identifying opportunities, threats, trends, and strategic uncertainties. The ultimate goal is to improve strategic choices – decisions as to where and how to compete.
- Segmentation (identifying customer groups that can support different competitive strategies) can be based on a variety of customer characteristics, such as benefits sought, customer loyalty, and applications.
- Customer motivation analysis can provide insights into what assets and competencies are needed to compete, as well as indicating possible SCAs.
- Unmet needs that represent opportunities (or threats) can be identified by asking customers, by accessing lead users, by ethnographic research, and by interacting with customers.

FOR DISCUSSION

1. Why do a strategic analysis? What are the objectives? What, in your view, are the three keys to making a strategic analysis helpful and important? Is there a downside to conducting a full-blown strategic analysis?
2. Consider the buyer 'hot buttons' described in the insert. What are the implications for Buitoni? What new business areas might be considered, given each hot button? Answer the same questions for a grocery store chain such as Safeway.
3. Consider the segments in the male shopper insert. Describe each further. What car would they drive? What kind of holiday would they take? What beer brand would they buy?
4. What is a customer buying at Harrods? At Banana Republic? At Zara?
5. Pick a company or brand/business on which to focus, such as cereals. What are the major segments? What are the customer motivations by segments? What are the unmet needs?

NOTES

1. 'Cleaning Products 3.0? Reckitt Benckiser Makes an Online Push to Connect with Young Consumers', *Marketing*, 14 July 2009.
2. This insert was inspired by Nanette Byrnes, 'Secrets of the Male Shopper', *Business Week*, 4 September 2006, pp. 45–53.
3. Clayton M. Christiansen, Scott Cook, and Taddy Hall, 'Marketing Malpractice: the Cause and the Cure', *Harvard Business Review*, December 2005, pp. 74–83.
4. Melinda Cuthbert, 'All Buyers Not Alike', *Business 2.0*, 26 December 2000.

5. Abbie Griffin and John R. Hauser, 'The Voice of the Customer', *Marketing Science*, Winter 1993, pp. 1–27.
6. C.K. Prahalad and Venkatram Ramaswamy, 'Co-opting Customer Competence', *Harvard Business Review*, January–February 2000, pp. 79–87.
7. Eric von Hippel, 'Lead Users: a Source of Novel Product Concepts', *Management Science*, July 1986, p. 802.
8. Richard J. Harrington and Anthony K. Tjan, 'Transforming Strategy One Customer at a Time', *Harvard Business Review*, March 2008, p. 67.
9. Elizabeth Sanders, 'Ethnography in NPD Research. How "Applied Ethnography" Can Improve Your NPD Research Process', *Visions Magazine*, 2006; available at: http://www.maketools.com/pdfs/EthnographyinNPDResearch_Sanders_02.pdf (accessed 12 October 2009).
10. Spencer E. Ante, 'The Science of Desire', *Business Week*, 5 June 2006, pp. 99–106.
11. Ian Pring, 'Forum – Going Underground: How Ethnography Helped the Tube Tunnel to the Heart of its Brand', *International Journal of Market Research*, 2007, **49**(6).
12. George S. Day, 'Creating a Superior Customer-Relating Capability', *Sloan Management Review*, Spring 2003, pp. 82–83.

CHAPTER THREE

Competitor Analysis

Competition is always a fantastic thing, and the computer industry is intensely competitive. Whether it's Google or Apple or free software, we've got some fantastic competitors and it keeps us on our toes.
—Bill Gates

If you know your strength it never becomes a weakness. If the market knows your strength then it becomes a weakness.
—Shailendra Singh

The ability to learn faster than your competitors may be the only sustainable competitive advantage.
—Arie de Geus

In the history of business there are many examples of how competitors, often unseen or unanticipated by industry incumbents, have emerged to capture significant market share and profits within industries. In the 1970s the American car market, the home of the world's greatest car firms, was significantly penetrated by Japanese car brands. The profitability and structure of the European airline industry was transformed in the 1990s by Ryanair and easyJet, start-up, low-cost carriers that few took seriously. In the early part of the twenty-first century the business model of the music industry was irrevocably changed by Napster, a previously unheard of company run by a college student using technology that all knew to be available. In more recent times, Microsoft, an earnings giant that created and led the personal computer industry, is being challenged by Google, and other competitors, who primarily give their operating systems and software away for free. What is common among the challengers in each case is a clear, formal or informal, understanding of where the weaknesses of their stronger adversaries lay and a parallel lack of understanding on the part of incumbents to see their rivals early enough to take action against them.

In parallel, as the BRIC economies (Brazil, Russia, India, and China) continue to develop as economic powerhouses, are similar mistakes being made by western managers again? How realistic is the assumption that India's threat lies mainly in its low-cost base when that economy graduated 112 000 engineers in 2004, with the number expected to double by 2010? How seriously should companies take the ambition of Chinese firms to take their place on the global stage when there is a national ambition to have 50 Chinese firms on the Fortune 500 list by 2010 (there were 24 in 2007 and 37 in 2009). It is widely expected that 100–125 places on the Fortune 500 list will be held by Chinese firms in 2020. Who will lose out and why?

Competitor analysis is the second phase of external analysis. Again, the goal should be insights that will influence the development of successful business strategies. The analysis should focus on the identification of threats, opportunities, or strategic uncertainties created by emerging or potential competitor moves, weaknesses, or strengths.

Competitor analysis starts with identifying current and potential competitors. There are two very different ways of identifying current competitors. The first examines the perspective of the customer who must make choices among competitors. This approach groups competitors according to the degree to which they compete for a buyer's choice. The second approach attempts to place competitors in strategic groups on the basis of their competitive strategy.

After competitors are identified, the focus shifts to attempting to understand them and their strategies. Of particular interest is an analysis of the strengths and weaknesses of each competitor or strategic group of competitors. Figure 3.1 summarizes a set of questions that can provide a structure for competitor analysis.

WHO ARE THE COMPETITORS?

- Against whom do we usually compete? Who are our most intense competitors? Less intense but still serious competitors? Makers of substitute products?
- Can these competitors be grouped into strategic groups on the basis of their assets, competencies, and/or strategies?
- Who are the potential competitive entrants? What are their barriers to entry? Is there anything that can be done to discourage them?

EVALUATING THE COMPETITORS

- What are their objectives and strategies? Their level of commitment? Their exit barriers?
- What is their cost structure? Do they have a cost advantage or disadvantage?
- What is their image and positioning strategy?
- Which are the most successful/unsuccessful competitors over time? Why?
- What are the strengths and weaknesses of each competitor or strategic group?
- What leverage points (or strategic weaknesses or customer problems or unmet needs) could competitors exploit to enter the market or become more serious competitors?
- Evaluate the competitors with respect to their assets and competencies. Generate a competitor strength grid.

Figure 3.1 Questions to Structure Competitor Analysis

IDENTIFYING COMPETITORS – CUSTOMER-BASED APPROACHES

One approach to identifying competitor sets is to look at competitors from the perspective of customers – what choices are customers making? A Nespresso coffee machine buyer could be asked what brand would have been purchased had the Nespresso offering not been available. A buyer for a nursing home meal service could be asked what would be substituted for granulated potato buds if they increased in price. A sample of sports car buyers could be asked what other cars they considered and perhaps what other dealers they actually visited.

Product-Use Associations

Another approach that provides insights is the association of products with specific-use contexts or applications. Perhaps 20 or 30 product users could be asked to identify a list of use situations or applications. For each use context they would then name all the products that are appropriate. Then, for each product they would identify appropriate use contexts so that the list of use contexts would be more complete. Another group of respondents would then be asked to make judgements about how appropriate each product is for each use context. Then, products would be clustered according to the similarity of their appropriate use contexts. Thus, if Cadbury's Time-Out or the Indian snack brand Kurkure were regarded as appropriate for snack occasions, they would compete primarily with products similarly perceived. The same approach will work with an industrial product that might be used in several distinct applications.

Both the customer-choice and product-use approaches suggest a conceptual basis for identifying competitors that can be employed by managers even when marketing research is not available. The concept of alternatives from which customers choose and the concept of appropriateness to a use context can be powerful tools in helping to understand the competitive environment.

Indirect Competitors

In most instances, primary competitors are quite visible and easily identified. Heineken competes with Carlsberg, Stella Artois, Guinness, and other beers. CNN competes with other international news channels – Sky News, Bloomberg, CNBC, and BBC World. Airbus competes with Boeing. The competitor analysis for this group should be done with depth and insight.

In many markets, however, customer priorities are changing, and indirect competitors offering customers product alternatives are strategically relevant. Understanding these indirect competitors can be strategically and tactically important, as the following examples demonstrate:

- As mobile phones become more feature laden with MP3 players, cameras, and videos, handset manufacturers such as Nokia have had to expand their understanding of competitors to include consumer electronics firms such as Sony and Apple.

- Coke focused on Pepsi and ignored for many years the emerging submarkets in water, iced tea, and fruit-based drinks. The result was a missed opportunity and the eventual need to pursue an expensive and difficult catch-up strategy.
- While newspapers globally have traditionally competed in particular geographic regions, using wide distribution and well-known columnists to drive sales, the global availability of quality news coverage through websites of the BBC, CNN, and newspapers such as *The Daily Telegraph* (United Kingdom) reduced the value they provide and the willingness of consumers to pay for them.
- While Nescafé, Maxwell House, and others competed for supermarket business using coupon promotions, other firms, such as India's Barista Coffee and Australia's Gloria Jean's and Starbucks, succeeded in selling a very different kind of coffee in different ways. These chains are in turn now threatened by gourmet coffee makers sold for home use (such as Nespresso) and by alternatives offered by chains like McDonald's.
- On-line music providers were largely ignored by the major music labels until they gradually became major players.

The energy drinks market includes direct competitors such as Lucozade, Red Bull, Powerade, and dozens of smaller, niche firms. There are also a host of indirect competitors, many with very similar products: bottled water brands like Evian, soft-drink brands like 7-Up and Sprite, and juice brands like Tropicana. Understanding the positioning and new product strategies of these indirect competitors will be strategically important to businesses in the energy drinks category.

Both direct and indirect competitors can be further categorized in terms of how relevant they are, as determined by similar positioning. Thus, bottled water will be more relevant to Powerade than to Red Bull because of the former's positioning as an aid to sports hydration.

The competitive analysis in nearly all cases will benefit from extending the perspective beyond the obvious direct competitors. By explicitly considering indirect competitors, the strategic horizon is expanded, and the analysis more realistically mirrors what the customer sees. In the real world, the customer is never restricted to a firm's direct competitors, but instead is always poised to consider other options.

A key issue with respect to strategic analysis in general, and competitor analysis in particular, is the level at which the analysis is conducted. Is it at the level of a business unit, the firm, or some other aggregation of businesses? Because an analysis will be needed at all levels at which strategies are developed, multiple analyses might ultimately be necessary. For example, Walkers' Sensations range is positioned as the 'posh crisp' for an everyday treat. Strategy development for this brand would benefit from a competitor analysis of luxury crisps, such as premium and kettle crisps, with other crisp brands being considered as indirect competitors.

IDENTIFYING COMPETITORS – STRATEGIC GROUPS

The concept of a strategic group provides a very different approach towards understanding the competitive structure of an industry. A strategic group is a group of firms that:

- over time pursue similar competitive strategies (for example, the use of the same distribution channel, the same type of communication strategies, or the same price/quality position);
- have similar characteristics (e.g. size, aggressiveness);
- have similar assets and competencies (such as brand associations, logistics capability, global presence, or research and development).

For example, there have historically been three strategic groups in the European airline business. One strategic group consists of the flag carriers. These are large and medium-sized airlines with established brands, some of them strong. Historically, they dominated the airline travel market in Europe and competed using services, destinations, and their participation in alliances such as Oneworld and the Star Alliance. The large players within this group are British Airways, Air France-KLM, and Lufthansa. The second tier of airlines includes British Midland, Aer Lingus, Alitalia, and Iberia. All are historically strong but suffering from their lack of scale and the impact of low-cost carriers.

In fact, many industries are populated by premium-dominated volume entries such as China Airlines in airlines or Budweiser in beer, low-cost entries such as India's Air Deccan in airlines, and niche groups such as timeshare planes and low-alcohol and craft beers.

Each strategic group has mobility barriers that inhibit or prevent businesses from moving from one strategic group to another. An ultrapremium group has the brand reputation, product, and manufacturing knowledge needed for the health segment, access to influential veterinarians and retailers, and a local customer base. Private-label manufacturers have low-cost production, low overheads, and close relationships with customers. It is possible to bypass or overcome the barriers, of course. A private-label manufacturer could create a branded entry, especially if markets are selected to minimize conflicts with existing customers. The barriers are real, however, and a firm competing across strategic groups is usually at a disadvantage.

A member of a strategic group can have exit as well as entry barriers. For example, assets such as plant investment or a specialized labour force can represent a meaningful exit barrier, as can the need to protect a brand's reputation.

The mobility barrier concept is crucial because one way to develop a sustainable competitive advantage is to pursue a strategy that is protected from competition by assets and competencies that represent barriers to competitors. Consider the PC and server market. Dell and others have marketed computers direct to consumers by telephone and the Internet. They developed a host of assets and competencies to support their direct channels, including an impressive product support system. Competitors such as HP – which has used indirect channels involving retailers and systems firms – have developed a very different set of assets and competencies. HP and Dell have both struggled to cross the channel barriers.

Using the Strategic Group Concept

The conceptualization of strategic groups can make the process of competitor analysis more manageable. Numerous industries contain many more competitors than can be analysed individually. Often it is simply not feasible to consider 30 competitors, to say nothing of hundreds. Reducing this set to a small number of strategic groups makes the analysis compact, feasible, and more usable. For example, in the wine industry, competitor analysis by a firm like BRL Hardy might examine three strategic groups: jug wines, premium wines (€12–20), and superpremium wines (over €25). Little strategic content and insight will be lost in most cases, because firms in a strategic group will be affected by and react to industry developments in similar ways. Thus, in projecting future strategies of competitors, the concept of strategic groups can be helpful.

Strategic groupings can refine the strategic investment decision. Instead of determining in which industries to invest, the decision can focus on what strategic group warrants investment. Thus, it will be necessary to determine the current profitability and future potential profitability of each strategic group. One strategic objective is to invest in attractive strategic groups in which assets and competencies can be employed to create strategic advantage.

Ultimately, the selection of a strategy and its supporting assets and competencies will often mean selecting or creating a strategic group. Thus, a knowledge of the strategic group structure and dynamics can be extremely useful.

POTENTIAL COMPETITORS

In addition to current competitors, it is important to consider potential market entrants, such as firms that might engage in:

1. *Market expansion.* Perhaps the most obvious source of potential competitors is firms operating in other geographic regions or in other countries. A snack food company may want to keep a close eye on a competing firm in a nearby country, for example.
2. *Product expansion.* The leading Chinese food and agribusiness firm, COFCO, began its life as an agricultural commodity trader and used related product expansion, including reintroducing foreign wines and Coca-Cola to the Chinese market, as a driver of growth. COFCO has been included in the Fortune 500 list of the world's leading enterprises since 1994.
3. *Backward integration.* Customers are another potential source of competition. For example, Kingspan, an Irish company active in the manufacture of insulation products, has acquired dozens of manufacturers of components over the years, including a manufacturer of insulation materials.
4. *Forward integration.* Suppliers attracted by margins are also potential competitors. Sony, for example, has very successfully opened a chain of retail stores. Suppliers, believing they have the critical ingredients to succeed in a market, may be attracted by the margins and control that come with integrating forward.

5. *The export of assets or competencies.* A current small competitor with critical strategic weaknesses can turn into a major entrant if it is purchased by a firm that can reduce or eliminate those weaknesses. Predicting such moves can be difficult, but sometimes an analysis of competitor strengths and weaknesses will suggest some possible synergistic mergers. A competitor in an above-average growth industry that does not have the financial or managerial resources for the long haul might be a particularly attractive candidate for merger.
6. *Retaliatory or defensive strategies.* Firms that are threatened by a potential or actual move into their market might retaliate. Thus, Microsoft has made several moves (including into the Internet space), in part to protect its dominant software position.

COMPETITOR ANALYSIS – UNDERSTANDING COMPETITORS

Understanding competitors and their activities can provide several benefits. First, an understanding of the current strategy strengths and weaknesses of a competitor can suggest opportunities and threats that will merit a response. Second, insights into future competitor strategies may allow the prediction of emerging threats and opportunities. Third, a decision about strategic alternatives might easily hinge on the ability to forecast the likely reaction of key competitors. Finally, competitor analysis may result in the identification of some strategic uncertainties that will be worth monitoring closely over time. A strategic uncertainty might be, for example, 'Will competitor A decide to move into the Chinese market?'.

As Figure 3.2 indicates, competitor actions are influenced by eight elements. The first of these reflects financial performance, as measured by size, growth, and profitability.

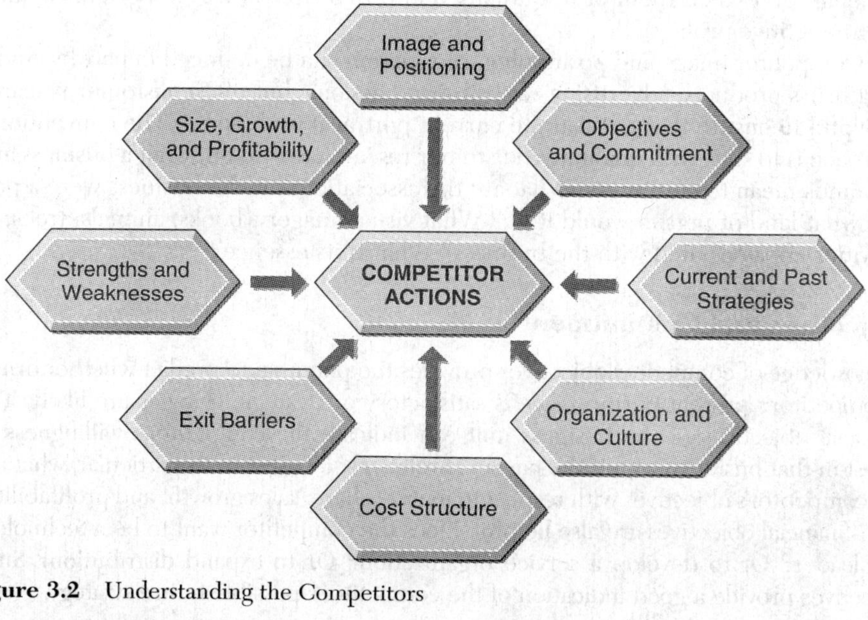

Figure 3.2 Understanding the Competitors

Size, Growth, and Profitability

The level and growth of sales and market share provide indicators of the vitality of a business strategy. The maintenance of a strong market position or the achievement of rapid growth usually reflects a strong competitor (or strategic group) and a successful strategy. In contrast, a deteriorating market position can signal financial or organizational strains that might affect the interest and ability of the business to pursue certain strategies. To provide a crude sales estimate for businesses that are buried in a large company, take the number of employees and multiply it by the average sales per employee in the industry. For many businesses, this method is very feasible and remarkably accurate.

After size and growth comes profitability. A profitable business will generally have access to capital for investment unless it has been designated by the parent to be milked. A business that has lost money over an extended time period or has experienced a recent sharp decrease in profitability may find it difficult to gain access to capital either externally or internally.

Image and Positioning Strategy

A cornerstone of a business strategy can be an association, such as being the strongest truck, the most durable car, the smallest consumer electronics equipment, or the most effective cleaner. More often, it is useful to move beyond class-related product attributes to intangibles that span product class, such as quality, innovation, sensitivity to the environment, or brand personality.

In order to develop positioning alternatives, it is helpful to determine the image and brand personality of the major competitors. Weaknesses of competitors on relevant attributes or personality traits can represent an opportunity to differentiate and develop advantage. Strengths of competitors on important dimensions may represent challenges to exceed them or to outflank them. In any case, it is important to know the competitive profiles.

Competitor image and positioning information can be deduced in part by studying a firm's products, advertising, website, and actions, but often customer research is helpful to ensure that an accurate current portrayal is obtained. The conventional approach is to start with qualitative customer research to find out what a business and its brands mean to customers. What are the associations? If the business were a person, what kind of person would it be? What visual imagery, books, animals, trees, or activities are associated with the business? What is its essence?

Objectives and Commitment

A knowledge of competitor objectives provides the potential to predict whether or not a competitor's present performance is satisfactory or strategic changes are likely. The financial objectives of the business unit can indicate the competitor's willingness to invest in that business even if the payout is relatively long term. In particular, what are the competitor's objectives with respect to market share, sales growth, and profitability? Non-financial objectives are also helpful. Does the competitor want to be a technological leader? Or to develop a service organization? Or to expand distribution? Such objectives provide a good indication of the competitor's possible future strategy.

The objectives of the competitor's parent company (if one exists) are also relevant. What are the current performance levels and financial objectives of the parent? If the business unit is not performing as well as the parent, pressure might be exerted to improve or the investment might be withdrawn. Of critical importance is the role attached to the business unit. Is it central to the parent's long-term plans, or is it peripheral? Is it seen as a growth area, or is it expected to supply cash to fund other areas? Does the business create synergy with other operations? Does the parent have an emotional attachment to the business unit for any reason? Deep pockets can sometimes be accompanied with short arms; just because resources exist does not mean they are available.

Current and Past Strategies

The competitor's current and past strategies should be reviewed. In particular, past strategies that have failed should be noted, because such experiences can inhibit the competitor from trying similar strategies again. Also, a knowledge of a competitor's pattern of new product or new market moves can help anticipate its future growth directions. Is the strategy based on product line breadth, product quality, service, distribution type, or brand identification? If a low-cost strategy is employed, is it based on economies of scale, the experience curve, manufacturing facilities and equipment, or access to raw material? What is its cost structure? If a focus strategy is evident, describe the business scope.

Organization and Culture

Knowledge about the background and experience of the competitor's top management can provide insight into future actions. Are the managers drawn from marketing, engineering, or manufacturing? Are they largely from another industry or company? Premier Foods, a UK firm that owns many strong brands including Oxo, Branston, Ambrosia and Crosse and Blackwell, has employed a number of marketers previously employed by Heinz.[1] This insight provides some sense of how the brands mentioned and others owned by Premier might be managed in the future.

An organization's culture, supported by its structure, systems, and people, often has a pervasive influence on strategy. A cost-oriented, highly structured organization that relies on tight controls to achieve objectives and motivate employees may have difficulty innovating or shifting into an aggressive, marketing-oriented strategy. A loose, flat organization that emphasizes innovation and risk-taking may similarly have difficulty pursuing a disciplined product-refinement and cost-reduction programme. In general, as Chapter 15 will make clearer, organizational elements such as culture, structure, systems, and people limit the range of strategies that should be considered.

Cost Structure

Knowledge of a competitor's cost structure, especially when the competitor is relying on a low-cost strategy, can provide an indication of its likely future pricing strategy and its staying power. The following information can usually be obtained and can provide insights into cost structures:

- the number of employees and a rough breakdown of direct labour (variable labour cost) and overheads (which will be part of fixed costs);
- the relative costs of raw materials and purchased components;
- the investment in inventory, plant, and equipment (also fixed cost);
- sales levels and number of plants (on which the allocation of fixed costs is based);
- outsourcing strategy.

Exit Barriers

Exit barriers can be crucial to a firm's ability to withdraw from a business area, and thus are indicators of commitment. They include:[2]

- specialized assets – plant, equipment, or other assets that are costly to transform to another application and therefore have little salvage value;
- fixed costs, such as labour agreements, leases, and a need to maintain parts for existing equipment;
- relationships with other business units in the firm, resulting from the firm's image or from shared facilities, distribution channels, or sales force;
- government and social barriers – for example, governments may regulate whether a railroad can exit from a passenger service responsibility, or firms may feel a sense of loyalty to workers, thereby inhibiting strategic moves;
- managerial pride or an emotional attachment to a business or its employees that affects economic decisions.

NINTENDO – SUCCESS THAT STARTED WITH COMPETITOR ANALYSIS

The story of the Nintendo business strategy and brand is nothing short of astounding, and competitive analysis played an important part. BrandJapan, an annual survey over eight years of the strength of over 1000 Japanese brands, had seen a remarkable stability in the cast of characters occupying the top two dozen positions. Then came Nintendo. In the 2005 findings, Nintendo was ranked 135 in the survey. From that point on, its status rose to 66 in 2006, to 5 in 2007, and finally to the number one position in 2008, a position it held with a value of over 93 while the next seven brands were bunched at 82–84. During the 2004–2008 period, its stock price went up more than five-fold, and at one point its market cap was behind only Toyota in Japan. Why? What drove this performance?

The products were clearly the drivers. Nintendo DS, released in December 2004, was a compact portable game console characterized by an innovatively intuitive touch-pen method. It was supported by the Touch! Generations series, which included game titles such as *Nintendogs*, *Animal Crossing*, and *Brain Age* aimed at a wide target market including young females and even seniors. Then came Wii, a new form of game that incorporated user movement into gaming. With a wireless controller and the Wii remote, which detects movement in three dimensions, the user can dance, golf, box, play a guitar, and so on and so forth. Opponents can be sourced in other locations, even in other countries. In fact, the DS and Wii, with their supporting games, created a new market categorized as 'casual games' – video games that require fewer skills and less experience and are characterized by simple and intuitive rules. The new casual game category went from 1% of the market to over 20% by 2005.[3]

But what was behind the Nintendo innovation success? Why was it able to beat such formidable competitors in this space as Sony and Microsoft? One principal reason was the acceptance of a realistic and astute analysis of the two competitors – Sony (Playstation) and Microsoft (Xbox). Nintendo recognized that Sony and Microsoft had, and would have, equipment that had better technology – higher-performance, higher-resolution, and higher-quality graphics – that appealed to the heavy users, i.e. young males. They were focused on that objective and invested in chips, software, manufacturing, and hardware to keep delivering. As a result, Sony and Microsoft had a definitive edge with respect to the teen and early-20s user, the hard-core heavy user group. Given this reality, Nintendo took a different course, a low-tech route, even though that meant that the heavy user segment might have to be ceded to the two competitors.

Nintendo decided to refocus its target population away from the hard-core young males, who were into action games and high-quality graphics, towards a broader audience, less concerned with ever-improving graphics. The key for this group would be a wide array of easy-to-use games that would move beyond the action genre and include some learning vehicles. One goal was to make the mother a participant and an advocate rather than a cynic and an opponent. Another was to involve the whole family so that the games were not simply the boys' domain. The strategy went against the conventional one of focusing on the heavy user and trying to better competitor's offerings.

A strategy, no matter how good, requires implementation, and that means people. Nintendo was blessed with a talented group that was extremely good at creating games. The new strategy liberated this group to be creative and fulfil its potential. Furthermore, a new CEO, a key ingredient, was brought in, a young, energetic entrepreneurial person. With exceptional people and organizational skills, he was able to gain acceptance and excitement around the new strategy and marshal the talent needed to implement it.

Assessing Strengths and Weaknesses

Knowledge of a competitor's strengths and weaknesses provides insight that is key to a firm's ability to pursue various strategies. It also offers important input into the process of identifying and selecting strategic alternatives. One approach is to attempt to exploit a competitor's weakness in an area where the firm has an existing or developing strength. The desired pattern is to develop a strategy that will pit 'our' strength against a competitor's weakness. Conversely, a knowledge of 'their' strength is important, so it can be bypassed or neutralized.

One firm that developed a strategy to neutralize a competitor's strength was a small software firm that lacked a retail distribution capability or the resources to engage in retail advertising. It targeted value-added software systems firms selling total software and sometimes hardware systems to organizations such as investment firms or hospitals.

These value-added systems firms could understand and exploit the power of the product, integrate it into their systems, and use it in quantity. The competitor's superior access to a distribution channel or resources to support an advertising effort were thus neutralized.

The assessment of a competitor's strengths and weaknesses starts with an identification of relevant assets and competencies for the industry and then evaluates the competitor on the basis of those assets and competencies. We now turn to these topics.

COMPETITOR STRENGTHS AND WEAKNESSES

What Are the Relevant Assets and Competencies?

Competitor strengths and weaknesses are based on the existence or absence of assets or competencies. Thus, an asset such as a well-known name or a prime location could represent a strength, as could a competency such as the ability to develop a strong promotional programme. Conversely, the absence of an asset or competency can represent a weakness.

To analyse competitor strengths and weaknesses, it is thus necessary to identify the assets and competencies that are relevant to the industry. As Figure 3.3 summarizes, four sets of questions can be helpful.

1. ***What businesses have been successful over time? What assets or competencies have contributed to their success? What businesses have had chronically low performance? Why? What assets or competencies do they lack?***
   By definition, assets and competencies that provide SCAs should affect performance over time. Thus, businesses that differ with respect to performance over time should also differ with respect to their assets and competencies. Analysis of the causes of the performance usually suggests sets of relevant competencies and assets. Typically, the superior performers have developed and maintained key assets and competencies that have

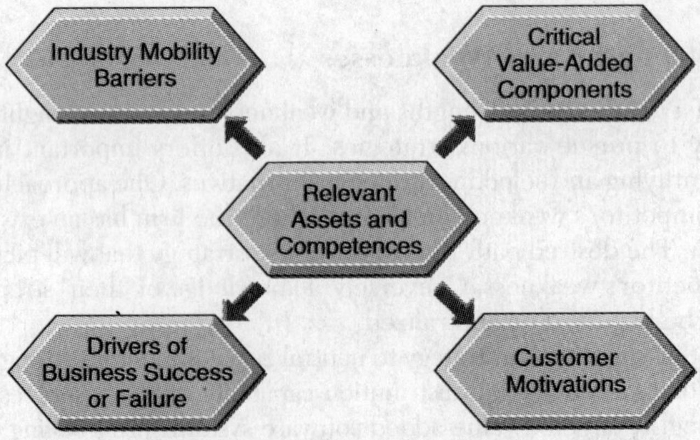

Figure 3.3 Identifying Relevant Assets and Competencies

been the basis for their performance. Conversely, weakness in several assets and competencies relevant to the industry and its strategy should visibly contribute to the inferior performance of the weak competitors over time. For example, in the car industry, one of the top performers, BMW, has superior driving technology, quality, and R&D, consistently strong performance, and credibility as a premium auto manufacturer, based on decades of innovations all reflecting the BMW idea.

2. ***What are the key customer motivations? What is needed to be preferred? What is needed to be considered?***
Customer motivations usually drive buying decisions and thus can dictate what assets or competencies potentially create meaningful advantages. In the heavy equipment industry, customers value service and parts back-up. Caterpillar's promise of '24-hour parts service anywhere in the world' has been a key asset because it is important to customers. Apple has focused on motivating designers to produce user-friendly design platforms. Brands need also to have points of parity on key motivating dimensions in order to be considered. While offering such characteristics may not determine winners, a deficiency will eliminate it from being considered. Hyundai, for example, needs to be perceived as having adequate quality. A series of 'best car' awards in 2009 did not necessarily vault the brand to a superior position, but for many it did get rid of the 'inadequate' perception.
3. ***What assets and competencies represent industry mobility (entry and exit) barriers?***
Strategic groups are characterized by structural stability even when one group is much more profitable than the others. The reason is mobility barriers, which can be both entry barriers and exit barriers. Some groups have assets and competencies that will be difficult and sometimes impossible to duplicate by those seeking to enter. International deep-water oil-well drilling firms, for example, have technology, equipment, and people that domestic on-shore firms cannot duplicate. These assets also represent exit barriers because there is no other use to which they could be put.
4. ***What are the significant value-added components in the value chain?***
A firm that can excel on a critical value-added component can have a sustainable advantage. The component can be critical because of its cost, such as package handling for DHL or the call centre at Dell. Or it can be critical because of the customer benefit it generates or effects, such as the ordering system at Amazon or the ingredients of a Henkel detergent. In examining the value chain, it is helpful to start with suppliers and end with the customer use experience while charting all the components in between. The components can be found throughout the organization and that of its partners. For eBay, for example, operations, customer support, auction services, plus the operations of those selling goods are all potential candidates.

A Checklist of Strengths and Weaknesses

Figure 3.4 provides an overview checklist of the areas in which a competitor can have strengths and weaknesses. The first category is innovation. One of the strengths of Google is its ability to develop innovative products that can be accessed on-line, usually for free. Its new products normally have a distinct technological advantage. In a highly technical industry, the percentage spent on R&D and the emphasis along the basic/applied continuum can be indicators of the cumulative ability to innovate. The outputs of the process in terms of product characteristics and performance capabilities, new products, product modifications, and patents provide more definitive measures of the company's ability to innovate.

The second area of competitor strengths and weaknesses is manufacturing and operations. A major area of strength of Inditex, owner of the Zara retail chain, has

INNOVATION
- Technical product or service superiority
- New product capability
- R&D
- Technologies
- Patents

MANUFACTURING/OPERATIONS
- Cost structure
- Effective and flexible operations
- Efficient operations
- Vertical integration
- Workforce attitude and motivation
- Capacity
- Outsourcing

FINANCE – ACCESS TO CAPITAL
- From operations
- From net short-term assets
- Ability to use debt and equity financing
- Parent's willingness to finance

MANAGEMENT
- Quality of top and middle management
- Knowledge of business
- Culture
- Strategic goals and plans
- Entrepreneurial thrust
- Planning/operation system
- Loyalty – turnover
- Quality of strategic decision making

MARKETING
- Product quality reputation
- Product characteristics/differentiation
- Brand name recognition
- Breadth of the product line – systems capability
- Customer orientation
- Segmentation/focus
- Distribution
- Retailer relationship
- Advertising/promotion skills
- Sales force
- Customer service/product support

CUSTOMER BASE
- Size and loyalty
- Market share
- Growth of segments served

Figure 3.4 Analysis of Strengths and Weaknesses

been manufacturing. This is based on its culture, work processes, and ability to reduce inventory and costs. Carrefour has developed operational capacity and efficiency, based in part by working closely with suppliers, that are significant advantages. In addition to potential cost advantages, superior processes and systems at both Inditex and Carrefour provide strategic and tactical flexibility.

The third area is finance, the ability to generate or acquire funds in the short as well as the long run. Companies with deep pockets (financial resources) have a decisive advantage because they can pursue strategies not available to smaller firms. This is especially true in times of stress. Firms with a strong balance sheet can seize opportunities. Operations provide one major source of funds. What is the nature of cash flow that is being generated and will be generated, given the known uses for funds? Cash or other liquid assets and the deep pockets of a parent firm are important sources as well.

Management is the fourth area. Controlling and motivating a set of highly disparate business operations are strengths for Nestlé, GE, India's Reliance Industries and other firms that have successfully diversified. The quality, depth, and loyalty (as measured by turnover) of top and middle management provide an important asset for others. Another aspect to analyse is the culture. The values and norms that permeate an organization can energize some strategies and inhibit others. In particular, some organizations, such as Indian giants like Infosys and Wipro, possess both an entrepreneurial culture that allows them to initiate new directions and the organizational skill to nurture them. The ability to set strategic goals and plans can represent significant competencies. To what extent does the business have a vision and the will and competence to pursue it?

The fifth area is marketing. Often the most important marketing strength, particularly in the high-tech field, involves the product line: its quality reputation, breadth, and the features that differentiate it from other products. Brand image and distribution have been key assets for businesses as diverse as Puma, Mercedes-Benz, and UBS. The ability to develop a true customer orientation can be an important strength. For Danone, two of its strengths are consumer understanding and brand building. Another strength can be based on the ability and willingness to advertise effectively. The success of Diesel clothing, Singapore Airlines, and San Miguel beer of the Phillipines is due in part to an ability to generate superior advertising. Other elements of the marketing mix, such as the sales force and service operation, can also be sources of sustainable competitive advantage. One of Caterpillar's strengths is the quality of its global dealer network. Yet another possible strength, particularly in the high-tech field, is an ability to stay close to its customers.

The final area of interest is the customer base. How substantial is the customer base and how loyal is it? How are the competitor's offerings evaluated by its customers? What are the costs that customers will have to absorb if they switch to another supplier? Extremely loyal and happy customers are going to be difficult to dislodge. What are the size and growth potentials of the segments served?

The Competitive Strength Grid

With the relevant assets and competencies identified, the next step is to scale your own firm and the major competitors or strategic groups of competitors on those assets and competencies. The result is termed a competitive strength grid and serves to summarize the position of the competitors with respect to assets and competencies.

A sustainable competitive advantage is almost always based on having a position superior to that of the target competitors in one or more assets or competence areas that are relevant both to the industry and to the strategy employed. Thus, information about each competitor's position with respect to relevant assets and competencies is central to strategy development and evaluation.

If a superior position does not exist with respect to assets and competencies important to the strategy, it probably will have to be created, or the strategy may have to be modified or abandoned. Sometimes there simply is no point of difference with respect to the firms regarded as competitors. A competency that all competitors have will not be the basis for an SCA. For example, flight safety is important among airline passengers, but, if airlines are perceived to be equal with respect to pilot quality and plane maintenance, it cannot be the basis for an SCA. Of course, if some airlines can convince passengers that they are superior with respect to antiterrorist security, then an SCA could indeed emerge.

The Luxury Car Market

A competitor strength grid is illustrated in Figure 3.5 for the luxury car market. The relevant assets and competencies are listed on the left, grouped as to whether they are considered keys to success or are of secondary importance. The principal competitors are shown as column headings across the top. Each cell could be coded as to whether the brand is strong, above average, average, below average, or weak in that asset or competence category. The figure uses an above average, average, and below average scale.

The resulting figure provides a summary of the hypothetical profile of the strengths and weaknesses of 10 brands. BMW and Lexus have enviable positions.

Analysing Submarkets

It is often desirable to conduct an analysis for submarkets or strategic groups and perhaps for different products. A firm may not compete with all other firms in the industry but only with those engaged in similar strategies and markets. For example, a competitive strength grid may look very different for the safety submarket, with Volvo having more strength. Similarly, the handling submarket may also involve a competitive grid that will look different, with BMW having more strength.

The Analysis Process

The process of developing a competitive strength grid can be extremely informative and useful. One approach is to have several managers create their own grids independently. The differences can usually illuminate different assumptions and information bases. A reconciliation stage can disseminate relevant information and identify and structure strategic uncertainties. For example, different opinions about the quality reputation of a competitor may stimulate a strategic uncertainty that justifies marketing research. Another approach is to develop the grid in a group setting,

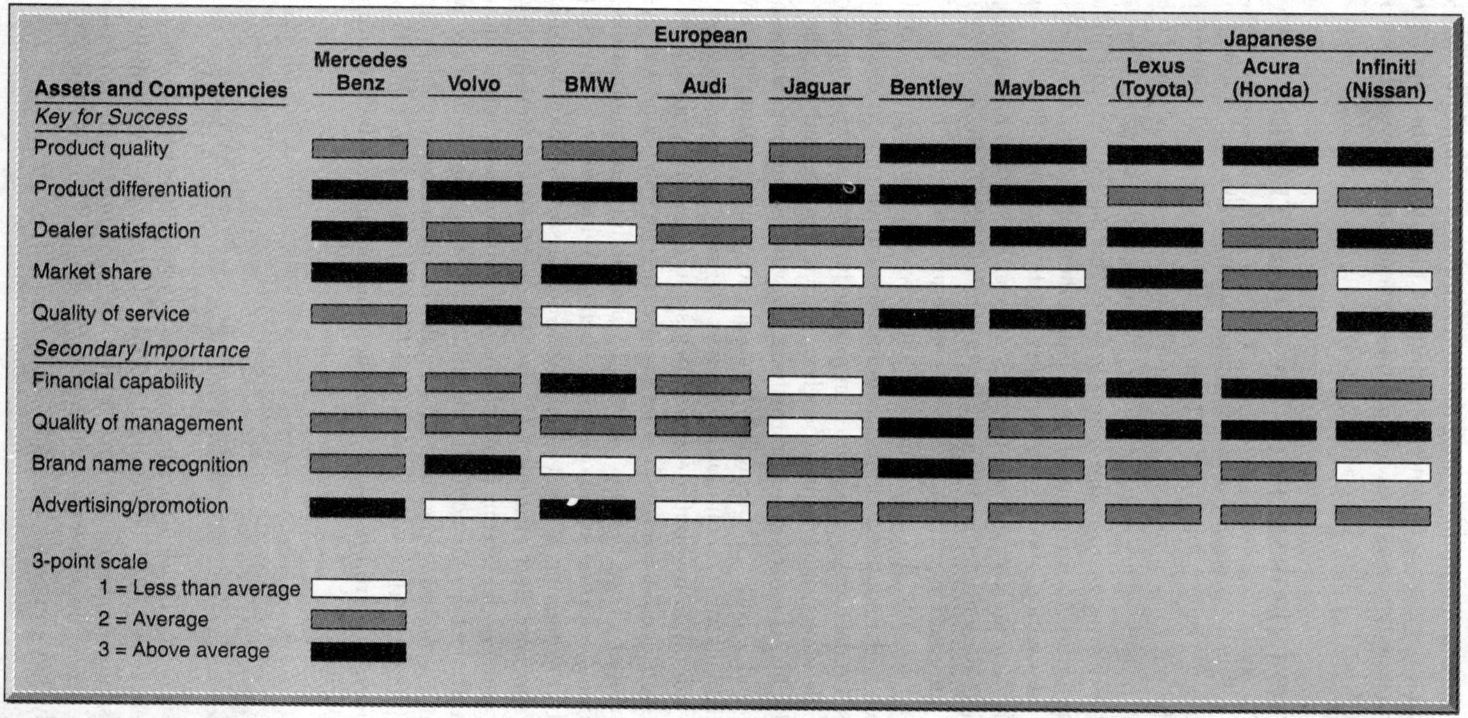

Figure 3.5 Illustrative Example of a Competitive Strength Grid for the European Luxury Car Market

perhaps supported by preliminary staff work. When possible, objective information based on laboratory tests or customer perception studies should be used. The need for such information becomes clear when disagreements arise about where competitors should be scaled on the various dimensions.

OBTAINING INFORMATION ON COMPETITORS

A competitor's website is usually a rich source of information, and the first place to look. The strategic vision (along with a statement about values and culture) is often posted, and the portfolio of businesses is usually laid out. The way that the latter is organized can provide clues as to business priorities and strategies. When Nestlé emphasizes the role of health and wellness in food, that says something about their likely future priorities for investment and management attention. The website can also provide information about such business assets as plants, global access, and brand symbols. Research on the competitor's site can be supplemented with search engines and access to articles and financial reports about the business.

Detailed information on competitors is generally available from a variety of sources. Competitors usually communicate extensively with their suppliers, customers, and distributors, with equity analysts and shareholders, and with government legislators and regulators. Contact with any of these can provide information. Monitoring of trade magazines, trade shows, advertising, speeches, annual reports, and the like, can be informative. Technical meetings and journals can provide information about technical developments and activities. Thousands of databases accessible by computer now make available detailed information on most companies.

Detailed information about a competitor's standing with its customers can be obtained through market research. For example, regular telephone surveys could provide information about the successes and vulnerabilities of competitors' strategies. Respondents could be asked questions such as: Which store is closest to your home? Which do you shop at most often? Are you satisfied? Which has the lowest prices? Best specials? Best customer service? Cleanest stores? Best-quality meat? Best-quality produce? And so on. Those chains that were well positioned on value, on service, or on product quality could be identified, and tracking would show whether they were gaining or losing position. The loyalty of their customer base (and thus their vulnerability) could be indicated in part by satisfaction scores and the willingness of customers to patronize stores even when they are not the most convenient or the least expensive.

KEY LEARNINGS

- Competitors can be identified by customer choice (the set from which customers select) or by clustering them into strategic groups (firms that pursue similar strategies and have similar assets, competencies, and other characteristics). In either case, competitors will vary in terms of how intensely they compete.

- Competitors should be analysed along several dimensions, including their size, growth and profitability, image, objectives, business strategies, organizational culture, cost structure, exit barriers, and strengths and weaknesses.
- Potential strengths and weaknesses can be identified by considering the characteristics of successful and unsuccessful businesses, key customer motivation, and value-added components.
- The competitive strength grid, which arrays competitors or strategic groups on each of the relevant assets and competencies, provides a compact summary of key strategic information.

FOR DISCUSSION

1. Consider the newspaper industry. Identify the competitors to *The Financial Times* and organize them in terms of their intensity of competition.
2. Evaluate Figure 3.5. What surprises are there in the figure? What are the implications for Bentley? For Audi?
3. Pick a company or brand/business on which to focus. What business is it in? Who are its direct and indirect competitors? Which in each category are the most relevant competitors?
4. Consider the automobile industry. Identify competitors to Land Rover SUVs and organize them in terms of their intensity of competition. Also, organize them into strategic groups. What are the key success factors for the strategic groups? Do you think that will change in the next five years?

NOTES

1. Claire Murphy, The Trouble with Heinz, *Marketing*, 14 June 2006, pp. 26–28.
2. Michael E. Porter, *Competitive Strategy*, New York, NY, The Free Press, 1980, pp. 20–21. The concept of exit barriers will be discussed again in Chapter 14.
3. Study by Enterbrain mentioned in *Nikkei Business Daily*, 23 July 2007.

CHAPTER FOUR

Market/Submarket Analysis

As the economy, led by the automobile industry, rose to a new high level in the twenties, a complex of new elements came into existence to transform the market: installment selling, the used-car trade-in, the closed body, and the annual model. (I would add improved roads if I were to take into account the environment of the automobile.)
—*Alfred P. Sloan, Jr, General Motors*

Vision is the art of seeing things invisible.
—*Jonathan Swift*

To be prepared is half the victory.
—*Miguel Cervantes*

Market analysis builds on customer and competitor analyses to make some strategic judgements about a market (and submarket) and its dynamics. One of the primary objectives of a market analysis is to determine the attractiveness of a market (or submarket) to current and potential participants. Market attractiveness, the market's profit potential as measured by the long-term return on investment achieved by its participants, will provide important input into the product market investment decision. The frame of reference is all participants.

Microsoft, for example, has entered the search engine market with its Bing brand, which will compete directly with Google. One factor in its decision was an analysis of the search engine market and its growth trajectory, but perhaps more importantly its future role as a window on the world of cloud computing, the next deep pool of profit in the information industry. Of course, participating in an attractive market will not guarantee success for all competitors. Whether a market is appropriate for a particular firm is a related but very different question, depending not only on the market attractiveness but also on how the firm's strengths and weaknesses match up against those of its competitors. Microsoft would have at least to approximate the technological advantage of Google and provide a reason for customers to use Bing rather than Google.

A second objective of market analysis is to understand the dynamics of the market. The need is to identify emerging submarkets, key success factors, trends, threats, opportunities, and strategic uncertainties that can guide information-gathering and analysis. A key success factor is an asset or competency that is needed to play the game. If a firm has a strategic weakness in a key success factor that isn't neutralized by a well-conceived strategy, its ability to compete will be limited. The market trends can include those identified in customer or competitor analysis, but the perspective here is broader, and others will usually emerge as well.

DIMENSIONS OF A MARKET/SUBMARKET ANALYSIS

The nature and content of an analysis of a market and its submarkets will depend on context, but will often include the following dimensions:

- emerging submarkets;
- actual and potential market and submarket size;
- market and submarket growth;
- market and submarket profitability;
- cost structure;
- distribution systems;
- trends and developments;
- key success factors.

Figure 4.1 provides a set of questions structured around these dimensions that can serve to stimulate a discussion identifying opportunities, threats, and strategic uncertainties. Each dimension will be addressed in turn. The chapter concludes with a discussion of the risks of growth markets.

EMERGING SUBMARKETS

The management of a firm in any dynamic market requires addressing the challenge and opportunity of relevance, as described in the boxed insert below. In essence, the challenge is to detect and understand emerging submarkets and to identify those that are attractive to the firm, given its assets and competencies, and then to adjust offerings and brand portfolios in order to increase their relevance to the chosen submarkets. The opportunity is to influence these emerging submarkets so that competitors become less relevant.

In Chapter 12, characteristics of new business areas or submarkets will be detailed. Knowing these characteristics can help detect and analyse emerging submarkets. They include offerings that:

- provide a lower price point – low-cost carrier airlines;
- serve non-users – Kodak Brownie camera;

- serve niche markets – performance snowboards;
- provide systems solutions – home cinema systems;
- serve unmet needs – Lexus car buying experience;
- respond to a customer trend – fortified energy drinks;
- leverage a new technology – Gillette Fusion razors.

ACTUAL AND POTENTIAL MARKET OR SUBMARKET SIZE

A basic starting point for the analysis of a market or submarket is the total sales level. If it is reasonable to believe that a successful strategy can be developed to gain a 15% share, it is important to know the total market size. Among the sources that can be

SUBMARKETS

Are submarkets emerging defined by lower price points, the emergence of niches, systems solutions, new applications, a customer trend, or new technology? How should the submarket be defined?

SIZE AND GROWTH

Important submarkets? What are the size and growth characteristics of a market and submarkets? What submarkets are declining or will soon decline? How fast? What are the driving forces behind sales trends?

PROFITABILITY

For each major submarket, consider the following: Is this a business area in which the average firm will make money? How intense is the competition among existing firms? Evaluate the threats from potential entrants and substitute products. What is the bargaining power of suppliers and customers? How attractive/profitable are the market and its submarkets both now and in the future?

COST STRUCTURE

What are the major cost and value-added components for various types of competitor?

DISTRIBUTION SYSTEMS

What are the alternative channels of distribution? How are they changing?

MARKET TRENDS

What are the trends in the market?

KEY SUCCESS FACTORS

What are the key success factors, assets, and competencies needed to compete successfully? How will these change in the future? How can the assets and competencies of competitors be neutralized by strategies?

Figure 4.1 Questions to Help Structure a Market Analysis

RELEVANCE

All too frequently, in spite of retaining high levels of awareness, attitude, and even loyalty, a brand loses market share because it is not perceived to be relevant to emerging submarkets. If a group of customers want hybrid cars, it simply does not matter how good they think your firm's SUV is. They might love it and recommend it to others, but if they are interested in a hybrid because of their changing needs and desires, then your brand is irrelevant to them. This may be true even if your firm also makes hybrids under the same brand. The hybrid submarket is different to SUVs and has a different set of relevant brands.

Relevance for a brand occurs when two conditions are met. First, there must be a perceived need or desire by customers for a submarket defined by some combination of an attribute set, an application, a user group, or other distinguishing characteristic. Second, the brand needs to be among the set considered to be relevant for that submarket by the prospective customers.

Winning among brands within a submarket, however, is not enough. There are two additional relevance challenges. One is to make sure that the submarket associated with the brand is relevant. The problem may not be that the customer picks the wrong brand, but rather that the wrong submarket (and brand set) is picked. The second challenge is to make sure that the brand is considered by customers to be an option with respect to a submarket. This implies that a brand needs to be positioned against the submarket in addition to whatever other positioning strategies may be pursued. It must also be visible and be perceived to meet minimal performance levels.

Nearly every marketplace is undergoing change – often dramatic, rapid change – which creates relevance issues. Examples appear in nearly every industry, from computers, consulting, airlines, power generators, and financial services to snack food, beverages, pet food, and toys. Hardware, paint, and flooring stores struggle with the reality of B&Q. Xerox and Kodak face a relevance challenge as a variety of other firms (including HP, Microsoft, and Canon) are carving up the digital imaging world. Think about pay telephones, print newspapers, and national postal services and the relevance issues posed to firms in those sectors. Relevance is an issue, as well, for brands attempting to open up new business arenas, such as Mitsubishi's electric car, hybrid cars, or Nivea's venture into the men's skincare market.

The key to managing such change is twofold. First, a business must detect and understand emerging submarkets, projecting how they are evolving. Second, it must maintain relevance in the face of these emerging submarkets. Businesses that perform these tasks successfully have organizational skills at detecting change, the organizational vitality to respond, and a well-conceived brand strategy.

There is also the option of creating or influencing the emergence of submarkets that will serve to make competitors less relevant. Apple did it with their iPod, Tesco did it with their on-line store and home delivery service, Magners/Bulmer's did it twice with the introduction of the original pint bottle and Bulmer's Light, and Guinness did it with their canned Guinness draught, which used a widget to improve product quality. Creating and owning subcategories can only occur when the right firm, armed with the right idea and offering, is ready to act at the right time. But when it happens, it can be a strategic home run.[1]

helpful are published financial analyses of the firm, customers, government data, and trade magazines and associations. The ultimate source is often a survey of product users in which the usage levels are projected to the population.

Potential Market – the User Gap

In addition to the size of the current, relevant market or submarket, it is often useful to consider the potential size. A new use, new user group, or more frequent usage could dramatically change the size and prospects for the market or submarket.

There is unrealized potential for the cereal market in Europe, as consumers buy only about 25% as much cereal as their US counterparts. If technology allowed cereals to be used more conveniently away from home by providing shelf-stable milk products, usage could be further expanded. Of course, the key is not only to recognize the potential but also to have the vision and programme in place to exploit it. A host of strategists have dismissed investment opportunities in industries because they lacked the insight to see the available potential and take advantage of it.

Ghost Potential

Sometimes an area becomes so topical and the need so apparent that potential growth seems assured. As a Lewis Carroll character observed, 'What I tell you three times is true'. However, this potential can have a ghostlike quality caused by factors inhibiting or preventing its realization. For example, the demand for computers exists in many underdeveloped countries, but a lack of funds and the absence of suitable technology inhibit buying. Many dot-com firms such as Boo.com and Pets.com were the beneficiaries of considerable hype, but failed because the growth of their application never materialized.

Small Can Be Beautiful

Some firms have investment criteria that prohibit them from investing in small markets. Unilever, Diageo, and Nestlé, for example, have historically looked to new products that would generate large sales levels within a few years. Yet in an era of micromarketing, much of the action is in smaller niche segments. If a firm avoids them, it can lock itself out of much of the vitality and profitability of a business area. Furthermore, most substantial business areas were small at the outset, sometimes for many years, and, as noted in Chapter 12, some become attractive niche submarkets. Avoiding the small market can thus mean that a firm must later overcome the first-mover advantage of others.

Further, there is evidence recounted in the book *The Long Tail* by Chris Anderson that many markets have changed so that the small niche business is economically viable and should not be automatically ignored.[2] The music, entertainment, and broadcasting areas illustrate the fact that the tail – the offerings that are not the large hit products – is extensive and collectively important. Netflix, the US-based online DVD rental firm, for example, carries 55 000 titles, and 21% of its sales come from titles that do not appear in retail stores (which stock under 3000 titles). Rhapsody, the subscription-based streaming service operated by RealNetworks, offers more that 1.5 million music tracks and gets 41% of its sales from tracks not available in retail stores. Companies limited by retailers to a small selection can provide access to a full line from their websites; KitchenAid, for example, offers its products in some 50 colours. With eBay, Amazon, Google, and others, the economics of marketing small niche items has changed. The fact that some 25 000 items are introduced in the supermarket stores each year and car makers offer some 250 different models indicates that niche marketing is viable outside the Internet world.

There is a downside to having too many niche offerings. First, companies can create operating and marketing costs that can be debilitating when the offerings are too extensive. Second, customers can become overwhelmed by the confusion of too many choices and rebel – looking for the equivalent of Colgate's Total, a product that simplified decision-making in a cluttered environment. Thus, many firms are trimming lines that have become too large. Nevertheless, the analysis of niche markets needs to reflect the new reality that customers have faster and more extensive access to information than before, and products are accessible in ways not feasible too many years ago.

MARKET AND SUBMARKET GROWTH

After the size of the market and its important submarkets have been estimated, the focus turns to growth rate. What will be the size of the markets and submarkets in the future? If all else remains constant, growth means more sales and profits, even without increasing market share. It can also mean less price pressure when demand increases faster than supply and firms are not engaged in experience curve pricing, anticipating future lower costs. Conversely, declining sales can mean reduced sales and often increased price pressure as firms struggle to hold their shares of a diminishing pie.

It may seem that the strategy of choice would thus be to identify and avoid or disinvest in declining situations and to identify and invest in growth contexts. Of course, the reality is not that simple. In particular, declining product markets can represent a real opportunity for a firm, in part because competitors may be exiting and disinvesting, instead of entering and investing for growth. The firm may attempt to become a profitable survivor by encouraging others to exit and by becoming dominant in the most viable segments.

The other half of conventional wisdom, that growth contexts are always attractive, can also fail to hold true. Growth situations can involve substantial risks. Because of the importance of correctly assessing growth contexts, a discussion of these risks is presented at the end of this chapter.

Identifying Driving Forces

In many contexts, the most important strategic uncertainty involves the prediction of market sales. A key strategic decision, often an investment decision, can hinge on not only being correct but also understanding the driving forces behind market dynamics.

Addressing most key strategic uncertainties starts with asking on what the answer depends. In the case of projecting sales of a major market, the need is to determine what forces will drive those sales. For example, the sales of a new consumer electronics device may be driven by machine costs, the evolution of an industry standard, or the emergence of alternative technologies. Each of these three drivers will provide the basis for key second-level uncertainties.

In the wine market, the relationship of wine to health and the future demand for premium reds might be driving forces. One second-level strategic uncertainty might then lead one to ask on what the demand for premium red will depend.

Forecasting Growth

Historical data can provide a useful perspective and help to separate hope from reality. Accurate forecasts for new packaged goods can be based on the timing of trial and repeat purchases. Durable goods forecasts can be based on projecting initial sales patterns. However, care needs to be exercised. Apparent trends in data, such as those shown in Figure 4.2, can be caused by random fluctuations or by short-term economic conditions, and the urge to extrapolate should be resisted. Furthermore, the strategic interest is not in projections of history but rather in the prediction of turning points, times when the rate and perhaps direction of growth change.

Sometimes, leading indicators of market sales may help in forecasting and predicting turning points. Examples of leading indicators include:

- *Demographic data.* The number of births is a leading indicator of the demand for education, and the number of people reaching the age of 65 is a leading indicator of the demand for retirement homes.
- *Sales of related equipment.* Personal computer and printer sales provide a leading indicator of the demand for supplies and service needs.

Market sales forecasts, especially of new markets, can be based on the experience of analogous industries. The trick is to identify a prior market with similar characteristics. Sales of colour televisions might be expected to have a pattern similar to sales of black-and-white televisions, for example. Sales of a new type of snack might look to the history of other previously introduced snack categories or other consumer products, such as cereal bars or energy bars. The most value will be

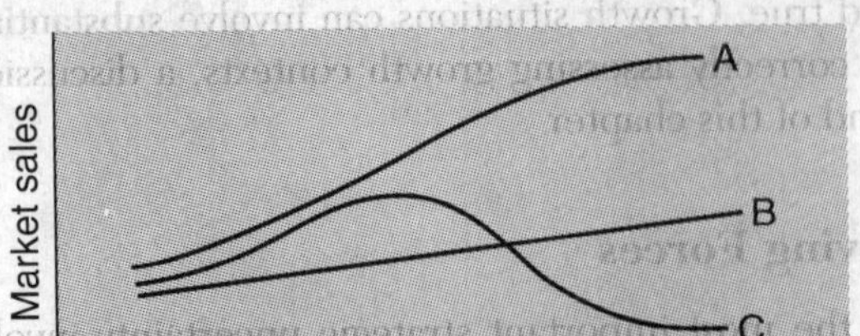

Figure 4.2 Sales Patterns

obtained if several analogous product classes can be examined and the differences in the product class experiences related to their characteristics.

Submarket Growth

Submarket growth is usually critical because it affects investment decisions and value propositions. That involves identifying and analysing current and emerging submarkets. While the beer category is flat, imports are declining and craft beers are showing significant growth. Among restaurants, quick-service restaurants in Europe saw a revival in 2009 owing to recessionary pressure. At the same time, Yum! Brands, owner of the KFC and Pizza Hut brands among others, expects to enjoy sales growth in excess of 20% in China as consumers there continue to discover the value of convenience foods.

Detecting Maturity and Decline

One particularly important set of turning points in market sales occurs when the growth phase of the product life cycle changes to a flat maturity phase and when the maturity phase changes into a decline phase. These transitions are important indicators of the health and nature of the market. Often they are accompanied with changes in key success factors. Historical sales and profit patterns of a market can help to identify the onset of maturity or decline, but the following are often more sensitive indicators:

- *Price pressure caused by overcapacity and the lack of product differentiation.* When growth slows or even reverses, capacity developed under a more optimistic scenario becomes excessive. Furthermore, the product evolution process often results in most competitors matching product improvements. Thus, it becomes more difficult to maintain meaningful differentiation.
- *Buyer sophistication and knowledge.* Buyers tend to become more familiar and knowledgeable as a product matures, and thus they become less willing to pay a premium price to obtain the security of an established name. Airline travellers have gained more confidence and knowledge over the years in their ability to select which airline offers the cheapest price; the Internet, websites, and travel agents like SAYIT that search for the cheapest flights for customers have resulted in a reduction in the value of brand names like KLM and Lufthansa as search cues.
- *Substitute products or technologies.* The sales of personal TV services like Sky+ and TiVo provide an indicator of the decline of VCRs.
- *Saturation.* When the number of potential first-time buyers declines, market sales should mature or decline.
- *No growth sources.* The market is fully penetrated and there are no visible sources of growth from new uses or users.
- *Customer disinterest.* The interest of customers in applications, new product announcements, and so on, falls off.

MARKET AND SUBMARKET PROFITABILITY ANALYSIS

Economists have long studied why some industries or markets are profitable and others are not. Harvard economist and business strategy guru Michael Porter applied his theories and findings to the business strategy problem of evaluating the investment value of an industry, market, or submarket.[3] The problem is to estimate how profitable the average firm will be. It is hoped, of course, that a firm will develop a strategy that will bring above-average profits. If the average profit level is low, however, the task of succeeding financially will be much more difficult than if the average profitability were high.

Porter's approach can be applied to any industry, but it also can be applied to a market or submarket within an industry. The basic idea is that the attractiveness of an industry or market, as measured by the long-term return on investment of the average firm, depends largely on five factors that influence profitability, shown in Figure 4.3:

- the intensity of competition among existing competitors;
- the existence of potential competitors who will enter if profits are high;
- substitute products that will attract customers if prices become high;
- the bargaining power of customers;
- the bargaining power of suppliers.

Each factor plays a role in explaining why some industries are historically more profitable than others. An understanding of this structure can also suggest which key success factors are necessary to cope with the competitive forces.

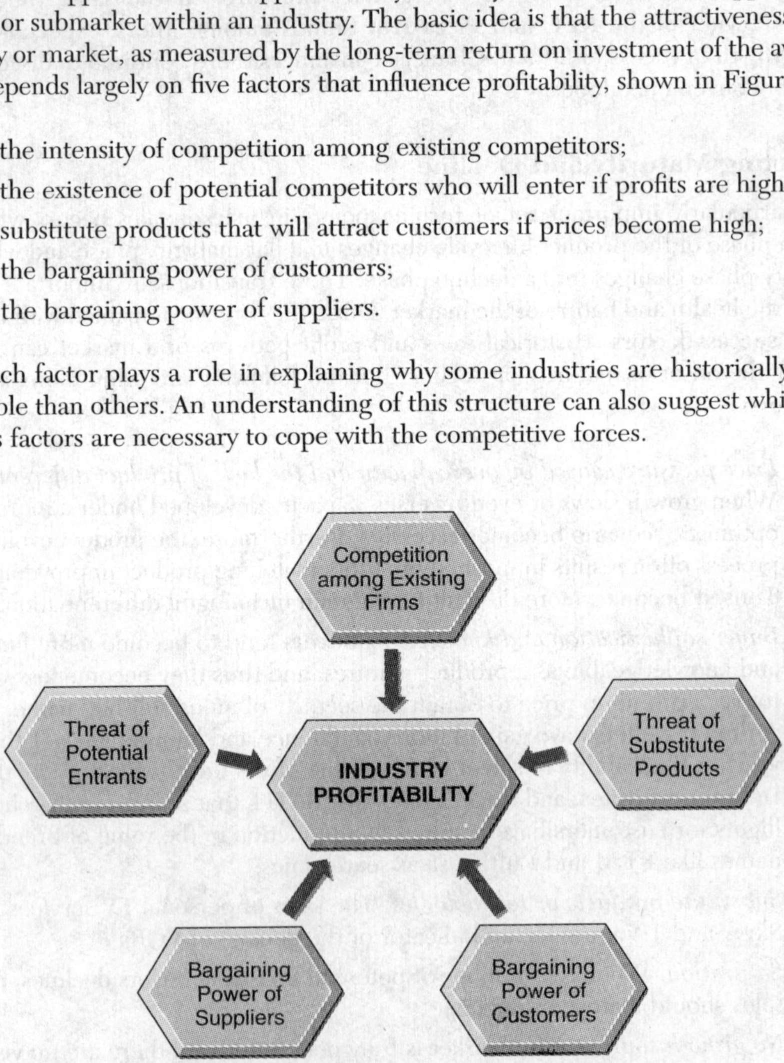

Figure 4.3 Porter's Five-Factor Model of Market Profitability

(*Source*: The concept of five factors is due to Michael E. Porter. See his book *Competitive Advantage*, New York, The Free Press, 1985, Chapter 1.)

Existing Competitors

The intensity of competition from existing competitors will depend on several factors including:

- the number of competitors, their size, and their commitment;
- whether their product offerings and strategies are similar;
- the existence of high fixed costs;
- the size of exit barriers.

The first consideration is how many competitors are already in the market or making plans to enter soon. The more competitors that exist, the more competition intensifies. Are they large firms with staying power and commitment, or small and vulnerable ones? The second consideration is the amount of differentiation. Are the competitors similar, or are some (or all) insulated by points of uniqueness valued by customers? The third factor is the level of fixed costs. A high-fixed-cost industry, like telecommunication or airlines, experiences debilitating price pressures when overcapacity becomes large. Finally, one should assess the presence of exit barriers such as specialized assets, long-term contract commitments to customers and distributors, and relationships to other parts of a firm.

One major factor in the shakeouts that occurred in many industries during and after the financial crisis of 2008/9 was an excessive number of competitors. Easy access to capital and buoyant levels of consumer demand meant that, in many industries, barriers to entry were lowered, and that products with low levels of differentiation could succeed, at least initially.

Potential Competitors

Chapter 3 discusses identifying potential competitors that might have an interest in entering an industry or market. Whether potential competitors, identified or not, actually do enter depends in large part on the size and nature of barriers to entry. Thus, an analysis of barriers to entry is important in projecting likely competitive intensity and profitability levels in the future.

Various barriers to entry include required capital investment (the infrastructure required to produce solar power or nuclear energy), economies of scale (the success of Microsoft is largely based on scale economies), distribution channels (Henkel and Danone have access to customers that is not easily duplicated), and product differentiation (Singapore Airlines and Mandarin Oriental Hotels have highly differentiated product offerings based on Asian service culture that protect them from new entrants).

Substitute Products

Substitute products compete with less intensity than do the primary competitors. They are still relevant, however, as the discussion in Chapter 3 made clear. They can influence the profitability of the market and can be a major threat or problem. Thus plastics, glass, and fibre-foil products exert pressure on the metal can market. Electronic alarm systems are substitutes for the security guard market. E-mail provides a threat to some portion of the express-delivery market of DHL and India's DTDC. Substitutes that show a steady improvement in relative price/performance and for which the customer's cost of switching is minimal are of particular interest.

Customer Power

When customers have relatively more power than sellers, they can force prices down or demand more services, thereby affecting profitability. A customer's power will be greater when its purchase size is a large proportion of the seller's business, when alternative suppliers are available, and when the customer can integrate backwards and make all or part of the product. Thus, tyre manufacturers face powerful customers in the car firms. Soft-drink firms sell to fast food restaurant chains that have strong bargaining power. Wal-Mart has enormous power over its suppliers. It can dictate prices and product specifications; if companies resist, other suppliers are usually willing to comply. Because something like 15% of all Procter & Gamble sales go through Wal-Mart (a proportion that approaches 30% for some categories), even P&G is subject to customer power.

Supplier Power

When the supplier industry is concentrated and sells to a variety of customers in diverse markets, it will have relative power that can be used to influence prices.

Power will also be enhanced when the costs to customers of switching suppliers are high. Thus, the highly concentrated oil industry is often powerful enough to influence profits in customer industries that find it expensive to convert from oil. However, the potential for regeneration, whereby industries can create their own energy supplies, perhaps by recycling waste, may have changed the balance of power in some contexts.

COST STRUCTURE

An understanding of the cost structure of a market can provide insights into present and future key success factors. The first step is to conduct an analysis of the value chain presented in Figure 4.4 to determine where value is added to the product (or service). As suggested in this figure, the proportion of value added attributed to one value chain stage can become so important that a key success factor is associated with that stage. It may be possible to develop control over a resource or technology. More likely, competitors will aim to be the lowest-cost competitor in a high value-added stage of the value chain. Advantages in lower value-added stages will simply have less leverage. Thus, in the metal can business, transportation costs are relatively high, and a competitor that can locate plants near customers will have a significant cost advantage.

It may not be possible to gain an advantage at high value-added stages. For example, a raw material, such as flour for bakery firms, may represent a high value

Production Stage	Markets That Have Key Success Factors Associated with the Production Stage
• Raw material procurement	• Gold mining, winemaking
• Raw material processing	• Steel, paper
• Production fabricating	• Integrated circuits, tyres
• Assembly	• Clothing, instrumentation
• Physical distribution	• Bottled water, metal cans
• Marketing	• Branded cosmetics, alcohol
• Service back-up	• Software, automobiles
• Technology development	• Razors, medical systems

Figure 4.4 Value Added and Key Success Factors

added, but because the raw material is widely available at commodity prices, it will not be a key success factor. Nevertheless, it is often useful to look first at the highest value-added stages, especially if changes are occurring. For example, the cement market was very regional when it was restricted to rail or truck transportation. With the development of specialized ships, however, waterborne transportation costs dropped dramatically. Key success factors changed from local ground transportation to production scale and access to the specialized ships.

DISTRIBUTION SYSTEMS

An analysis of distribution systems should include three types of question:

- What are the alternative distribution channels?
- What are the trends? What channels are growing in importance? What new channels have emerged or are likely to emerge?
- Who has the power in the channel, and how is that likely to shift?

Sometimes the creation of a new channel of distribution can lead to a sustainable competitive advantage. A dramatic example is the success that Tesco's on-line operation experienced, which gave it an advantage over its competitors. Unlike other home grocery delivery offerings, the Tesco.com offering quickly impacted on profitability because it started out using existing stores to manage its logistics rather than building a dedicated network that would have taken time and significant resources to develop. In 2009, Tesco.com reported a year-on-year sales increase of 20% to £1.9 billion, with profits of £109 million. Thus, it is useful to consider not only existing channels but also potential ones.

An analysis of likely or emerging changes within distribution channels can be important in understanding a market and its key success factors. The increased sale of wine in supermarkets made it much more important for winemakers to focus on packaging and advertising.

MARKET TRENDS

Often, one of the most useful elements of external analysis comes from addressing the question as to the market trends. The question has two important attributes: it focuses on change, and it tends to identify what is important. Strategically useful insights almost always result. A discussion of market trends can serve as a useful summary of customer, competitor, and market analyses. It is thus helpful to identify trends near the end of market analysis.

While the global soft-drink market stagnated, non-carbonated beverages grew sharply, and sales of herb- and vitamin-fortified beverages exploded. Not surprisingly, the major soft-drink companies sought to obtain a position in these trendy categories. Reports that dark chocolate is heart healthy have seen sales of dark and premium chocolate brands, such as Green & Blacks, explode. Other chocolate makers scrambled to redo their lines and yet create products with authenticity.

Trends versus Fads

It is crucial to distinguish between trends that will drive growth and reward those who develop differentiated strategies and fads that will only last long enough to attract investment (which is subsequently underemployed or lost forever). Schwinn, the classic name in bicycles, proclaimed mountain biking a fad in 1985, with disastrous results to its market position and, ultimately, its corporate health.[4] The mistaken belief that certain food trends such as low carb represented a long-term trend caused strategists to invest in new products and acquisitions that ultimately failed.

One firm, the Zandl Group, suggests that three questions can help detect a real trend, as opposed to a fad:[5]

1. *What is driving it?* A trend will have a solid foundation with legs. Trends are more likely to be driven by demographics (rather than pop culture), values (rather than fashion), lifestyle (rather than a trendy crowd), or technology (rather than media).
2. *How accessible is it in the mainstream?* Will it be constrained to a niche market for the foreseeable future? Will it require a major change in ingrained habits? Is the required investment in time or resources a barrier (perhaps because the product is priced too high or is too hard to use)?
3. *Is it broadly based?* Does it find expression across categories or industries? Eastern influences, for example, are apparent in healthcare, food, fitness, and design – a sign of a trend.

Faith Popcorn observes that fads are about products, while trends are about what drives consumers to buy products. She also suggests that trends (which are big and broad, lasting an average of 10 years) cannot be created or changed, only observed.[6]

Still another perspective on fads comes from Peter Drucker, who opined that a change is something that people do, whereas a fad is something people talk about. The implication is that a trend demands substance and action supported by data, rather than simply an idea that captures the imagination. Drucker also suggests that the leaders of today need to move beyond innovation to be change agents – the real payoff comes not from simply detecting and reacting to trends, even when they are real, but from creating and driving them.[7] The marketing guru Seth Godin offers a further insight when he suggests that those who buy into fast-moving trends are often fickle early adopters who are unlikely to continue buying something that is adopted by the mainstream. The implication is that, to avoid your product becoming a fad, it is important to sell to the difficult-to-sell-to middle of the market.[8]

KEY SUCCESS FACTORS

An important output of market analysis is the identification of key success factors (KSFs) for strategic groups in the market. These are assets and competencies that provide the basis for competing successfully. There are two types. *Strategic necessities* do not necessarily provide an advantage, because others have them, but their absence will create a substantial weakness. The firm needs to achieve a point of parity with respect to strategic necessities. The second type, *strategic strengths*, are those at which a firm excels, the assets or competencies that are superior to those of competitors and provide a base of advantage. The set of assets and competencies developed in competitor analysis provides a base from which key success factors can be identified. The points to consider are which are the most critical assets and competencies now and, more importantly, which will be most critical in the future.

It is important not only to identify KSFs but also to project them into the future and, in particular, to identify emerging KSFs. Many firms have faltered when KSFs changed and the competencies and assets on which they were relying became less relevant. For example, for industrial firms, technology and innovation tend to be most important during the introduction and growth phases, whereas the roles of systems capability, marketing, and service back-up become more dominant as the market matures. In consumer products, marketing and distribution skills are crucial during the introduction and growth phases, but operations and manufacturing become more crucial as the product settles into the maturity and decline phases.

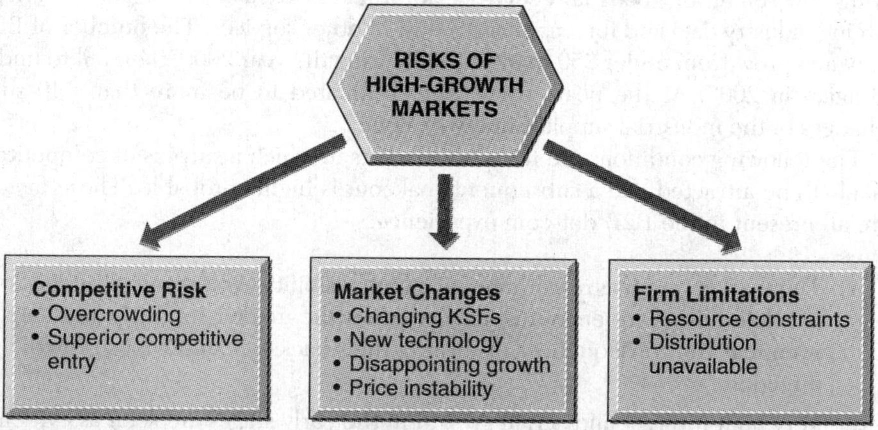

Figure 4.5 Risks of High-Growth Markets

RISKS IN HIGH-GROWTH MARKETS

The conventional wisdom that the strategist should seek out growth areas often overlooks a substantial set of associated risks. As shown in Figure 4.5, there are the risks that:

- The number and commitment of competitors may be greater than the market can support.
- A competitor may enter with a superior product or low-cost advantage.
- Key success factors might change and the organization may be unable to adapt.
- Technology might change.
- The market growth may fail to meet expectations.
- Price instability may result from overcapacity or from retailers' practice of pricing hot products low to attract customers.
- Resources might be inadequate to maintain a high growth rate.
- Adequate distribution may not be available.

Competitive Overcrowding

Perhaps the most serious risk is that too many competitors will be attracted by a growth situation and enter with unrealistic market share expectations. The reality may be that sales volume is insufficient to support all competitors. Overcrowding has been observed in virtually all hyped markets, from railroads to airplanes, radio stations and equipment, televisions sets, and personal computers.

Overcrowding was never more vividly apparent (in retrospect, at least) than in the Internet bubble of the early 2000s. At one point there were at least 150 on-line brokerages, 1000 travel-related sites, and 30 health and beauty sites that were competing for attention. Dot-com business-to-business (B2B) exchanges were created for the buying and selling of goods and services, information exchanges, logistics services, sourcing industry data and forecasts, and a host of other services. The number of B2B companies grew from under 250 to over 1500 during the year 2000, then fell to under 250 again in 2003. At the peak, there were estimated to be more than 140 such exchanges in the industrial supplies industry alone.[9]

The following conditions are found in markets in which a surplus of competitors is likely to be attracted and a subsequent shakeout is highly probable. These factors were all present in the B2B dot-com experience:

1. The market and its growth rate have high visibility. As a result, strategists in related firms are encouraged to consider the market seriously and may even fear the consequences of turning their backs on an obvious growth direction.
2. Very high forecast and actual growth in the early stages are seen as evidence confirming high market growth as a proven phenomenon.

3. Threats to the growth rate are not considered or are discounted, and little exists to dampen the enthusiasm surrounding the market. The enthusiasm may be contagious when venture capitalists and stock analysts become advocates.
4. Few initial barriers exist to prevent firms from entering the market. However, there may be barriers to eventual success (such as limited retail space) that may not be evident at the outset.
5. Some potential entrants have low visibility, and their intentions are unknown or uncertain. As a result, the quantity and commitment of the competitors are likely to be underestimated.

Superior Competitive Entry

The ultimate risk is that a position will be established in a healthy growth market and a competitor will enter late with a product that is demonstrably superior or that has an inherent cost advantage.

Thus, the Apple Newton was first to market with a handheld computing device, but it failed in part because it was priced too high, badly designed, and too complex to use. The cheaper, better, and simpler Palm Pilot then won the market, even though it came later. It subsequently lost its leadership position to the Blackberry and iPhone. In mid-2009, Palm launched the Palm Pré smartphone to try and wrestle leadership of the category back from the RIM and Apple products.

Changing Key Success Factors

A firm may successfully establish a strong position during the early stages of market development, only to lose ground later when key success factors change. One forecast is that the surviving personal computer makers will be those able to achieve low-cost production through sourcing manufacture in low-cost countries, exploitation of the experience curve, and obtaining efficient, low-cost distribution – capabilities not necessarily critical during the early stages of market evolution. Many product markets have experienced a shift over time from a focus on product technology to a focus on process technology, operational excellence, and the customer experience. A firm that might be capable of achieving product-technology-based advantages may not have the resources, competencies, and orientation/culture needed to develop the demands of the evolving market.

Changing Technology

Developing first-generation technology can involve a commitment to a product line and production facilities that may become obsolete, and to a technology that may not survive. A safe strategy is to wait until it is clear which technology will dominate and then attempt to improve it with a compatible entry. When the principal competitors have committed themselves, the most promising avenues for the development of a sustainable competitive advantage become more visible. In contrast, the early entry has to navigate with a great deal of uncertainty.

Disappointing Market Growth

Many shakeouts and price wars occur when market growth falls below expectations. Sometimes the market was an illusion to begin with. Internet-based B2B exchanges did not provide value to firms that already had systems built with relationships that were, on balance, superior to the B2B exchanges. There was an absence of a compelling value proposition to overcome marketplace inertia. In other cases, the demand may be healthy, but the market is still hostile because competitors have built capacity to match overly optimistic expectations. Or the demand might simply take longer to materialize because the technology is not ready, or because customers are slow to change. Demand for electronic banking, for example, took many years longer than expected to materialize.

Forecasting demand is difficult, especially when the market is new, dynamic, and glamorized. In 2002 the future of the mobile phone industry was uncertain. The market was relatively new and there was a tremendous amount of technological optimism surrounding it. In addition to this there were doubts about the availability of new handsets, the capabilities of networks, and difficulty in forecasting demand for new services. This period was the eve of the introduction of digital audio and visual handsets, which posed a problem for providers in forecasting demand, deciding tariffs, design, and security. More recently, similar uncertainty surrounded the market for netbooks, the widespread adoption of which seems to be dependent upon the emergence of web-based applications and mobile networking.

Price Instability

When the creation of excess capacity results in price pressures, industry profitability may be short lived, especially in an industry such as airlines or steel, in which fixed costs are high and economies of scale are crucial. However, it is also possible that some will use a hot product as a loss leader just to attract customer flow.

CDs, a hot growth area in the late 1980s, fuelled the overexpansion of retailers who were very profitable when they sold CDs for about \$15. However, when Best Buy, a home electronics chain, decided to sell CDs for under \$10 to attract customers to their locations, and when Circuit City followed suit, the result was a dramatic erosion in margins and volume and the ultimate bankruptcy of a substantial number of the major CD retailers. A hot growth area had spawned a disaster, not by a self-inflicted price cut, but by price instability from a firm that chose to treat the retailing of CDs as nothing more than a permanent loss leader.

Resource Constraints

The substantial financing requirements associated with a rapidly growing business are a major constraint for small firms. Royal Crown's Diet-Rite cola lost its leadership position to Coca-Cola's Tab and Diet Pepsi in the mid-1960s when it could not match the advertising and distribution clout of its larger rivals. Furthermore, financing requirements frequently are increased by higher than expected product development and market entry costs and by price erosion caused by aggressive or desperate competitors.

The organizational pressures and problems created by growth can be even more difficult to predict and deal with than financial strains. Many firms have failed to survive the rapid growth phase because they were unable to obtain and train people to handle the expanded business or to adjust their systems and structures.

Distribution Constraints

Most distribution channels can support only a small number of brands. For example, few retailers are willing to provide shelf space for more than four or five brands of a houseware appliance. As a consequence, some competitors, even those with attractive products and marketing programmes, will not gain adequate distribution, and their marketing programmes will become less effective.

A corollary of the scarcity and selectivity of distributors as market growth begins to slow is a marked increase in distributor power. Their willingness to use this power to extract price and promotion concessions from manufacturers or to drop suppliers is often heightened by their own problems in maintaining margins in the face of extreme competition for their customers. Many of the same factors that drew in an overabundance of manufacturers also contribute to overcrowding in subsequent stages of a distribution channel. The eventual shakeout at this level can have equally serious repercussions for suppliers.

KEY LEARNINGS

- The emergence of submarkets can signal a relevance problem or opportunity.
- Market analysis should assess the attractiveness of a market or submarket, as well as its structure and dynamics.
- A usage gap can cause the market size to be understated.
- Market growth can be forecast by looking at driving forces, leading indicators, and analogous industries.
- Market profitability will depend on five factors: existing competitors, supplier power, customer power, substitute products, and potential entrants.
- Cost structure can be analysed by looking at the value added at each production stage.
- Distribution channels and trends will often affect who wins.
- Market trends will affect both the profitability of strategies and key success factors.
- Key success factors are the skills and competencies needed to compete in a market.
- Growth-market challenges involve the threat of competitors, market changes, and firm limitations.

FOR DISCUSSION

1. What are the emerging submarkets in the adult snack food industry? What are the alternative responses available to confectionery and snack companies such as Cadbury and Walkers, assuming they want to stay relevant to customers interested in healthier eating?
2. Identify markets in which actual sales and growth were less than expected. Why was that the case? Identify markets where a sales collapse was sudden. Explain why this happened.
3. Why are some brands able to fight off competitors in high-growth markets and others are not?
4. Pick a company or brand/business on which to focus. What are the emerging submarkets? What are the trends? What are the strategic implications of the submarkets and trends for the major players?
5. What considerations go into forecasting when sales of dark chocolate will peak?

NOTES

1. For more details on the relevance concept, see David A. Aaker, 'The Brand Relevance Challenge', *Strategy & Business*, Spring 2004, and David A. Aaker, *Brand Portfolio Strategy*, New York, NY, The Free Press, 2004, Chapter 3.
2. Chris Anderson, *The Long Tail*, New York, NY, Hyperion, 2006.
3. This section draws on Michael E. Porter, *Competitive Advantage*, New York, NY, The Free Press, 1985, Chapter 1.
4. Scott Davis of Prophet Brand Strategy suggested the Schwinn case.
5. Irma Zandl, 'How to Separate Trends from Fads', *Brandweek*, 23 October 2000, pp. 30–35.
6. Faith Popcorn and Lys Marigold, *Clicking*, New York, NY, HarperCollins, 1997, pp. 11–12.
7. James Daly, 'Sage Advice – Interview with Peter Drucker', *Business 2.0*, 22 August 2000, pp. 134–144.
8. Seth Godin's Blog, 'Fast In Fast Out', available at: http://sethgodin.typepad.com/seths_blog/2009/06/fast-in-fast-out.html (accessed 5 September 2009).
9. George S. Day, Adam J. Fein, and Gregg Ruppersberger, 'Shakeouts in Digital Markets: Lessons for GB2B Exchanges', *California Management Review*, Winter 2003, pp. 131–133.

CHAPTER FIVE

Environmental Analysis and Strategic Uncertainty

There are fish in the sea better than have ever been caught.
—*Traditional Irish saying*

Everyone experiences tough times, it is a measure of your determination and dedication how you deal with them and how you can come through them.
—*Lakshmi Mittal, Indian industrialist*

If you're not confused, you're not paying attention.
—*Tom Peters*

Nestlé, the Swiss-based global food giant, has identified health, wellness, and nutrition as key drivers of its organic growth strategy. In taking this position, the firm ultimately seeks to take advantage of growth in the global population from 6.5 billion in 2005 to 9 billion by 2050. Two issues arise here. The first is the need for healthier diets in the western world. This is a broad concern for most consumers today, but, as populations age, the associated health challenges make the need for food that promotes health and wellness a huge force. Second is the increasing prosperity of those living in the new economies, which, over the medium term means that a whole new group of consumers will be coming to the market with basic nutritional needs. This market alone may be worth €70 billion. Nestlé's decision to focus on health, wellness, and nutrition is based on projecting existing environmental trends and acting upon them.

In this chapter, the focus changes from the market to the environment surrounding the market. Being curious about the area outside the business is one route to generating creative ideas that could lead to products and strategies. It is also a way to anticipate threats and put a strategy in place, as Nestlé are doing, to neutralize them. The goal is to identify and evaluate trends and events that will affect strategy either directly or indirectly.

The direct impact of an observed trend will be of interest, but it is important to look at indirect impact as well.[1] For example, increasing oil prices will affect costs of a firm and its suppliers. However, pursuing the indirect implications can generate additional insights. What about the rising use of oil by China and India? Will they deal with their needs through political alliances or actions? Will that affect prices and availability? Will conservation gain impetus and make a difference? Will new technologies affect the supply? What about wind and solar power? Where are the oil profits going to be invested? Such questions will result in a depth of understanding and raise options that take the strategic conversation to a whole new level.

Environmental analysis is by definition very broad and involves casting a wide net (Figure 5.1). Any trend that will potentially have an impact on strategy is fair game. As a practical matter, the analysis requires some discipline to make sure that it does not become like an out-of-control fishing expedition that occupies time and generates reports but provides little real insight and actionable information.

TECHNOLOGY TRENDS

- To what extent are existing technologies maturing?
- What technological developments or trends are affecting or could affect the industry?

CONSUMER TRENDS

- What are the current or emerging trends in lifestyles, fashions, and other components of culture? Why? What are their implications?
- What demographic trends will affect the market size of the industry or its submarkets? What demographic trends represent opportunities or threats?

GOVERNMENT/ECONOMIC TRENDS

- What are the economic prospects and inflation risks for the countries in which the firm operates? How will they affect strategy?
- What changes in regulation are possible? What will their impact be?
- What are the political risks of operating in a governmental jurisdiction?

GENERAL EXTERNAL ANALYSIS QUESTIONS

- What are the significant trends and future events?
- What threats and opportunities do you see?
- What are the key areas of uncertainty as to trends or events that have the potential to impact on strategy? Evaluate these strategic uncertainties in terms of their impact.

SCENARIOS

- What strategic uncertainties are worth being the basis of a scenario analysis?

Figure 5.1 Environmental Analysis

Although environmental analysis has no bounds with respect to subject matter, it is convenient to provide some structure in the form of three areas of inquiry that are often useful: technological trends, consumer trends, and government/economic forces. The analysis should not be restricted to these topics. Nevertheless, in the following sections, each of these three will be discussed and illustrated.

After describing environmental analysis, the last of the four dimensions of external analysis, the chapter will turn to the task of dealing with strategic uncertainty, a key output of external analysis. Impact analysis and scenario analysis are tools that help to evolve that uncertainty into strategy. Impact analysis – the assessment of the relative importance of strategic uncertainties – is addressed first. Scenario analysis – ways of creating and using future scenarios to help generate and evaluate strategies – follows.

TECHNOLOGY TRENDS

One dimension of environmental analysis is technological trends or technological events occurring outside the market or industry that have the potential to impact strategies. They can represent opportunities and threats to those in a position to capitalize. For example, technology advances have enabled customers and others to co-create offerings, have generated real options to cable television, and have changed the face of energy competition.

Transformational, Substantial, and Incremental Innovations

Trends, both market and environmental, can stimulate innovation, which can take several forms. In particular, Foster and Kaplan distinguish between incremental, substantial, and transformational innovation.[2] These differ in terms of how new they are and how much wealth they represent for the business. In general, substantial innovations have 10 times the impact of incremental innovations; the impact of transformational innovations is 10 times greater again.

An incremental innovation makes the offering more attractive or profitable but does not fundamentally change the value proposition or the functional strategy. Adding additional sails to the clipper ships of the late nineteenth century made them better, but fundamentally they remained the same mode of transport. Adding flavours and package innovations to a line of toothpaste is incremental innovation that adds energy and choice but requires little change in the business model. It is important to track incremental innovation and to recognize competitors skilled in it, as it can lead to a forecast of who will be strong competitors in the future. Because firms good at incremental innovation are committed to their business model, they are unlikely to drive real change in the industry.

A transformation innovation will provide a fundamental change in the business model, likely involving a new value proposition and a new way to manufacture, distribute, and/or market the offering. It is likely to make the assets and competencies of established firms irrelevant. The advent of steam power, which ultimately spelled the end of sail-powered transport, was a transformational innovation. The car, easyJet, FedEx, the business model of Inditex (the owner of Zara and Massiom Dutti), and Cirque du Soleil represent innovations that have transformed markets.

Transformational innovations, which sometimes take decades to emerge, are critical to analyse because they represent new competitive landscapes and often attract customers who were on the sidelines because the prior offering was too expensive or lacked some critical element.

Substantial innovations are in between in newness and impact. They often represent a new generation of products, such as the Airbus A380 or Windows 7, that make existing products obsolete for many. Cisco introduced a videoconference technology called telepresence that uses massive amounts of bandwidth to provide a high-fidelity experience and should expand the usage of videoconferencing. In these cases, the basic value proposition and business model were enhanced but not changed. Substantial innovations are much more common than transformational innovations and involve major changes in the competitive landscape.

Innovations that are transformational or even substantial are often championed by new entrants into the industry. Incumbent firms – especially successful ones – are incentivized to focus on incremental innovation to protect and improve their profitable niche in the market. Their people, culture, and mix of assets and competencies are unlikely to support a transformational innovation. As a result, when transformational innovations make their appearance, the reaction of incumbent firms is denial, supported by a belief that improvements in the early offerings would not happen. So the fixed phoneline handset makers have not made the transition to mobile phone manufacturing, arcade game manufacturers have not made the transition to the home console or on-line gaming market, and the leaders in the photographic film market lag behind the leaders in digital photography.

Forecasting Technologies

It is often easy to compile a list of technologies in the wings; the hard part is sorting out the winners from the losers. The experience of the retail sector may provide some guidance. Among the big winners were the 1936 invention of the shopping trolley (which allowed customers to buy more and do so more easily) and the UPC scanner (which improved checkout and provided a rich information source). Among the losers were monitors positioned by the checkout counters in supermarkets and screens attached to shopping carts that could highlight specials and guide shoppers, and efforts to create home-delivery Internet supermarkets.

Retail expert Ray Burke drew upon a variety of research sources to develop a set of guidelines for separating winners from losers. Although his context is retailing, any organization exploring new technologies can benefit from considering each of the guidelines:[3]

- *Use technology to create an immediate, tangible benefit for the consumer.* The benefit, in short, needs to be perceived as such. TV shopping channels were designed to help entertain, but consumers saw them as an intrusive annoyance.
- *Make the technology easy to use.* Consumers resist wasting time and becoming frustrated, and too often new technologies are perceived as doing exactly these things. Research shows that it takes customers an average of

20–30 minutes just to learn how to shop in most text-based Internet grocery-shopping systems.

- *Execution matters: prototype, test, and refine.* One in-store kiosk had no way to inform frustrated customers that it had run out of paper. A bank found customers more receptive to an interactive videoconferencing system when the screens were placed in inviting locations.
- *Recognize that customer response to technology varies.* One bank found that ATM customers rejected videoconferencing options because they actually did not want to interact with humans. Some retailers use loyalty cards to provide receipts and promotions tailored to individual customers.

Impact of New Technologies

Certainly, it can be important, even critical, to manage the transition to a new technology. The appearance of a new technology, however, even a successful one, does not necessarily mean that businesses based on the prior technology will suddenly become unhealthy.

A group of researchers at Purdue University studied 15 companies in five industries in which a dramatic new technology had emerged:[4]

- diesel-electric locomotives versus steam;
- transistors versus vacuum tubes;
- ballpoint pens versus fountain pens;
- nuclear power versus boilers for fossil-fuel plants;
- electric razors versus safety razors.

Two interesting conclusions emerged that should give pause to anyone attempting to predict the impact of a dramatic new technology. First, the sales of the old technology continued for a substantial period, in part because the firms involved continued to improve it. Safety-razor sales have actually increased 800% since the advent of the electric razor. Thus, a new technology may not signal the end of the growth phase of an existing technology. In all cases, firms involved with the old technology had a substantial amount of time to react to the new technology.

Second, it is relatively difficult to predict the outcome of a new technology. The new technologies studied tended to be expensive and crude at first. Furthermore, they started by invading submarkets. Transistors, for example, were first used in hearing aids and pocket radios. In addition, new technologies tended to create new markets instead of simply encroaching on existing ones. Throwaway ballpoint pens and many of the transistor applications opened up completely new market areas.

CONSUMER TRENDS

Consumer trends can present both threats and opportunities for a wide variety of firms. For example, a dress designer conducted a study that projected women's lifestyles. It predicted that a more varied lifestyle would prevail, that more time

COULD TEENAGERS REALLY HAVE THE ANSWERS?[5]

In the summer of 2009, a 15-year-old (15 years and 9 months actually) was on a work experience placement at Morgan Stanley in London. As part of his placement he was asked to write a piece on how teenagers consume media. The result was a paper that so struck the Morgan Stanley analysts that they made it available to clients. The paper provides a number of significant insights that have the potential to shape the future of the media. Teenagers do not read newspapers and few listen to radio. The advent of services such as the BBC iPlayer means that fewer are watching TV. Gaming is becoming more popular with girls owing to the rise of the Nintendo Wii. Teenagers listen to a great deal of music but are generally unwilling to pay for it, preferring to download and share. The report concluded with a 'what is hot' section (including touch screens and mobile phones with huge capacity for music) and a 'what is not' section (including anything with wires and devices with less than 10 hours of battery life). While Morgan Stanley claimed no statistical or research background for the paper, the clarity of the messages and the starkness of the insights meant that they had a significant impact on how people think about the current and future use of media in this segment.

would be spent outside the home, and that those who worked would be more career oriented. These predictions had several implications relevant to the dress designer's product line and pricing strategies. For example, a growing number and variety of activities would lead to a broader range of styles and larger wardrobes, with perhaps somewhat less spent on each garment. Furthermore, consumers' increased financial and social independence would probably reduce the number of follow-the-leader fashions and the perception that certain outfits were required for certain occasions.

Cultural Trends

Faith Popcorn has uncovered and studied cultural trends that, in her judgement, will shape the future. Her efforts provide a provocative view of the future environment of many organizations. Consider, for example, the following trends:[6]

- *Cocooning.* Consumers are retreating into safe, cozy, 'homelike' environments to shield themselves from the harsh realities of the outside world. This trend supports on-line and catalogue shopping, home security systems, gardening, and smart homes.
- *Fantasy adventure.* Consumers crave low-risk excitement and stimulation to escape from stress and boredom. Responsive firms offer theme restaurants, exotic cosmetics, adventure travel, fantasy clothes that suggest role-playing, fantasy-based entertainment, and fantasy cars.
- *Pleasure revenge.* Consumers are rebelling against rules to cut loose and savour forbidden fruits (for example, indulgent ice creams, cigars, martinis, tanning salons, and furs).

- *Small indulgences.* Busy, stressed-out people are rewarding themselves with affordable luxuries that will provide quick gratification: fresh-squeezed orange juice, chocolate-dipped Tuscan biscotti, crusty bread, and upscale fountain pens. For the financially well off, the range of possibilities might include Porsche flatware, Louis Vuitton bags, or Range Rover night-vision binoculars.
- *Down-ageing.* Consumers seek symbols of youth, renewal, and rejuvenation to counterbalance the intensity of their adult lives. The over-55 crowd going to school and participating in active sports (including iron man competitions and outdoor adventures) reflect this trend, but it really extends to a wide age group who favour products, clothing, activities, and entertainment that capture the nostalgia of youth.
- *Being alive.* Consumers focus on the quality of life and the importance of wellness, taking charge of their personal health rather than delegating it to the healthcare industry. Examples of this include the use of holistic medical approaches, vegetarian products and restaurants, organic products, water filters, and health clubs.
- *99 lives.* Consumers are forced to assume multiple roles to cope with their increasingly busy lives. Retailers serving multiple needs, ever-faster ways to get prepared food, a service that manages your second home and prepares it for visits, noise neutralizers, e-commerce, and yoga are all responsive to this trend.

There is a trend towards tribing, the affinity towards a social unit that is centred around an interest or activity and is not bound by conventional social links. These can range from festivals like *La Dolce Vita,* an Italian festival in London designed to entertain and create an Italian experience for all who like to indulge in Italian food and wine and learn about living in Italy, to the *Bulldog Bash* biker event held in England annually by bikers wishing to celebrate hard rock music, custom motorcycles, and similar lifestyle activities.

However, the greatest change agent in the marketing profession is the emergence of social media such as Facebook, Twitter, and LinkedIn. These new media have created an opportunity for individuals to circulate and gather information and share experiences about new and existing products. Collectively, they are driving marketing towards more open and authentic relationships with customers. Additionally, sharing sites such as TripAdvisor provides an opportunity for consumers to review services and advise others.

Being Green

Increasingly, firms are assessing strategy and markets on the basis of the environmental cost and impact of their involvement. Concern for the environment is important to business for three reasons. First, citizens are generally more concerned about the impact of society and business on the global ecosystem. Tangibly, consumers may be less willing to buy a brand that is harmful to the environment and less willing to pay a premium for a brand that does not have established environmental credentials. Second, every business needs to be assured of supply of essential raw materials, such as ingredients or fuel. As there is the possibility that such inputs might become scarce, more expensive, or unavailable entirely, it is imperative that alternative arrangements be made. Finally, as the environment moves up the agenda, the willingness of government to intervene and impose sanctions and taxes on those damaging the environment will increase. The European Union's Emissions Trading Scheme (ETS) imposes emission caps on certain industries with particularly high emissions and provides an opportunity for companies to trade their carbon and meet their emission targets, although this process has not been without criticism. Organizations such as The CarbonNeutral Company have worked with clients like British Sky Broadcasting, DHL, and O2 to go beyond regulatory limits and achieve carbon-neutral status.

A firm's response will depend on the organization and what it can do. Some companies with a legacy of concern for the environment and social responsibility will find it comfortable to increase investment in environmental programmes. For others it will require a cultural change that is not easy. What is feasible and appropriate will depend on the nature of the business. Are cost savings associated with environmental actions? As the boxed insert describes, Marks & Spencer discovered, to its surprise, that an ambitious environmental programme was associated with tangible cost savings. Will customer demand provide sales and margins associated with green products and services? If there is a business rationale behind going green, it is much easier to justify and create momentum. If not, the rationale will need to be more indirect, based on the value of being an industry leader, on making employees proud, and on improving relationships – if not bonding – with those customers (and others such as government officials) that are environmentally sensitive.

Another issue is getting credit for environmental programmes. Many firms have developed programmes with meaningful investment and substance behind them, but their efforts are invisible. One survey found that American consumers rated Dell as the top green consumer electronics brand, followed by Apple, HP, and Microsoft.[7] Greenpeace, in contrast, looking at what firms are actually doing, rated these same firms 12th, 14th, 13th, and 17th (second from the bottom) respectively, while the top firms were actually Nokia and Sony-Erickson. Why? This is probably due to a halo effect caused by brand visibility and perceived marketing success, coupled with an absence of contrary information.

What can be done to make green efforts more visible? One answer is branding. Consider three firms that have used a brand to help them get credit for creating programmes and initiatives that are meaningful and worthwhile. BP has repositioned the corporate brand around a tagline, 'Beyond Petroleum', that captures its concern for the environment and its commitment to reach out beyond petroleum (which contributes to global warming) for energy solutions. Toyota has long had substantial environmental initiatives that have been largely invisible. However, as the Prius has become the leading hybrid, it has served to make the firm's innovation in the hybrid space prominent and thus affected the Toyota brand. Finally, the Korean firm LG has developed a global sustainability initiative, focusing on reducing hazardous substances, recycling, and developing take-back programmes under the 'Life's Good When It's Green' brand.

MARKS & SPENCER PLAN A

In 2007 Marks and Spencer launched a five-year environmental programme, Plan A,[8] which consisted of 100 environmental initiatives for the company, its suppliers, and customers to commit to. The plan is divided into five areas of action: climate change, waste, sustainable raw materials, fair partners, and health. As an example of the detail of the plan, in the area of waste the company committed to reducing packaging and the use of plastic carrier bags. Also, under the climate change heading, the company committed itself to becoming carbon neutral by 2012. Some of its commitment required partnership with other organizations. The Marks & Spencer Oxfam Clothes Exchange programme was the most prominent among these. With more than 1 million tons of clothing thrown out each year, customers are invited to bring their clothes to an Oxfam store to be resold, and an additional incentive of a £5 Marks & Spencer shopping voucher is provided. Customers were also invited to take part and advised to travel with the environment in mind, turn their thermostats down, use less water, and recycle their furniture.

In 2009, the half-way point in the plan, the company reported some significant results in its annual *How We Do Business*. Of the original 100 initiatives, 39 had been achieved and 24 extended to more ambitious goals. Only one initiative had been suspended. However, the most significant result was financial. At its inception, Marks & Spencer had been willing to invest £200 million in Plan A; by 2009, the programme had become cost positive owing to cost savings.

Why are Marks & Spencer and so many other firms undertaking such initiatives? The first reason is often a realization from the CEO or other senior leader that this is simply the right thing to do. Second, customer interest in dealing with what they perceive as their own challenge to respond to environmental stewardship leads them to turn to their favourite brands to find a way. Increasingly, a third reason is coming to the fore – initiatives such as *this don't cost money, they save it*. Combined, these three provide a compelling business case for engaging with the challenge of the environment.

The experience of Marks & Spencer raises some interesting issues. What is the responsibility of a for-profit organization to contribute to solving the problems of the nation and the world? Is the business of business to make profits, with other objectives being left to the government? What are the problems worth addressing? How should they be addressed? How does an individual business determine what programmes will be effective or even helpful when the problems being addressed are so complex?

Some firms may not want to be visible. If, like Coke, they have a broad audien with large segments that are indifferent to or even negative about being gree (because they associate it with higher prices or a political agenda they oppose), cred for environmental actions may not be a net positive. Others, like The Body Shop an Green & Black's, have found that being a prominent believer in the green moveme raises expectations and increases the risk that they will make a visible misstep. Tl deforestation of South America, for example, is a complex problem, and some actio made with good intentions could have unintended consequences that would crea bad publicity.

Demographics

Demographic trends can be a powerful underlying force in a market, and they can be predictable. Among the influential demographic variables are age, income, education, and geographic location.

The older demographic group is of particular interest because it is growing rapidly and is blessed not only with resources but also with the time to use them. The over-65 population in Europe will grow from 115 million in 2005 to 136 million in 2020. The over-80 group will grow from 25 million to over 36 million in the same time period, and its members will be much more likely to live independently. In Asia, a broadly similar situation prevails. In 2000, the average age in Asia was 29 years. In 2050, this will have increased to 40 years, and the percentage of over-65s will have grown to 18% of the population and the under-15s will have dropped from 30% to 19%. As women tend to outlive men, so their portion of the population increases sharply over age groups; within the 80-year-old group there are only 30 men per 100 women. In Asia, for those aged 75 years and above the figure is roughly 70 men per 100 women.

Between 1975 and 1995, the European Union's population grew by over 6%, but from 1995 to 2025 this growth is expected to halve to 3.7%. In this regard, Asia tells a different story, with the total Asian population expected to grow by 1.35 billion between 1995 and 2025.

To profit from this trend, marketers must move away from the image of the over-50s as being a slippers and blanket-over-the-knee market. In France, Danone has targeted the senior market with its Actimel brand and its promise to boost immune systems. In the cosmetics market, L'Oréal and Revlon have both developed products targeted at older women and used mature stars such as Catharine Deneuve, Diane Keaton, Jane Fonda, and Susan Sarandon to endorse and promote them.

Demographic trends are magnified when they are quantified by industry. The impact of ageing is dramatically different across industries according to an Italian study.[9] The demand for healthcare, housing, and energy in Italy will increase by 32, 24, and 21%, respectively, from 2005 to 2020. During that same time period, the demand for toys/sports will fall by 41%, for motorcycles by 36%, and for education by 23%.

Ethnic populations in Europe are rising rapidly, and some analysts believe that immigration could be the magic bullet that will solve Europe's labour problem. For example, the UK population is set to rise by about 5 million people over the next 25 years, with immigrants accounting for two-thirds of this growth. This has implications for a range of organizations such as supermarket owners who may need to adjust their product lines to stock more ethnic products.

The nuclear family, which was once traditional in European homes, has declined rapidly owing to various technological and social developments and changes (for example, contraception, abortion, the Internet, TV, women's emancipation, education, and changes in cultural values). This has led to an increase in the prevalence of one-parent families, and 55% of females in the European Union are now employed outside the home. One implication of this demographic evolution is an increased demand for DIY services, home help, domestic cleaners, meal preparation, and child minding.

GOVERNMENT/ECONOMIC TRENDS

Economic Recessions

Economic forecasts will affect strategy. Very different types of investment and strategy are needed when the economic climate is healthy to when it is under stress. Furthermore, it is far better and sometimes imperative to put in place strategies before a strong or weak economy hits, because when it is in progress it can be too late. Thus, it becomes important to forecast the demand in general and the demand within the sectors that are most relevant to the business. Good forecasting means having links to authoritative voices, a broad-based information system, and a clear understanding of leading indicators.

It is of particular importance to forecast and adjust to recessions, especially deep ones, because they can threaten survival and can provide rare opportunities for major changes in competitive position. This means that the balance sheet and cash position need to be buttressed, which in turn means that firms need to cut budgets and programmes, sometimes radically. Marketing is particularly vulnerable because its budget appears to be discretionary. Adjusting marketing to gain short-term financial benefits has its own risks. Some observations:

- First, as the boxed insert details, a recession can be an opportunity to introduce products or marketing programmes because the media environment will be less cluttered and competitors will be less motivated and able to respond.
- Second, cutting marketing budgets and programmes across the board, the easy route, is guaranteed to be suboptimal. Rather, a budget crunch is an opportunity to develop and nurture the effective and identify and defund the ineffective. There is almost always a significant portion of the budget that is going to products, countries, segments, media, or programmes that have an unacceptable return on investment (ROI). Funding is based on wishful thinking, historical momentum, or organizational power. The actual market impact of a budget reduction can be minimized by identifying those budget areas in which marketing performance is mediocre or worse and stopping supporting them. The cost of ineffective marketing may exceed targeted budget cuts.

  In measuring ROI, the difficult part is to ensure that measurement is not dominated by immediate sales or its surrogates promoting programmes damaging to the brand franchise and inhibiting programmes with a longer time horizon. One FMCG firm developed an analytical model based on access to daily store sales. The model drove the firm to price prohibitions as they delivered immediate sales bumps. As a result, customers learned to wait for the next promotion, and after two years the business and brand were visibly deteriorating and the model was discarded. The fact is that some marketing efforts, both positive and negative, have been shown to have effects only with a two- and three-year delay. Surrogates for long-term health of the business such as the size and loyalty level of the loyal segment or brand health indicators such as image, differentiation, and energy of the brand can help.

- Third, it is important to find ways to communicate value, often a necessity during tough economic times, without hurting the brand. Shouting price and deals is the wrong course because it announces that the brand is not worth the price. One way is to divert attention to value subbrands such as the BMW One Series. Another is to bundle services to provide extra value at the same price, such as free shipping by Amazon. Still another is to demonstrate the value of quality – Fairy washing-up liquid encourages buyers by promising to do more with less. Finally, the frame of reference can be changed – other products can become the comparison standard; for example, KFC's Family Value Meal versus home cooking or satellite movie channels rather than an expensive night out.
- Fourth, the tendency is to think budgets, i.e. how much is spent, while the need is to change programmes, i.e. to find new programmes that are more effective. Marketing needs to elevate its game to move beyond competence to excellence. In many cases, how a budget is spent can be up to four times more important than how much is spent. When budgets become tight, the challenge of creating home run programmes or reducing costs without sacrificing impact needs to be a priority. That means enhancing the creativity of the organization, sharing programmes between organizational units, and considering different media, particularly digital media and social technology.

Government Regulations

The addition or removal of legislative or regulatory constraints can pose major strategic threats and opportunities. For example, the ban on some ingredients in food products or cosmetics has dramatically affected the strategies of numerous firms. The impact of governmental efforts to reduce piracy in industries such as software (more than one-fourth of all software used is copied) and DVDs is of crucial importance to those affected. Global and national regulation and deregulation in banking, energy, and other industries are having implications for the firms involved. The car industry is affected by fuel-economy standards and by taxes based on emissions. The relaxation of regulatory constraints in India and China can have enormous implications for global firms.

Global Events

In an increasingly global economy with interdependencies in markets and in the sourcing of products and services, possible political hot spots need to be understood and tracked. A book by Ian Bremmer and Preston Keat, *The Fat Tail: The Power of Political Knowledge for Strategic Investing*, identifies the growth of political shocks and surprises in affecting business outcomes. They note the obvious desirability of anticipating those shocks and having strategies to deal with them. In order to anticipate such changes, managers need to take a broader but shorter perspective on trouble. Rather than projecting the political situation for 20 years, leaders should focus on one- and two-year scenarios and on understanding these in detail. Effective

RECESSION OPPORTUNITIES TO GAIN MARKET POSITION

Opportunities to gain market position will occasionally emerge in times of economic stress, sometimes caused by that stress. In that case, it might pay to be aggressive with some portion of the marketing budget.

In rare cases, it might be worthwhile to consider increasing the budget. In fact, numerous empirical studies of marketing budget changes during recessions have shown that, on average, there is a strong correlation between the marketing budget during a recession and the performance of the business both during and in the years after the recession. This evidence, coupled with many case studies, suggests that being aggressive rather than defensive can pay off – when there is a product, position, or programme that can be leveraged to gain market position.

What type of firms are likely to benefit from being aggressive? They would include:

- Firms that can be positioned as a value brand. In 2008, Tesco gained market share against its rivals by focusing on keeping prices low and maintaining or growing sales rather than growing profits as its competitors did. The ambition was to benefit from customer loyalty as the economy moved into recovery.
- Firms that enjoy an offering that has points of relevant superiority. During the recession following the 2008 financial crisis, Reckitt Benckiser continued to introduce consumer products, each driven by improving performance for consumers, a core strength of the company.
- Firms that have a new product that is changing the industry or affecting the firm's competitive position.
- Firms that have a particularly effective marketing programme. In 2008, Nestlé, Heinz, and Unilever all used their strong brands to push through price increases and improve profitability.
- Firms that have a balance sheet advantage over rivals – when competitors are unable to respond, the chance of improving market position with aggressive marketing increases. For example, most Indian banks, through careful management in the 2000s, today have superior financial strength compared with some of their main competitors.

In the American market, Hyundai in 2009 had most of these factors in hand.[10] Along with a heritage as a value brand, it was recognized as a leader with award-winning models, including the luxury Genesis, the first 'car return' policy if you got laid off, a 10-year warranty, and a relatively strong financial position. Hyundai increased advertising by 38% as its rivals on average decreased theirs by 7%. Its sales sharply increased while their competitors' sales were declining, some by close to 40%.

strategies for dealing with these challenges include geographic diversification among risk areas and the creation of effective mechanisms to allow for information to impact on decision-making within the organization.[11] A prudent strategy is one that is both diversified and flexible, so that a political surprise will not be devastating.

Cultivating Vigilance

There is a strong tendency to fail to understand important trends or predict future events.[12] How could the great flag-carrying airlines have ever allowed their industry to be taken over by low-cost carriers? Why did the early leaders of the mobile phone industry not anticipate the emergence of the customer needs that enabled the iPhone or the Blackberry to gain leadership of the smartphone market.

One reason is that executives are focused on execution and have little attention span left for what 'might be'. Another is that there is a natural perceptual bias towards ignoring or distorting information that conflicts with the strategic model of the day and collecting supporting information. Still another is the support of 'groupthink' within the organization – it is awkward to point out that basic assumptions may be wrong.

Research on organizational vigilance suggests some ways that leaders and organizations can improve:

- *Be curious, externally focused, and connected.* What is happening in areas that will impact the business? Travel, observe, and interact with people of all types.
- *Look to secondary as well as primary effects*. Johnson & Johnson has a strategy process termed Frameworks that looks at major issues facing corporate and individual business leaders. Working in teams, intensive research leads to multiple perspectives and unanticipated solutions to problems. It is also important to make sure that silo units are communicating so that in-house information is shared.
- *Create discovery mechanisms.* Texas Instruments holds a 'Sea of Ideas' meeting each week to recognize emerging needs and innovation at the fringe of their business. One such meeting led to the development of a low-power chip for mobile phones.
- *Force a long-term perspective.* Get away from the day-to-day executional issues and programmes.

DEALING WITH STRATEGIC UNCERTAINTY

Strategic uncertainty, uncertainty that has strategic implications, is a key construct in external analysis. A typical external analysis will emerge with dozens of strategic uncertainties. To be manageable, they need to be grouped into logical clusters or themes. It is then useful to assess the importance of each cluster in order to set priorities with respect to information-gathering and analysis. Impact analysis, described in the next section, is designed to accomplish that assessment.

Sometimes the strategic uncertainty is represented by a future trend or event that has inherent unpredictability. Information-gathering and additional analysis will not be able to reduce the uncertainty. In that case, scenario analysis can be employed. Scenario analysis basically accepts the uncertainty as given and uses it to drive a description of two or more future scenarios. Strategies are then developed for each. One outcome could be a decision to create organizational and strategic flexibility so that, as the business context changes, the strategy will adapt. Scenario analysis will be detailed in the final section of this chapter.

IMPACT ANALYSIS – ASSESSING THE IMPACT OF STRATEGIC UNCERTAINTIES

An important objective of external analysis is to rank the strategic uncertainties and decide how they are to be managed over time. Which uncertainties merit intensive investment in information-gathering and in-depth analysis, and which merit only a low-key monitoring effort?

The problem is that dozens of strategic uncertainties and many second-level strategic uncertainties are often generated. These strategic uncertainties can lead to an endless process of information-gathering and analysis that can absorb resources indefinitely. Today, most publishing companies are concerned about the impact of on-line publishing as well as lifestyle patterns, educational trends, geographic population shifts, and printing technology. Any one of these issues involves a host of subfields and could easily spur limitless research. For example, on-line publishing might involve a variety of issues including the willingness of advertisers to pay for ads in on-line publications, the likelihood of customers paying for on-line content, and the impact of free competition.

The extent to which a strategic uncertainty should be monitored and analysed depends on its impact and immediacy:

1. The impact of a strategic uncertainty is related to:
   - the extent to which it involves trends or events that will impact upon existing or potential businesses;
   - the importance of the businesses involved;
   - the number of businesses involved.
2. The immediacy of a strategic uncertainty is related to:
   - the probability that the trends or events involved will occur;
   - the timeframe of the trends or events;
   - the reaction time likely to be available, compared with the time required to develop and implement appropriate strategy.

Impact of a Strategic Uncertainty

Each strategic uncertainty involves potential trends or events that could have an impact on present, proposed, and even potential businesses. For example, a strategic uncertainty for a beer firm could be based on the future prospects of the microbrewery market. If the beer firm has both a proposed microbrewery entry and an imported beer positioned in the same area, trends in the microbrewery beer market could have a high impact on the firm. The trend towards natural foods may present opportunities for a sparkling water product line for the same firm and be the basis of a strategic uncertainty.

The impact of a strategic uncertainty will depend on the importance of the impacted business to a firm. Some businesses are more important than others. The importance of established businesses may be indicated by their associated sales, profits, or costs. However, such measures might need to be supplemented for proposed or growth businesses for which present sales, profits, or costs may not reflect the true value to a firm. Finally, because an information-need area may affect several businesses, the number of businesses involved can also be relevant to a strategic uncertainty's impact.

Immediacy of Strategic Uncertainties

Events or trends associated with strategic uncertainties may have a high impact but such a low probability of occurrence that it is not worth actively expending resources to gather or analyse information. Similarly, if occurrence is far in the future relative to the strategic decision horizon, then it may be of little concern. Thus, the harnessing of tide energy may be so unlikely or may occur so far in the future that it is of no concern to a utility.

Finally, there is the reaction time available to a firm, compared with the reaction time likely to be needed. After a trend or event crystallizes, a firm needs to develop a reaction strategy. If the available reaction time is inadequate, it becomes important to anticipate emerging trends and events better so that future reaction strategies can be initiated sooner.

Managing Strategic Uncertainties

Figure 5.2 suggests a categorization of strategic uncertainties for a given business. If both the immediacy and impact are low, then a low level of monitoring may suffice. If the impact is thought to be low but the immediacy is high, the area may merit monitoring and analysis. If the immediacy is low and the impact high, then the area

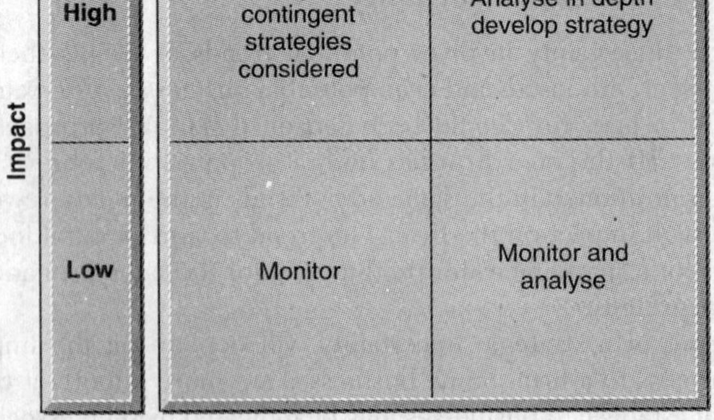

Figure 5.2 Strategic Uncertainty Categories

requires monitoring and analysis in more depth, and contingent strategies may be considered but not necessarily developed and implemented. When both the immediacy and potential impact of the underlying trends and events are high, then an in-depth analysis will be appropriate, as will the development of reaction plans or strategies. An active task force may provide initiative.

SCENARIO ANALYSIS

Scenario analysis can help deal with uncertainty. It provides an alternative to investing in information to reduce uncertainty, which is often an expensive and futile process. By creating a small number of marketplace or market context scenarios and assessing their likelihood and impact, scenario analysis can be a powerful way to deal with complex environments.

There are two types of scenario analysis. In the first type, strategy-developing scenarios, the object is to provide insights into future competitive contexts, then use these insights to evaluate existing business strategies and stimulate the creation of new ones. Such analyses can help create contingency plans to guard against disasters – an airline adjusting to a terror incident, for example, or a pharmaceutical company reacting to a product safety problem. They can also suggest investment strategies that will enable the organization to capitalize on future opportunities caused by customer trends or technological breakthroughs.

In the second type of analyses, decision-driven scenarios, a strategy is proposed and tested against several scenarios that are developed.[13] The goal is to challenge the strategies, thereby helping to make the go/no-go decision and suggesting ways to make the strategy more robust in withstanding competitive forces. If the decision is to enter a market with a technology strategy, alternative scenarios could be built around variables such as marketplace acceptance of the technology, competitor response, and the stimulation of customer applications.

In either case, a scenario analysis will involve three general steps: the creation of scenarios, relating those scenarios to existing or potential strategies, and assessing the probability of the scenarios (see Figure 5.3).

Identify Scenarios

Strategic uncertainties can drive scenario development. The impact analysis will identify the strategic uncertainty with the highest priority for a firm. A manufacturer of a medical imagery device may want to know whether a technological advance will allow its machine to be made at a substantially lower cost. A farm equipment manufacturer or ski area operator may believe that the weather – the prospect of a continuing

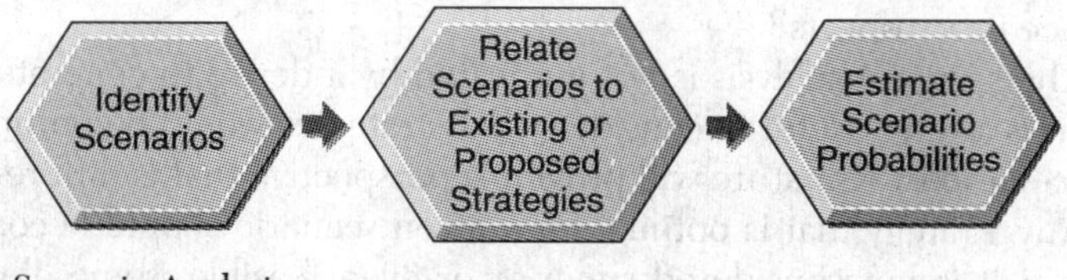

Figure 5.3 Scenario Analysis

drought, for example – is the most important area of uncertainty. A server firm may want to know whether a single software standard will emerge or multiple standards will coexist. The chosen uncertainty could then stimulate two or more scenarios.

A competitor scenario analysis can be driven by the uncertainly surrounding a competitor's strategy. For example, could the competitor aggressively extend its brand? Or might it divest a product line or make a major acquisition? Perhaps the competitor could change its value proposition, or become more aggressive in its pricing.[14]

When a set of scenarios is based largely on a single strategic uncertainty, the scenarios themselves can usually be enriched by related events and circumstances. Thus, an inflation-stimulated recession scenario would be expected to generate a host of conditions for the appliance industry, such as price increases and retail failures. Similarly, a competitor scenario can be comprehensive, specifying such strategy dimensions as product market investment, acquisition or joint ventures, pricing, positioning, product, and promotions.

It is sometimes useful to generate scenarios based on probable outcomes: optimistic, pessimistic, and most likely. The consideration of a pessimistic scenario is often useful in testing existing assumptions and plans. The aura of optimism that often surrounds a strategic plan may include implicit assumptions that competitors will not aggressively respond, the market will not fade or collapse, or technological problems will not surface. Scenario analysis provides a non-threatening way to consider the possibility of clouds or even rain on the picnic.

Often, of course, several variables are relevant to the future period of interest. The combination can define a relatively large number of scenarios. For example, a large greetings-card firm might consider three variables important: the success of small boutique card companies, the life of a certain card type, and the nature of future distribution channels. The combination can result in many possible scenarios. Experience has shown that two or three scenarios are the ideal number with which to work; any more, and the process becomes unwieldy and any value is largely lost. Thus, it is important to reduce the number of scenarios by identifying a small set that ideally includes those that are plausible/credible and those that represent departures from the present substantial enough to affect strategy development.

Relate Scenarios to Strategies

After scenarios have been identified, the next step is to relate them to strategy – both existing strategies and new options. If an existing strategy is in place, it can be tested with respect to each scenario. Which scenario will be the best one? How bad will the strategy be if the wrong scenario emerges? What will its prospects be with respect to customer acceptance, competitor reactions, and sales and profits? Could it be modified to enhance its prospects?

Even if the scenario analysis is not motivated by a desire to generate new strategy options, it is always useful to consider what strategies would be optimal for each scenario. A scenario by its nature will provide a perspective that is different from the status quo. Any strategy that is optimal for a given scenario should become a viable option. Even if it is not considered superior or even feasible, some elements of it might be captured.

Estimate Scenario Probabilities

To evaluate alternative strategies, it is useful to determine the scenario probabilities. The task is actually one of environmental forecasting, except that the total scenario may be a rich combination of several variables. Experts could be asked to assess probabilities directly. A deeper understanding will often emerge, however, if causal factors underlying each scenario can be determined. For example, the construction equipment industry might develop scenarios based on three alternative levels of construction activity. These levels would have several contributing causes. One would be the interest rate. Another could be the availability of funds to the home-building sector, which in turn would depend on the emerging structure of financial institutions and markets. A third cause might be the level of government spending on roads, energy, and other areas.

KEY LEARNINGS

- Environmental analysis of technology and consumer and government/economic trends can detect opportunities or threats relevant to an organization.
- The green movement provides opportunities to connect to customers and employees.
- Impact analysis involves assessing systematically the impact and immediacy of the trends and events that underlie each strategy uncertainty.
- Scenario analysis, a vehicle to explore different assumptions about the future, involves the creation of 2–3 plausible scenarios, the development of strategies appropriate to each, the assessment of scenario probabilities, and the evaluation of the resulting strategies across the scenarios.

FOR DISCUSSION

1. What did the fax machine replace, if anything? What will replace (or has replaced) the fax machine? When will the fax machine disappear?
2. Develop a scenario based on the proposition that electric cars will continue to improve and take 15% of the automotive market in a few years. Analyse it from the point of view of an energy company like Shell, or a car company like Mercedes.
3. Consider mobile computing using smartphones. Will this change the use of desktop computers? Laptop computers? Netbook computers? How? Will it change the type of computers made?
4. Pick a company or brand/business on which to focus. What are the major trends that come out of an environmental analysis? What are the major areas of uncertainty? How would a major company in the industry handle those best?

5. Focusing on the airline industry, develop a list of strategic uncertainties and possible strategic actions.
6. Consider Cisco's 'telepresence' in videoconferencing, which upgrades the quality of the experience. Will it change the incidence of usage? What is driving the usage (or lack of usage) of videoconferencing?
7. Address the questions posed in the Marks & Spencer insert.
8. Visible criticism has been levelled at the bottled water industry, including the claim that their product is not better than tap water in many locales (some brands are even said to have an unpleasant aftertaste), and that the plastic bottles are carbon costly to make and are not biodegradable. What programmes would you consider to combat these arguments if you were responsible to the Nestlé Pure Life brand?

NOTES

1. Ram Charan, 'Sharpening Your Business Acumen', *Strategy & Business*, Spring 2006, pp. 49–57.
2. Richard Forster and Sarah Kaplan, *Creative Destruction*, New York, NY, Currency, 2001.
3. Raymond Burke, 'Confronting the Challenges that Face Bricks-and-Mortar Stores', *Harvard Business Review*, July–August 1999, pp. 160–167.
4. Arnold Cooper, Edward Demuzilo, Kenneth Hatten, Elijah Hicks, and Donald Tock, 'Strategic Responses to Technological Threats', *Academy of Management Proceedings*, 1976, pp. 54–60.
5. 'How Teenagers Consumer Media', *Media & Internet*, Morgan Stanley, 10 July 2009.
6. Faith Popcorn and Lys Marigold, *Clicking*, New York, NY, HarperCollins, 1997, pp. 11–12.
7. Wendy Melillo and Steve Miller, 'Companies Find It's Not Easy Being Green', *BrandWeek*, 24 July 2006.
8. http://plana.marksandspencer.com/.
9. Stefano Proverbio, Sven Smit, and S. Patrick Viguerie, 'Dissecting Global Trends: an Example from Italy', *McKinsey Quarterly*, 2008, (2), pp. 14–16.
10. Janet Stilson, 'Passing Lane', *Adweek Media*, 6 April 2009, pp. 7–10.
11. 'Beyond Economics: Factoring Politics Into Investment Strategies', *McKinsey Quarterly*, May 2009; available at: http://www.mckinseyquarterly.com/Beyond_economics_Factoring_politics_into_investment_strategies_2337 (accessed 6 September 2009).
12. George Day and Paul Schoemaker, 'Are You a "Vigilant Leader"?', *MIT Sloan Management Review*, Spring 2008, pp. 43–51.
13. Hugh Courtney, 'Decision-Driven Scenarios for Assessing Four Levels of Uncertainty', *Strategy & Leadership*, 2003, **31**(1), pp. 14–16.
14. Liam Fahey, 'Competitor Scenarios', *Strategy & Leadership*, 2003, **31**(1), pp. 32–44.

CHAPTER SIX

Internal Analysis

We have met the enemy and he is us.
—*Pogo*

Self-conceit may lead to self-destruction.
—*Aesop, 'The Frog and the Ox'*

The fish is last to know it swims in water.
—*Chinese proverb*

Should the existing strategy be enhanced, expanded, altered, or replaced? Are existing assets and competencies adequate to win? An internal analysis of the business will help the strategist address these questions. This exploration is similar in scope to an analysis of a competitor or strategic group, but much richer and deeper because of its importance to strategy and because much more information is available.

Just as strategy can be developed at the level of a business, a group of businesses, or the firm, internal analysis can also be conducted at each of these levels. Of course analyses at different levels will differ from each other in emphasis and content, but their structure and thrust will be the same. The common goal is to identify organizational strengths, weaknesses, and constraints and, ultimately, to develop responsive strategies, either exploiting strengths or correcting or compensating for weaknesses.

Four aspects of internal analysis will be discussed in this chapter. The first, financial performance, provides an initial approximation as to how the business is doing. The second, an analysis of other performance dimensions such as customer satisfaction, product quality, brand association, relative cost, new products, and employee capability, can often provide a more robust link to future profitability. The third is an analysis of the strengths and weaknesses that are the basis of current and future strategies. The fourth is an identification and prioritization of the threats and opportunities facing the firm. The final section explores the relationship between strategy and the analysis of the organization, its competitors, and the market. It suggests that successful strategy is when organization strengths are matched against market needs and competitor weaknesses.

FINANCIAL PERFORMANCE – SALES AND PROFITABILITY

Internal analysis often starts with an analysis of current financials – measures of sales and profitability. Either can signal a change in the market viability of a product line and the ability to produce competitively. Furthermore, they provide an indicator of the success of past strategies and thus can often help in evaluating whether strategic changes are needed. In addition, sales and profitability at least appear to be specific and easily measured. As a result, it is not surprising that they are so widely used as performance evaluation tools.

Sales and Market Share

A sensitive measure of how customers regard a product or service can be sales or market share. After all, if the value proposition to a customer changes, sales and share should be affected, although there may be an occasional delay caused by market and customer inertia.

Sales levels can be strategically important. Increased sales can mean that the customer base has grown. An enlarged customer base, if we assume that new customers will develop loyalty, will mean future sales and profits. Increased share can provide the potential to gain SCAs in the form of economies of scale and experience curve effects. Conversely, decreased sales can mean decreases in customer bases and a loss of scale economies.

A problem with using sales as a measure is that it can be affected by short-term actions, such as promotions by a brand and its competitors. Thus, it is necessary to separate changes in sales that are caused by tactical actions from those that represent fundamental changes in the value delivered to the customer, and it is important to couple an analysis of sales or share with an analysis of customer satisfaction and loyalty, which will be discussed shortly.

Profitability

The ultimate measure of a firm's ability to prosper and survive is its profitability. Although both growth and profitability are desirable, establishing a priority between the two can help guide strategic decision-making.

A host of measures and ratios reflect profitability, including margins, costs, and profits. Building on the assets employed leads to the return on assets (ROA) measure, which can be decomposed with a formula developed by General Motors and DuPont in the 1920s.

$$\text{ROA} = \frac{\text{profits}}{\text{sales}} \times \frac{\text{sales}}{\text{assets}}$$

Thus, return on assets can be considered as having two causal factors. The first is the profit margin, which depends on the selling price and cost structure. The second is the asset turnover, which depends on inventory control and asset utilization.

The determination of both the numerator and denominator of the ROA terms is not as straightforward as might be assumed. Substantial issues surround each, e.g. the distortions caused by depreciation and the fact that book assets do not reflect intangible assets, such as brand equity, or the market value of tangible assets.

Measuring Performance: Shareholder Value Analysis

The concept of shareholder value, an enormously influential concept during the past two decades, provides an answer to this question. Each business should earn an ROA (based on a flow of profits emanating from an investment) that meets or exceeds the costs of capital, which is the weighted average of the cost of equity and cost of debt. Thus, if the cost of equity is 16% and the cost of debt is 8%, the cost of capital will be 12% if the amount of debt is equal to the amount of equity; if there is only one-fourth as much debt as equity, then the cost of capital will be 14%. If the return is greater than the cost of capital, shareholder value will increase, and if it is less, shareholder value will decrease.

Some of the routes to increasing shareholder value are as follows:

- Earn more profit by reducing costs or increasing revenue without using more capital.
- Invest in high-return products (this, of course, is what strategy is all about).
- Reduce the cost of capital by increasing the debt to equity ratio or by buying back stock to reduce the cost of equity.
- Use less capital. Under shareholder value analysis, the assets employed are no longer a free good, so there is an incentive to reduce them. If improved just-in-time operations can reduce the inventory, it directly affects shareholder value.

The concept of shareholder value is theoretically valid.[1] If a profit stream can b estimated accurately from a strategic move, the analysis will be sound. The probler is that short-term profits (known to affect stock return and thus shareholder wealth are easier to estimate and manipulate than long-term profits. Investors who assum that short-term profits predict longer-term profits pay undue attention to the fo mer, as does the top management of a company with numerical targets to meet. Th discipline to invest in a strategy that will sacrifice short-term financial performan for long-term prospects is not easy to come by, especially if some of the futu prospects are in the form of options. For example, the investment by Itali jewellery company Bulgari into a joint venture with Marriott International In to create Bulgari Hotels and Resorts gave it the option to expand its brand name in a different sector. When Diageo bought the Chalone Wine Group, it bought tl option to enhance its business in the alcoholic beverage area specifically in tl North American wine business.

The impact of reducing investment is also not without risks. When, for example, Coca-Cola sold off its bottlers to reduce investment and improve shareholder value, its control of the quality of its products may have been reduced. Similar challenges face firms every time they outsource. In general, investment reduction often means outsourcing, with its balancing act between flexibility and loss of control over operations. A company that outsources its call centre reduces its control over customer interaction.

One danger of shareholder value analysis is that it reduces the priority given to other stakeholders such as employees, suppliers, and customers, each of whom represents assets that can form the basis for long-term success. It can be argued that the shareholder has the least at risk because he or she is very likely diversified and thus has only a small part of a portfolio at risk. In contrast, employees, suppliers, and sometimes customers have more to lose if the firm fails. Furthermore, the shareholder does not in any practical way have any influence over the management of the firm. Thus, it might be reasonable to elevate the priority of other stakeholders. P&G, for one, puts customers first, arguing in part that, if customers are delighted with the products, shareholders will benefit in the long term. Other firms have explicitly put employees first, assuming that, if they are productive, shareholders will eventually benefit. Making the shareholders the first priority can lead to programmes such as cost reduction, possibly involving degradation of the customer experience, that result in short-term profits and therefore enhance shareholder value but undercut the firm's strength in the long term.

In fact, shareholder value management has met with very mixed results. However, one study of the experience of 125 firms found similarities among those that had applied shareholder value concepts successfully:[2]

- The companies gave priority to shareholder value over other goals, particularly growth goals.
- They provided intensive training on shareholder value throughout the organization and made it a practical tool for business managers at all levels. The philosophy was not restricted to the executive suite.
- They were disciplined in identifying the drivers of shareholder value. For example, for a call centre, drivers could be the length of time to answer calls and the quality of responses.
- They reduced overheads by adapting the current accounting system and integrating shareholder value analysis with strategic planning.

These firms found a variety of benefits. First, the concept led to value-creating divestments that otherwise would not have occurred. Second, firms were able to transfer corporate planning and decision-making to decentralized business units because all units tended to use the same logic, metrics, and mindset. Third, the business investment horizon tended to be longer, with projects with multiyear time-frames being approved. Fourth, the new recognition that capital had a cost tended to generate better strategic decisions.

PERFORMANCE MEASUREMENT – BEYOND PROFITABILITY

One of the difficulties in strategic market management is developing performance indicators that convincingly represent long-term prospects. The temptation is to focus on short-term profitability measures and to reduce investment in new products and brand images that have long-term payoffs.

The concept of net present value represents a long-term profit stream, but it is not always operational. It often provides neither a criterion for decision-making nor a useful performance measure. It is somewhat analogous to preferring €6 million to €4 million. The real question involves determining which strategic alternative will generate €6 million and which will generate €4 million.

It is necessary to develop performance measures that will reflect long-term viability and health. The focus should be on the assets and competencies that underlie the current and future strategies and their SCAs. What are the key assets and competencies for a business during the planning horizon? What strategic dimensions are most crucial: to become more competitive with respect to product offerings, to develop new products, or to become more productive? These types of question can help identify performance areas that a business should examine. Answers will vary depending on the situation, but, as suggested by Figure 6.1, they will often include customer satisfaction/brand loyalty, product/service quality, and brand/firm associations, relative cost, new product activity, and manager/employee capability and performance.

Customer Satisfaction/Brand Loyalty

Perhaps the most important asset of many firms is the loyalty of the customer base. Measures of sales and market share are useful but potentially inaccurate indicators of

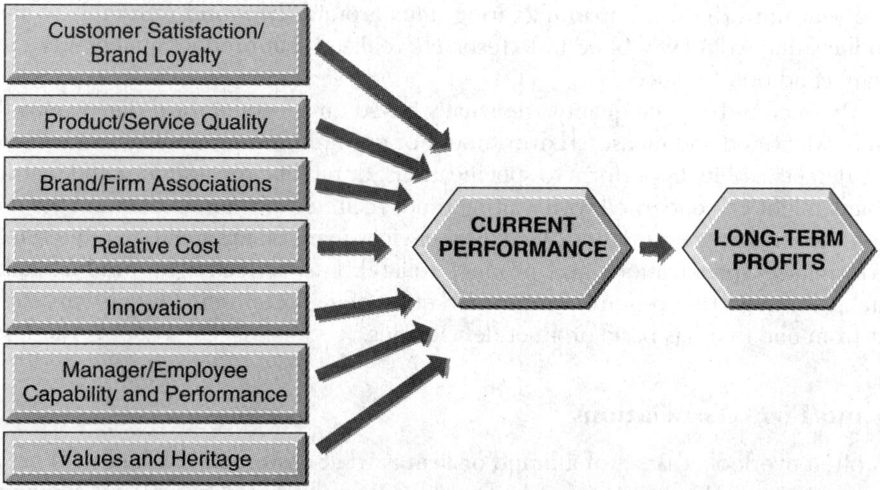

Figure 6.1 Performance Measures Reflecting Long-Term Profitability

how customers really feel about a firm. Such measures can reflect market inertia and are noisy, in part, because of competitor actions and market fluctuations. Measures of customer satisfaction and brand loyalty are much more sensitive and provide diagnostic value as well.

Guidelines for Measuring Satisfaction and Loyalty

First, problems and causes of dissatisfaction that may motivate customers to change brands or firms should be identified. In fact, the most sensitive and insightful information comes from those who have decided to leave a brand or firm. Thus, exit interviews for customers who have abandoned a brand can be productive. Second, there is a big difference between a brand or firm being liked and the absence of dissatisfaction. The size and intensity of the customer group that truly likes a brand or firm should be known. Third, the lifetime value of a customer, based on their usage level and the time period that they are expected to be attached to the firm's offerings, is often a useful concept. Estimation of lifetime value for key segments can be illuminating. Fourth, measures should be tracked over time and compared with those of competitors. Relative comparisons and changes are most important.

Product and Service Quality

A product (or service) and its components should be critically and objectively compared both with the competition and with customer expectations and needs. How good a value is it? Can it really deliver superior performance? How does it compare with competitor offerings? How will it compare with competitor offerings in the future, given competitive innovations? One common failing of firms is to avoid tough comparisons with a realistic assessment of competitors' current and potential offerings. A newly appointed CEO of a snack food firm once put all programmes on hold for a year until the firm's manufacturing units around the world were able to make products that would win blind taste tests. He realized that product quality was a necessary condition for success.

Product and service quality are usually based on several critical dimensions that can be identified and measured over time. For example, a car manufacturer can measure defects, ability to perform to specifications, durability, repairability, and features. A bank might be concerned with waiting time, accuracy of transactions, and the quality of the customer experience. A medical devices manufacturer can examine relative performance specifications and product reliability as reflected by product failure data. A business that requires better marketing of a good product line is very different from one that has basic product deficiencies.

Brand/Firm Associations

An often overlooked asset of a brand or firm is what customers think of it. What are its associations? What is its perceived quality? Perceived quality, which is sometimes very different from actual quality, can be based on experience with past products or services and on quality cues, such as retailer types, pricing strategies, packaging, advertising, and typical customers. Is a brand or firm regarded as expert in a product or technology area (such as designing and making sailing boats)? Innovative? Expensive? For the upper middle classes? Is it associated with a country, a user type, or an application area (such as racing)? Such associations can be key strategic assets for a brand or firm.

Associations can be monitored by regularly asking customers to describe their use experiences and to tell what a brand or firm means to them. The identification of changes in important associations will likely emerge from such efforts. Structured surveys using a representative sample of customers can provide even more precise tracking information.

Relative Cost

A careful cost analysis of a product (or service) and its components, which can be critical when a strategy is dependent on achieving a cost advantage or cost parity, involves tearing down competitors' products and analysing their systems in detail. The Japanese consultant Kenichi Ohmae suggested that such an analysis, when coupled with performance analysis, can lead to one of the four situations shown in Figure 6.2.[3]

If a component such as a car's braking system or an on-line retailer's logistics operation is both more expensive than and inferior to that of the competition, a strategic problem requiring change may exist. An analysis could show, however, that the component is such a small item in terms of both cost and customer impact that it should be ignored. If the component is competitively superior, however, a cost reduction programme may not be the only appropriate strategy. A value analysis, in which the component's value to the customer is quantified, may suggest that the point

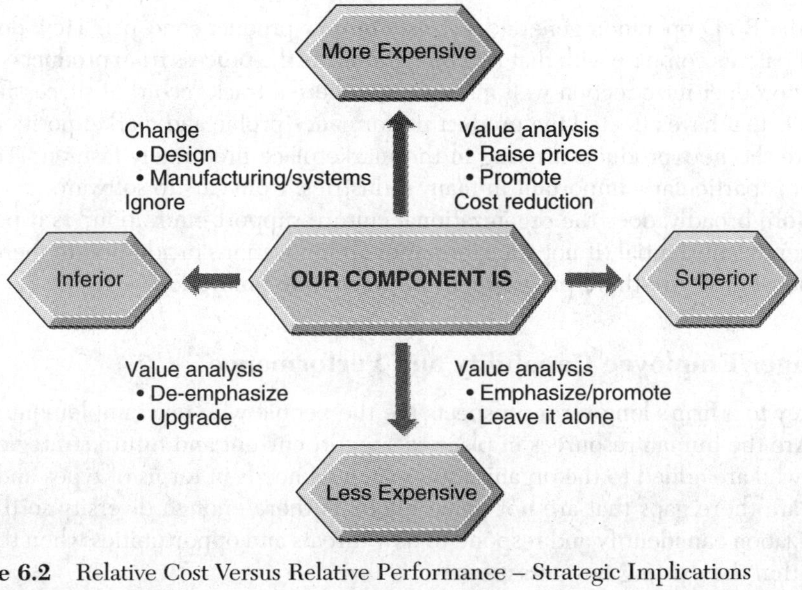

Figure 6.2 Relative Cost Versus Relative Performance – Strategic Implications

of superiority could support a price increase or promotion campaign. If, on the other hand, a component is less expensive than that of the competition but inferior, a value analysis might suggest that it be de-emphasized. Thus, for a car with a cost advantage but handling disadvantage, a company might de-emphasize its driving performance and position it as an economy car. An alternative is to upgrade this component. Conversely, if a component is both less expensive and superior, a value analysis may suggest that the component be emphasized, perhaps playing a key role in positioning and promotion strategies.

Sources of Cost Advantage

The many routes to cost advantage will be discussed in Chapter 8. They include economies of scale, the experience curve, product design innovations, and the use of a no-frills product offering. Each provides a different perspective to the concept of competing on the basis of a cost advantage.

Average Costing

In average costing, some elements of fixed or semi-variable costs are not carefully allocated but instead are averaged over total production. Average costing can provide an opening for competitors to enter an otherwise secure market. Large customers can be much more profitable than small ones, and premium-priced products and offerings can be more lucrative than value-priced ones. A product line that is subsidizing other lines is vulnerable, representing an opportunity to competitors and thus a potential threat to a business.

Innovation

Does the R&D operation generate a stream of new product concepts? How does the flow of patents compare with that for competitors? Is the process from product concept to new product introduction well managed? Is there a track record of successful new products that have affected the product performance profile and market position?

Are the new products arriving in the marketplace in a timely fashion? Time to market is particularly important in many industries, from cars to software.

More broadly, does the organizational culture support innovation? Is it possible to generate substantial (if not transformational) innovations in addition to incremental innovations? Are there programmes to precipitate innovation?

Manager/Employee Capability and Performance

Also key to a firm's long-term prospects are the people who must implement strategies. Are the human resources in place to support current and future strategies? Do those who are added to the organization match its needs in terms of types and quality or are there gaps that are not being filled? Is there enough diversity so that the organization can identify and respond to new threats and opportunities when they are not within the existing business arena?

An organization should be evaluated not only on how well it obtains human resources but also on how well it nurtures them. A healthy organization will consist of individuals who are motivated, challenged, fulfilled, and growing in their professions. Each of these dimensions can be observed and measured by employee surveys and group discussions. Certainly, the attitude and ability of employees was a key factor in the rapid and profitable growth of Google over the past 10 years. In sales-driven industries such as pharmaceuticals and animal feed, the ability to sustain positive salesperson performance and attitude is usually a key success factor.

Values and Heritage

The firms with strong performance over time usually have a well-defined set of values that are both known and accepted within the organization, values that are more than simply increasing financial return. Strong values that guide and even inspire are enhanced if they are supported by a well-known and relevant heritage. Values and a heritage not only create a strong and consistent brand and support the business strategy. In fact, when business falters, one tactic that often works is to return to the roots of the business – to what made it strong in the first place. When McDonald's faltered, a turnaround was based in part on their historic core values of service, people, convenience, quality, and good prices.

Values provide a reason to believe for employees and will influence the brand as a result. Among the values that are often influential are the organizational associations discussed in Chapter 9, such as innovation, social responsibility, concern for the customer, quality, service, being global, and being environmentally responsible.

Having a heritage based on a founder or on early success can be a guide and a value anchor. Consider the Godrej Group, one of India's leading conglomerates, which retains the commitment to innovation of its founder Ardeshir Godrej. Most recently, the company introduced a range of environmentally friendly refrigerators to the Indian market. Ireland's leading retailer, Dunnes Stores, retains the emphasis on market-leading value, which was the strategic driver of the founder of the company, Ben Dunne Sr.

STRENGTHS AND WEAKNESSES

In developing or implementing strategy, it is important to identify the assets and competencies that represent areas of strength and weakness. A successful strategy needs to be based on assets and competencies because it is generally easier for competitors to duplicate what you do rather than who you are. Furthermore, current assets and competencies, as illustrated in Chapter 11, can be leveraged to create new businesses.

Figure 3.4 had a partial list of the types of asset and competence that an organization might develop. There were more than three dozen, organized under the categories of innovation, manufacturing, access to capital, management, marketing, and customer base. This checklist is a good place to start when identifying the most relevant assets and competencies, as are the motivating questions introduced in Chapter 3, which identify assets and competencies important to customers, those developed by successful competitors, and those representing large or important parts of the value-added chain.

Each asset or competence relevant to the business, such as a new product development capability, access to low-cost labour, an innovative culture, brand strength, or a loyal customer base, should be evaluated as to its strength and impact. Is it dominant in that it provides a point of advantage that has endured and is likely to remain so in the future?

The service delivery capability of Disney, for example, is so superior that other firms study its operation. Is the organization willing to invest to make the asset or competence dominant into the future? Certainly, Disney has shown this willingness over many decades. The investment commitment needs to be factored into the financial resource picture. It may mean that resources for new ventures will be limited.

Is it strong but vulnerable? Are others catching up? Should the firm attempt to invest to regain a dominant position so that it is a point of advantage? If so, what programme is implied, and at what cost? Or should the firm retreat so that the asset or competence is simply a modest advantage over some competitors and a point of parity with respect to others?

Is the asset or competence adequate, a point of parity? Is it strong enough for customers not to avoid the firm because of it? If so, is that a satisfactory long-term position? Can advantage be achieved on other dimensions? What investment is implied to maintain the current strength so that it does not become a point of disadvantage? Product quality is often in this situation. If H&M, for example, can deliver quality adequate enough for customers not to use a quality judgement as a reason to exclude H&M from their consideration set, the battle will shift to other dimensions on which Target is likely to excel.

Is it a liability? Is it holding back the firm from gaining and retaining customers? Consider the Korean automobile firms whose quality and social acceptability deficit precluded people from buying their products. They needed to convert this liability to a point of parity.

BENCHMARKING

Comparing the performance of a business component with others is called *benchmarking*. The goal is to generate specific ideas for improvement, and also to define standards at which to aim. One target may be competitors: what cost and performance levels are they achieving, and how? Knowing your deficits with respect to the competition is the first step to developing programmes to eliminate them. Best-practice companies are another target. Thus, many benchmark against Disney in terms of delivering consistent service in their theme parks, or Amazon as the standard for Internet e-commerce operations and customer support. Looking outside one's own industry is often a way to break away from the status quo and thereby create a real advantage.

THREATS AND OPPORTUNITIES

The other half of an internal analysis is the identification of threats and opportunities. In the external analysis, a host of potential threats and opportunities will have been identified. The internal challenge is to determine which are most relevant for the firm's business and to prioritize them. The dimensions used to manage strategic uncertainty in general, immediacy and impact, are appropriate when assessing threats and opportunities.

Those threats that are imminent and have high impact should drive a strategic imperative, a programme that has the highest priority. If there is a visible quality problem, fixing that problem and thus addressing the associated threat need to be a high priority. When the threat is of low impact or is not immediate, a more measured response is possible. For example, when the Mercedes A-Class was introduced to the market, Mercedes failed to spot a problem with the car's high centre of gravity. A reporter from a Swedish motor journal rolled over while test-driving it, and leading customers across Europe began to cancel their orders. This required Mercedes to make strategic moves to recall cars and fit (for free) ESP systems and different tyres to rectify the problem.

The most extreme threat is one that potentially makes obsolete the business model. As e-book devices, such as Amazon Kindle and the Sony E-book, become popular with regular readers, the business model of the paper book industry appears doomed. With multiple and expensive layers in the supply chain (writers, agents, publishers, bookshops, and customers), the ability of e-book formats to capture much of the value for themselves appears to be great. It does not take a great deal of imagination to create a scenario in which authors sell directly and only in e-book format. Having dominated the industry for over a century, could existing publishers have done a better job of preparing for this new reality?

Threats can come in the form of a strategic problem or a liability. Strategic problems, events, or trends adversely affecting strategy generally need to be addressed aggressively and corrected, even if the fix is difficult and expensive. Strategic liabilities – the absence of an asset (such as good location) or competence (for example, new-product introduction skills) – usually require a different response. A business often copes over time with a liability by adjusting strategies in a way that will neutralize that liability.

An opportunity can similarly be evaluated as to whether its impact will be immediate and major. If so, the organization should be set up to move quickly and decisively. One study found that most organizations are presented with a 'golden opportunity' only once or twice a decade. The mark of a firm that can adapt to new conditions and still come out a market leader is recognizing and reacting to such opportunities. Opportunities that have a low impact or are in the future may justify serious investment and perhaps an experimental entry into a new business area to gain information, but the resource commitment is likely to be more modest.

In general, lost opportunities are costly and are only too common. As Drucker once said, managers need to spend more time on opportunities and less on solving problems.

FROM ANALYSIS TO STRATEGY

In making strategic decisions, inputs from a variety of assessments are relevant, as the last several chapters have already made clear. However, the core of any strategic decision should be based on three types of assessment. The first concerns organizational strengths and weaknesses. The second evaluates competitor strengths, weaknesses, and strategies, because an organization's strength is of less value if it is neutralized by a competitor's strength or strategy. The third assesses the competitive context, the customers and their needs, the market, and the market environment in order to determine how attractive the selected market will be, given the business strategy.

The goal is to develop a strategy that exploits business strengths and competitor weaknesses and neutralizes business weaknesses and competitor strengths. The ideal is to compete in a healthy, growing industry with a strategy based on strengths that are unlikely to be acquired or neutralized by competitors. Figure 6.3 summarizes how these three assessments combine to influence strategy.

Vodafone's decision to sell its Japanese business in 2006 illustrates these strategic principles.[4] Vodafone had originally entered the Japanese market through the acquisition of J-phone, Japan's third-place player, in 2001. The logic of the acquisition was twofold: to take advantage of Vodafone's global economies of scale to grow in the Japanese market, and to use the advanced business model of the Japanese market to drive its activities in other markets. The latter worked well, but problems arose in the former. Plans to switch the Japanese market to the 3G technology used in Europe did not work. Consumers were unenthusiastic about the handsets on offer, and so Vodafone had to develop a Japan-specific range of phones, undermining the economies-of-scale

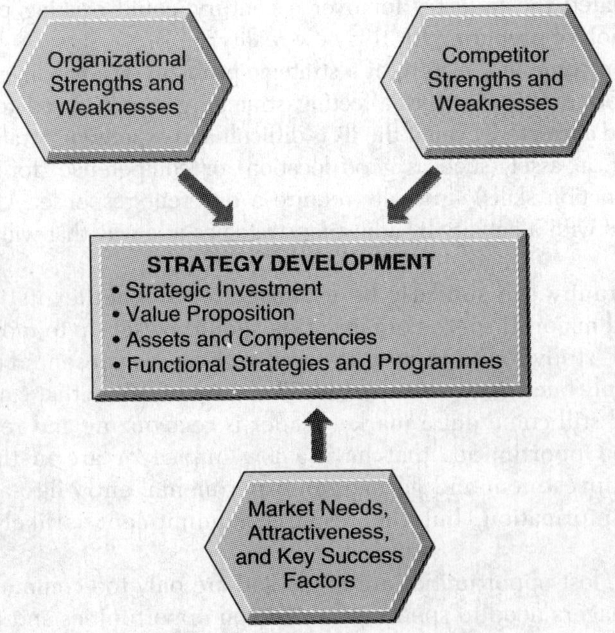

Figure 6.3 Structuring Strategic Decisions

aspect of their business model. In competitive terms, Vodafone faced two strong incumbents in NTTDoCoMo and KDDI, and the Japanese government created three new mobile phone licences and introduced new legislation to allow consumers to keep their numbers when they switched providers, a move likely to encourage switching behaviour. Finally, the market for phone services was changing rapidly. Vodafone had built its strategy on being a global mobile-only provider. In 2001 this looked like a winning strategy, but by 2006 this seemed questionable as a key success factor, as the market had switched to being able to provide customers with converged services of mobile, fixed line, broadband and TV. Faced with such a decision environment, the move to sell the Japanese business offered an opportunity for Vodafone to re-evaluate its overall position and to find a more competitive way to deploy its assets and competencies.

KEY LEARNINGS

- Sales and profitability analysis provide an evaluation of past strategies and an indication of the current market viability of a product line. Shareholder value holds that the flow of profits emanating from an investment should exceed the cost of capital (which is the weighted average of the cost of equity and cost of debt). Routes to achieving shareholder value – such as downsizing, reducing assets employed, and outsourcing – can be risky when they undercut assets and competencies.
- Performance assessment should go beyond financials to include such dimensions as customer satisfaction/brand loyalty, product/service quality, and brand/firm associations, relative cost, new product activity, and manager/employee capability and performance.
- Assets and competencies can represent a point of advantage, a point of parity, or a liability. Threats and opportunities that are both imminent and important should trigger strategic imperatives, programmes with high priority.

FOR DISCUSSION

1. Explain shareholder value analysis. Why might it help firms? Why might it result in bad decisions?
2. Look at the quotations that begin Chapters 2 to 6. Which one do you find the most insightful? Why? Under what circumstances would its implications not hold?
3. What performance measures would you consider most important for Chinese food firm COFCO? For French car firm Renault?
4. Conduct a strengths, weaknesses, opportunities, and threats (SWOT) analysis for Vodafone.

NOTES

1. For an excellent review of the risks of shareholder value, see Allan A. Kennedy, *The End of Shareholder Value*, Cambridge, MA, Perseus Publishing, 2000.
2. Philippe Haspeslagh, Tomo Noda, and Fares Boulos, 'It's Not Just About the Numbers', *Harvard Business Review*, July–August 2001, pp. 65–73.
3. Kenichi Ohmae, *The Mind of the Strategist*, New York, NY, Penguin Books, 1982, p. 26.
4. 'Not-So-Big is Beautiful', *The Economist*, 9 May 2006; 'Calling for a Rethink', *The Economist*, 26 January 2006.

CASES FOR THE END OF PART I

Case 1

UNDERSTANDING AND WORKING WITH INDUSTRY TRENDS. THE FUTURE OF NEWSPAPERS

As the first decade of the twenty-first century ended, the global newspaper industry was in turmoil. The sector had changed little in the previous 100 years – sourcing and printing daily news on paper for distribution and sale. The advent of the Internet, citizen journalism, and new media technologies had disrupted newspapers' dominance over the way people sourced, shared, and consumed information, specifically daily news stories. In the developed world, unit sales for papers were tailing off, and consequently advertising revenues dwindled as readership was lost to the Internet. People were actively seeking out free content or niche news on-line. That trend had culminated in shrinking margins and dozens of business closures between 2006 and 2009 as many of the leading titles in the United States and Europe crumbled under the burden of their unsustainable cost structures, often costing four times as much to reach 1000 people by print than on-line.

However, the global picture was more attractive for the contemporary business model. Markets in India and China were growing steadily – of the world's 100 best-selling daily newspapers, some 74 were published in Asia, and 62 of those were from India, China, and Japan. Furthermore, new technologies like the Kindle Electronic Paper device and the rise of freesheet newspapers seemed to offer hope that those who could adapt to a wired world could survive over the long term by radically reinventing themselves to cope with a market where consumers were accustomed to high-quality, free information. However, not all businesses had fared equally. The *New York Times* and *The Washington Post*, stalwarts of American journalism, both struggled in maintaining their bricks-and-mortar presence, but the *Post*'s diversification into educational publishing had dampened the effect of falling newspaper stock market valuations.[1] Meanwhile, high-quality targeted products like *The Financial Times* and the *Wall Street Journal* had actually prospered, in spite of the 'webocratization' of daily news, charging premiums for content on a subscription basis. Crystallizing the nature of the problem, one commentator observed, 'The peculiar fact about the current crisis is that, even as big papers have become less profitable, they've arguably become more popular'.[2]

---

[1]'Future of Newspapers', Wikipedia, available at: http://en.wikipedia.org/wiki/Future_of_newspapers#cite_note-20 (accessed 1 December 2009).

[2]James Surowiecki, 'News You Can Lose', *The New Yorker*, 22 December 2008, available at: http://www.newyorker.com/talk/financial/2008/12/22/081222ta_talk_surowiecki (accessed 1 December 2009); in 'Future of Newspapers', Wikipedia, available at: http://en.wikipedia.org/wiki/Future_of_newspapers#cite_note-69 (accessed 1 December 2009).

Newspaper Business

As a conduit of news, information, and opinion, newspapers have played a central role in society for centuries. Napoleon Bonaporte recognized the power that newspapers wielded, preferring to face a thousand artillery guns rather than four angry broadsheets. Advertising was the main revenue stream in the standard business model. Supporting advertising was revenue from classified ads and finally unit sales. By the 1990s, the press had grown so large and lucrative that Rupert Murdoch described his global newspaper portfolio as 'rivers of gold'.[3] Investors believed newspapers were the cornerstone to the new emerging media empires which would incorporate television, print, film, and on-line assets into one massive story-weaving machine. A wave of mergers and acquisitions ensued in the late 1990s and early 2000s, which drove prices for prestigious titles to record levels. Dow Jones, for example, sold Rupert Murdoch's News Corp International *The Wall Street Journal* for $5.6 billion in 2007.

The newspaper industry has long been seen as a cyclical one, tied closely as it is to advertising and economic fortunes. It was this fact combined with newspapers' resilience to the proliferation of television that led owners to dismiss the gravity of the threat posed by Web 2.0 and interactive technologies. Over the course of the twentieth century, little had changed in the format of newspaper reporting and packaging, but the strengths and weaknesses of newspapers as a form of communication were highlighted by the rapid adoption of the Internet as a competing source of information in the late 1990s.

Internet Kills the Daily Newspaper

Henry Fielding, the eighteenth-century English author and dramatist, observed that 'a newspaper consists of just the same number of words whether there be any news in it or not'. This characterized one of the format's main drawbacks – dynamism. Television and the Internet could be updated in almost real time. These channels could also enhance a story with moving images, sound, and links to other content in the case of the Internet. Twitter, the short-form text-based mobile blogging technology, had taken that immediacy factor to a new level, with many cases of world-interest stories breaking via Twitter networks long before mainstream media could cover the same story.

In respect of advertising, both television and the Internet offered businesses more compelling models. Again, the Internet seemed by far the best-suited medium, amalgamating the benefits of television with the ability to target advertisements specifically related to a user's search terms while accessing the web's vast information resources. This quality was particularly valuable in the case of classified advertisements, prompting the birth of many localized classifieds websites such as Craigslist and Gumtree, for example.

---

[3]'Who Killed the Newspaper?', *The Economist Magazine*, 24 August 2006, available at: http://www.economist.com/opinion/displaystory.cfm?story_id=7830218 (accessed 1 December 2009).

Such drastic alterations to the business model behind modern commercial journalism had implications for the quality of the product being created. Starved of advertising revenues and weighed down by high costs, many newspapers could ill-afford to invest in ventures like investigative journalism, foreign reporting bureaux, or even quality editorial work, stimulating a potentially vicious circle of poor service and poor returns.

Of course, newspapers were well positioned to go on-line, and many embraced the Internet, offering extra content on-line and even access to their archives, sometimes for a premium. The problem remained as to how to earn money from proprietary content on-line, because in cyberspace newspapers faced stiff competition for reader's attentions. Low set-up costs permitted alternative sources and niche journalism to propagate in the forms of on-line newspapers like *The Huffington Post* and more pervasively with the popularity of blogging software, which, in tandem with cheap video cameras, had given rise to the citizen journalist phenomenon. In combating the proliferation of citizen journalism, newspapers were quick to point out the value of accountability, credibility, and professional journalistic standards to which established titles would naturally adhere whether in print or pixels. It was a valid point – in spite of their financial woes, both *The New York Times* and *The Washington Post* ranked among the world's top 20 global news sites, indicating the brand retained significant equity, even if the content was free.

But more worrying for newspapers was the effect of on-line news aggregators such as *Google News*, a technology that amalgamated news stories from across the web into one convenient interface for busy 'netizens', or frequent web users. In so doing, *Google News* earned an estimated US$100 million in advertising revenue with very little outlay. The flipside of that equation was the transfer of value away from the content producers to the content provider. While newspapers could also earn advertising revenues on-line, the return was far lower than that required, primarily because advertising remained a buyer's market in cyberspace.

Future Options

> Simply put, if cable and satellite broadcasting, as well as the Internet, had come along first, newspapers as we know them probably would never have existed.
>
> *Warren Buffett*[4]

A number of specific avenues for opportunity faced the industry, including new technologies, new real-world strategies, and, of course, new on-line business models. Within some of these categories, a number of opportunities arose. The fundamental issue, however, remained the same: identifying the value in sourcing, creating, and disseminating news stories to audiences and how to extract that value before someone else did.

---

[4]Buffeted: Newspapers Are Paying the Price for Shortsighted Thinking', *American Journalism Review*, October–November 2007, available at: http://www.ajr.org/Article.asp?id=4416 (accessed 1 December 2009); in 'Future of Newspapers', Wikipedia, available at: http://en.wikipedia.org/wiki/Future_of_newspapers#cite_note-32 (accessed 1 December 2009).

New Technologies

Newsprint was an outdated technology whose cost had begun to rise, placing pressure on newspapers already struggling to keep production costs in line. Furthermore, pixels offered a richer experience than newsprint. Technologies like Kindle, the electronic wireless reading device developed by Amazon, appealed to some in the industry as an ideal way to overcome these problems and bypass some competitive threats posed by the Internet. The purchase price for a Kindle device was high enough for any deal to require newspapers to subsidise the cost to the reader. This subsidy, in conjunction with the unit rental fee due to Amazon, would leave little annual revenue accruing to the newspaper from each device. Other electronic readers were coming onto the market, but cost remained a universal issue with such appliances. Furthermore, smartphones capable of accessing the Internet via Wi-Fi technologies were fast becoming mainstream products and were more likely to be adopted owing to multiple functionalities. E-readers could not ignore this real long-term trend. Speculatively, next-generation technologies such as augmented realities and virtual realities promised the possibility of harnessing the experience of reading a physical newspaper in a digitized format optimizing the best of both worlds.

New Strategies

One option facing those businesses with cash or backed-by-market confidence was to seek synergies through mergers and acquisitions. In other industries, consolidation provided for stability, but in journalism it raised questions about integrity and the impact on independent news reporting. Aside from the moral implications, markets had recently responded negatively to new merger activity. For example, McClatchy, the third largest newspaper business in the United States, announced the purchase of Knight-Ridder for several billion in 2005 and went on to lose 98% of its market value.

Another option for newspapers was to print less often, saving on costs and focusing on high-value editions such as Weekend sections or Friday business sections. This could be coupled with a daily on-line edition to retain readership throughout the week. Such a strategy would allow publishers to charge a premium and retain brand presence in the market. Alternatively, some within the industry were excited by the high circulation figures gained by freesheets, especially among younger urban readers – a key next-generation target audience that had proven difficult to reach with traditional titles. Crucially, in spite of their popularity, freesheets were entirely dependent on advertising revenues and analysts remained unconvinced of the sustainability of that business model, especially in a volatile global economy.

International market expansion was another real opportunity for larger businesses, targeting growth markets like India, China, and perhaps Africa. Independent News and Media plc, for example, had already entered the Indian market with a view to stabilising revenues from its media portfolio. Television ownership and Internet penetration remained well below western averages, although phenomenal economic growth in both China and India indicated that emerging middle classes in both countries could soon rival those in the developed world in terms of living standards. In that regard, newsprint's long-term future was not guaranteed in these markets either. On the other hand, in China, governmental control over freedom of speech and foreign ownership of Chinese businesses limited scope for growth as well.

Digital Strategies

Again, the digital world presented a number of possible scenarios that newspapers could consider towards long-term sustainable profitability. Publishing exclusively on-line, as the *Seattle Post-Intelligencer* and the *Christian Science Monitor* had done, would allow businesses to slash overheads, leverage their brand equity, and perhaps add on services and products for which fees could be charged, such as crossword puzzles, archive access, rich media, extra reportage, or financial market information. Some businesses had been more successful than others in this strategy, those with a clear focus offering a niche product. One prospect was the development of an iTunes-style interface that could sell stories or content piecemeal in return for micro-payments, but newspapers had yet to make such a system work.

Instead, strength in unity seemed to offer businesses a real prospect of retaining value in their content. Journalism Online was such a venture, founded by industry veterans, the organization signed up 500 newspapers in a bid to coordinate a pan-industry subscription model for member's content on-line. Launched in 2009, its success would take time to evaluate.

Being a generalist on-line discounted the value of the publication's brand owing to the widespread availability of most news stories through a myriad of portals, aggregators, and news feeds.

Another challenge facing papers considering an entirely on-line presence was the emergence of citizen journalism such as OhMyNews, a Korean venture that sourced its stories from a wide pool of some 50 000 private citizens and professional journalists who earned a nominal sum for any story that was published. By creating an open-source-style newspaper on-line, founder Oh Yeon-ho, an experienced journalist, aimed to challenge the conservative status quo in Korea's press. In 2009 the website published about 200 stories daily, averaging about 16 million hits from 1.2–2 million readers. It was a textbook example of the power and appeal of the Internet in democratizing story writing and news reporting. Ultimately, OhMyNews proved so influential in helping to elect Korean President Roh that he snubbed the established press to grant OhMyNews his first presidential interview. This blend of professional journalism and citizen journalism offered tantalizing prospects to businesses that were prepared to invest in radically new models in reporting.

The decline in advertising and sales revenues in the bricks-and-mortar world of newsprint was an unmistakable and terminal one, and was really a matter of timing. As readers and businesses migrated on-line, the challenges inherent in understanding and exploiting a radically different communications channel that embraced interactivity were particularly difficult for established newspaper titles to adapt to. Those companies that had adapted earlier on were still faced with declining on-line revenues, as the global economic downturn affected all sectors of advertising. Apart from the cyclicality of advertising and consequently newspaper sales, the fundamental sources of value in the industry were shifting, and it seemed that only those businesses that could reposition themselves away from older norms and viewpoints had any chance for long-term survival in the brave net world.

QUESTIONS

1. What trends are driving consumers away from newspapers? Which of these are supported by underlying consumer trends? Identify these trends.
2. Which of these trends will be around in five years? How would you forecast the probability that the trend will persist for that long?
3. What are the threats and opportunities represented by these trends for other news organizations such as the BBC and CNN?
4. Given your analysis, could a move to charge for content on-line succeed on a wide scale?

BIBLIOGRAPHY

1. Kenneth Li, 'Newspapers Join Online Payment Platform', *Financial Times*, 14 August 2009, available at: http://www.ft.com/cms/s/0/5e64a656-885f-11de-82e4-00144feabdc0 .html?nclick_check=1 (accessed 27 January 2010).
2. Jeremy Caplan, in *Time Magazine* on-line, available at: http://www.time.com/time/business/article/0,8599,1566014,00.html (accessed 1 December 2009).
3. 'Who Killed the Newspaper?', The Economist Magazine, 24 August 2006, available at: http://www.economist.com/opinion/displaystory.cfm?story_id=7830218 (accessed 1 December 2009).
4. 'Future of Newspapers', in Wikipedia, available at: http://en.wikipedia.org/wiki/Future_of_newspapers#cite_note-32 (accessed 1 December 2009).
5. Miguel Helft, 'Newspapers Worldwide (Minus U.S.) Oppose Google–Yahoo Deal', in *New York Times* on-line blogs, 15 September 2008, available at: http://bits.blogs.nytimes.com/2008/09/15/newspapers-worldwide-minus-us-oppose-google-yahoo-deal/?ref=technology (accessed 1 December 2009).
6. 'Newspapers and the Kindle, in *Financial Times* on-line blogs, 8 May 2009, available at: http://blogs.ft.com/techblog/2009/05/lex-newspapers-and-the-kindle/ (accessed 1 December 2009).
7. Andrew Edgecliffe-Johnson, 'Google Chief Urges Newspapers to Use Technology to Boost Revenue', *Financial Times*, 8 April 2009, available at: http://www.ft.com/cms/s/0/bc9e25a4-23d2-11de-996a-00144feabdc0.html (accessed 1 December 2009).
8. Andrew Edgecliffe-Johnson and Kenneth Li, *Financial Times*, 7 May 2009, available at: http://www.ft.com/cms/s/0/db6c8cb2-3b30-11de-ba91-00144feabdc0.html (accessed 1 December 2009).

9. Robert Anderson and Christopher Mason, 'Newspapers Face Fresh Pricing Pressures', *Financial Times*, 17 November 2008, available at: http://www.ft.com/cms/s/0/88ffa868-b446-11dd-8e35-0000779fd18c.html (accessed 1 December 2009).

10. Ben Fenton, 'Free Newspapers are in the Frontline Trenches of This War', *Financial Times*, 17 March 2009, available at: http://www.ft.com/cms/s/0/8cef0ff2-1294-11de-b816-0000779fd2ac.html (accessed 1 December 2009).

11. Andrew Edgecliffe-Johnson, 'When Newspapers Fold', *Financial Times*, 16 March 2009, available at: http://www.ft.com/cms/s/0/d00f013a-1261-11de-b816-0000779fd2ac.html (accessed 1 December 2009).

12. Ben Fenton, 'Upmarket Newspapers Profit from Tough Economic Times', *Financial Times*, 20 February 2009, available at: http://www.ft.com/cms/s/0/d6807a92-feef-11dd-b19a-000077b07658.html (accessed 1 December 2009).

Case 2

EVALUATING AND ASSESSING THE IMPLICATIONS OF A NEW BUSINESS MODEL. SPOTIFY – IDENTIFYING A NEW VALUE PROPOSITION

In August 2009, Spotify, a three-year-old Swedish-owned music download business with 1 million customers worldwide, announced a significant breakthrough. It had gained global approval from Apple Corp. to sell its Spotify Application through Apple's on-line Application Store (App Store). Commentators wondered why Apple would allow Spotify to use its proprietary distribution channel to offer a product that many assumed directly competed with Apple's cash cow, iTunes.

Commenting on Spotify's achievements, Ged Day, founder of earlier music download site Bleep.com, crystallized a core issue for the on-line music industry: 'The market leader isn't iTunes. The market leader is free'.[1] Indeed, Daniel Ek, founder of Spotify, had cited other 'freemium'-based business models as the inspiration for Spotify, whereby members could access any of 6 million music tracks free, on a listen-only basis. In exchange for access to unlimited free music, customers accepted three minutes of advertising for every one hour of playtime. A $20 million investment by the owner of the UK-based 3 mobile phone network, Li Ka-Shing, valued Spotify at $250 million. However, advertising revenues had barely exceeded $100 000, leaving industry analysts to speculate as to whether Spotify was sustainable, let alone what kind of a threat it could pose to Apple's iTunes, by far the dominant force in this rapidly changing industry.

Music Industry: a Turbulent Rebirth

Like the stars it promised to make or break, the music industry was in flux. The advent of the Internet, digital music formats and players, file-sharing technologies that bypassed copyright laws, and royalty-fee payments put pressure on music studios to reinvent their business models. The balance of power had shifted towards the music listener, and the pace of change was unforgiving. In fact, by 2009, music industry analysts foretold the demise of the Digital Music Player (DMP), a flash-in-the-pan product category that had emerged 10 years previously with the launch in 1998 of Saehan's MPMAN, capable of storing just 32 MB of data. However, it was Apple's iPod product line and iTunes on-line music store that had revolutionized the way consumers purchased and listened to music products on a mass-market scale. Music studios liked it because sales were traceable and thus income generating, and consumers liked it because it was easy to access and use and easy to purchase from with confidence. By 2007, Apple's iPods, capable of storing thousands of songs, controlled 68% of the US domestic market, and iTunes accounted for 75–80% of legal music downloads globally.[2]

---

[1]Joseph Menn and Tim Bradshaw, 'Double Blow for Music Sites from Ads and Labels', *Financial Times*, 30 March 2009, available at: http://www.ft.com/cms/s/0/99d32942-1cc1-11de-977c-00144feabdc0.html (accessed 1 December 2009).

[2]Charles Arthur, 'Twilight of the iPods', The Guardian, 9 September 2009, available at: http://www.guardian.co.uk/technology/2009/sep/09/apple-ipod-digital-music-sales (accessed 1 December 2009).

Three years later, sales of iPods appeared to have plateaued,[3] and the convergence of technologies in appliances such as smartphones, like Apple's own iPhone, was again set to transform the way people bought and enjoyed their music. Smartphones were multimedia devices that allowed access to email, the Internet, navigation, game-playing, music, and video playback. The implication of this was that each activity would come into competition with the others in retaining the user's attention.

This phenomenon explained why the music industry had begun to promote initiatives like Nokia's 'Comes With Music', whereby handset buyers received free music for a year with their phone. Commenting on such measures, one analyst asserted, 'I don't think "Comes With Music" would have been licensed three years ago'.[4] Spotify, because of its relationships with music studios and telecommunications companies, seemed well placed to catch the new wave, however. It offered several benefits. It eliminated the need to store and potentially lose large collections of music and customized playlists, because everything was stored on the Internet. Furthermore, it could bypass the contentious issue of file sharing at the post-purchase stage: a niggling problem for music studios that iTunes never fully addressed because of its limited Digital Rights Management (DRM) technologies.

That limitation in the iTunes model gave rise to a number of listen-only services like Ruckus, SpiralFrog, and Spotify in 2006. Each of these new entrants offered free music on a listen-only basis in return for exposure to advertising. The advertising revenue sharing deal for music studios was less than lucrative, but studios were anxious to exploit any income opportunity available to them. With the downturn in the global economy in 2008, however, and subsequent cutbacks in the advertising industry, Ruckus and SpiralFrog were forced to shut down operations in early 2009. At the same time, speculation was rife that Spotify was seeking funding to enter the US market, and the iPhone Application Store approval was the linchpin in that emerging strategy.

Spotify Company Background

Based in London, Spotify was founded by Swedish entrepreneurs Daniel Ek and Martin Lorentzon. Ek was former chief technology officer of Stardoll, a social network for teenage girls, and Lorentzon had cofounded digital advertising network TradeDoubler. The newly formed company, with offices in London, Luxembourg, and Stockholm, offered two core services: an ad-supported, free, listen-only music player with access to 6 million tracks and a premium version for $12 monthly subscription. The premium version was free of advertisements and allowed users to customize playlists as well as gain sneak previews. After downloading Spotify's application to their computers, listeners could select genres, create playlists, or simply listen to music 'streamed' over the Internet. Users could not download or copy songs to MP3 players.

---

[3]Charles Arthur, 'Twilight of the iPods', The Guardian, 9 September 2009, available at: http://www.guardian.co.uk/technology/2009/sep/09/apple-ipod-digital-music-sales (accessed 1 December 2009).

[4]Charles Arthur, 'Twilight of the iPods', The Guardian, 9 September 2009, available at: http://www.guardian.co.uk/technology/2009/sep/09/apple-ipod-digital-music-sales (accessed 1 December 2009).

To control the customer base, Spotify was offered on an invitation basis only. In its three years of operation, Ek estimated the company had spent $7500 on marketing, leveraging instead word of mouth and its members-only model to build a buzz in the press and the on-line blogosphere. The audience was growing by about 25% a month since its launch in March 2009, reaching the 1 million mark by August of the same year.

Critical to its business model was the cooperation of major music labels, which Ek secured after extensive negotiations lasting two years (18 months longer than he had expected). Under the terms of the agreements reached, Spotify committed to paying a royalty for every song played, regardless of advertising revenue earned. Nevertheless, not all artists were happy with the deal. Some icons and many less established and unsigned artists decried Spotify's system, which seemed to reward established stars poorly and discriminate against lesser-known musicians by paying them even less per song. Furthermore, in 2009, the UK royalty collection agency PRS announced a revised royalty fee structure, which more than halved payments per song payed on-line (but not downloaded) to 0.085 pence from 0.22 pence. In return for this, PRS had accepted a greater percentage of advertising revenue, jumping from 8 to 10.5%.

It was evident from the collapse of competitors that an ad-supported model was not sustainable in an uncertain economic climate. Furthermore, with revenues from advertising underperforming, Spotify realized that, in order to grow and fund that growth, it needed to secure relationships with suppliers and other business network partners. By the end of summer 2009, an equity deal was agreed with one major music label, and a partnership had been formed with another company to sell tracks alongside its ad-supported and subscription-based services. Management was confident that the next phase of their strategy could be implemented.

Next-Generation Spotify

In its short history, the company had grown and changed rapidly. In terms of the future directions, it was faced with a number of complementary opportunities: entering the US market, launching a mobile-phone-friendly version of its software, and partnering with investor Li Ka-Shing to develop new business opportunities.

US Market

Spotify management was keen to enter the US market and knew that, in addition to their existing portfolio of services, a smartphone application was essential. Hence, approval from Apple to sell via its on-line App Store was critical, as it was by far the largest smartphone application retailer, with 65 000 different applications for sale, cataloguing 1 billion units sold in its first year of operation. Independently of Spotify, Apple had recently been criticized for blocking an application by Google to sell Google Voice via the App Store. Google Voice would have allowed someone to receive calls to various numbers all in one place, simplifying communications for busy professionals, for example. As a result, experts believed Apple could ill-afford to draw more bad press, opening a window of opportunity for Spotify to push its application through. Furthermore, it was understood that Apple would earn a percentage of revenues generated by Spotify's iPhone application while also earning income from sales of Apple hardware like iPhones and Mac computers.

iPhone Application

According to author and Internet expert Chris Anderson, in an ideal 'freemium' system, premium services would earn revenue from just 5% of its customer base.[5] Still others believed the best way was to monetize an application – whether by charging for the application or by a subscription to the service. While Ek championed the free model, he was also concerned with 'how you package music so that fans are prepared to pay for it'. The application would offer both free and premium options. In an era of mobile communications, Spotify knew a mobile application was central to their long-term growth, but also they believed consumers would be willing to pay a premium for such a service free of ads. In this respect, the application would let users compile and share playlists with other Spotify members, facilitating a community aspect to the technology. Furthermore, and crucially, users could store playlists in the cache of their handsets' memory for playback off-line. This, it was felt, would be a key selling point, especially in the United States where the quality of mobile network connectivity was poorer than in Europe.

Partnership with INQ

The Li Ka-Shing foundation, which had invested $20 million in Spotify, was headed by Chinese entrepreneur Li Ka-Shing, also chairman of Hutchison Whampoa, the owner of 3 as well as the mobile handset maker INQ. The investment presented significant areas for potential synergy between the three companies. 3, the smallest mobile operator in the UK market, had differentiated itself by offering media-based packages including Skype offers, and a partnership with Spotify was appealing. Prebundling Spotify with 3 handsets could help boost sales for both, while Spotify could also encourage other mobile operators to stock INQ's phones to address enhanced competition from the 3 network. Going down this mobile route would place Spotify in direct competition with MusicStation, which already supplied UK leader Vodafone and handset maker SonyEricsson.

Considerations

Spotify seemed to have anticipated and addressed the nebulous pattern of change in the world music and telecommunications industries. It was well placed to take advantage of the convergence of media consumption habits because of its technologies and its business partnerships. But its revenue model was fraught with uncertainties and seemed to rely heavily on investor confidence rather than income from the market. While aspects of Spotify's business model presented a serious challenge to iTunes, the

---

[5] Robert Andrews, 'Free or Fee – Which Way Should Tech Media Companies Go?', *The Guardian*, 2009, available at: http://www.guardian.co.uk/tech-media-invest-100/free-or-fee (accessed 27 January 2010).

latter had proved itself to be a robust business model earning a steady stream of income from millions of transactions daily at its global shopfront. Spotify's move to market a premium mobile application service represented a move to capture some of that value, but serious concerns remained as to whether such a strategy could achieve the scale necessary to pay suppliers and investors and contribute to the company's bottom line.

QUESTIONS

1. Who are the industries and firms for which Spotify's new business model is a threat? What is the nature of the threat? How would you go about evaluating it? How can you forecast the impact? What similar examples from history can provide insights? How do they differ? What prevents existing firms from participating in the new business model?
2. Will Spotify's business model expand the market for music, bringing in new customers, or will it simply replace the existing business?
3. What are the strategic options for Spotify to use its transformational business model?
4. Evaluate the branding and positioning of Spotify. How would you advise Spotify to manage its branding to drive growth?

BIBLIOGRAPHY

1. Tim Bradshaw and Samantha Pearson, 'Spotify Hopes to Steer Fans Away from Piracy', *Financial Times*, 1 March 2009, available at: http://www.ft.com/cms/s/0/117e0bd0-0690-11de-ab0f-000077b07658.html (accessed 1 December 2009).
2. Tom Mitchell, Tim Bradshaw, and Andrew Edgecliffe-Johnson, 'Music Service Spotify Wins High-profile Backing', *Financial Times*, 3 August 2009, available at: http://www.ft.com/cms/s/0/d890cbea-8066-11de-bf04-00144feabdc0.html (accessed 1 December 2009).
3. Tim Bradshaw, 'Spotify Looks to iPhone Revenue', *Financial Times*, 4 September 2009, available at: http://www.ft.com/cms/s/0/841a1b66-98e9-11de-aa1b-00144feabdc0.html (accessed 1 December 2009).
4. Joseph Menn and Tim Bradshaw, 'Apple Approves Spotify's Rival Music Service', *Financial Times*, 28 August 2009, available at: http://www.ft.com/cms/s/0/f729fd76-9360-11de-b146-00144feabdc0.html (accessed 1 December 2009).
5. Maija Palmer, 'Britons Keep Connected Despite Recession', *Financial Times*, 6 August 2009, available at: http://www.ft.com/cms/s/0/78fb1a4e-8207-11de-9c5e-00144feabdc0.html (accessed 1 December 2009).
6. Helienne Lindvall, 'Behind the Music: the Real Reason Why the Major Labels Love Spotify', *The Guardian*, 17 August 2009, available at: http://www.guardian.co.uk/music/musicblog/2009/aug/17/major-labels-spotify (accessed 1 December 2009).
7. Tim Bradshaw and Salamander Davoudi, 'Online Music Wins Boost from Cut in Fees', *Financial Times*, 27 May 2009, available at: http://www.ft.com/cms/s/0/42bd5778-4a56-11de-8e7e-00144feabdc0.html (accessed 1 December 2009).

8. Charles Arthur, 'Twilight of the iPods', *The Guardian*, 9 September 2009, available at: http://www.guardian.co.uk/technology/2009/sep/09/apple-ipod-digital-music-sales (accessed 1 December 2009).

9. Eliot Van Buskirk, 'U.S. Exclusive: Hands-On with the Spotify iPhone App', in *Wired Magazine* on-line, July 2009, available at: http://www.wired.com/epicenter/2009/07/spotify-iphone-app/ (accessed 1 December 2009).

10. Joseph Menn and Tim Bradshaw, 'Double Blow for Music Sites from Ads and Labels', *Financial Times*, 30 March 2009, available at: http://www.ft.com/cms/s/0/99d32942-1cc1-11de-977c-00144feabdc0.html (accessed 1 December 2009).

11. Robert Andrews, 'Free or Fee – Which Way Should Tech Media Companies Go?', *The Guardian*, 2009, available at: http://www.guardian.co.uk/tech-media-invest-100/free-or-fee (accessed 1 December 2009).

12. Robert Andrews, 'Li Ka-Shing Confirms Spotify Stake, Will Tie Up with 3, INQ', *The Guardian*, 21 August 2009, available at http://www.guardian.co.uk/media/pda/2009/aug/21/spotify-mobilephones (accessed 1 December 2009).

Case 3

COMPETING AGAINST INDUSTRY GIANTS. COMPETING AGAINST TESCO

Tesco is the largest supermarket retailer in the United Kingdom, the fourth largest retailer in the world behind Wal-Mart, Carrefour, and Home Depot, and the world's largest on-line grocery retailer. Since 1999, it has been the United Kingdom's most profitable retailer. In the third quarter of 2009 it had a 31% share of the UK grocery market, down slightly on the previous year. Its gross turnover for the full year 2008/9, reported in February 2009, was up 13.5% at £59.4 billion, with pretax profits of £3.12 billion. In 2009 it had 4308 stores in 14 countries worldwide (including more than 2300 in the United Kingdom) and almost half a million employees worldwide. In 2007 it was estimated that over £1 in every £7 of UK retail sales was spent in Tesco.

Tesco was established in London by Jack Cohen, a veteran from World War I, who, upon returning from military service, opened a stall in East London in 1919. Gradually, his business began to grow to include markets all over London. He also began wholesale trade, and the first line of Cohen-brand goods placed on the market was tea. Five years later, the first 'Tesco' brand appeared – 'Tesco' contained the initials of the owner of the firm, Mr T.E. Stockwell, who supplied the firm with tea, and the first two letters of Jack Cohen's surname. In 1929, Cohen opened the first Tesco store in North London. In 1934, he purchased land to construct a modern head office and warehouse employing new ways of materials inventory control, a first for the country. During World War II, Jack Cohen once again demonstrated vision when he launched (before the government did) food rationing to make sure everyone received an equal food supply.

In 1947, Tesco was floated on the London Stock Exchange. The first Tesco self-service store opened in 1948, the first supermarket opened in Essex in 1956, and the first superstore opened in West Sussex in 1968. The company began selling petrol in 1974, and in 1995 it introduced the loyalty Clubcard, which helped push its market share and is the United Kingdom's most popular loyalty reward scheme, with 10 million accounts. Tesco began its international quest for expansion in 1994, when it took over Scottish supermarket chain William Low and then proceeded to expand into Central Europe, Ireland, and East Asia. In its international expansion it has used both acquisition, such as the purchase of the Quinnsworth and Crazy Prices stores in Ireland in 1997, and joint ventures with local retailers, for example, in Thailand with Tesco Lotus.

Tesco began specializing in food, later moving into areas such as clothing, consumer electronics, financial services, Internet services, customer telecoms, and fuel services. The company expanded its services in the 1990s and 2000s by using a joint venture strategy. In 1994, for example, Tesco began operating an Internet service, Tesco.com, and in 2001 it became involved with a US internet grocery retailing company called GroceryWorks. Today it has the world's biggest on-line market, offering not only Tesco grocery products but also a wide range of services from its telecom services and financial services to extra services offered in partnership with other companies, such as flights, holidays, electricity, gas, music, and DVD rental. In 2003 it launched a UK telecoms division by partnering with existing telecoms; for example,

Tesco Mobile was launched as a joint venture with O2. In 2004 it launched a broadband service as a joint venture. In April 2006, Tesco announced that it had signed up one and a half million customers for a telecom account that included mobile, fixed-line, and broadband accounts. Tesco also entered into a joint venture with Royal Bank of Scotland to provide customers with a financial service called Tesco Personal Finance. By 2006 it managed over five million customer accounts. In 2008 the company announced plans to accelerate its growth in the financial services business.

The founder, Jack Cohen, was determined to get people to patronize his stores by particular strategies. He signed Tesco up to Green Shield Stamps in 1963, which was a sales promotion technique used in the United Kingdom in the 1960s and 1970s. However, customers began to realize that, although they were accumulating stamps, grocery prices were being increased in supermarkets to cover the cost of the scheme. So Tesco abandoned this approach for a simpler value-for-money approach, using the money invested in Green Shield stamps to implement cost reductions.

Initially, Jack Cohen's successful approach was to use the selling proposition 'pile it high and sell it cheap', but by the middle of the 1970s this strategy had caused Tesco cost problems and the company was beginning to overstretch itself. Middle-class customers were also beginning to have a poor perception of Tesco stores as a result of this, which in the late 1970s led Tesco to face a crisis over the negative image that was associated with the brand, so much so that consultants advised that it rebrand its store name. It did not accept this as an option, and the managing director at the time, Ian MacLaurin, instead fought to change the company strategy and revitalize the brand. Over two or three decades, Tesco, using a range of innovative schemes, managed to develop its brand name and grow to become the leading supermarket chain in 2006.

The key to Tesco's success and growth over the past three decades lies in its change of strategy and image. Firstly, it needed to achieve a difficult feat, to appeal to all segments of the market – lower, middle, and upper classes – with an 'inclusive offer' strategy. This was based on a plain vision of selling high-quality goods at a reasonable price. Tesco most obviously managed to achieve this by offering four differing levels of its own-brand products. The 'Finest' range of premium products was introduced in 1998. This was followed by the 'Tesco Organic' range, which was introduced in 2006. Following this was the 'Tesco Healthy Living' range. Finally, the 'Value' range, to appeal to the price-conscious customer, which in 2008 and 2009 was deployed very successfully to meet the challenges of a sharp recession. By developing a wide range of own brands, Tesco succeeded in changing customers' perceptions of own-brand products, which allowed the company to achieve higher profit margins than it did for other branded products. Secondly, the company mantra has shifted from maximizing shareholder value to maximizing customer value. While the underlying objective is naturally to make higher profits, this is specifically done while focusing on customer service. Tesco believes that it needs continuously to improve the standard of services provided and respond to customers' needs. Its offers reflect trends of a new lifestyle, stressing health and environment in relation to customer, employees, and business partners. Thirdly, Tesco has developed a diversification strategy based on four main areas: innovating and expanding in the core UK grocery market and into areas like convenience stores;

innovating through expansion into non-food businesses like consumer electronics, clothing, health, beauty, CDs, and DVDs, and even developing its non-food Finest and Value ranges; expanding into retail services like personal finance telecoms and utilities by entering into joint ventures with major players in these industry sectors; finally, expanding internationally, which accounted for more than 25% of sales in 2008/9, with plans for further expansion in international markets including India and China.

But what does the future hold for Tesco? For years, retail companies have battled it out over price and value propositions. However, recently the shift in competition has moved from price to the environment, with all the chains trying to prove their green credentials and caring image. The new consumer trend of being more concerned about the environment is having a significant impact on Tesco's strategies. For example, Tesco reports annually on its performance in a Corporate Responsibility report. It continues to make acquisitions to grow its business internationally. The company weathered the storm of the international recession of 2008/9 well, but how would consumers change after this, and what would the implications be for the investments Tesco had in place? Tesco is clearly a company firing on all cylinders, but it still has more to do.

FOR DISCUSSION

Supermarkets in the United Kingdom must expect a more competitive Tesco in the future, and these supermarkets need to understand Tesco and how it competes. Which of the strategies that led to Tesco's success could be used in the future? What future direction is Tesco likely to pursue? Are there plans to expand its business into new industries and product lines? Consider two competitors in the UK market, ASDA and Sainsbury's, who need to design a strategy that will help them increase their industry market share and compete with Tesco.

ASDA

ASDA became a subsidiary of Wal-Mart in 1999 and is the United Kingdom's second largest retailer. It was founded in 1965 by a group of Yorkshire farmers to provide an outlet for their farm produce. As other supermarkets moved upmarket in the 1970s and 1980s, ASDA remained relatively focused on low prices. In the late 1980s, ASDA tried to expand its product offering to include a clothing line to help it compete, but this got off to a slow start. In the recession of the early 1990s, ASDA was on the brink of collapse until the introduction of aggressive marketing practices to back up the stores' pledge. Sales increased, and by 1995 it had become the United Kingdom's number three supermarket group. Instead of expanding internationally, ASDA stayed in the United Kingdom and focused on building its range. In 1999, ASDA was bought out by Wal-Mart, and in 2000 an ASDA hypermarket in Bristol was refurbished to become the first Wal-Mart store in the United Kingdom. Two more were launched in 2001. In 2009, ASDA had a market share of roughly 16% through the operation of ASDA/Wal-Mart Supercentres, ASDA Living Stores, ASDA George stores, and ASDA Direct.

Sainsbury's

Sainsbury's was once the market leader in the United Kingdom, but it is now ranked third largest retailer, having been overtaken by Tesco in 1995 and ASDA in 2003. Sainsbury's was established as a partnership by John James Sainsbury and his wife in 1869 in London, initially selling basic products like eggs and bacon. In 1922 it was incorporated as a private company, and in 1973 it floated on the stock exchange. In the 1980s the company began to expand overseas when it acquired US chain Shaw's. However, in the early 1990s, Sainsbury's expansion threatened to take away its competitive edge in its core markets, and the company experienced some difficulties. This, combined with Tesco's aggressive strategy, saw Sainsbury's lose its number one spot. The company's fortunes improved after the launch of a recovery programme in 2004. In mid-2009 it had roughly 15% market share, sales of £20 billion and profits of £616 million, up 15% on the previous year. Sainsbury's had historically adopted a market approach of retaining a middle-to-upper-class image, with such a wide lead on quality that it did not need to position itself to customers on price as it was not interested in attracting lower-income customers. However, since Sainsbury's lost its number one position to Tesco in 1995, it has had to reconsider its strategy to be more customer focused and, in effect, closer to Tesco's. In 2009 the company saw five pathways to future growth: great food at fair prices, accelerating growth of complementary non-food and services, reaching more customers through additional channels, growing supermarket space, and active property management.

QUESTIONS

1. What are the strengths and weaknesses of Tesco from ASDA's and Sainsbury's perspective?
2. What strategies should each company adopt to compete with Tesco, and what strategies should they avoid?
3. Does Tesco have any areas of weakness or strategies that ASDA and Sainsbury's could exploit?
4. Are there any market segments that Tesco is not currently serving that ASDA and Sainsbury's could exploit?

PART II

CREATING, ADAPTING, AND IMPLEMENTING STRATEGY

CHAPTER SEVEN

Creating Advantage, Synergy, and Commitment versus Opportunism versus Adaptability

All men can see the tactics whereby I conquer, but what none can see is the strategy out of which great victory is evolved.
—*Sun-Tzu, Chinese military strategist*

Our work is certainly challenging, but we are not under any pressure except for the pressure to outperform.
—*Li Ka-Shing*

The possibilities are numerous once we decide to act and not react.
—*George Bernard Shaw*

Our attention now shifts from strategic analysis to the development of a business strategy. What strategic alternatives should be considered? What assets and competencies, target segments, value propositions, and functional strategies? What investment and disinvestment decisions should be raised? These questions will be the focus of the remainder of the book. One goal will be to provide a wide scope of available strategic alternatives in order to increase the likelihood that the best choices will be considered. Even a poor decision among superior alternatives is preferable to a good decision among inferior alternatives.

The remaining nine chapters in this book are shown in Figure 7.1. This chapter will discuss the concept and creation of a sustainable competitive advantage (SCA), the key to a successful strategy. It then turns to the challenge of creating and leveraging synergy as one basis for an SCA. Finally, four very different strategic philosophies – strategic commitment, strategic opportunism, strategy adaptability, and strategic intent – are

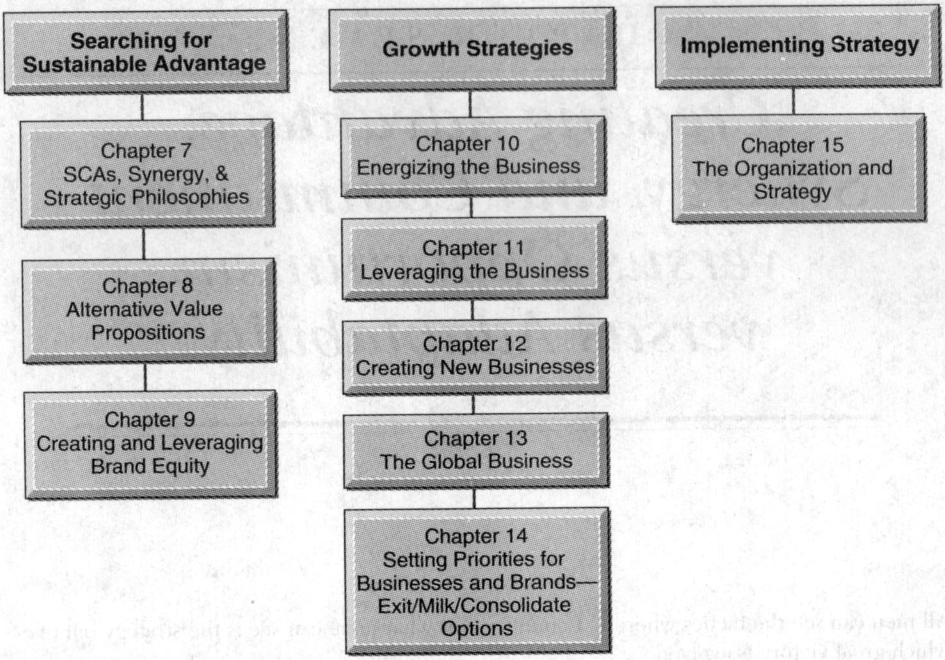

Figure 7.1 Creating and Implementing Strategy

presented, which collectively offer a useful perspective on strategy and strategic choices.

Chapter 8 provides an overview of alternative value propositions. A value proposition is often an umbrella concept under which the supporting assets and competencies and functional strategies and programmes can be grouped. In that sense, it represents a good overview of alternative strategies. Chapter 9 describes how to create and leverage a key asset, brand equity. The next four chapters present growth strategies: energizing the business (Chapter 10), leveraging the business (Chapter 11), creating new business models (Chapter 12), and going global (Chapter 13). Chapter 14 discusses setting priorities among business units and making disinvestment decisions, a key determinate in providing growth resources. Finally, Chapter 15 introduces organizational and implementation issues.

THE SUSTAINABLE COMPETITIVE ADVANTAGE

As defined earlier in this book, a sustainable competitive advantage is an element (or combination of elements) of the business strategy that provides a meaningful advantage over both existing and future competitors (see Figure 7.2). Carrefour, the French hypermarket, has a cost advantage because of its scale economies, market power, logistical efficiencies, value reputation, and international market assets. Ryanair has a point-to-point travel model that provides for low-cost, convenient, reliable, uncomplicated travel. Particularly in China, Lenovo's status as a global

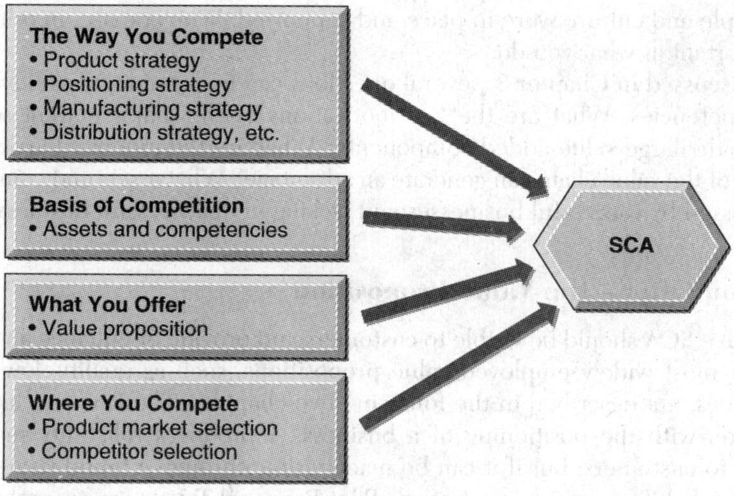

Figure 7.2 The Sustainable Competitive Advantage

Chinese brand and its ownership of low-cost manufacturing facilities in China provide it with a competitive advantage when competing against other global giants such as HP.

An SCA needs to be both meaningful and sustainable. It should be substantial enough to make a difference; a marginal superiority in quality, especially when 'good' quality is good enough for most customers, will not generate an SCA. Meanwhile, sustainability (in the absence of an effective patent) means that any advantage needs to be supported and enhanced over time. There needs to be a moving target for competitors. For example, Gillette maintained its technological superiority in razors over a long time period with innovation after innovation, making copying its competitive advantage difficult.

An SCA will in part depend on the functional strategies and programmes, how you compete. Carrefour's hypermarket format, Ryanair's point-to-point system, and Lenovo's brand and manufacturing model all have SCAs based in part on their functional strategies and programmes. In these cases and others, however, an effective SCA will also involve other aspects of the business strategy – assets and competencies, the value proposition, and the selection of the product market.

The Basis of Competition: Assets and Competencies

The assets and competencies of an organization represent the most sustainable element of a business strategy, because these are usually difficult to copy or counter. There is no point in pursuing a quality strategy, for example, without the design and manufacturing competencies needed to deliver quality products. Anyone can try to distribute cereal or detergent through supermarkets, but few have the competencies in logistics, shelf-space management, and promotions or relationships with supermarket buyers and managers that make product distribution efficient and effective. Similarly, Pacha, the international dance club chain, could not succeed unless the right people and culture were in place and supported. Who you are, in other words, is as important as what you do.

As discussed in Chapter 3, several questions can help to identify relevant assets and competencies. What are the key motivations of the major market segments? What are the large value-added components? What are the mobility barriers? What elements of the value chain can generate an advantage? What assets and competencies are possessed by successful businesses and lacking in unsuccessful businesses?

What You Offer – the Value Proposition

An effective SCA should be visible to customers and provide or enhance a value position. The most widely employed value propositions, such as quality, low price, or social values, are described in the following two chapters. The key is to link a value proposition with the positioning of a business. A product's reliability may not be apparent to customers, but if it can be made visible through a brand strategy, it can support a reliability positioning strategy. Pilot Pens and Toyota are examples of firms whose reliability positioning is supported by advertising that communicates the value proposition provided by their product design and performance.

A reputation for delivering a value proposition can be a more important asset than the substance that underlies that reputation. A business with such a reputation can falter for a time, and the market will either never become aware of the weakness or will forgive the firm. Conversely, competitors often have a much easier time in matching the quality or performance of a market offering than in convincing customers that they indeed have done so. Enduring impressions are why a visible value proposition that is meaningful to customers is strategically valuable.

A solid value proposition can fail if a key ingredient is missing. Procter & Gamble's Pringles potato chips had a host of assets, such as a consistent product, long shelf life, a crushproof container, and national distribution. The problem was that these attributes were valued only if the taste was perceived to be good. As a result, Pringle's ability to penetrate the snack market was limited for decades until it made progress in terms of both actual and perceived taste. Lexus sales in Europe were originally inhibited by the lack of diesel models, but were later significantly boosted by the availability of a Lexus hybrid.

Where You Compete: the Product Market Served

An important determinant for an SCA is the choice of the target product market. A well-defined strategy supported by assets and competencies can fail because it does not work in the marketplace. One way to create marketplace value is to be relevant to customers. The most relevant long-term trend driving the food industry today is the need to feed people in a way that promotes wellness.

The scope of the business also involves the identity of competitors. Sometimes an asset or competency will form an SCA only given the right set of competitors. Thus, it is vital to assess whether a competitor or strategic group is weak, adequate, or strong with respect to assets and competencies. The goal is to engage in a strategy that will match up with competitors' weak points in relevant areas.

SCAs versus Key Success Factors

What is the difference between key success factors (KSFs), introduced in Chapters 1 and 4, and SCAs? A KSF is an asset or competence needed to compete. An SCA involves an asset or competence that is the basis for a continuing advantage. For example, a comic firm, like Marvel Comics, needs to have a wide range of characters to draw upon to maintain reader interest, so a character pool is a KSF. Marvel has turned its deep pool of characters into an SCA by branding a range of Marvel character movies. The strength of this brand was ultimately reflected in the €2.8 billion acquisition of Marvel by Disney in 2009. A KSF for value-priced economy cars is the ability to control costs in order to create profit margins. Hyundai's ability in this regard is markedly superior to its competitors, and thus it becomes an SCA.

To be a winner at poker requires skill, nerve, and money. It also requires a player to ante – to put up a certain amount of money just to see the cards and engage in betting. A KSF can be an ante in terms of the marketplace. Creating a website with an excellent user interface may have been an SCA for Apple with its iTunes store in the early 2000s. As other firms, such as Spotify, enter the market with similarly easy-to-use websites, this becomes a KSF but not a basis for an SCA. Instead of winning the competitive hand, a KSF merely buys an organization a seat at the table.

Reviewing the concepts of points of parity (POPs) and points of differentiation (PODs), introduced in Chapter 1, will provide additional insight into this distinction.[1] PODs are strong, favourable, and unique brand associations based on some attribute or benefit associations. IKEA, for example, provides home furnishings at accessible prices with unique designs that require customers handle and assemble the products. A POP, in contrast, is an association that is not necessarily unique to the brand. POPs may be necessary to present a credible offering within a certain category, as in the case of ATMs and convenient hours for a bank. A POP might also be designed to negate a competitor's point of distinction. A functional food brand such as Benecol, for example, seeks to create parity with regard to taste, thereby negating the taste POD of its competitors and leading customers to base their selection on its own POD (namely, the ability to reduce cholesterol). An SCA is analogous to a POD, whereas a KSF can be analogous to either a POP or a POD.

What Business Managers Name as Their SCAs

Managers of 248 distinct businesses in the service and high-tech industries were asked to name the SCAs of their business.[2] The objectives were to identify frequently employed SCAs, to confirm that managers could articulate them, to determine whether different managers from the same businesses would identify the same SCAs, and to find how many SCAs would be identified for each business. The responses were coded into categories. The results, summarized in Figure 7.3, provide some suggestive insights into the SCA construct.

The wide variety of SCAs mentioned, each representing distinct competitive approaches, is shown in the figure. Of course, the list did differ by industry. For high-tech firms, for example, name recognition was less important than technical superiority, product innovation, and installed customer base. The next two chapters discuss several SCAs in more detail.

	High-Tech	Service	Other	Total
1. Reputation for quality	26	50	29	105
2. Customer service/product support	23	40	15	78
3. Name recognition/high profile	8	42	21	71
4. Retain good management and engineering staff	17	43	5	65
5. Low-cost production	17	15	21	53
6. Financial resources	11	26	14	51
7. Customer orientation/feedback/ market research	13	26	9	48
8. Productline breadth	11	23	13	47
9. Technical superiority	30	7	9	46
10. Installed base of satisfied customers	19	22	4	45
11. Segmentation/focus	7	22	16	45
12. Product characteristics/differentiation	12	15	10	37
13. Continuing product innovation	12	17	6	35
14. Market share	12	14	9	35
15. Size/location of distribution	10	11	13	34
16. Low-price/high-value offering	6	20	6	32
17. Knowledge of business	2	25	4	31
18. Pioneer/early entrant in industry	11	11	6	28
19. Efficient, flexible production/ operations adaptable to customers	4	17	4	25
20. Effective sales force	10	9	4	23
21. Overall marketing skills	7	9	7	23
22. Shared vision/culture	5	13	4	22
23. Strategic goals	6	7	9	22
24. Powerful well-known parent	7	7	6	20
25. Location	0	10	10	20
26. Effective advertising/image	5	6	6	17
27. Enterprising/entrepreneurial	3	3	5	11
28. Good coordination	3	2	5	10
29. Engineering research and development	8	2	0	10
30. Short-term planning	2	1	5	8
31. Good distributor relations	2	4	1	7
32. Other	6	20	5	31
Total	315	539	281	1,135
Number of businesses	68	113	67	248
Average number of SCAs	4.63	4.77	4.19	4.58

Figure 7.3 Sustainable Competitive Advantages of 248 Businesses

Most of the SCAs in Figure 7.3 reflect assets or competencies. Customer base, quality reputation, and good management and engineering staff, for example, are business assets, whereas customer service and technical superiority usually involve sets of competencies.

For a subset of 95 of the businesses involved, a second business manager was independently interviewed. The result suggests that managers can identify SCAs with a high degree of reliability. Of the 95 businesses, 76 of the manager pairs gave answers that were coded the same, and most of the others had only a single difference in the SCA list.

Another finding is instructive – the average number of SCAs per business was 4.58, suggesting that it is usually not sufficient to base a strategy on a single SCA. Sometimes a business is described in terms of a single competency or asset, implying that being a quality-oriented business or a service-focused business explains success. This study indicates, however, that it may be necessary to have several assets and competencies.

THE ROLE OF SYNERGY

Synergy between business units can provide an SCA that is truly sustainable because it is based on the characteristics of a firm that are unique. A competitor might have to duplicate the organization in order to capture the assets or competencies involved.

Olam International is a global, integrated, supply-chain manager of agricultural products and food ingredients. It is the world's leading supplier of cashew nuts and sesame seeds and has effectively used synergy to build and grow its business. An important part of the SCA of Olam is the presence of managers 'up country' in agricultural areas and villages in Africa. Over time, it has used this presence to move into multiple African countries and to develop expertise in multiple agricultural commodities. It has also integrated down the value chain and begun processing raw cashew in Africa rather than exporting, thus saving on transport costs, as the product is lighter when it is exported from Africa, and improving the value of the product sold.

Sony exploits the synergy of its many product groups by showcasing them together in its Sony Centres in Europe and Australia. The ships are outfitted with Sony entertainment products, including television sets, cinemas, and sound equipment. The result is an integrated package that has the cumulative impact of reinforcing Sony's role of providing high-quality and technologically advanced entertainment.

Synergy can be generated by leveraging assets and competences. Amazon has leveraged its warehouse, ordering, and distribution system over hundreds of products and allows other firms to use its system, which generates more scale and margin dollars. Disney leverages its brand and its global connection to children and families over a wide variety of offerings including EuroDisney, Hong Kong Disneyland Resort, and its movie arm, which produces films like *Pirates of the Caribbean*, and through TV programmes such as *Hannah Montana*.

Synergy means that the whole is more than the sum of its parts. In this context, it means that two or more businesses (or two or more product market strategies) operating together will be superior to the same two businesses operating independently. In terms of products, positive synergy means that offering a set of products will generate a higher return over time than would be possible if each of the products were offered separately. Similarly, in terms of markets, operating a set of markets within a business will be superior to operating them autonomously.

As a result of synergy, the combined businesses will have one or more of the following:

1. Increased customer value and thus increased sales.
2. Lower operating costs.
3. Reduced investment.

Generally, the synergy will be caused by leveraging some commonality in the two operations, such as:

- *Customers and sometimes customer applications (potentially creating a systems solution)*. Danone leverages a commitment to customer focus with scientific research across all of its products.
- *A sales force or channel of distribution*. Henkel's channels support products across its three business groups.
- *A brand name and its image*. Billabong uses its brand and its evocation of Australian life and values to sell ranges of clothing around the world.
- *Facilities and methods used for manufacturing, offices, or warehousing*. The Tesco system works in various geographies.
- *R&D efforts*. The divisions of Phillips draw upon the resources of Phillips Design when developing new products and strategy.
- *Staff and operating systems*. All the divisions of Market Facts, the global market intelligence firm, access its statistical staff and operation systems.
- *Marketing and marketing research*. Diageo market research technology helps all Diageo product lines.

Synergy is not difficult to understand conceptually, but it is slippery in practice, in part because it can be difficult to predict whether synergy will actually emerge. Often, two businesses seem related, and sizable potential synergy seems to exist but is never realized. Sometimes the perceived synergy is merely a mirage or wishful thinking, perhaps created in the haste to put together a merger. At other times, the potential synergy is real, but implementation problems prevent its realization. Perhaps there is a cultural mismatch between two organizations, or the incentives are inadequate. In Chapter 11, the difficulties of realizing potential synergy will be revisited.

Alliances

Obtaining instant synergy is a goal of alliances. Pairing a fast food outlet with a petrol company, for example, provides traffic and added value for the petrol company and valuable locations for the fast food firm. Dentsu, the largest Japanese advertising agency, has more than a hundred alliances – many based on partial ownership – that allow it to offer a broader communication solution to clients.

Alliances are often the key to a successful Internet strategy. Facebook and Amazon have many major alliances and thousands of smaller ones that combine to help them reach their goals of driving Internet traffic and offering differentiated value to their visitors. Chapter 13, on global strategies, covers the difficult process of putting together alliances and joint ventures and making them work.

Core Assets and Competencies[3]

A firm's asset or competency that is capable of being the competitive basis of many of its businesses is termed a core asset or competency and can be a synergistic advantage. Consider a tree metaphor, in which the root system is the core asset or competency, the trunk and major limbs are core products, the smaller branches are business units, and the leaves and flowers are end-products. You may not recognize the strength of a competitor if you simply look at its end-products and fail to examine the strength of its root system. Core competence represents the consolidation of firm-wide technologies and skills into a coherent thrust. A core asset, such as a brand name or a distribution channel, merits investment and management that span business units.

Consider, for example, the core competencies of Sony in miniaturization, Ryanair in long-term cost reduction in operations, Phillips in the design of consumer electronics, Volvo in vehicle safety, Samsung in semiconductors (which underlies its product innovation in consumer electronics and cell phones), and Saab in turbocharging, safety, and green technology. Each of these competencies underlies a large set of businesses and has the potential to create more. Each of these firms invests in competence in a variety of different ways and contexts. Each would insist on keeping its primary work related to the core competency in-house. Outsourcing would risk weakening the asset, and each firm would rightfully insist that there is no other firm that could match its state-of-the-art advances.

Highly effective business processes often represent a core competence that can be applied across businesses, leading to a sustainable advantage. One such process is the new product development and introduction process. The tense relationship between retailers and brand owners is often attributed to retailer brands and the threat they present to the price and quality expectations of other brands. However, a significant additional tension arises around the demonstrated ability of retailers to identify new product opportunities and exploit them very quickly. The 12 weeks that it can take a retailer to develop and launch a new product provides it with a real advantage when compared with the up to 18 months that a manufacturer brand owner might take. Another is the management of international operations, considered an SCA by Nestlé, which sells brands in every country in the world and uses an advanced IT system called GLOBE to integrate the decision-making of country managers and corporate headquarters and to provide real-time information on customers to achieve this. Tesco has used its supply-chain management skills to drive costs out of its business model and to drive its competitiveness in the marketplace. One of the capabilities that Henkel deploys is its ability successfully to manage global brands such as Sellotape and Persil as well as local/regional brands such as Somat or Flink.

Developing superior capabilities in key processes involves strategic investments in people and infrastructure, the use of cross-functional teams, and clear performance targets. True process improvement does not occur without control and ownership of the parts of the process. Thus, the virtual corporation, which draws pieces from many sources in response to the organizational task at hand, is not a good model for capabilities-based competition.

STRATEGIC COMMITMENT, OPPPORTUNISM, AND ADAPTABILITY

There are three very different philosophies or approaches to the development of successful strategies and sustainable competitive advantages, which can be labelled strategy commitment, strategy opportunism, and strategic adaptability. Descriptions of each, summarized in Figure 7.4, provide a good perspective on choices as to management style, processes, and philosophy of business. There is no right way; given the right context, people, culture, and strategy, each can work. In fact, most firms use some combination of the three. In addition, the concept of strategic intent provides a fourth perspective on strategy.

Strategic Commitment

Strategic commitment involves a passionate, disciplined loyalty to a clearly defined business strategy that can result in an ever-stronger and more profitable business over time. This 'stick-to-your-knitting' focus avoids being distracted by enticing opportunities or competitive threats that involve expending resources and do not advance the core strategy. Aldi, with its single-minded focus on costs and value, has excelled with a strategic commitment philosophy. China's COFCO has a focus on establishing itself as a global supplier of food inputs.

Google established its position with a single-minded focus on the search engine while its competitors, such as Yahoo and Microsoft, were expanding their services in order to drive traffic and exploit their customer visits. Google based its strategy on several core beliefs. One was the unwavering drive to be the best search engine, as exemplified by the concept that 'it's best to do one thing really, really well' and 'best is a starting point not an endpoint'.[4] Another was the value of focus on the user in order to deliver a simple interface, fast loading, placement based on popularity rather than bribes, and advertising that appeared much like relevant content.

Organizational Characteristics	Strategic Commitment	Strategic Opportunism	Strategic Adaptability
Perspective	Continuous improvement	Opportunistic	Adapt to changing marketplace
Orientation	Commitment	Fast response	Being relevant
Leadership	Charismatic	Tactical	Visionary
Structure	Centralized	Decentralized	Flat
Future perspective	Long term	Short term	Medium term
People	Eye-on-ball	Entrepreneurial	Diverse
Risk	Lose relevance	Also ran	Misread trends

Figure 7.4 Three Strategic Philosophies

Strategic commitment is based on the assumption that the future will be sufficiently like the past for today's effective business model also to be successful in the future. There is a long-term perspective – the focus is on the future in investment decisions and strategy development. The planning horizon may extend two, five, or more than 10 years into the future, depending on the business involved.

There should be an understanding and buy-in throughout the organization as to what the strategy is and why it is persuasive, achievable, and worthwhile. In particular, people should know and believe in the value proposition, the target market, the functional strategies, and the role of assets and competencies. The business rationale should be more than achieving financial objectives; there should be a purpose that is valued, if not inspirational.

Execution and improving the strategy are the keys to success. The emphasis is on continually improving (rather than changing) the existing implementations of the strategy, reducing the cost, improving efficiency, enhancing the value proposition, improving customer satisfaction, and strengthening the assets and competencies. Each year, the operations and the output should be better than the last. Japanese firms such as Shiseido or Canon call this continuous improvement *kaizen* and have built successful companies around it. In pursuing continuous improvement, what is needed is incremental rather than transformational or even substantial innovation. The goal is improvement of the existing strategy rather than the creation of a new strategy. In that regard, the information needs are on technology developments and consumer attitudes within the framework of the existing competitive context.

Strategic commitment places demands on the organization and its people, culture, structure, and systems. In general, a centralized organization that can be disciplined in resource allocation and keep it 'on strategy' will be helpful, as will the presence of a strong, charismatic leader who can sell the vision to relevant constituencies inside and outside the organization. The people should be specialized, each with skills that will advance the strategy and its underlying assets and competencies. The culture should revolve around the strategic vision that is supporting the strategy. It should go beyond financial goals to include those that will inspire those implementing the strategy.

Strategic commitment has some commonalities with strategic intent, a concept conceived by Hamel and Prahalad nearly two decades ago, namely a clear strategic vision and commitment to that vision.[5] There are some meaningful differences as well. Strategic intent was more oriented towards a firm starting from an also-ran or entry position rather than enhancing an established or leading position. It therefore encouraged transformational rather than incremental innovation in order to change the existing market order. It also advocated stretching the organization to identify and develop new SCAs. The focus was on overcoming the major competitor in part with a sustained obsession with winning at all levels of the organization and a clear idea as to what winning would entail.

Strategic Stubbornness

The risk of the strategic commitment route, as suggested by Figure 7.5, is that the vision may become obsolete or faulty and its pursuit may be a wasteful exercise in strategic stubbornness. Of the host of pitfalls that could prevent a vision from being realized, three stand out:

Strategic Approach	Strategic Risk
Strategic commitment	Strategic stubbornness
Strategic opportunism	Strategic drift
Strategic adaptability	Strategic blunders; misread trends

Figure 7.5 Vision Versus Opportunism

- *Implementation barriers.* The picture of the future may be substantially accurate, but the firm may not be able to implement the strategy required. Many food and commodity firms recognize that Africa offers great opportunity as a location for sourcing and production. However, the challenges of governance and logistics make strategy very difficult to implement in many African countries.
- *Faulty assumptions of the future.* The vision might be misguided because it is based on faulty assumptions about the future. For example, it was hoped that the concept of customer loyalty cards and programmes used by retailers like Tesco and Boots would encourage brand loyalty and customer retention, and that customer behaviour could be modified to the retailer's advantage. However, while many retailers spend a small fortune on the programmes, there is little evidence that the financial gains and brand loyalty that they expected have materialized, with the main benefit emerging in the form of an improvement in the quality and quantity of data about customer purchases and behaviour.
- *A paradigm shift.* A third problem occurs when there is a paradigm shift, perhaps brought about by a transformational innovation. For example, computers changed from mainframes to minicomputers to workstations to servers. In the semiconductor industry, the vacuum-tube business first gave way to transistors and then, in sequence, to semiconductors, integrated circuits, and microprocessors. In both cases, each new paradigm brought with it a remarkable change in the cast of characters. It was extremely rare for a leader in one paradigm to be a leader in the next, often because of strategic stubbornness.

New operating models can also change the paradigm. The Internet, particularly sites such as Facebook, Twitter, and Myspace, has changed the way people communicate and consume media. This has left newspapers and the print media generally to fight in a declining, unprofitable segment. Napster and later on-line music sites changed the way people listened to music and the formats in which they were willing to accept the product. For example, the album may no longer be a relevant format in which to sell music. Following on from this, Apple changed the way portable music is stored and listened to with the introduction of its iPod. This has reduced the power of traditional music companies and left bricks-and-mortar music stores with a challenge to maintain relevance. Low-cost airlines such as easyJet have changed the way consumers in all segments buy tickets and travel. Websites like daft.ie, Rentamatic.co.uk, and propertyworld.com changed the way people look for property to buy and rent, challenged newspaper listings, and reduced the role of estate and letting agents as sources of information. The emergence and popularity of the fairtrade movement has forced supermarkets not only to stock fairtrade products but also to examine how they source their products.

In each case, it is no coincidence that the new paradigm has been dominated by new entries or by entries that had been considered insignificant niche players by the leading companies.

Strategic Opportunism

Strategic opportunism is driven by a focus on the present. The premise is that the environment is so dynamic and uncertain that it is at least risky, and more likely futile, to predict the future and invest behind those predictions. The more prudent and profitable route is to detect and capture opportunities when they present themselves, with the goal of achieving immediate profits. When short-term successes flow, the long term will take care of itself, as at least some of these short-term winners will grow to major businesses, and the rest, in the aggregate, will not be a burden.

One key to success in strategic opportunism is an entrepreneurial culture and the willingness to respond quickly to opportunities as they emerge. The people should be entrepreneurial, sensitive to new opportunities and threats, and fast to react. The organization needs to be decentralized, with people empowered to experiment and invest behind emerging opportunities. The culture needs to support empowered managers, new ventures, and change. The strategy will be dynamic, and change will be the norm. New products will be continuously explored or introduced, and others de-emphasized or dropped. New markets will be entered, and disinvestment in existing ones will always be an option. The organization will be on the lookout for new synergies and assets and competencies to be developed.

Another key is to be close to the market. The management team needs to be talking to customers and others about the changing customer tastes, attitudes, and needs. Information systems must monitor customers, competitors, and the trade to learn of trends, opportunities, problems, and threats as they appear. Information-gathering and analysis should be both sensitive and on-line. Frequent, regular meetings to analyse the most recent developments and news may be helpful. The organization should be quick to understand and act on changing fundamentals.

Strategic opportunism provides several advantages. One is that the risk of missing emerging business opportunities is reduced. Firms such as Kellogg's in cereals, Ryanair in travel, and Google in information management all seek emerging niche segments and develop brands tailored to speciality markets. Thus, Ryanair is constantly adding and eliminating destinations according to demand of travellers and the emergence of new trends in travel. Google is constantly introducing mainstream and niche products such as Google Earth, Google Maps, and Google Scholar. Another advantage is that the risk of strategic stubbornness is also reduced.

Strategic opportunism tends to generate a vitality and energy that can be healthy, especially when a business has decentralized R&D and marketing units that generate a stream of new products. Within easyGroup, for example, new businesses are continually created and evaluated with respect to their prospects. HP is another firm that believes in decentralized entrepreneurial management. These decentralized firms are often close to the market and technology and are willing to pursue opportunities.

Strategic opportunism results in economies of scope, with assets and competencies supported by multiple product lines. Adidas, which applies its brand assets and competencies in product design and customer sensing to a wide range of product markets, is an example. Its strategy revolves around marketing sports footwear, clothing, and accessories for running, basketball, football, tennis, and training. It focuses its attention on innovative footwear and uses the opportunity of celebrity sponsorship to promote its range. This association with high-profile individuals, a superior product design, and one of the world's most widely recognized brand names allows them to develop strong emotional ties and relationships with customers. Adidas has strategic flexibility, which characterises successful, strategically opportunistic firms.

Strategic Drift

The problem with the strategic opportunism model is that, as suggested by Figure 7.5, it can turn into strategic drift. Investment decisions are made incrementally in response to opportunities rather than directed by a vision. As a result, a firm can wake up one morning and find that it is in a set of businesses for which it lacks the needed assets and competencies and that provide few synergies.

At least three phenomena can turn strategic opportunism into strategic drift:

- A short-lived, transitory force may be mistaken for one with enough staying power to make a strategic move worthwhile. If the force is so short lived that a strategy does not pay off or does not even have a chance to get into place, the result will be a strategy that is not suitable for the business or the environment.
- Opportunities to create immediate profits may be rationalized as strategic when, in fact, they are not. For example, an instrumentation firm might receive many requests from some of its customers for special-purpose instruments that could conceivably be used by other customers but that have little strategic value for the company. Such opportunities might result in a sizable initial order, but could divert R&D resources from more strategic activities.
- Expected synergies across existing and new business areas may fail to materialize owing to implementation problems, perhaps because of culture clashes or because the synergies were only illusions in the first place.

A drive to exploit core assets or competencies might not work. As a result, new business areas would be in place without the expected sustainable advantages.

Strategic drift not only creates businesses without needed assets and competencies but also can result in failure to support a core business that has a good vision. Without a vision and supporting commitment, it is tempting to divert investment into seemingly sure things that are immediate strategic opportunities. Thus, strategic opportunism can be an excuse to delay investment or divert resources from a core vision.

One example of strategic drift is a firm that designed, installed, and serviced custom equipment for steel firms. Over time, steel firms became more knowledgeable and began buying standardized equipment mainly on the basis of price. Gradually, the firm edged into this commodity business to retain its market share. The company finally realized it was pursuing a dual strategy for which it was ill-suited. It had too many overheads to compete with the real commodity firms, and its ability to provide upscale service had eroded to the point where it was now inferior to some niche players. Had there been a strategic vision, the firm would not have fallen into such a trap.

Another example is a discounter that did well when operating a limited product line in a local market with a low-cost message. The customer value was clear, and the hands-on management style was effective. However, when the firm expanded its geographic and product scope, the management systems were no longer adequate and the value proposition became fuzzy as well. It had drifted into a business requiring assets and competencies it did not have.

Strategic Adaptability

Strategic adaptability, like strategic opportunism, is based on the assumption that the market is dynamic, the future will not necessary mimic the past, and an existing business model, however successful, may not be optimal in tomorrow's marketplace. Unlike strategic opportunism, however, there is also an assumption that it is possible to understand, predict, and manage responses to market dynamics that emerge, and even create or influence them.

Strategic adaptability is about managing relevance, a topic introduced in Chapter 4. As the market dynamics evolves and the niches and submarkets emerge, one goal is to adapt the offering so that it maintains its relevance. The firm wants to avoid investing in four-by-fours when the market is shifting to hybrid and electric cars. Another is to seize opportunities to influence the creation of markets and submarkets. One study determined that such an opportunity occurs about once or twice a decade on average, and that the window of opportunity is often short. A strategically adaptable firm does not want to miss such an opportunity. In that respect, it is more likely to go beyond incremental innovation to substantial and even transformational innovation if that is what it takes to create new markets.

A firm that aspires to being strategically adaptable needs to have competence in identifying and evaluating trends, a culture that supports aggressive response, and organizational flexibility so that business creation and modification can occur quickly.

Identifying and Evaluating Trends

The strategically adaptable firm needs to have a good external sensing mechanism to detect underlying customer trends and market dynamics involving drivers; for example, the organization will need to be able to distinguish fads from trends and to evaluate the substance, dynamics, and implications of those trends. This is not an easy assignment. Being close to the customer, through direct contact and through research, will be important.

Adaptation-supporting Culture

When trends are detected, the strategically adaptable firm needs to have a culture that supports aggressive response to opportunities represented by the trend analysis. This means that innovation, entrepreneurship, and experimentation should be valued and that it is okay to fail. Innovation is a mindset, but it also involves an R&D capability, in-house or with alliance firms, to provide the potential to broaden the firm's offerings. The entrepreneurial style should be supported by organizational structures and reward systems that encourage managers to exploit opportunities with action-oriented strategies. There has to be some ability to tolerate a 'ready, fire, aim' mentality and to allow pilot tests to thrive. Unlike strategic opportunism, the short-term product will be less important than the priority of getting the offering right and establishing a value position in the emerging market.

Strategic Flexibility

Strategic adaptability usually requires flexibility so that the firm will be ready when a window of opportunity arises. Strategic flexibility – the ability to adjust or develop strategies to respond to external or internal changes – can be achieved in a variety of ways, including participating in multiple product markets and technologies, having resource slack, and creating a flexible brand portfolio.

Participation in multiple product markets or technologies means that the organization is already 'on the ground' in different arenas and has purchased strategic options. Thus, if it appears that demand will shift to a new product market or that a newer technology will emerge, the organization can simply expand its current product market rather than start from zero, with all the risks and time required. An organization may also participate in business areas with weak returns in order to gain the strategic flexibility to deal with possible market changes. For example, GM's investment in Saturn resulted in a very modest return. However, having Saturn could allow GM some very nice competitive options if gas supplies were curtailed by OPEC or by a war.

Investing in underused assets provides strategic flexibility. An obvious example is maintaining liquidity [as with the world's largest bank lender, Industrial and Commercial Bank of China, which had 8.9 trillion yuan (US$ 1.3 trillion or €890 billion) in deposits at the end of March 2009] so that investment can be funnelled swiftly to opportunity or problem areas. Maintaining excess capacity in distribution, organizational staffing, or R&D can also enhance a firm's ability to react quickly.

A flexible brand portfolio may be needed so that brand assets will be in place to support a move in a new direction. Such flexibility can be based on a strong umbrella brand; Quiksilver not only has the Quiksilver brand but also other brands like Roxy and DC, which can be the basis of a growth platform. It can also be based on a system of endorsed brands, subbrands, and branded features, such as Google's portfolio, which includes Google Chrome, Gmail, Google Latitude, and others. The idea is to have a portfolio robust enough for a new offering not to have to create a brand asset in order to compete.

Two firms that have shown strategic adaptability are Nucor and Charles Schwab. In the 1970s, facing price pressures from fully integrated steel firms plus efficient Japanese brands, Nucor developed a strategy of producing joists (higher-value products used in construction) in rural minimills that employed non-unionized labour and used scrap steel as raw material. For a decade, this model made Nucor a strategic and financial success. By the mid-1980s, however, others had started to copy the strategy, scrap steel was no longer as plentiful, and aluminium had made serious inroads into traditional steel markets. In response to these changes, Nucor again reinvented the paradigm by focusing on flat-rolled, upmarket products using a scrap steel substitute, and drawing on iron ore in Brazil and a processing plant in Trinidad.

Microsoft has had similar success, although it did not abandon the old vision, but rather augmented it with a new direction. Microsoft's focus progressed from operating systems to applications to the Internet. Other firms, such as News International, the BBC, and Tesco, have all adopted a dynamic vision in their strategy, which has left them well positioned to engage with the Internet age. Each of these firms chose not to abandon the old vision, but rather to augment it with a new direction.

Strategy Blunders – Misreading Trends

Investing behind trends and emerging submarkets is inherently risky because of the uncertainty and judgement involved and because the execution of the strategy is often difficult.

An error in interpreting a trend or emerging submarket can result in a substantial blunder that can damage or even cripple the firm. Not only will resources be wasted that could have been productively used elsewhere, it can also have a deleterious impact on the brand assets and on the internal culture. A visible failure can inhibit future strategy choices. The food industry is replete with examples of failed products that were intended to take advantage of trends, such as low fat and low carb, but turned out not to be as long-term as first thought.

In addition to a trend being misinterpreted, there is an execution issue. The most astute and insightful analysis can lead to a strategy that simply cannot be implemented. Consider the acquisition of Chrysler by Daimler in 1998 for US$ 37 billion – and sold in 2007, paying US$ 650 million for the privilege. The opportunity, as Daimler originally saw it, was to create a globally integrated car firm and to achieve synergies at every level of the new organization. The failure of this concept was at least in part due to the inability to execute behind the strategy. The two organizations faced difficulties in a number of areas including branding, as Daimler had historically sold premium brands such as Mercedes-Benz, while Chrysler was a mass-market brand. In addition, the German firm was unable to enhance the efficiency of Chrysler factories or to develop new models as the light trucks market, where Chrysler was strong, went into decline. Even had the vision been on target, the execution difficulties would have resulted in failure.

Blended Philosophies

There are firms that have a dominant strategic philosophy. It can be argued that Google and Starbucks are primarily strategic commitment firms, that General Mills is more in the strategic opportunistic group, and that P&G and GE are strategically adaptable. But it is not that simple. Most firms are a blend. They engage in strategic commitment in one business arena, strategic opportunism in another, and strategic adaptability in yet another.

Starbuck's ice cream is available in supermarkets and Starbuck's coffee can be had on some airlines, reflecting strategy opportunism. Furthermore, Starbuck's has a soluble coffee, Via, in supermarkets and in Starbuck's kiosks at airports and in supermarkets, indicating some strategic adaptability. Google has adopted an adaptability strategy by acquiring a host of capabilities and firms along with some strategic opportunism based on knowing about traffic flows from its database. Among its many acquisitions were YouTube, Dodgeball (mobile social networking), and Double Click (an Internet advertising agency).

While General Mills has a strong opportunistic philosophy, it also has a strategic commitment with respect to the Cheerios brand and has pursued strategy adaptability with respect to health trends. GE is strategically adaptable, but it too has commitment to business units such as jet engines and has been opportunistic in its acquisition strategy over the years.

The philosophies can also overlap within a business. Toyota, for example, has a very real strategic commitment with respect to some of its business strategy elements.[6] All Toyota businesses believe passionately that their ability to execute *kaizen* (continuous improvement), internal innovation enhanced by trial and error experimentation, and putting the customer first, informed by first-hand customer contact, are the basis for strategy. At the same time, Toyota has elements of strategic adaptability. In particular, it has a presence in virtually all automotive markets. Thus, Toyota is participating in a wide variety of niches and is unlikely to be caught on the wrong side of an emerging trend. Furthermore, its conservative finance strategy, resulting in considerable cash reserves, allows it flexibility.

The real question is not which philosophy to have. The real challenge is which blend of philosophies makes sense to provide a successful and coherent strategic path to success.

KEY LEARNINGS

- To create an SCA, a strategy needs to be valued by the market and supported by assets and competencies that are not easily copied or neutralized by competitors. The most common SCAs are quality reputation, customer support, and brand name.
- Synergy is often sustainable because it is based on the unique characteristics of an organization.

- Strategic commitment, involving a 'stick-to-your-knitting' focus on a clearly articulated strategy, is based on an assumption that the business model needs to be refined and improved and not changed.
- Strategic opportunism assumes that the environment is so dynamic and uncertain that it is futile to predict the future and invest behind those predictions. The more prudent and profitable route is to detect and capture opportunities when they present themselves, with the goal of achieving immediate profits.
- Strategic adaptability, based on the assumption that it is possible to understand, predict, and manage responses to market dynamics that emerge, and even create or influence them, is about managing relevance.

FOR DISCUSSION

1. What is a sustainable competitive advantage? Identify SCAs for LinkedIn, Henkel, Lenovo, and HSBC.
2. Pick a product class and several major brands. What are each brand's points of parity and points of difference? Relate POPs to KSFs, and the PODs to SCAs.
3. What is synergy? What are the sources of synergy? Give examples. Why is it so elusive?
4. What is strategic commitment? Can you name examples that fit, besides those mentioned in the book? What examples of strategic stubbornness come to mind? Why are good strategists so blind to this problem? How does strategic commitment differ from strategic intent? Illustrate with examples.
5. What is the difference between strategic opportunism and strategic adaptability? Can you give examples of each? What is the difference between the risks of both? Can you give examples of firms that have experienced drift or misread trends?
6. Examine a major firm and determine its philosophy blend. Where does each of its philosophies become visible?

NOTES

1. Keller introduced points of parity in the branding context in Kevin Lane Keller, *Strategic Brand Management*, 2nd edition, Upper Saddle River, NJ, Prentice Hall, 2003, pp. 131–136.
2. David A. Aaker, 'Managing Assets and Skills: the Key to a Sustainable Competitive Advantage', *California Management Review*, Winter 1989, pp. 91–106.

3. C.K. Prahalad and Gary Hamel, 'The Core Competence of the Corporation', *Harvard Business Review*, May–June 1990, pp. 79–91. This book uses the phrase 'core assets and competencies', which is an extension of the term 'core competencies' used in Prahalad and Hamel's article.
4. The quotes come from The Google Corporate Information site on Google.com, May 2009.
5. Gary Hamel and C.K. Prahalad, 'Strategic Intent', *Harvard Business Review*, May–June 1989, pp. 63–76.
6. A good source for the Toyota strategy is Emi Osono, Norihiko Shimizu, and Hirotaka Takeuchi, *Extreme Toyota*, New York, NY, John Wiley & Sons, Inc., 2008.

CHAPTER EIGHT

Alternative Value Propositions

Finding new ways, more clever ways, to interrupt people doesn't work.
—*Seth Godin*

You've got to look for a gap where competitors in a market are lazy and have lost contact with the readers or the viewers.
—*Rupert Murdoch*

You can't depend on your eyes when your imagination is out of focus.
—*Mark Twain*

A business strategy, as defined in Chapter 1, involves four components: the product market investment decision, the customer value proposition, the organization's assets and competencies, and functional strategies and programmes. For a given industry and organizational context, a strategist will have uncountable ways to compete. Alternative markets, submarkets, product extensions, and new product arenas can always be considered. A bewildering variety of customer value propositions, each with its own nuances and spins, will represent strategy variants. Hundreds of conceivable assets and competencies can be developed, nurtured, exploited, and combined, and there are potentially thousands of viable functional strategies and programmes.

Usually, however, business strategies cluster around a limited number of value propositions for a product market, supported by assets and competencies and functional strategies and programmes. These value propositions include a superior attribute or benefit (Mercedes' prestige), appealing design (TOD's footwear), offering a complete systems solution (DHL supply-chain solutions), social responsibility (Marks &

Spencer Plan A), a superior customer relationship (Singapore Airlines), a specialist niche (LinkedIn), superior value (Aldi), superior quality (Toyota), a familiar brand (Nestlé), and a strong personality (Kingfisher Airlines). Each of these value propositions needs to be adapted to a given context, but all should potentially affect customer–firm relationships.

Looking at business strategies through the lens of value propositions provides a way to consider a broad set of strategies. As a summary indicator of complex strategies, value propositions provide a shorthand way to visualize a business strategy. Reflecting on a value proposition and its implied target markets, assets, competencies, and functional strategies is easier than dealing with complete detailed business strategy. As a result, more strategies can be considered, and creating multiple alternatives is a way to make sure that superior ones are allowed to surface.

Considering strategies at the level of a value proposition also allows a firm to make preliminary evaluative judgements as to the problems that will have to be overcome, the investments required, the appeal in the marketplace, and the fit with the organization. Thus, some strategies can be rejected or put on hold before a lot of resources have been invested.

A business may select more than one value proposition – choosing to walk and chew gum at the same time, so to speak. It is not an either/or situation. In fact, most successful strategies will represent an integration of several value propositions. A solid understanding of each, however, can guide you not only in making the decision as to which to include but also in specifying their respective roles and priorities in the overall strategy. Which should be dialled up? How should various propositions interact?

Although multiple value propositions can be supported and employed, there is a limit as to how many can be addressed – it is not credible or feasible to create or communicate too many value propositions simultaneously. More than two or three will generally stretch resources too thinly, and the customer will become confused and sceptical.

BUSINESS STRATEGY CHALLENGES

Which value proposition or propositions – with their supporting target market, assets, competencies, and functional strategies – should form the basis for a business strategy? To answer this question, each value proposition should be challenged with respect to whether it contains a real and perceived value proposition and whether it is feasible, relevant, and sustainable. The goal of this analysis is to identify not only the potential impact of the strategic option but also its limitations and feasibility.

Is There a Real Customer Value Proposition?

A successful business strategy needs to add value for the customer, and this value needs to be real rather than merely assumed. For example, the British supermarket chain Iceland tried to develop its product line by stocking only organic own-label products, but this backfired as their core market could not afford these products. Bic tried to extend its familiar brand name into a disposable underwear product line, but the Bic brand name, which is synonymous with stationery and lighters, did not extend well to this new product line and failed.

Value is more likely to be real if it is driven from the customer's perspective rather than from that of the business operation. How does the point of differentiation affect the customer's experience of buying and using the product? Does it serve to reduce cost, add performance, or increase satisfaction? The concepts of unmet needs and customer problems, outlined in Chapter 2, are relevant. Does market research confirm that value is added from the customer's perspective?

Is There a Perceived Customer Value Proposition?

Furthermore, the value proposition must be recognized and perceived as worthwhile by the customers. Delivering a value proposition is pointless unless customers know about it and believe it. For example, a customer may be unaware that phone calls made via Skype are free or that listing a product for sale on eBid is free. This may occur because customers have not been exposed to the information, because the information was not packaged in a memorable and believable way, or because the attribute or service was not considered to be relevant or of value.

The perceived value problem is particularly acute when the customer is not capable of judging the added value easily. Customers, for example, cannot evaluate airline safety or the skill of a dentist without investing significant time and effort. Instead, the customer will look for signals, such as the appearance of the aircraft or the professionalism of the dentist's front office. The firm's task, then, is to manage the signals or cues that imply added value.

Is the Strategy Feasible?

If the value proposition is aspirational, is it feasible? It is one thing to create the perfect strategy with respect to customers, competitors, and the marketplace. It is another to execute that strategy effectively. The strategy may require assets and capabilities that are currently inadequate or do not exist, and programmes to develop or upgrade them may turn out to be unrealistic. Alliance partners to fill the gap may be difficult to find or to work with. Furthermore, an objective analysis of the customer trends, competitor strengths, or market dynamics may reveal that any strategic success will be short lived.

Is the Value Proposition Relevant to Customers?

A business has to make what customers want to buy. The product or service has to be considered relevant to the markets in which the business chooses to compete. It does no good, for example, to produce the best ready meals if customers are interested in fresh food. If a business has a value proposition that is of secondary interest to customers, the latter may look elsewhere, even if the business is executing its value proposition effectively. If the products are considered passé or inferior, the business will lack relevance.

Is the Value Proposition a Point of Difference That Is Sustainable?

Does the value proposition represent a point of superiority over the competition? Or is it simply a point of parity, with the customer believing that the offerings are acceptable but not superior with respect to the value proposition? And if there is a point of difference, is it sustainable? Sustainability is often a tough challenge, because most points of differentiation are easily copied. One route to a sustainable advantage is to own an important product dimension, perhaps with the aid of a branded differentiator (such as the Philips CoolSkin range of electric razors, which incorporates a Nivea lotion dispenser that reduces friction and ensures a closer shave), as described in Chapter 10. A second route would be to create a programme of continuous investment and improvement that enables the strategy to remain a moving target, always ahead of competitors or poised to leapfrog them. Third, a business could create points of differentiation that are based on unique assets and competencies of the organization, which are inherently difficult to copy.

Overinvestment in a value-added activity may pay off in the long run by discouraging competitors from duplicating a strategy. For example, competitors might be deterred from developing a service back-up system that is more extensive than current customers expect. The same logic can apply to a broad product line. Some elements of that line might be unprofitable, but still might be worth retaining if they plug holes that competitors could use to provide customer value.

ALTERNATIVE VALUE PROPOSITIONS

While there are an infinite number of business strategy variants in any context, certain value propositions with supporting strategy elements tend to be used most often. In this chapter, a snapshot of a handful of value propositions will be described, as noted in Figure 8.1. They are among the most commonly used, and their description provides a glimpse of the scope of choices available to the business strategist.

Two of the value propositions – quality and value – will be discussed in some detail. Each is frequently employed, has led to performance successes, and is associated with a body of knowledge and experience. Two more – brand familiarity and delivering emotional/self-expressive benefits – will be covered in the next chapter, and another – being global – is the subject of Chapter 13.

A Superior Attribute or Benefit

If a product or service attribute or benefit is central to the purchase and use of an offering, one strategic option is to dominate or even own that attribute. Rolex, the Swiss watchmaker, has long dominated the prestige end of the watch market and has strong credibility in this space. Nivea has a historical position as a leader in the skincare market and has been able to use this successfully to enter and achieve a leadership position in the rapidly developing men's skincare market. In each case, the attribute is relevant to customers, and the brands are clearly positioned on that attribute.

If such an option is to be viable over time, it needs to be protected against competitors. Having patent protection is one route. Nestlé's fastest-growing product,

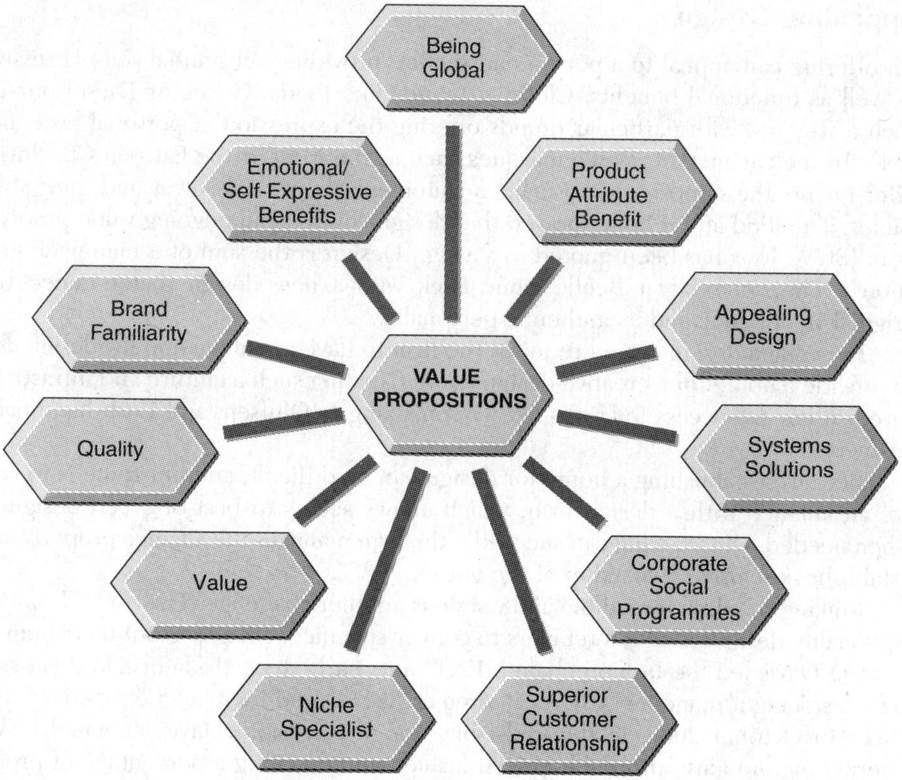

Figure 8.1 Alternative Value Propositions

Nespresso, relies on patented technology. Another route is to have a programmatic investment strategy in order to maintain the real and perceived edge. Rolex has taken this route and invested in a design process for new watches that can take up to five years. This initiative allows them to maintain a competitive edge in the market through delivering on its brand promise of quality and prestige.

Another route to owning an attribute over time is to brand it and then actively manage that brand and its promise. For example, iDrive provides a visible, branded point of differentiation for BMW cars. Again, this concept will be elaborated in Chapter 10.

A superior and more relevant value proposition is often found by broadening the perspective beyond raw attributes and benefits. Crayola has fine-quality crayons and other drawing instruments for children. However, it reframed its value proposition to be about colourful fun and creativity in the lives of children and changed from an art products company to a visual expressions company. The ice cream market was transformed when manufacturers realized that adults ate ice cream as well as children and began to introduce brands such as the Mars ice cream bar and Magnum. Such changes have a host of implications with respect to products and customer relationships. They can include self-expressive and social benefits, as discussed in the next chapter.

Appealing Design

An offering can appeal to a person's aesthetics, providing substantial self-expressive as well as functional benefits. Clothing brands like Prada, Gucci, or Diesel pursue such a strategy, with particular brands offering the expression of personal taste and style. In the car market, iconic marques such as the Mini or the Citroen C3 Pluriel offer buyers the opportunity to make a statement about themselves and their style values. The iPod and iPhone showed that design could be an ongoing value proposition. (Steve Jobs has been quoted as saying, 'Design is the soul of a manmade creation'.) The Volkswagen Beetle came back with a new design that retained the original Beetle look and its authentic personality.

Pursuing a design option requires the firm to have a real passion for design and to provide a home for a creative design team. Creating such a culture and infrastructure is a key to success for firms like Dyson, Bang & Olufsen, and Lush handmade cosmetics.

Because establishing a home for design can be difficult, another route is to create an alliance with a design firm, which allows access to best-of-breed designers when needed. Outsourcing can succeed if the firm manages the alliance properly and establishes exclusive ownership of the output.

Making the design credible and visible is another challenge. The use of branded personality designers allows retailers to convey specific messages about their brands. George Davis led the fashion chain NEXT in its early days. He later had great success designing a range for ASDA (George at ASDA) and for Marks & Spencer (Per Una). In October 2009, in the midst of a tough recession, Davis launched GIVe, offering high-quality, affordably priced fashion and donating a percentage of profits to charitable causes. The credibility of his design and retails skills meant that few doubted that the venture would be a success.

Systems Solutions

A compelling value proposition can be based on moving from selling products to selling systems solutions, based on packaging products that work together to create a total system. Competitors selling ad hoc products, even though they might be superior, will be at a disadvantage. B&Q offers a one-stop place to deliver home improvement projects. Sony, because it makes a complete line of home entertainment products, offers customers total system design and a single source for upgrades and service.

Especially in the business-to-business space, many firms are trying to move from being component suppliers to being systems solution players. One reason is that a systems-based organization will be more likely to control the customer relationship. Another is a need to capture greater margins in a context where components are becoming commodities. But the ultimate reason is that customers demand it. Simply bundling products, though, is rarely enough. To deliver value to the customer, a firm must offer not only product breadth but also a systems orientation and expertise, and it must be willing and able to deliver a high level of customer service. In Chapter 12 the potential of forming a new submarket of those desiring systems instead of components is discussed.

Corporate Social Programmes

IKEA has supported world causes like UNICEF for children's rights in India, the WHO immunization programmes, and environmental causes like Global Forest Watch. The German company Bayer collaborates with National Geographic to focus on the development of new sources of water supply; they also have committed to a youth environmental programme and to Global Compact, an initiative for human rights. Boots supports Cancer Research UK with their SunSmart campaign and fund-raises for Breast Cancer Care and Children in Need. In each case, these firms have used their involvement with society both to express their corporate values and to enhance their corporate image.

CEOs believe that corporate social responsibility (CSR) can pay off. In one survey, more than 90% thought that socially responsible management creates shareholder value.[1] In another study, 300 firms judged to have high commitment to CSR had a slightly higher stock return during a two-year period beginning in October 2000.[2] Providing a more direct measurement, a UK study compared the marketplace performance of three energy companies. Two of these, BP and Shell, were perceived as environmentally friendly, while the third, Esso, had visibly taken the position that renewable energy was not a viable solution and that the Kyoto international accords on the environment were flawed. Greenpeace subsequently attacked Esso with a high-profile 'StopEsso' campaign. A subsequent Greenpeace poll found that the proportion of British petrol buyers who said they regularly used Esso stations dropped by 7% during the year of the campaign.[3]

There are good reasons why CSR could influence profitability. First, many people fundamentally want to have a relationship with good people who can be trusted, and they perceive that CSR programmes reflect a firm's values. Second, a strong and visible CSR programme can deliver to customers self-expressive benefits, particularly for the core group of customers who have strong feelings about environmental issues. Certainly, many drivers of Toyota's Prius, the leading hybrid car, achieve significant self-expressive benefits. In fact, the glamorous CEO of The Body Shop Japan drives a Prius as a statement about both herself and her firm. With Prius as the flagship of dozens of environmental programmes, Toyota has taken the leadership position with respect to the visibility of CSR in both Japan and North America. Nokia, one of the top-ranked world leaders with respect to CSR, integrates various socially responsible programmes into its business, including community initiatives like the International Youth Foundation and environmental initiatives like its Eco Declaration, which details the materials used in the products and assists in their ultimate recycling and disposal. Third, a CSR programme can add energy and make a boring brand interesting. Finally, a CSR programme can also be defensive, in that it can help a firm deal with an accident or criticism by activists concerning social responsibility issues.

Ad hoc programmes, though, are not the way to pursue CSR. Rather, the programmes need to be focused, meaningful, consistent over time, and hopefully branded. All firms will give lip service and some resources towards CSR. However, the firms that stand out, such as Toyota and BP, have a real commitment – even a passion – and find ways to make it visible.

There are challenges in pursuing a CSR strategy. One, perhaps the most serious, involves creating unreasonable expectations. If a firm is visible and active with regard to CSR, people will expect it to be flawless. Given the complexity of the issues, however, a firm can be making strides and still be criticized. BP can make significant investments in renewable energy relative to its competitors, for example, but some may correctly point out that the investment is still small relative to BP's size. Adidas can make progress in addressing the labour practices of its foreign suppliers, but still draw fire because problems remain. Another challenge is to make CSR programmes visible, linked to the firm, and relevant to customers. Chapter 10, on energizing the business, will elaborate on this.

Superior Customer Relationship

All firms place an emphasis on the customer. A few, however, create an experience that connects the offering to the customer on a more involving and passionate level. For these firms, customer intimacy is a strategic option. Facebook offers customers a superior customer relationship, allowing users to keep in contact with old and new friends, express themselves through their hobbies and interests, but most importantly to do so entirely on their own terms. Some local hardware stores create offerings, specialized services, and personal customer relationships that allow them to prosper while competing with 'big boxes' such as B&Q, Hornbach (Germany), or Castorama (France). Harrods has generated a customer link by offering personalized service and a shopping experience that often delights rather than merely satisfies. Apple and Logitech have similarly connected by providing products that generate a 'Wow!' response.

Firms that create intimacy understand customers at a deep level. They deliver an experience that is satisfying on several levels, going beyond functional benefits to provide emotional, social, and self-expressive benefits. The Mazda MX-5 is an iconic sports car that had a number of unofficial clubs and websites devoted to it. Mazda launched its own website, which allowed owners to interact with Mazda staff, as well as providing news about the car and a forum for interaction with other owners. Mazda relaunched its website with the objective of increasing the level of activity on the site. Through more frequent updating and closer monitoring of the forums, the number of unique visitors to the site rose by 150%, with a membership growth of 10% per month. Mazda's ambition is to use this deeper interaction to provide a better experience of the brand to its most loyal customers.[4]

The key to turning on customers and achieving intimacy might be resolving unmet needs in the marketplace – finding answers to annoyances that customers have tolerated because there was no option. For example, the car buying experience was often distasteful before some brands such as Ford and Lexus introduced a very different buying experience that became a basis for a new customer relationship. Lexus also earns loyalty with a dozen clever design features in its cars. Intimacy can also come from delight at an unexpected experience, such as the massages that come with Virgin's first-class seats and Harley-Davidson's biking parties. Or it could develop from an outstanding product such as the RIM Blackberry.

The highly loyal, even fanatical customer base sometimes created through an intimacy strategy needs active programmes for nurture and support. Harley-Davidson, for example, supports its Harley Owners' Groups (HOGs) with local and national events, clothing and accessories, and a website with a host of supporting services, including a trip planner and on-line photo centre. Virgin continually adds new features and services designed to support its image of being creative and willing to ignore convention in pursuit of enjoyable customer experiences.

Niche Specialist

Being a niche specialist means that the firm concentrates on one part of the market or product line and can emerge in virtually any arena. LinkedIn is a business-oriented social networking site intended to allow professionals to build and use a network of contacts. Alltech is one of the world's leading animal health companies but emphasizes natural solutions. Pandora is a niche player within the on-line music market in that it invites users to identify their favourite music and then makes recommendations as to what other music they would like and provides links to iTunes or Amazon where the music can be purchased. The Peninsula Hotel in Hong Kong uses a fleet of Rolls-Royce cars to transfer guests between the airport and the hotel, emphasizing their focus on the upscale segment.

Because a niche specialist by nature tends to avoid strategy dilution or distraction, it is more likely to pursue a strategic commitment strategy leading to a sustainable advantage. When internal investments, programmes, and culture have all been directed towards a single end and there is buy-in on the part of everyone in the organization, the result will be assets, competencies, and functional strategies that match market needs. There are no compromises or diluted investments. It is no accident that specialized retailers such as Victoria's Secret have been much more successful than department stores and others that are spread thinly. One reason is the strategic and operational advantages of focusing.

SHOULDICE HOSPITAL

Shouldice Hospital near Toronto only does hernia operations. Since its founding in 1945, over 300 000 operations have been conducted, with a 99% success rate. Measured by how often repeat treatment is needed, Shouldice is 10 times more effective than other hospitals. The surgical procedure used is branded as the Shouldice Technique.

The experience of the doctors and staff are appealing, but so are the Shouldice setting and its recovery programme. Located on a country estate, the hospital has a calming ambience and facilities tailored to the needs of recovering hernia patients. Patients walk to watch TV, to eat, and even to and from the operating room, because walking is good therapy for hernias. There is thus no need to deliver food to rooms, or to have wheelchair facilities. The length of a hospital visit at Shouldice is around half the norm elsewhere. No general anaesthesia is administered, because local anaesthesia is safer and cheaper for hernia operations.

By concentrating on one narrow segment of the medical market, Shouldice has developed a hospital that is proficient, inexpensive, and capable of delivering an extraordinary level of patient satisfaction. Patients are so pleased that the Shouldice Hospital annual reunion attracts some 1500 'alumni'.

A product focus can result in technical superiority because the people are developing and bringing to the market products that they are passionate about. When the products of a firm capture the imagination of its key people, they tend to be exciting, innovative, and of high quality.

A niche specialist strategy can translate into a value proposition for customers. First, a focused firm will have more credibility than a firm that makes a wide array of products, as demonstrated by Shouldice Hospital in hernia surgeries, LinkedIn in business networking, and Alltech in animal health. If you are really interested in the best, you will go to a firm that specializes in and has a passion for the business. Second, the bond between the loyal user and the brand will tend to be greater when the brand is focused and the people are seen to have a passion for their product. The reunions of Shouldice Hospital patients and the passion of Harley-Davidson customers would not happen without a focus strategy.

This list of strategic options could be extended in any given context. For now, we will explore two options, quality and value, in more detail.

SUPERIOR QUALITY

A quality strategy means that the brand – whether it be hotels, cars, or computers – will be perceived as superior to other brands in its reference set. The point of superiority spans the brand offerings, delivering exceptional quality across products and individual attributes. Usually, such superiority will be associated with a price premium. As the Lexus insert illustrates, perceived quality can be the driver of a business strategy.

LEXUS – A PASSION FOR EXCELLENCE

For more than a decade, Lexus has been among the leaders on a variety of objective quality indicators. Among the many reasons behind the Lexus achievement, several stand out. First, the Lexus concept was based on quality from its inception. Toyota launched Lexus in the early 1980s as a brand that would take automobile design, manufacturing, and retailing to a new level. Second, the brand delivered on the concept, as Lexus drew on assets and competencies developed by Toyota to make cars that were more reliable and had fewer defects. Third, a new dealer network offered the potential to break from industry norms and provide a pleasant buying experience. Fourth, the positioning of the Lexus brand (with the classic 'relentless pursuit of perfection' tagline) delivered the quality message consistently over the years. Finally, Lexus excelled in the new standard of quality, clever features, and rideability.

The challenge facing Lexus now is that, in spite of its success with a quality mission and message, it has failed to develop much personality in comparison with BMW, Mercedes, Jaguar, and Audi. When the latter brands gradually closed the quality gap over the years, the Lexus message became less compelling. In response, Lexus belatedly has tried to inject some emotional and self-expressive benefits, as demonstrated by its modified tagline, 'The passionate pursuit of perfection'. It has not been an easy task.

A quality value proposition, if based on substance, has a host of advantages. First, it provides an opportunity to be a leader in the category. Every category, including those with value offerings such as Aldi or Ryanair, will have a market leader, and that leader will almost always have to have a superior quality image. Second, perceived quality can drive people's perceptions on a wide variety of attribute dimensions because of the powerful halo effect. Third, it provides the motivation if not inspiration for employees to do what they should do anyway, strive to deliver the best possible product or service. A quality culture affects what people strive for. And it affects how the organization reacts to missteps. Fourth, it can foster innovation because quality is always a moving target. If quality is not a priority as evidenced by the value proposition, innovation will likely not be ongoing.

A bottom-line reason for a quality value proposition is that it simply pays off in terms of financial performance because it supports not only customer loyalty but also the price that can be charged. Aaker and Jacobson have demonstrated that perceived quality can drive stock return, a measure that truly reflects long-term performance.[5] They analysed annual measures of perceived quality obtained from the Total Research EquiTrend database for 35 brands (including IBM and Pepsi) for which sales were a substantial part of firm sales. They found that the impact of perceived quality on stock return was nearly as strong as the impact of ROI. Given that ROI is an established and accepted influence on stock return, the performance of perceived quality is noteworthy. It means that investors are able to detect and respond to programmes that affect intangible assets such as perceived quality. Figure 8.2 shows the dramatic relationship between perceived quality and stock return.

Superiority will be defined by customers. In nearly all contexts, a single overall indicator of quality exists, is relevant to customers, and in fact drives other, more specific dimensions of performance. To understand what drives perceived quality and actively to manage it, however, the underlying dimensions in any given context need to be determined.

Figure 8.3 lists several dimensions of product quality that are often relevant. Of course, each of these dimensions has multiple components (for example, performance for a printer will involve attributes such as speed, resolution, and capacity). Also, the list itself will depend on the context. Furthermore, the drivers of quality will undergo changes over time. Thus, it is important to keep monitoring customer trends, preferences, sources of dissatisfaction, and unmet needs.

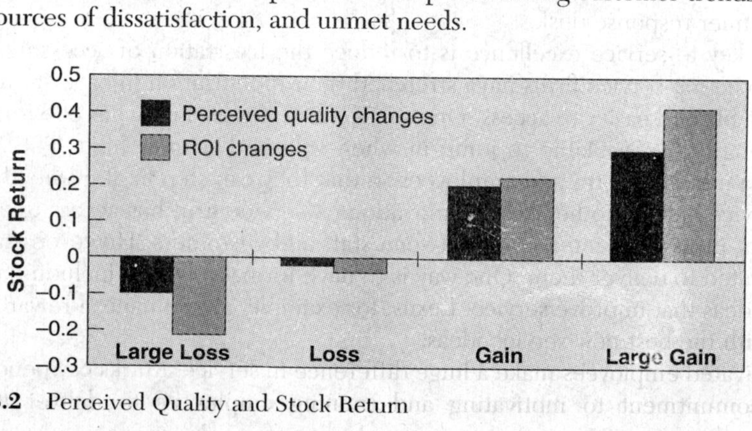

Figure 8.2 Perceived Quality and Stock Return

1. **Performance.** What are the specifications? How well is the task performed? Does the lawn mower cut grass well? Does the bank handle transactions with speed and accuracy?
2. **Conformance to specifications.** Does the product or service perform reliably and provide customer satisfaction?
3. **Features.** Does the product offer the latest features? Are there any 'Wow' attributes?
4. **Customer support.** Does the firm support the customer with caring, competent people and efficient systems?
5. **Process quality.** Is the process of buying and using the product or service pleasant, rather than frustrating and disappointing?
6. **Aesthetic design.** Does the design add pleasure to the experience of buying and using the product or service?

Figure 8.3 Product Quality Dimensions

Service Quality

In a service context – such as a bank, restaurant, or theme park – research has shown that quality is based in large part on the perceived competence, responsiveness, and empathy of the people with whom customers interact.[6] A successful organization therefore must deliver consistently on those dimensions. Delivering service quality, however, also means managing expectations. If expectations are too high, the service experience might be unsatisfactory, even if it is at a high level. Generating clarity about the service promise, whenever possible, will thus be helpful.

Delivering service quality starts with the culture of the organization. With the right culture, innovation and motivation will happen. A 2009 *Business Week* study of the top service firms, conducted in conjunction with J.D. Powers, illustrates how culture affects performance and the variety of ways that firms can improve customer service.[7]

Amazon, the top service company, backs up the sales of outside merchants, which represent about 30% of its volume, and terminates any that fail to measure up to Amazon standards. Amazon also attempts to make the customer experience so good that they never need to contact an employee. One way to make that contact positive when it is necessary is to have all employees spend two days every two years on the consumer response desk.

One key to service excellence is to reduce the frustration of accessing service. Many of the top service firms have stretched their organization in order to have service available and easier to access. One service firm, for example, has 300 former call service employees available to jump in when volume becomes high. The Marriott Hotel chain has cross-trained employees so that they can step in at events that need extra service help. Another key is innovation. A service firm has access to a host of sources of ideas from interaction between staff and customers. However, staff must be motivated to deliver them. One way is to have formal rewards, including recognition for ideas that improve service. Lexus, for example, gives financial rewards to the dealer with the best new service ideas.

Motivated employees make a huge difference in service. Marks & Spencer has a strong commitment to motivating and training employees to deliver excellent customer service:[8] This begins with the 'Our Service Style' training programme which every staff member is required to attend. One in six customer assistants acts as a coach for other staff, leading to continuous improvement on the shopfloor. The quality of the staff, the Marks & Spencer recruitment process, and a very low staff turnover by industry standards also contribute to the excellence of service offered by the retailer. Finally, the firm operates a rigorous monitoring of customer service via customer surveys and mystery shopping. It is possible, however, to create measures that are dysfunctional. For example, a company (not one of the top service firms) sought to improve the quality of its phone service by measuring the percentage of calls answered after the first ring. Unfortunately, the pressure to answer promptly caused agents to become abrupt and impatient with callers, and thus customer satisfaction suffered. The saying 'Be careful what you wish for' is especially true in performance measurement.

How is a quality reputation obtained? The answer is context specific but involves creating the right culture, processes, and people and then managing the way the result is communicated. Total quality management, managing quality signals, and managing quality missteps are relevant.

Total Quality Management

To pursue a quality strategic option successfully, a business must distinguish itself with respect to delivering quality to customers. To accomplish this goal, it needs a quality-focused management system that is comprehensive, integrative, and supported throughout the organization. Such a total quality management (TQM) system should incorporate a host of tools and precepts, including the following:

- The commitment of senior management to quality, which creates a culture, if not passion, to deliver high quality.
- Cross-functional teams empowered to make changes by initiating and implementing quality improvement projects.
- A process (rather than results) orientation. The goal is not a one-time quality enhancement, but to develop processes and cross-functional teams that will lead to quality improvements on an ongoing basis.
- A set of systems, such as suggestion systems, measurement systems, and recognition systems.
- A focus on the underlying causes of customer complaints and areas of dissatisfaction. One approach used in TQM is to explore a problem in depth by repeatedly asking, 'Why?'. This process has been dubbed 'the five whys'.
- The tracking of key quality measures – going beyond customer satisfaction to measures of loyalty and the willingness to recommend. Updating quality measures so that the focus is not on dimensions that have become industry standards and points of parity.
- The involvement of suppliers in the system through supplier audits, ratings, and recognition, as well as joint team efforts.

Signals of High Quality

Most quality dimensions, such as performance, durability, reliability, and serviceability, are difficult if not impossible for buyers to evaluate. As a result, consumers tend to look for attributes that they believe indicate quality. The fit-and-finish dimension can be such a quality signal. Buyers assume that, if a firm's products do not have good fit and finish, they probably will not have other, more important attributes. In pursuing a quality strategy, it is usually critical to focus on a visible dimension pivotal in affecting perceptions about more important dimensions that are very difficult to judge. Some examples:

- *Broadband Internet suppliers.* A professional attitude on the part of the installation team means quality.
- *Tomato juice.* Thickness means high quality.
- *Cleaners.* A lemon scent can signal cleaning power.
- *Supermarkets.* Produce freshness means overall quality.
- *Cars.* A solid door-closure sound implies good workmanship and a safe body.
- *Clothes.* Higher price means higher quality.
- *Airlines.* A stain on a seat can reflect on perceived maintenance standards.

Managing Quality Missteps

One somewhat ironic problem of achieving high actual and perceived quality is that expectations are raised and thus the potential for disappointment is higher. Because negative experiences are more salient than positive ones, a quality strategy needs to focus on avoiding them. The challenge is to seek points of annoyance and attempt to reduce their incidence and intensity. For example, in order to make even waiting in line at their respective locations bearable, Disney provides entertainment with its delightful characters, and Schwab provides stock news. More important than alleviating annoyances is to eliminate them. Disney has a system of reservations to eliminate the burden of long waits, and Schwab has direct numbers to call agents so that the pain of menus does not occur at least during the second call.

A much more serious threat to a quality reputation is the visible and dramatic brand misstep. While obtaining trust is too often overvalued as a brand attribute because it is not differentiating or energizing, the loss of trust can be monumental. The Schlitz story shown in the insert illustrates how a decision to reduce costs led to a loss of perceived quality that was disastrous.

Disaster management requires not only the right quality culture but also a contingency plan to deal with it. The gold standard is Johnson & Johnson's handling of the Tylenol poison incident – taking responsibility, removing the product from the shelves, and creating a visible packing solution. The action of US Airways after the miracle landing of a damaged plane on the Hudson river is a more recent role model.[9] The airline dispatched a 'Care Team' with over 100 members that had rehearsed for such incidents three times a year. They activated a special 800 number for passenger families and provided emergency cash, prepaid cell phones, and clothes. Passengers

SCHLITZ: WHEN PERCEIVED QUALITY FALTERS

The story of Schlitz beer dramatically illustrates the strategic power of perceived quality and how fragile it is. From a strong number two position in 1974 (selling 17.8 million barrels of beer annually), supported by a series of well-regarded 'go for the gusto' ad campaigns, Schlitz fell steadily until the mid-1980s, when it had all but disappeared (with sales of only 1.8 million barrels). The stock market value of the brand fell by more than a billion dollars.

The collapse can be traced to a decision to reduce costs by converting to a fermentation process that took four days instead of twelve, substituting corn syrup for barley malt, and using a different foam stabilizer. Word of these changes got into the marketplace. In early 1976, when bottles of flaky, cloudy-looking Schlitz beer appeared on the shelves, the condition was eventually traced to the new foam stabilizer. Worse still, in early summer of that same year, an attempted fix caused the beer to go flat after a few months on the shelf. In the fall of 1976, 10 million bottles and cans of Schlitz were 'secretly' recalled and destroyed. In spite of a return to its original process and aggressive advertising, Schlitz never recovered.

were escorted to alternative transportation or hotels. They followed up with a $5000 advance to cover expenses and a ticket refund without requiring them to waive legal rights, an unprecedented action. The result was a sharp uptick on a reputation that had been somewhat marginal.

The impact of a disaster can depend on the positioning of the firm. In a fascinating experiment, academic researchers Jennifer Aaker of Stanford, Susan Fournier of Boston University, and Adam Brasel of Boston College created two on-line film-processing firms with very different personalities, one exciting and the other sincere, and each experimental subject was randomly assigned to one of the sites.[10] In addition, after about 10 interactions, half of each of the two groups were informed, with regret, that their NetAlbum had been lost, and a week later they were informed that it had been found. With no service disrupt, six weeks later the sincere site was regarded more favourably than the exciting site. However, the exciting site was able to rebound from the disruption while the sincere site was not. One lesson is that building trust creates expectations, and service problems had better be few and minimal.

VALUE

In nearly every market, from appliances to economy sedans to toothpaste to booksellers to brokerage services, there will be a segment that is motivated by price. Even in high-end markets such as luxury cars, some brands (Lexus, for example) will stake out a value position. During recessionary times, the 'value segment' can become large. Whether it comprises 10 or 80% of the market, the value segment will usually be a significant one.

Ignoring the value segment can be risky because even healthy markets can evolve into situations where price grows in importance. In consumer electronics,

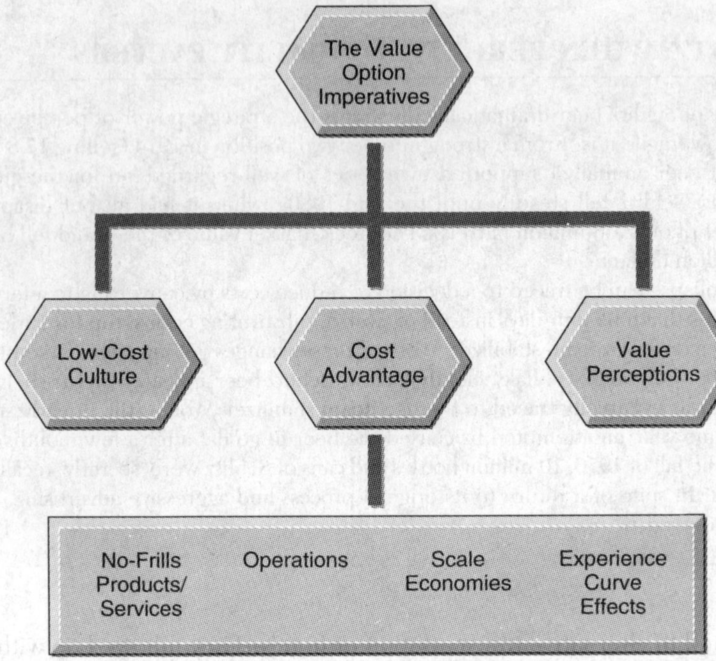

Figure 8.4 The Value Option

appliances, and other product arenas, competitors have created overcapacity, causing a need to create or maintain a critical mass in the market. Power retailers with their own brands as competitive tools are another potential contributing force. Thus, ignoring the value segment may not be an option. It may be necessary to participate, perhaps with a value brand or as a private label supplier, in order to maintain scale economies.

As Figure 8.4 suggests, to compete successfully in the value arena it is necessary to:

- have a cost advantage (or at least avoid a cost disadvantage);
- foster a cost culture in the organization;
- create a perception of value without eroding the quality perception to a point where the brand is not considered.

Each of these imperatives is explored further below.

Creating a Cost Advantage (or Avoiding a Cost Disadvantage)

Although there is a tendency to think of low cost as a single approach, there are actually many dimensions to cost control and thus many routes to a cost reduction. The successful low-cost firms are those that can harness multiple approaches, including the use of no-frills products/services, operational efficiency, scale economies, and the experience curve.

ALDI

Aldi is an international hard discount supermarket chain that was founded in Germany in 1946. Its goal is to provide products at aggressively low prices, and it has managed to establish a large market with this tactic. Aldi's price competitiveness stems from a cost-cutting, no-frills strategy. Aisles are left undecorated, and it is common to find empty shelves with the products simply placed on a pallet alongside them – once customers have cleared a pallet, it is replaced. Aldi has adopted a minimal staffing level, which is evident from the sometimes long checkout queues in its stores, although an efficient checkout system means that a long queue may not always mean a longer waiting time than other stores. Stores have no telephone listings, to reduce the time spent on answering the phone and minimizing the time that checkouts are left idle. Aldi tries to keep its stores as small as possible to avoid spending money on high land prices in urban areas. In most of Europe, Aldi does not advertise except in local papers or by direct mail, although they began advertising in the United Kingdom in 2005. With the introduction of the euro, customers generally believed that retailers used the changeover to increase prices of products, but Aldi included 'before' and 'after' prices on products and rounded the euro price down instead of up like other retailers. This earned them considerable goodwill among customers. Many of Aldi's products are own-brand labelled, with the number of other brands limited. Aldi offers special weekly buys, like 'Thursday Buys' or 'Sunday Buys', with exceptional discounts on clothing, toys, flowers, etc. Such strategies appear to be accepted by customers in exchange for the value that they receive from Aldi. While Aldi's brand reputation is associated with cheap shops selling poor-quality goods, the company countered in countries like Germany by introducing cookbooks that used only Aldi products, which altered the public's opinion of Aldi and its undeserved reputation.[11]

No-Frills Product/Service

One direct approach to low cost is simply removing all frills and extras from a product or service and using materials and components that are functionally adequate. Budget hotels like Jury's Inn and Hotel Formule 1 provide a service with limited extras and amenities. No-frills airlines like BMI Baby, Ryanair, and Air Deccan follow a similar strategy, offering no-frills services at a lower cost. Supermarket chains such as Tesco with their 'value lines', Kwik Save, and Iceland all provide own-label brands that offer a cheap, basic alternative to branded products. These products are adequate for consumers but may lack the aesthetic appeal of popular branded products and are generally not supported in a marketing sense. Value furniture lines like IKEA use self-service warehouses and self-assembly strategies to create sustainable cost advantages.

A major risk, especially in the service sector, is that competitors will position themselves against a no-frills offering by adding just a few features. In the low-cost airline market in the United States, JetBlue has made strong inroads by offering budget fares but offering inflight services such as snacks and inflight TV. The result of such strategies can be a feature war.

Operations

Enduring cost advantages can also be created through efficiencies in operations based on government subsidies, process innovation, distribution efficiency (like Tesco's supply-chain management system), access to target markets (Internet banking services appealing to young-to-middle-aged professionals, reducing their reliance on physical visits), outsourcing competencies, and the management of overheads.

To obtain significant operational economies, it is useful to examine the value chain and look for inherently high-cost components that could be eliminated or reduced by changing the way the business operates. The best example is the disintermediation of channel members. By selling direct and cutting out retailers, Spotify and iTunes strip large components out of the value chain. For instance, in the conventional bookstore model, about 30% of sold books are returned, representing a huge deadweight on costs. In the Amazon model, that proportion is reduced to 3% – an enormous potential saving.[12]

Another place to find operations-based cost savings is in the interface with a supplier or customer. Uniqlo (a Japanese Gap-like retailer) links its store sales and inventory to its factories in China to create breathtaking efficiencies. Similarly, Zara also links stores, warehouses, and design centres electronically to ensure swift response to customer trends, effective design, and efficient supply. Likewise, Procter & Gamble created an ongoing partnership with Wal-Mart, resulting in a continuous replenishment system for reordering, shipping, and restocking that minimizes shipping and warehouse costs, inventory, and out-of-stock conditions. Ten years after the partnership programme began, stock-keeping units were down 25%, sales staffing was down 30%, inventory was down 15%, and the programme was expanded to all major P&G customers.[13]

Scale Economies

The scale effect reflects the natural efficiencies associated with size. Fixed costs such as advertising, sales force overheads, R&D, staff work, and facility upkeep can be spread over more units. Furthermore, a larger operation can support specialized assets and activities (such as market research, legal staff, and manufacturing-engineering operations) dedicated to a firm's needs. Amazon has long based its business model on creating scale economies by driving sales higher.

When a business is too small to support needed assets or operations, the result can be a severe competitive disadvantage. The solution might be to prune or consolidate business units. Scale economy effects are particularly relevant in brand building, where each brand may seek a share of limited resources. In recent years, firms such as Nestlé, Unilever, P&G, and HP have deleted, consolidated, and prioritized brands in their portfolios in order to make sure that important brands are fully funded and developed. Perhaps the best known example of this is Unilever's 'Paths to Growth' strategy. The detail of this strategy was to reduce the brand portfolio from 1600 to 400 brands, with the new focus being on leading brands. The logic was that this reduction would provide growth-enhancing benefits including an improvement in the company's focus on customers and competitors, drive product innovation, and allow for improvements both in supply-chain management and in management information flows.

In retailing, scale can be obtained by combining business units. Yum! Brands has introduced dual-branded stores from its stable of KFC, Pizza Hut, Taco Bell, Long John Silver's, and A&W. Such dual-brand outlets can compete with McDonald's and Burger King for expensive sites that require a large annual sales volume.

The Experience Curve

The experience curve, empirically verified in hundreds of studies, suggests that, as a firm accumulates experience in building a product, its costs in real dollars will decline at a predictable rate. When the experience curve applies, the first market entry attaining a large market share will have a continuing cost advantage. The experience curve effect is based on the fact that, over time, people will learn to do tasks faster and more efficiently, that technological process improvements will occur, and that products will be redesigned to be simpler to build.

The classic experience curve is represented by the Ford Model T, introduced in 1908 as a reliable, easy-to-drive, and remarkably inexpensive car. The Model T, which sold over 15 million units, began its life priced at $850 (around $18 000 in modern dollars), but the price fell continually until in 1922 it cost less than $300, a price that served to expand the market dramatically. Because of the production-friendly and unchanging design, vertical integration, and the building of the huge River Rouge plant, production costs declined according to an 85% experience curve (that is, costs fell roughly 15% every time cumulative production doubled). Figure 8.5 presents the pattern.

Several issues need to be understood in working with the experience curve concept. First, the experience curve is not automatic. It must be proactively managed with efficiency improvement goals, quality circles, product design targets, and equipment upgrading. Furthermore, a late entry can often gain the same advantage as more experienced vendors simply by accessing the most recent design. Second, if the technology or market changes, the experience curve may become obsolete. The auto market in the early 1920s turned away from the Model T, and Ford had to close down for a year to retool in order to make what GM was offering and the market wanted. Third, the

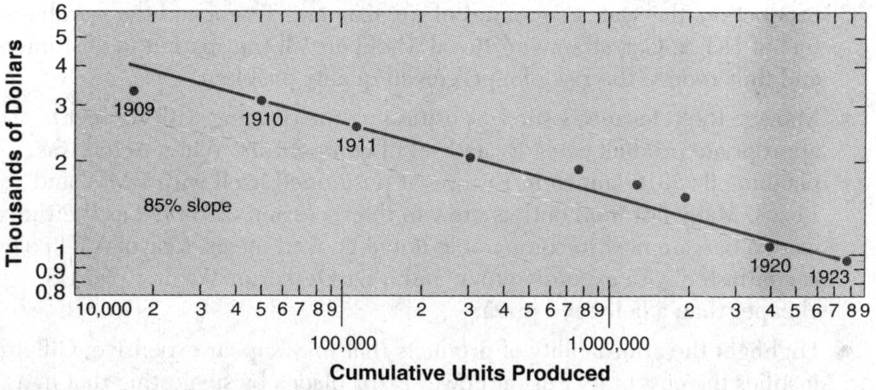

Figure 8.5 Price of Model T, 1909–1923 (average list price in 1958)

experience curve model implies that cost improvements, whatever their source, should be translated into low prices and higher share so that the business can stay ahead on the experience curve. Lower prices can trigger price wars, however, leading to reduced margins, as has occurred in consumer electronics numerous times.

A Low-cost Culture

A successful low-cost strategy is usually multifaceted and supported by a cost-oriented culture. Performance measurement, rewards, systems, structure, top management values, and culture are all fronts where cost reduction should be stressed. The single-minded focus needed is comparable with that required for total quality management. Such a commitment is evident at Ryanair, TK Maxx, Iceland, and other firms that have succeeded with a value strategy.

There are many examples of firms that decided to go into the low-cost world and failed because their cultures could never adapt. One large supermarket chain decided to create a discount beverage chain. When the chain failed to deliver on the promise and still be profitable, an analysis determined that the people and processes were not compatible with the cost structure needed to succeed in that market. A successful discount operation almost always requires a new organization with different culture, processes, and people.

Perceived Value

Managing prices and price perceptions is tricky, because price is often a quality cue and customers may perceive low price as a signal for inferior quality. If the quality is perceived to be unacceptably low, the offering will be deemed irrelevant to the customers' needs. This is particularly troublesome for offerings in categories where it is difficult to judge actual quality (perfume or motor oil, for example) and for premium brands in times of deep recessions where a value message is needed. So how to tell the value story without shouting price? Among the approaches that work:

- Communicate the substance behind the cost advantage – Dell's direct sales model, Ryanair's point-to-point travel and no-frills service, Ford's mass production, the scale economies of Amazon and Tesco, and the warehouse feel of IKEA, Carrefour, and Royal Ahold are all transparent to customers and thus reduce the risk of a perceived quality problem.
- Manage the relevance issue by positioning the offering with respect to the appropriate product category and set of competitors. When Acura was planning its 2010 launch in Europe, it positioned itself with BMW and Lexus. Many fast food outlets grew in the recession of 2008/9 as their meals were a bargain next to comparable home-cooked meals, Crayola's 64 colours is contrasted with expensive toys, and a Dr Oetker or Wagner pizza is cheaper than a delivered pizza.
- Highlight the affordability of products that may appear expensive. Gillette justifies the cost of its Fusion Power razor blades by suggesting that in a high-performance world its cost per week is affordable.

- Replace price reduction with bundled features or services that provide extra value at the same price, such as free shipping by Amazon.
- Demonstrate the value of quality – Bounty towels pay by doing more with fewer.
- Divert attention to value subbrands such as the BMW One Series, the Tesco value range, or Waitrose's Essentials.
- Manage the visible price points. Grocery stores have long learned that customers tend to be knowledgeable about a few categories and brands. Similarly, the major book chains pay close attention to best-selling books, because those are the ones most likely to receive a price comparison. Car manufacturers are concerned most with base prices and much less about accessories and options, because prices for the latter will be harder to compare.
- Bundle products to produce a viable value. Mobile phones now have multiple features, many of which can be added at low cost, that can enhance value perceptions.

KEY LEARNINGS

- Business strategies usually cluster around a limited number of value propositions, such as a superior attribute, appealing design, systems solutions, social responsibility, a superior customer relationship, a niche specialist, superior quality, and superior value. The value proposition should be real, believed, feasible, relevant, and sustainable.
- A value position needs to be communicated effectively and supported by a cost advantage, which can be based on a no-frills offering, operations, scale economies, and/or the experience curve.
- Superior quality, which has been shown to drive stock return, has to be continually addressed through processes and programmes and transferred into quality perceptions.

FOR DISCUSSION

1. Consider three industries, such as hotels or appliances or cars. For several of the firms in the industry, identify what value propositions are representing their strategy. Were there multiple propositions? Evaluate. Are they successful or likely to be successful?
2. Consider three of the following value propositions: systems solutions, corporate social responsibility, superior customer relationships, quality, and

value. For each of these, think of two firms not mentioned in the book that have pursued them. Which of the two firms has done better with respect to the five business strategy challenges? Discuss why and how that firm was able to do better.

3. Evaluate the quality strategy of Lexus with respect to the business strategy challenges. How might Lexus add more personality and emotion to its brand? Think of role models that have achieved a quality reputation and a strong personality.
4. Pick a product or service offering. How would you develop a set of customer survey questions that would measure its quality on an ongoing basis? How would you administer the survey?
5. Consider the NetAlbum experiment. What explanation would you propose?

NOTES

1. Stan L. Friedman, 'Corporate America's Social Conscience', *Fortune*, 23 June 2003, p. S6.
2. Stan L. Friedman, 'Corporate America's Social Conscience', *Fortune*, 23 June 2003, p. S4.
3. 'Esso – Should the Tiger Change Its Stripes?', *Reputation Impact*, October 2002, p. 16.
4. 'Brand Engagement', *Marketing*, 5 July 2006.
5. Valarie A. Zeithaml, *Service Quality*, Boston, MA, Marketing Science Institute, 2004.
6. Jena McGregor, 'When Service Means Survival', *Business Week*, 2 March 2009, pp. 26–40.
7. Jena McGregor, 'When Service Means Survival', *Business Week*, 2 March 2009, p. 31.
8. Marks & Spencer Annual Review and Financial Statement, 2006.
9. Jena McGregor, 'When Service Means Survival', *Business Week*, 2 March 2009, pp. 26–40.
10. Jennifer Aaker, Susan Fournier and S. Adam Brasel, 'When Good Brands Do Bad', *Journal of Consumer Research*, 2004, **31** (June), 1–18.
11. http://www.aldi.com/; http://biz.yahoo.com/ic/54/54910.html; 'Aldi', Wikipedia, http://en.wikipedia.org/wiki/Aldi (all accessed 1 December 2009).
12. Jena McGregor, 'When Service Means Survival', *Business Week*, 2 March 2009, pp. 126–40.
13. Material is drawn in part from Lawrence D. Milligan, 'Keeping It Simple, the Evolution of Customer-Business Development at Procter & Gamble', remarks made at the American Marketing Association Doctoral Symposium, Cincinnati, July 1997.

CHAPTER NINE

Building and Managing Brand Equity

You do not merely want to be considered just the best of the best. You want to be considered the only ones who do what you do.
—*Jerry Garcia, The Grateful Dead*

You cannot make a business case that you should be who you're not.
—*Jeff Bezos, Amazon*

Selling to people who actually want to hear from you is more effective than interrupting strangers who don't.
—*Seth Godin*

A business strategy is enabled by brand assets. A brand gives a firm permission to compete in product markets and services, and it represents the value proposition of the business strategy. Thus, it is strategically crucial to develop, refine, and leverage brand assets.

Anecdotes abound about the power of a brand to improve financial performance, but solid research also shows that, on average, building brands generates a payoff in terms of stock return. In fact, as noted in Chapter 8, the brand effect on stock return is nearly as large as that of accounting ROI in such diverse settings as large-cap, Internet, and high-tech firms. Furthermore, efforts to estimate the value of brand assets as compared with other intangible assets – like people and IT technology – and tangible assets reveal that the brand assets represent from 15% or so (Toyota and Banco Santander) to 30% (China Mobile) to more than 70% (Google and BMW) of the value of the firm. Even the lower number is significant strategically.

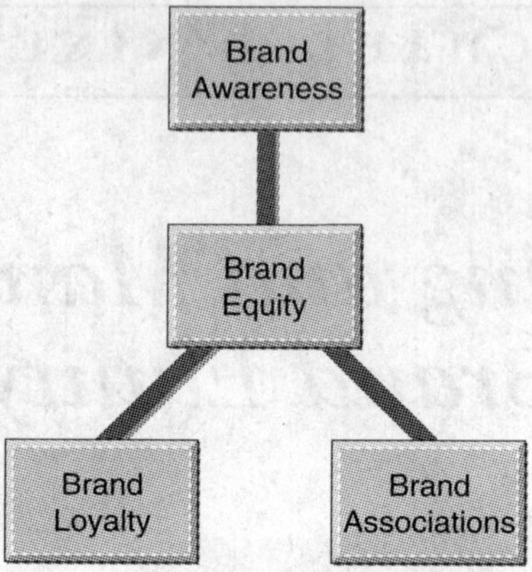

Figure 9.1 Brand Equity

Brand equity is the set of assets and liabilities linked to the brand. The conceptualization of brand equity, which occurred in the late 1980s, was pivotal because it changed the way that marketing was perceived. Where brand image could be delegated to an advertising manager, brand equity – as a key asset of the firm – needed to be elevated to part of the business strategy, the purview of the CEO. Its management was strategic and visionary instead of tactical and reactive, long term in orientation rather than short term, and involved a different set of metrics. It truly changed the role of marketing and the CMO.

There are three types of brand asset – brand awareness, brand loyalty, and brand associations (see Figure 9.1). Each creates formidable competitive advantages, and each needs to be actively managed.

BRAND AWARENESS

Brand awareness is often taken for granted, but it can be a key strategic asset. In some industries that have product parity, awareness, the third most mentioned SCA (see Figure 7.3), provides a sustainable competitive difference. It serves to differentiate the brands along a recall/familiarity dimension.

Brand awareness can provide a host of competitive advantages. First, awareness provides the brand with a sense of familiarity, and people like the familiar. For low-involvement products, such as soap or chewing gum, familiarity can drive the buying decision. Taste tests of products such as soft drinks show that a recognized name can affect evaluations even if the brand has never been purchased or used.

Second, name awareness can be a signal of presence, commitment, and substance, attributes that can be very important even to industrial buyers of big-ticket items and consumer buyers of durables. The logic is that, if a name is recognized, there must be a reason. The 'Intel Inside' programme was remarkably successful at creating a perception of advanced technology and earned a significant price premium for Intel for well over a decade, even though it did not communicate anything about the company or the product. Pure awareness power was at work.

Third, the salience of a brand will determine if it is recalled at a key time in the purchasing process. The initial step in selecting an advertising agency, a car to test drive, or a computer system is to decide on which brands to consider. The extreme case is name dominance, where the brand is the only one recalled when a product class is cued. Consider Greenpeace, Innocent smoothies, Band-Aid adhesive bandages, iPod, Google, Crayola crayons, Kleenex tissues, Hellman's mayonnaise, Philadelphia cream cheese, and V-8 vegetable juice. In each case, how many other brands can you name? How would you like to compete against the dominant brand?

Brand awareness is an asset that can be extremely durable and thus sustainable. It can be very difficult to dislodge a brand that has achieved a dominant awareness level. Customers' awareness of the Datsun brand, for example, was as strong as that of its successor, Nissan, four years after the firm changed its name.[1] Another study of familiarity asked homemakers to name as many brands of any type as they could; they averaged 28 names each. The ages of the brands named were surprising: more than 85% were over 25 years old, and 36% were more than 75 years old.[2]

There is a great deal of difference between recognition (have you ever heard of Brand X) and unaided recall (what brands of four-by-four can you name). Sometimes, recognition for a mature brand is not even desirable when unaided recall is low. In fact, brands with high recognition and low recall are termed graveyard brands. Without recall, they are not in the game; their high recognition means they are considered yesterday's news, and thus it is difficult for them to gain visibility and energy.

Because consumers are bombarded every day by more and more marketing messages, the challenge of building awareness and presence – and doing so economically and efficiently – is formidable, especially considering the fragmentation and clutter that exist in mass media. One route to visibility is to extend the brand over product categories. For that reason, firms such as Cadbury, Philips, Sony, Toshiba, and GE have an advantage because wide product scope provides brand exposure. Another route is to go beyond the normal media channels by using event promotions, publicity, sampling, and other attention-grabbing approaches. For example, consider the impact of Red Bull's Flugtag events, Honda's live event ad featuring skydivers spelling the Honda name to launch the new Accord in the UK market, Burger King's £95 burger featuring Wagyu beef and white truffles, and the Nespresso Club programme. All of these firms were able to increase their awareness levels much more effectively than if they had relied only on mass media advertising.

BRAND LOYALTY

An enduring asset for some businesses is the loyalty of the installed customer base (listed as item 10 in Figure 7.3). Competitors may duplicate or surpass a product or service, but they still face the task of making customers switch brands. Brand loyalty, or resistance to switching, can be based on simple habit (there is no motivation to change from the familiar gas station or supermarket), preference (people genuinely like the brand of cake mix or its symbol, perhaps based on use experience over a long time period), or switching costs. Switching costs would be a consideration for a software user, for example, when a substantial investment has already been made in training employees to learn a particular software system.

An existing base of loyal customers provides enormous sustainable competitive advantages. First, it reduces the marketing costs of doing business, as existing customers usually are relatively easy to hold – the familiar is comfortable and reassuring. Keeping existing customers happy and reducing their motivation to change is usually considerably less expensive than trying to reach new customers and persuading them to try another brand. Of course, the higher the loyalty, the easier it is to keep customers happy.

Second, the loyalty of existing customers represents a substantial entry barrier to competitors. Significant resources are required when entering a market in which existing customers must be enticed away from an established brand that they are loyal to or even merely satisfied with. The profit potential for the entrant is thus reduced. For the barrier to be effective, however, potential competitors must know about it; they cannot be allowed to entertain the delusion that customers are vulnerable. Therefore, signals of strong customer loyalty, such as customer interest groups, can be useful.

Third, a relatively large, satisfied customer base provides an image of a brand as an accepted, successful, enduring product that will include service back-up and product improvements. A set of loyal customers also provides reassurance to others. Customers find comfort in the fact that others have selected the brand.

Finally, brand loyalty provides the time to respond to competitive moves – it gives a firm some breathing room. If a competitor develops a superior product, a loyal following will allow the firm the time needed to respond by matching or neutralizing the offering. With a high level of brand loyalty, a firm can allow itself the luxury of pursuing a less-risky follower strategy.

The management of brand loyalty is a key to achieving strategic success. Firms that manage brand loyalty well are likely to:

- Measure the loyalty of existing customers. Measurement should include not only sensitive indicators of satisfaction but also measures of the relationship between the customer and the brand. Is the brand respected? Liked? Trusted? The ultimate measure is, will the customer recommend the brand to others?
- Conduct exit interviews with those who leave the brand, to locate points of vulnerability.
- Have a customer culture whereby people throughout the organization are empowered and motivated to keep the customer happy.
- Measure the lifetime value of a customer so expected future purchases are valued.
- Reward loyal customers with frequent-buyer programmes or special unexpected benefits or premiums.
- Make customers feel that they are part of the organization, perhaps through customer clubs.
- Have continuing communication with customers, using direct mail, the Internet, toll-free numbers, and a solid customer back-up organization.
- Manage customer touchpoints to ensure that the brand does not falter in key contexts.

- Protect the relationship with the loyal customer base during tough economic times when there are pressures on marketing budgets.

BRAND ASSOCIATIONS

The associations attached to a firm and its brands can be key enduring business assets, as they reflect the strategic position of the brand. A brand association is anything that is directly or indirectly linked in the consumer's memory to a brand (see Figure 9.2). Thus, Innocent smoothies could be linked to healthy living, having fun at work answering banana phones, grass and cow vans, helping to meet the five-a-day requirement, smoothies, thickees, and juice. All these associations potentially serve to make Innocent interesting, memorable, and appealing to its customers.

Product attributes and customer benefits are the associations that have obvious relevance because they provide a reason to buy and thus a basis for brand loyalty. Heinz is the slowest-pouring (thickest) ketchup, Absolut is a premium vodka, Skoda is a reliable car priced for value, Zara clothing is stylish and selective, London is a good place to visit and Lidl delivers value. Companies love to make product claims, for good reason. They often engage in shouting matches to convince customers that their offering is superior in some key dimension – Kelloggs Bran Flakes is a high-fibre cereal, or an Airbus plane has the best fuel economy.

There are several problems with such specmanship. First, a position based on some attribute is vulnerable to an innovation that gives your competitor more speed, more fibre, or a greater range. In the words of Regis McKenna, 'You can always get outspeced'.

Second, when firms start a specification shouting match, they all eventually lose credibility. After a while, customers start to doubt whether any aspirin is more effective

Associations	Brands
Attributes/Benefits	Volvo, Crest
Design	Jaguar, Calvin Klein
Systems Solution	Siebel, IBM
Social Programmes	Body Shop, McDonald's
Customer Relationships	Harrods, Ritz Carlton
Niche Specialists	Ferrari, Gold Violin
Quality	Lexus, Hertz
Value	Lide, Hyundai
Product Category	Google, Toyota's Prius
Breadth of Product Line	Amazon, Marriott
Organizational Intangibles	Marks & Spencer, Accenture
Emotional and Self-Expressive Benefits	BMW, Jaguar
The Experience	Blackberry, Heineken
Being Global	Visa, Ford
Being Contemporary	Spotify, Apple
Brand Personality	Mozilla Firefox, Singapore Airlines

Figure 9.2 Brand Associations

or faster acting than another. There have been so many conflicting claims that all of them are discounted.

Third, people do not always make decisions based upon a particular specification. They may feel that small differences in some attribute are not important, or they simply lack the motivation or ability to process information at such a detailed level.

Strong brands go beyond product attributes to develop associations on other dimensions that can be more credible and harder to copy. It is useful to understand some of these other dimensions and learn how they have been used by firms to create customer relationships and points of differentiation.

The value propositions described in the last chapter in addition to attributes or benefits – design, systems solutions, social programmes, customer relationships, niche specialist, quality, and value – are all prominent candidates for actual or aspirational associations. Several additional ones, all with a proven ability to drive successful firms, will be described to provide a feel for the scope of potential associations.

Product Category

The choice of a product category or subcategory to which a business will associate itself can have enormous strategic and tactical implications. Red Bull positioned itself within the energy drink category but associated itself with the energy needs that arise around extreme sports and rave/club culture. Prior to Red Bull, most soft drinks were positioned as wholesome family products, with energy drinks often being promoted by mainstream sports stars. Red Bull's edgier positioning effectively expanded the category, allowing the brand to build a position for itself as a drink for young people both to sustain them through the challenges of their lives and to mix with spirits. In approaching the category in this way, Red Bull avoided battles with direct competitors and enjoyed a significant price premium. LinkedIn positioned itself as a social networking site for business networking. This allowed it to grow and become profitable at a rapid rate. Having created the category, the firm benefited significantly from its leadership.

Maintaining Relevance

As suggested in Chapter 4, the relevance concept can help with the difficult task of managing an evolving category with emerging and receding subcategories. Relevance is, in essence, being perceived as associated with the product category in which the customer is interested. In the Brand Asset Valuator, the product of Young & Rubicam's mammoth study of global brands, relevance was one of four key dimensions identified (along with differentiation, esteem, and knowledge). If a business loses relevance, differentiation may not matter.

The ability of a firm to maintain relevance varies along a spectrum, as shown in Figure 9.3. At one extreme are trend neglectors – firms that miss or misinterpret trends, perhaps because they are too focused on a predetermined business model. Such firms are often characterized as having inadequate strategic analysis capability, organizational inflexibility, and/or a weak brand portfolio strategy; they eventually wake up in surprise to find their products are no longer relevant. At the other end of

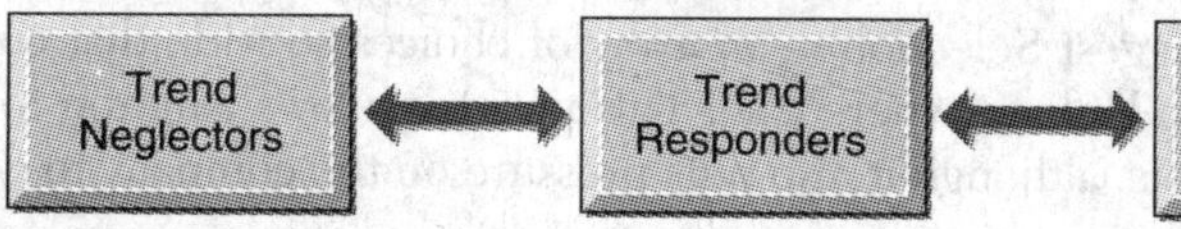

Figure 9.3 Staying Relevant

the spectrum are trend drivers, those firms that actually propel the trends that define the category (or subcategory). In the middle are trend followers, firms that track closely the trends and the evolution of categories and subcategories, making sure that their products stay current.

Virgin Atlantic Airlines, Zara, and Dyson have all been trend drivers. Virgin created a new subcategory by introducing and owning new services such as massage services in first class. Zara responds quickly to customer trends by manufacturing in Europe and designing clothing in-house. Dyson introduced a new suction-enhancing technology into vacuum cleaning that created new interest in the category, drove sales, and allowed Dyson to take the leadership position in many of the geographic markets in which it competes.

Trend responders – those firms that can recognize and evaluate trends, then create and implement a response – can sustain success in dynamic markets. Lego has evolved from being a wooden toy manufacturer in the early 1930s to its now famous brick manufacturing in the late 1940s to today selling video games and theme parks.

Google has evolved from its original position as a search engine to one where it is regarded as the organizer of information, providing access to a wide range of different types of information that was previously unavailable. Fuji Film was quick to adapt to the digital age and became a leader with its Super CCD high-quality image sensor for digital cameras, plus several other products such as digital photo printers.

Being a successful trend responder, however, is not easy. As suggested by Chapter 4, it can be difficult to identify and evaluate trends, separating the trends from the fads. It is also difficult to respond to emerging subcategories, especially if they start small and if the existing business and brand are established. Consider the difficulty that McDonald's, Burger King, KFC, and the other fast food giants have had in responding to the healthy eating trend. They are simply not good at product development and delivery in that arena because it is not in their DNA – they lack the people and culture to be successful. Even worse, their brand becomes a liability as they attempt to change perceptions ingrained by decades of doing what they do. Nevertheless, McDonald's, after several unsuccessful efforts to create salads, broke through with not only salads that worked but healthy desserts for concerned parents and even gourmet coffee to provide an alternative to Starbucks.

Breadth of Product Line

A broad product offering signals substance, acceptance, leadership, and often the convenience of one-stop shopping. For example, the strategic position that drove Amazon's operations and marketing was never about selling books, even at the beginning when it was simply a bookstore (Amazon had the vision to avoid calling itself books.com). Rather, the firm positioned itself as delivering a superior shopping/buying experience based on the 'Earth's Biggest Selection' – an array of choices so wide that customers would have no reason to look anywhere else. This position allows Amazon to enter a variety of product markets, although it also puts pressure on the company to deliver in each venue.

Breadth also works well as a dimension for other firms, such as Volkswagen, Tesco, and Hilti. Even under a strong brand, however, expanding the product offering involves risks. The firm may venture into business areas in which it lacks skills and competencies, the brand might be eroded, and resources needed elsewhere may be absorbed.

Organizational Intangibles

As already noted, attribute and benefit associations can often be easily copied. In contrast, it is difficult to copy an organization, which will be uniquely defined by its values, culture, people, strategy, and programmes. Organizational attributes such as being global (HSBC or British Airways), innovative (Logitech or Samsung), quality driven (Siemens or Patek Philippe), customer driven (Singapore Airlines or Mandarin Oriental Hotels), involved in community or social issues (Timberland or Godrej), or concerned about the environment (DSM or Telefonica) are usually more resistant to competitive claims than product – attribute associations.

A laboratory study of cameras demonstrated the power of an intangible attribute. Customers were shown two camera brands, one of which was positioned as being more technically sophisticated, and the other as easier to use. Detailed specifications of each brand, which were also provided, clearly showed that the easier-to-use brand in fact had superior technology as well. When subjects were shown both brands together, the easy-to-use brand was rated superior on technology by 94% of the subjects. However, when this brand was shown two days after exposure to the supposedly (but not actually) more sophisticated brand, only 36% felt that it had the best technology. Using technology as an abstract attribute dominated the actual specifications.

Emotional and Self-Expressive Benefits

Another way to move beyond attribute/functional claims is to create a position based on emotional or self-expressive benefits.

Emotional benefits relate to the ability of the offering to make the customer feel something during the purchase or use experience. The strongest brands often offer emotional benefits. Thus, a buyer or user can feel:

- safe travelling in a Saab;
- exhilarated while driving a TVR;
- energized while watching YouTube;
- important when shopping at Harrods;
- healthy when drinking Innocent smoothies;
- warm when buying or reading a Hallmark card;
- strong and rugged when driving a Range Rover.

Emotional benefits are all about the 'I feel ...' statement: I feel energized, I feel warm, I feel elegant. To see if an emotional benefit can play a role in differentiating a brand, try the 'I feel' question with customers. If the hard-core loyalists consistently come up with a particular emotional benefit associated with using the branch, then it should be considered as part of the strategic position of the brand.

Self-expressive benefits reflect the ability of the purchase and use of an offering to provide a vehicle by which a person can express him- or herself. To illustrate, a person might express a self-concept of being:

- adventurous or daring by owning Rossignol powder skis;
- hip by wearing Issey Miyake;
- sophisticated by wearing Tod's footwear;
- successful, in control, and a leader by driving a Mercedes;
- frugal and unpretentious by shopping at Aldi;
- competent by making calls using Skype;
- nurturing by buying Danone's Actimel for one's children to drink at school.

Self-expressive benefits are all about the 'I am ...' statement: I am successful, I am young, I am a great athlete. To see if a self-expressive benefit can play a role in differentiating a brand, try the 'I am' question with loyal customers and see if any consistent self-expressive benefits are associated with using the brand.

Contemporary art . Why is some contemporary art sold at astronomical prices? Why would a stuffed dead shark be worth $40 million and hung in the New York Metropolitan Museum? Why would a rectangular set of colour spots created by an artist's staff sell for $600 000? It is not objective quality, for sure. Experts could not agree as to whether a painting resembling a Jackson Pollock drip painting found at a flea market was authentic. Depending on their verdict, the painting would be worth a few thousand or $40 million. The same painting! How does an artist create a brand that can capture such a price premium? The answer is not simple but self-expressive, and social benefits without question play a predominant role.

The Experience

The experience of using the brand could include emotional or self-expressive benefits without any functional advantage, but when an experience combines two or even all three, it is usually broader and more rewarding. The experience at Tiffany's stores around the world includes a host of factors (such as the merchandise, the staff, the ambience, the service, and the sense of occasion) that combine to provide a pleasant, satisfying time and make a statement about shopping and buying at the store. The experience of using a Blackberry combines functional, emotional, and self-expressive benefits to provide a depth of connection that most competitor brands lack.

In addition to the breadth of its offering, Amazon is also positioned with respect to the experience it delivers. Its promise is to create a world-class shopping experience that is both efficient and enjoyable. The fast and easy selection, one-click ordering, special-occasion reminders, safe shopping guarantee, and reliable delivery lie behind the experience Amazon creates. The Amazon experience also provides emotional benefits by offering the excitement of discovering a book, CD, or other gift that is just right (as enhanced by its 'personalize item' recommendation). The Amazon river, representing the ultimate in discovery and adventure, provides an aspirational metaphor. One of the challenges for the Amazon brand is to make sure this emotional aspect is not submerged by the functional benefits the site provides.

Being Global

HSBC is a global financial institution. Visa is a global credit card. Lexus is a global car brand. Being global provides functional benefits in that you can access the services of HSBC or Visa anywhere. It also provides the prestige and assurance that comes from knowing that the firm has the capability of competing successfully throughout the world. Knowing that Lexus is strong in the United States helps it in Europe, where customers might otherwise look at it as a modest player. More information on global associations and strategy is provided in Chapter 13.

Being Contemporary

Most established businesses face the problem of remaining or becoming contemporary. A business with a long heritage is given credit for being reliable, safe, a friend, and even innovative if that is part of its tradition. However, it can also be perceived as 'your father's (or even grandfather's) brand'. The challenge is to have energy, vitality, and relevance in today's marketplace – to be part of the contemporary scene. The answer usually entails breaking out of the functional benefit trap. Approaches to add energy will be explored in Chapter 10.

When the US paper towel brand Bounty wished to enter the fast-growing, private-label-dominated UK market, it used new applications as its vehicle. The unique quality of Bounty was its strength when wet. Bounty used a series of commercials with the endline 'have you tried it wet yet' to emphasize the potential for Bounty to be used differently to other paper towels. The advertising led to paper towels being used for a wider variety of tasks, with more sheets being used each day and growth in the number of sheets used per task.[3]

Brand Personality

As with human beings, a business with a personality tends to be more memorable and better liked than one that is bland, nothing more than the sum of its attributes. And like people, brands can have a variety of personalities, such as being professional and competent (BBC and EDF), upmarket and sophisticated (Prada and Tod's), trustworthy and genuine (*The Financial Times* and Gor-Tex), exciting and daring (Porsche and Diesel), or active and tough (Timberland and Ponsse). Certainly, Ryanair is a brand whose strategic position includes a strong personality.

Vespa has a strong personality reflecting its Italian coolness, freedom seeking, and youthfulness. The experience of riding a Vespa allows people to express their personality, and so, even prior to its relaunch in the United States in 2000, there were two dozen shops dedicated to repairing and renovating old Vespas. In order to drive its sales, Vespa has introduced two new elements to the brand personality. First, working with local government officials to educate them in 'Vespanomics' or the particularly strong environmental logic behind encouraging people to travel by scooter. Second, they have adopted a direct-to-consumer communications approach using a blog, Vespaway, to establish a dialogue with users, potential users, and admirers.[4]

Ryanair is a brand with an exceptionally strong personality with a single message – Ryanair means the cheapest fares. Much of the personality of the brand has been created and exists through the personality of the CEO Micheal O'Leary. There is more to it than this. For many people around Europe, Ryanair is the brand that made flying feasible for them, enabling visits to family friends at a cost that was very affordable. For others, Ryanair is the brand that made owning a holiday home a possibility, as it allowed them to access part of Europe that they previously could not. For yet others, Ryanair has made travel an easy commodity. While the customer service level may not be as in a five-star hotel, when a passenger complies with the rules, travel is easy and people have grown to love the brand and the firm because it delivers exactly what it promises – the cheapest fares.

LYNX

'How do you turn a £2.19 deodorant into a youth icon? Then, how do you keep it there. Just ask Lynx'.[5] Lynx, marketed as Axe in Europe, is Europe's number one deodorant for men. It is Lever's leading male grooming brand and is sold in more than 50 countries. The success of Lynx is down to its ability to capture a particular emotion among its target market of young men. Lynx recognized that young men were more interested in the confidence smelling well gave them when meeting girls than in the functional benefits of freshness that other deodorant brands offered. Thus, Lynx adopted a simple message: 'use Lynx and get the girl'.[6] To execute this theme, Lynx has used both product innovation and advertising to create and sustain its brand equity. Product innovation at Lynx is simple – it offers six varieties of deodorant and introduces a new one each year, with the weakest from the previous year being culled. With constant product innovation, new users and old have ongoing opportunities to engage and re-engage with the brand.[7]

In advertising terms, Lynx has created some of the most iconic advertising of the past 20 years. Although the creative side of Lynx advertising is a vital part of the story, the strategy side is probably more so. Following its introduction in 1985, Lynx used advertising themes that reflected the view of masculinity that prevailed in society at the time. The advertising themes were of man as hero and conqueror and were responsible for the enormous success of the brand at the start of its life. The man got the girl but he did so in a heroic fashion. However, research in the early 1990s showed that Lynx was in danger of becoming the Brut of the 1990s.[8] That is a brand whose understanding of masculinity was far from current and had become a burden. The response from Lynx and its advertising agency was to seek to monitor and update their understanding of masculinity

(*Continued*)

as it evolved. This led Lynx to commercials that mirrored the 'new lads' culture of the mid- to late 1990s, the emergence of lads with girls culture of the late 1990s, and more recent themes such as seduction. Prior to the England versus Sweden game in the 2006 World Cup, Lynx launched its 'Billion' commercial. The ad featured an uncountable number of young women running, swimming, and climbing to get to a fellow alone on a beach spraying himself with two cans of Lynx. The closing headline 'spray more, get more' reflected the current interpretation of 'use Lynx and get the girl'. The ad was featured on the Lynx website and a variety of other websites and became a phenomenon over the summer of 2006.

The benefits of these efforts have been a brand that was launched at a 50% price premium and has managed to maintain that premium. In addition, in econometric modelling, Lynx outsells own-brand products more than threefold, with its price premium retained; if the price were reduced to that of own-label brands, its brand equity would allow it to outsell own labels 4.7-fold.[9] The youth target market presents a particular challenge, as the market must be recaptured every five years or so. In 1990, Lynx was used by 32.7% of 15–19 year olds, in 1996 by 72.1%, and in 2001 by 81.5%,[10] in each case a different cohort of users and in each case a very high level of penetration.

The Lynx case demonstrates the strategic value that building and maintaining brands and creating brand equity confer on the owners of a business. The development of brand image involves the marketer in breathing life into an inanimate product, thereby endowing it with a distinct personality and human characteristics in the eyes of the consumer. Branding results in an invisible, yet magnetic relationship between brand and consumer that must of necessity involve the brand in the world of the consumer. The concept of brands as social signals is now well accepted, with congruity between brand and user self-image regarded as a key motivational factor in consumer choice. So much so that it has been suggested that brands are part of consumers and consumers are part of brands.[11] The case of Lynx demonstrates how a brand can become integral to the life of a consumer, a valuable tool indeed in the creation of competitive advantage.

BRAND IDENTITY

Creating and managing a brand requires a brand strategy, at the heart of which is the *brand identity*, which provides direction, purpose, and meaning for the brand. A brand identity is a set of brand associations that the firm aspires to create or maintain, an aspirational external brand image. These associations represent what the brand aspires to stand for and imply a promise to customers from the organization. Brand identity differs from brand image in that it could include elements that are not present in the current image (you now make trucks as well as cars) or even conflict with it (you aspire to have a quality reputation that is superior to the current perceptions).

The brand identity can best be explained in terms of three steps. These steps assume that a comprehensive strategic analysis has been done. Customer, competitor, and internal analyses are particularly critical to the development of a brand identity.

1. *What the brand stands for.* The first step is to create a set of 6–12 distinct associations that are desired for the brand. The process starts by putting

Value creation	In-depth understanding of customers
Flexible	Close to customers
Resourceful	Team oriented
Dynamic	Partner with customers
Broad capability	Collaborator
Committed to excellence	Open communication
Best-of-breed	Multicultural
World class	Risk-sharing partner
Gets job done	Diversified workforce
Experienced	Technology that works
Confident	Global
Competent	Bold (without arrogance)
Straightforward	World health

Figure 9.4 Partial List of Aspirational Associations for Ajax

down all the associations desired, given what is known about the customers, competitors, and the business strategy going forward. A list of more than two dozen is shown in Figure 9.4 for a business-to-business service company, here termed Ajax. In actuality, the list more often contains 50–100. During this process there is no attempt to zero in on categories of associations, although there is an effort to make sure that organizational intangibles and personality dimensions are at least considered.

These items are then grouped, and each group is given a label. Ajax was created with a set of half a dozen acquisitions, each of which continued to operate somewhat autonomously. It was becoming clear, though, that customers preferred a single-solution firm with broad capabilities. The new Ajax strategy was to orient its service to broad customer solutions and to get its operating units to work together seamlessly. The strategy represented a significant change in culture and operations. With respect to the brand identity, the elements 'partner with customers', 'customized solutions', 'collaborative', and 'close to customers' were clustered and given the name Team Solutions, which became one of eight identity elements. The brand goal was to provide a face to customers that matched this new strategy.

2. *The core identity.* The second step is to prioritize the brand identity elements. The most important and potentially the most impactful are classified as *core identity* elements. The core identity elements will be the primary drivers of the brand-building programmes. They will be the focus of the brand investments, as they are the most critical to the success for the businesses that they are supporting. The balance of the elements are termed the *extended identity.* They serve to help define the brand, make decisions as to what actions and programs are compatible with the brand, and drive minor programs that will have lesser impact and take modest resources.

In developing the core and extended identity, four criteria should guide the process. Identity elements are sought that:

- *Resonate with the target market.* Ultimately the market dictates success, and thus the identity should resonate with customers. It is useful to think in terms of how customers relate to the brand over time rather than simply what drives purchase decisions. Also, consider emotional and self-expressive benefits in addition to functional ones.
- *Differentiate from competitors.* Differentiation is often the key to winning. There should be some points of differentiation throughout the brand identity so that there is always an answer to the question as to how our brand is different.
- *Provide parity where competitors have an advantage that is compelling to customers.* It is not always necessary to be different or better on all dimensions. There may be some dimensions where the goal is simply to be close enough so that this dimension is no longer a reason not to buy the brand. Hyundai need not, for example, be equal to Toyota in quality; it just needs to be close enough for its quality image not to prevent purchase.
- *Reflect the strategy and culture of the business.* Ultimately, the brand needs to enable and support the strategy of the business. Particularly when the strategy represents a change from the status quo, and requires a change in brand image, the brand identity needs to reflect the new strategy. The brand identity should also support and reflect the culture and values of the firm, because it is the organization that has to deliver on the aspirational brand promise.

3. *The brand essence.* The core identity compactly summarizes the brand vision. However, it is often useful to provide even more focus by creating a *brand essence*, a single thought that captures the heart of the brand. The purpose of an essence is to communicate the brand internally. Thus, while there are times when an external tagline, designed to communicate the message of the day externally, can and does represent the essence, that is often not the case. Figure 9.5 shows the final brand identity for Ajax, including the brand essence.

A good brand essence will capture much of the brand identity from a different perspective, will provide a tool to communicate the identity, and will inform and inspire those inside the organization. Consider 'I am', the brand essence of Orange mobile phones in the United Kingdom. This brand essence statement is intended to convey the contemporary relationship between people and their phones. In particular, the role that users play in cocreating the brand experience and the need to feel that they are in control of the brand.

Nescafe's 'coffee at its brightest' brand essence is intended to communicate particularly to younger people, who have developed their relationship with coffee through cafes, and to reassure them that the quality of their coffee experience will not be compromised by using instant.

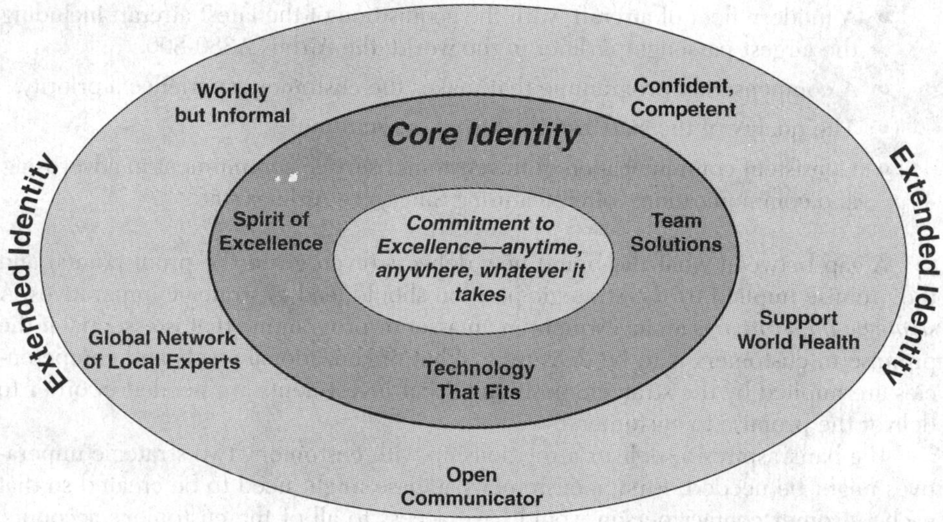

Figure 9.5 The Ajax Brand Identity

A key essence choice is whether to focus on what the brand is or on what it does for customers. The former, such as O2's 'we are better connected' or Audi's 'Vorsprung durch Technik' (Advantage through Technology) would tend to involve functional benefits; the latter, such as L'Oréal's 'because you're worth it' or BMW's 'ultimate driving machine' tend to look to emotional and self-expressive benefits.

Proof Points and Strategic Initiatives

A brand identity should not simply reflect something that appeals to customers. Rather, the firm needs to be willing to invest behind it and create products and programmes that will deliver on the promise. To that end, each identity element should have proof points and/or strategic initiatives associated with it.

Proof points are programmes, initiatives, and assets already in place that provide substance to the strategy position and help communicate what it means. Billabong is a vibrant brand offering clothing and accessories for board sports enthusiasts. Proof points include the brand's Australian heritage of outdoor activities, a flagship store geared to boarding, ongoing acquisition of relevant brands in the category, and association with high-credibility surfers, skateboarders, and other boarders. Singapore Airlines has a customer service position supported by the following proof points:

- A commitment from senior management that strategy decisions will be evaluated in terms of how they impact on customer service.
- A historical reputation for customer service.
- Innovation in service-enhancing technology such as in-flight entertainment and beds in business class.

- A modern fleet of aircraft, with the acquisition of the latest aircraft including the largest passenger airliner in the world, the Airbus A380-800.
- A compensation programme that makes the customer experience a priority.
- The quality of the staff and the hiring programme.
- Consistent communication of the customer service commitment in advertising and communications, often featuring Singapore Airlines staff.

A gap between what the brand now delivers (even given the proof points) and the promise implied by the strategic position should lead to strategic imperatives. A *strategic imperative* is an investment in an asset or programme that is essential if the promise to customers is to be delivered. What organizational assets and competencies are implied by the strategic position? What investments are needed in order to deliver the promise to customers?

If a bank aspires to deliver a relationship with customers, two strategic imperatives might be needed. First, a customer database might need to be created so that each customer contact person would have access to all of the customer's accounts. Second, a programme might be needed to improve the interpersonal skills of customer contact people, including both training and measurement.

The Role of the Brand Identity

The need to articulate a brand identity and position introduces discipline and clarity into the strategy formulation process. The ultimate strategy is usually more precise and elaborated as a result. However, the brand identity and position have other, more explicit roles to play.

One role is to drive and guide strategic initiatives throughout the organization, from operations to product offering to R&D project selection. The overall strategic thrust captured by the identity and position should imply certain initiatives and programmes. For example, given that we want to be an e-business firm, what tools and programmes will customers expect from us? Initiatives and programmes that do not advance the identity and position should be dispensed with.

A second role is to drive the communication programme. A strategic identity and position that truly differentiate the product and resonate with customers will provide not only punch and effectiveness to external communication, but consistency over time because of the long-term perspective.

A third role is to support the expression of the organization's values and culture to employees and business partners. Such internal communication is as vital to success as reaching out to customers. Lynn Upshaw suggests asking employees and business partners two questions:

- Do you know what the business stands for?
- Do you care?

Unless the answers to these questions are yes – that is, employees and business partners understand and believe in the business strategy – the strategy is unlikely to fulfil its potential. Too many businesses drift aimlessly without direction, appearing to stand for nothing in particular. Lacking an organizational sense of soul and a sound strategic position, they always seem to be shouting 'on sale', attached to some deal, or engaging in promiscuous channel expansion.

Multiple Brand Identities

Arbitrarily insisting that a brand identity should apply to all products or market segments can be self-defeating. Rather, consideration should be given to adapting it to each context. One approach is to augment the brand identity to make it appropriate to a specific context. For example, Honda is associated with youth and racing in Japan while being more family-oriented in the United States and being a premium mass-market car in Europe, but all three positions share a focus on quality and motor expertise. Another approach is to define one of the brand identity elements differently in disparate contexts. Quality for Samsung electronics might be different to quality at Samsung Heavy Industries, but high standards apply to both.

The Brand Position

The brand position represents the communication objectives – what parts of the identity are to be actively communicated to the target audience. The conceptualization of a brand position independent of a brand identity frees the latter to become a rich, textured picture of the aspirational brand. The brand identity does not have to be a compact view appropriate to guide communication.

The brand position will be inherently more dynamic than the brand identity. As the strategy and market context evolve and communication objectives are met, new ones become appropriate. A series of four or five positions over many years may be required to achieve the brand identity.

One fundamental choice that strategists often encounter is whether to create a position that is credible or aspirational. In the case of Ajax, the firm's energy and over-the-top quality was legendary and created a value proposition with both functional and emotional components. An associated brand position would be credible, compelling, and relatively easy to implement. However, it would not move the needle as far as supporting the new strategy. A position around collaboration and team solutions, on the other hand, would be on-strategy but would also not be credible for a firm noted as being arrogant and silo driven, and would be expensive and maybe even infeasible. The choice depends on the answers to two questions. Does the firm have programmes in place to deliver on the new promise? Is the market ready to accept the changed firm? If the answer to either question is no, it might be prudent to delay the aspirational position.

Another positioning choice is whether to emphasize points of differentiation or points of parity. The answer will depend on which direction will affect the target market. If the brand has a well-established image on a point of differentiation (such as value for Aldi or safety for Volvo), it may be more effective to attempt to create a point of parity on another dimension that is holding it back (quality for Aldi or styling for Volvo).

KEY LEARNINGS

- Brand equity, a key asset for any business, consists of brand awareness, brand loyalty, and brand associations.
- Awareness provides a sense of familiarity, credibility, and relevance, in that customers are more likely to consider brands that are top-of-mind.
- A core loyal customer base reduces the cost of marketing, provides a barrier to competitors, supports a positive image, and provides time to respond to competitor moves.
- Brand associations can and should go beyond attributes and benefits to include such associations as brand personality, organizational intangibles, and product category associations.
- The brand identity represents aspirational associations. The most important of these, the core identity, should be supported by proof points and/or strategic imperatives and should be the driver of strategic programmes, including product development.
- While the identity represents long-term aspirational associations and is multidimensional, the position represents the short-term communication objectives and is more focused.

FOR DISCUSSION

1. Explain how each of the three brand equity dimensions provides value to the firm. Explain how they provide value to customers.
2. What is the difference between identity and position? Develop alternative positioning statements for Ajax. Include a tagline and the rationale for that tagline.
3. Create a brand identity for Lynx. Are there potential dimensions that are inconsistent with the brand's personality? If so, how is that handled? How has the identity been brought to life? What are the proof points? Why don't more brands emulate Lynx's brand-building programmes?
4. Pick out three brands from a particular industry. How are they positioned? Which is the best in your view? Does that brand's positioning provide any emotional or self-expressive benefits? How would you evaluate each brand's positioning strategy? Hypothesize proof points and strategic imperatives for each brand.
5. Imagine you have been asked to design a concept hotel. Think of themes stimulated by magazines or movies, and discuss how you would design a hotel around each concept. For each theme, choose five words that reflect that theme.

NOTES

1. David A. Aaker, *Managing Brand Equity* , New York, NY, Free Press, 1991, p. 57.
2. Leo Bogart and Charles Lehman, 'What Makes a Brand Name Familiar?', *Journal of Marketing Research* , February 1973, pp. 17–22.
3. Sam Dias and Fiona Keyte, 'How Advertising Caused a Seismic Change in the UK's Use of Paper Towels', IPA Effectiveness Awards, 2004. (www.WARC.com) © 2006 Copyright and database rights owned by WARC.
4. www.Vespa.com
5. Michael Kelly and Matthew Gladstone, 'Lever Faberge – Lynx', Advertising Effectiveness Awards, 2002. (www.WARC.com) © 2006 Copyright and database rights owned by WARC.
6. Michael Kelly and Matthew Gladstone, 'Lever Faberge – Lynx', Advertising Effectiveness Awards, 2002. (www.WARC.com) © 2006 Copyright and database rights owned by WARC.
7. Michael Kelly and Matthew Gladstone, 'Lever Faberge – Lynx', Advertising Effectiveness Awards, 2002. (www.WARC.com) © 2006 Copyright and database rights owned by WARC.
8. Michael Kelly and Matthew Gladstone, 'Lever Faberge – Lynx', Advertising Effectiveness Awards, 2002. (www.WARC.com) © 2006 Copyright and database rights owned by WARC.
9. Michael Kelly and Matthew Gladstone, 'Lever Faberge – Lynx', Advertising Effectiveness Awards, 2002. (www.WARC.com) © 2006 Copyright and database rights owned by WARC.
10. Michael Kelly and Matthew Gladstone, 'Lever Faberge – Lynx', Advertising Effectiveness Awards, 2002. (www.WARC.com) © 2006 Copyright and database rights owned by WARC.
11. Michael Kelly and Matthew Gladstone, 'Lever Faberge – Lynx', Advertising Effectiveness Awards, 2002. (www.WARC.com) © 2006 Copyright and database rights owned by WARC.

CHAPTER TEN

Energizing the Business

It was our duty to expand. Those who cannot or will not join us are to be pitied. What we want to do, we can do and will do, together. A glorious future!
—Ingvar Kamprad, Founder IKEA

Many of the failures are people who did not realize how close to success they were before they gave in.
—Thomas Edison

Where there is no wind, row.
—Portuguese proverb

Businesses need growth, and not only for financial reasons. Certainly shareholders, employees, and partners look to enhance sales and profits. However, growth also introduces vitality to an organization by providing challenges and rewards. An organization that cannot improve and grow may not even be viable. Furthermore, improving performance by cutting costs and downsizing risks the morale of the employees and partners, as well as cutting the muscle needed to create and support growth opportunities.

There are four ways to grow a business, as suggested by Figure 10.1. The first, covered in Chapter 11, is about leveraging the current business. That can mean taking the existing products into new markets, finding new products or services for the existing customer base, or leveraging assets such as brand equity or competencies such as managing the supermarket channel. The second way, introduced in Chapter 12, is to create a new business by finding a white space in the market or by transformational innovation, a business for which a substantial competitive advantage will exist and persist. The third, presented in Chapter 13, entails going global, leveraging the business into new countries to create a broader market or creating new or improved assets and competencies that will lead to sustainable advantage in a global marketplace.

Figure 10.1 Growth Strategies

The fourth route to growth, the subject of this chapter, is to energize the existing business, an attractive growth avenue because an established firm has market and operating experience, assets, competencies, and a customer base on which to build. Developing new products or entering new markets is inherently risky and can stretch the firm in ways that may dilute the existing strategy and culture. An existing business can be energized by:

- innovating to improve the offering;
- energizing the brand and marketing;
- increasing existing customers' usage.

INNOVATING THE OFFERING

The ultimate business energizer is to improve the offering through innovation. Innovation, whether incremental, substantial, or transformational, will serve to create a dynamic around the business.

One focus of innovation can be to improve the customer experience. At the O2 Arena in London, 'O2 Angels' meet and greet customers, answer questions, and solve problems that arise during their visit to the venue. This is quite a unique feature — such venues are often large and impersonal places to visit. Look at all the touchpoints, value each in terms of customer impact and performance, and create programmes to turn problem areas into points of superiority and make them more visible. Exceeding expectations with respect to the value proposition may generate momentum.

A second focus can be to enhance the product through innovation. Tesco has added a variety of businesses, including financial services, telecoms and fuel, to its basic model of selling food in order to drive growth. Such activity provides vitality and credibility to the business. Product innovation involves understanding unmet needs, the organizational support, and the ability to evaluate proposed improvements in terms of customer relevance.

A third approach is to introduce line extensions. New flavours, packaging, sizes or services can add energy, interest, and the creation of new segments. Look for segments that are making do with the current offering and would prefer another option

Consider trends that are leaving your offering behind. Line extensions need to balance their value with the risk that the added cost might become a burden and that customers might rebel over the added confusion and complexity. Colgate made significant gains when it introduced Total, which simplified a purchase decision for consumers faced with a bewildering array of choices for toothpaste.

How can the organization create the sense and substance of continuous innovation rather than sporadic episodes of improvement in the product or service that are quickly copied and blend into the cluttered marketplace, resulting in a transient advantage? A basic answer is to create an organizational culture that builds innovation into the business strategy and views it as a basis for winning over time. That is certainly true for the most innovative companies, as reported by Business Week, Apple, Google, Toyota, Microsoft, Nintendo, IBM, HP, Research in Motion, Nokia, Wal-Mart, Amazon, P&G, Tata, Sony, and Reliance Industries.[1] These and other firms have become skilled in reaching outside their organization to other firms, even firms in other countries, to enhance the ability to innovate. Vodafone has developed a new web portal, betavine, which invites anyone to submit mobile phone applications and to test those submitted by others. While the developer retains the rights to the apps, Vodafone benefits from getting sight of new ideas and identifying possible future collaborators while also keeping a keen eye on the horizon of development.[2] In addition, the firms are good at branding their innovations.

Branding the innovation helps communication, adds credibility, and, most importantly, provides the potential to own an innovation so that it provides a point of differentiation over time. The concept of a branded differentiator provides a guide to branded innovation.[3]

Branded Differentiators

A *branded differentiator* is an actively managed, branded feature, ingredient or technology, service, or programme that creates a meaningful, impactful point of differentiation for a branded offering over an extended time period.

For example, in 1999 the Westin Hotel chain created the Heavenly Bed, a custom-designed mattress set (by Simmons) with 900 coils, a cozy down blanket adapted for climate, a comforter with a crisp duvet, high-quality sheets, and five goosedown pillows. The Heavenly Bed became a branded differentiator in a crowded category in which differentiation was a challenge.

A branded differentiator does not occur simply by slapping a name on a feature. The definition suggests rather demanding criteria that need to be satisfied. In particular, a branded differentiator needs to be meaningful (that is, to matter to customers) and impactful (that is, to make more than a trivial difference). The Heavenly Bed was meaningful in that it was truly a better bed and addressed the heart of a hotel's promise – to provide a good night's sleep. It was also impactful. During the first year of its life, those hotel sites that featured the Heavenly Bed had a 5% increase in customer satisfaction, a noticeable increase in perceptions of cleanliness, room decor, and maintenance, and increased occupancy.

A branded differentiator also needs to warrant active management over time and justify brand-building efforts. It should be a moving target. The Heavenly Bed has received that treatment with an active and growing set of brand-building programmes. The reception to the bed was so strong that Westin starting selling it; in 2004, some 3500 beds were sold. Imagine, selling a hotel bed. Think of the buzz. The concept has been extended to the Heavenly Bath, with dual shower heads plus soap and towels. The Heavenly Online Catalog is a place to connect and order all the branded products.

The Heavenly Bed was developed and owned by Westin. It is not always feasible to develop such products and brands, in part because the time and resources may not be available and in part because it is simply difficult. An alternative is to explore alliances in order to create branded differentiators with instant credibility. The Ford Explorer Eddie Bauer Edition, for example, was an offering that sold more than 1 million vehicles in the United States over two decades. It was successful from the outset because the Eddie Bauer brand (a premium-quality outdoor clothing brand) was established with associations of style, comfort, and the outdoors. Ford never could have achieved that success with its own brand (the Ford Explorer LeatherRide, for example). It would be difficult to imbue such a brand with the self-expressive benefits offered by the Eddie Bauer brand, even if the necessary brand-building resources and time had been available.

An effective differentiator needs to augment or buttress the product with something that is meaningful to the customer and capable of influencing choice and loyalty. Audi's Quattro feature is a four-wheel-drive technology first used in rally cars in the late 1970s but later used in production vehicles. The technology supports a powerful drive, which is much in demand. Relatively few differentiators in the car market have delivered so directly on what they promised for such a long period.

A branded differentiator, as suggested by Figure 10.2 and by the definition, will be either a feature, an ingredient or technology, a service, or a programme affecting the offering. A branded feature, such as BMW's iDrive, often provides a graphic way to signal superior performance. The iDrive system is a single knob controller located in the centre panel that allows the driver to control various systems within the car such as air conditioning and stereo systems.

A branded ingredient (or component or technology) such as Intel Inside, Gore-Tex, or adiPRENE can add credibility even if customers do not understand how the ingredient works, just because someone believed it was worth branding.

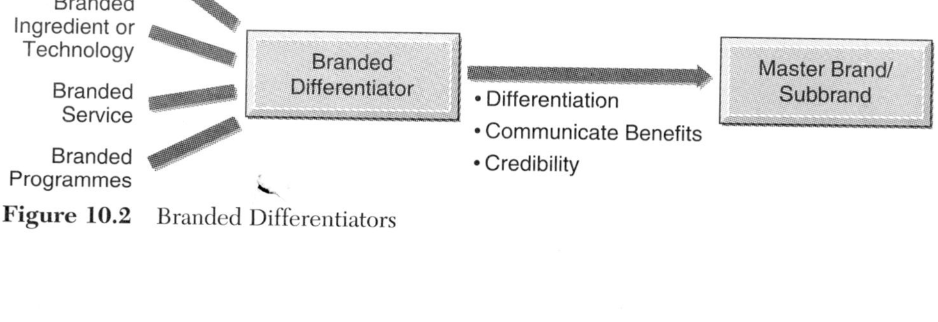

Figure 10.2 Branded Differentiators

A further example of a branded service is the BMW Connected Drive, which provides drivers with information the moment it is required. A branded programme such as the Harley-Davidson Ride Planner can provide a way to deepen customer relationships.

A valued feature, ingredient or technology, service, or programme will serve to differentiate a product, whether or not it is branded. Why brand it? For one reason: a brand can add credibility and legitimacy to a claim. The brand specifically says that the benefit was worth branding, that it is not only meaningful but impactful. The ability of a brand to add credibility was rather dramatically shown in a remarkable study of branded attributes. Carpenter, Glazer, and Nakamoto, three prominent academic researchers, found that the inclusion of a branded attribute (such as 'Alpine Class' fill for a down jacket, 'Authentic Milanese' for pasta, and 'Studio Designed' for compact disc players) dramatically affected customer preference towards premium-priced brands. Respondents were able to justify the higher price because of the branded attributes, even though they had no idea why the attributes were superior.[4]

A second reason is that a brand name makes communication easier. A branded feature such as Oral B's Action Cup provides a way to crystallize feature details, making the feature easier to both understand and remember. Communication is particularly difficult with a service or programme such as iTunes DJ, a feature of iTunes that selects music for you to listen to. For those wishing to listen to music but unsure what to listen to in often vast collections, the service is very welcome. The iTunes DJ brand communicates not only what the service does but also the energy and personality of the brand, what it is. In general, a branded service can help capture the essence and scope of a concept that otherwise could be multidimensional and complex and directed to an audience that simply does not care enough to make any effort.

Finally, brand equity around the point of differentiation creates a basis for a sustainable competitive advantage. A competitor may be able to replicate the feature, ingredient or technology, service, or programme, but if it is branded, they will need to overcome the power of the brand. Other hotels can create great beds and even brand them, but only one hotel will ever have the Heavenly Bed and the authenticity that goes with it. Only one music service has the iTunes DJ. It helps to make the branded differentiation a moving target, continually improving and enhancing it so that copying will be more difficult and the danger of becoming stale will be reduced.

Amazon developed a powerful feature, the ability to recommend books, or whatever, on the basis of a customer's interests as reflected by his or her purchase history and the purchase history of those that bought similar offerings. But they never branded it. How tragic is that? As a result, the feature basically became a commodity that is an expected feature of many e-commerce sites. If Amazon had branded it and then actively managed that brand, improving the feature over time, it would have become a lasting point of differentiation that today would be invaluable. They missed a golden opportunity. They did not make that same mistake with One-Click, a branded service that plays a key role in defining Amazon in what has become a messy marketplace.

CREATIVE THINKING METHODS

Not all growth strategies are obvious. In fact, the obvious ones are likely to be marginal in terms of likely success and impact, so it is useful to look for breakthrough ideas. Methods and concepts of creative thinking can help in this process. Among the guidelines suggested most often are the following:

- Pursue creative thinking in groups, as multiple perspectives and backgrounds can stimulate unexpected results.
- Begin with warm-up exercises that break down inhibitions. To make whimsy acceptable, for example, ask individuals to identify what animal expresses their personality and to imitate the sound made by that animal. To stretch minds, ask someone to start a story based on two random words (e.g. *blue* and *sail*), then ask the group to create a position for a brand based on that story.
- Focus on a particular task, such as how to build or exploit an asset (a brand name, for example) or a competence (such as the ability to design colourful plastic items).
- Develop options without judging them. Discipline in avoiding evaluation while generating alternatives is a key to creative thinking.
- Engage in lateral thinking to change the perspective of the problem. Make a list of associations with the brand or the use setting and take sets of two as a point of departure, the more incongruous the fit the better, or simply pick a random object (such as *tiger* or the Sydney Opera House) to stimulate a new line of thought.
- Evaluate the options based on potential impact without regard to how feasible they are.
- Engage in a second stage of creative thinking aimed at improving the success chances of an attractive option – possibly one with high potential impact that seems too expensive or too difficult to implement.
- Evaluate the final choices not just rationally ('What do the facts say?') but emotionally ('What does your gut say?').
- Create an action plan to go forward.

ENERGIZE THE BRAND AND MARKETING

The best way to energize a business is by improving the offering through innovation. However, that route is not always open. In many cases, successful innovations, even healthy efforts, budgets, and partners, are elusive. And innovations that really make a difference, that rise above those that simply maintain a market position, are even rarer. Furthermore, some businesses compete in product categories that are either mature or boring or both. If you make hot dogs or marketing insurance, it is hard to conceive of new offerings that are going to energize the marketplace. So the need then is to look beyond the offering for ways to make the brand interesting, involving, dynamic, enthusiastic, and even a topic of conversation. Some suggestions:

- *Involve the customer.* Programmes that involve the customer elevate the energy level of the brand and business. ASDA is embracing the era of 'democratic consumerism' with three initiatives: 'Chosen by You', an opportunity for consumers to offer views on the design of clothing and household items for the following season; 'Bright Ideas', a cash reward scheme with participants receiving 5% of any money saved by the retailer; the 'Aisle Spy' blog, where ASDA buyers and staff will regularly post updates on their activities and invite customer responses.[5] Peugeot's My Peugeot website invites existing customers to register to find out more about the features of their car and new information about Peugeot, and to be reminded of servicing. BMW has tracks allowing you to drive their cars.
- *Go retail.* A brand can tell its story best if it can control the context. The Apple store is a good part of the success of its products and brand because it presents the Apple line in a way that is completely on-brand. The power of Apple stores in driving the brand is best demonstrated by the announcement by Microsoft in 2009 that it was to open a chain of branded stores. Brands such as Diesel, Prada, and Chinese sports brand Li Ning use flagship stores in major cities around the world to communicate core brand values to customers in a controlled and authentic fashion. Latest products and promotions will often appear in these stores first.
- *Publicity events.* Publicity events can be a way to gain visibility and provoke conversation. Consider the Red Bull Flugtag competition which invites participants to fly their home-made aircraft off a pier, or when Rynair sent a tank to easyJet headquarters, declaring war on its competitor's prices, or Lotus Cars' 2008 'faceless people' stunt which saw people who looked to have no faces turning up at prominent summer events in London. The message to consumers was that you are nobody until you own a Lotus. In each case, millions were exposed to the brand in such a way as to emphasize its connection and vitality.
- *Promotions to attract new customers.* While existing customers may view the brand as old hat, new customers not only provide sales growth but also new eyes. It is, of course, difficult to attract customers, particularly if the brand is already well known. BMWFilms and later BMW Audibooks were both particularly intended to attract non-users to the brand and to provide them with an alternative view of the brand experience. BMWFilms had more than 100 million viewers between 2001 and 2005, when the movies were officially withdrawn from the BMW site. These films still remain popular on Internet sites.

Another approach, very different to trying to make the brand or business interesting or involving, is to find something with energy, attach your brand to it, and build a marketing programme around the connection. Find a branded energizer.

Branded Energizers

A *branded energizer* is a branded product, promotion, sponsorship, symbol, programme, or other entity that by association significantly enhances and energizes a target brand. The branded energizer and its association with the target brand are actively managed over an extended time period.

As Figure 10.3 and the definition suggest, a branded energizer can be a wide variety of branded entities and should have several characteristics. First, a branded energizer should itself have energy and vitality as opposed to being lethargic. An effective branded energizer should fare well when asked whether it would be described as being:

- interesting versus stale;
- youthful versus mature;
- interesting versus boring;
- dynamic versus unchanging;
- contemporary versus traditional;
- assertive versus passive;
- involving versus separated.

Second, the branded energizer needs to be connected to the master brand, even if, unlike a branded differentiator, it is not part of the master brand offering and does not promise any functional benefits. This connection task can be difficult and expensive.

One connection route is to use a subbrand such as Ronald McDonald House, where the master brand has a connection in the name. A second is to select a programme or activity that is so 'on-brand' that it makes the link easier to establish. A baby-oriented programme would require little effort to connect to Gerber, Nutricia, Milupa, or Cow and Gate. A third is simply to forge the link by consistently building it over time with significant link-building resources.

Third, a branded energizer should significantly enhance as well as energize the target brand and should not detract or damage the brand by being 'off-brand' or making

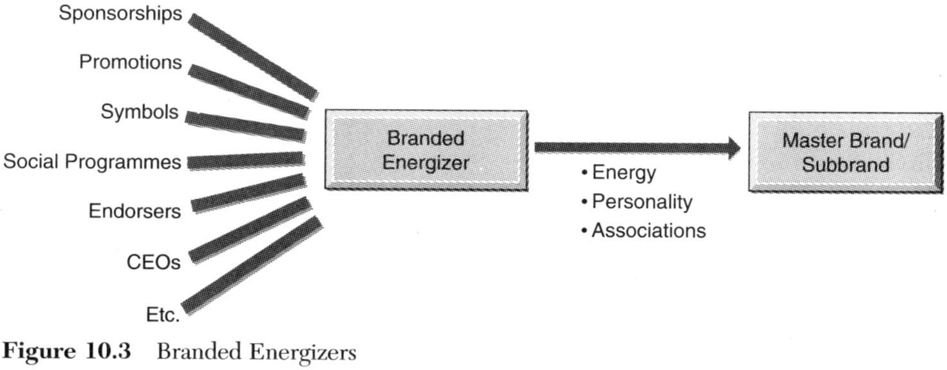

Figure 10.3 Branded Energizers

customers uncomfortable. Offbeat, underdog brands such as Red Bull, Innocent, and easyJet, which are perceived as unpredictable to begin with, have more leeway. 'Senior' brands, in contrast, can develop branded energizers that are edgier than the parent brand but have a lot of options foreclosed.

Fourth, the problems of finding and managing internal branded energizers leads firms to look outside the organization. The challenge is to find an external energizer brand that is linked into the lifestyle of customers, that will have the required associations to energize and enhance, that is not tied to competitors, that can be linked to the target brand, and that represents a manageable alliance. The task takes discipline and creativity.

Fifth, branded energizers (like branded differentiators) represent a long-term commitment; the brands involved should be expected to have a long life and merit brand-building investments. If the energizers are internally developed, the cost of brand-building will have to be amortized over a long enough period to make it worthwhile. If they are externally sourced, the cost and effort of linking them to the parent brand will take time as well. And they need to be actively managed over time so that they can continue to be successful in their roles. The concepts of branded energizers and differentiators do *not* provide a rationale to add brands indiscriminately.

There are many types of branded energizer. Some of the most useful include sponsorships, symbols, endorsers, promotions, programmes, and even CEOs.

Branded Sponsorships

The right sponsorship, handled well, can energize a brand and create strong relationships with customers. In the United Kingdom, O2 has effectively used sponsorship to achieve a variety of marketing objectives.[6] Early in its life, sports sponsorship was very effective in building awareness of the O2 brand. However, in 2006 there was a concern that mobile phones were becoming a commodity, and that its brand could be drawn into a no-win battle against a number of aggressive competitors. To head this off, the firm changed its objectives and set out to be not only the leading mobile phone brand but also one of the overall most loved brands in the United Kingdom. There was also a need for the brand to be sufficiently large to cope with the convergence of technology, content (particularly music), and communication. To achieve this objective, O2 developed a sponsorship concept involving the rebranding of the Millennium Dome in London as the O2 Arena. Working with the owners of the venue, they designed an exceptional customer experience, encouraged people to come to the O2 before concerts to soak up the atmosphere, and selected great acts and events to feature there. This resulted in the O2 brand being raised above the mobile phone category and in customers being allowed to have an in-depth interaction with the brand. The brand thus moved significantly up the list of most loved brands in the United Kingdom.

When E.ON entered the UK energy market, it had strong brand values that committed it to changing energy use for the better. As part of its campaign, it began sponsoring the FA Cup in England, perhaps the most famous cup competition in club football in the world. Its challenge was to use this sponsorship to achieve its objective of changing how energy was used. To achieve this, it developed the 'carbonfootyprint' campaign, which invited football fans to commit themselves to making a series of energy-saving measures on a website of the same name. Prizes were offered for those who entered. As the FA Cup competition progressed, E.ON intensified its advertising. The result was more than 160 000 pledges of change. The company estimates that the result was a saving of 2200 tons of CO_2.[7]

A sponsorship can provide the ultimate in relevance, the movement of a brand upwards into an acceptable if not into a leadership position. A software firm trying unsuccessfully to make a dent into the European market became a perceived leader in a few months when it sponsored one of the top three bicycle racing teams. Part of Samsung's breakthrough from being just another Korean price brand to becoming a global brand was its sponsorship of the Olympics. It says so much about the brand, so much more than product advertising could ever say. Tracking data confirm that well-conceived and well-managed sponsorships can make a difference. The Visa lead in perceived credit card superiority went from 15 percentage points prior to the Olympics to 30 points during the Olympics and to 20 points one month after – huge movements in what are normally very stable attitudes.[8]

A significant problem with sponsorship – indeed, with any external branded energizer – is linking it to the brand. DDB Needham's Sponsor-Watch, which measures such linkage, has shown that sponsorship confusion is common.[9] Of the 102 official Olympic sponsors tracked since 1984, only about half have built a link (defined as having sponsor awareness of at least 15% and at least 10% higher than that of a competitor who was not a sponsor, hardly demanding criteria). Those successful at creating links, such as Visa and Samsung, surround the sponsorship with a host of brand-driven activities including promotions, publicity events, website content, newsletters, and advertising over an extended time period.

Although most sponsorships are external to the firm, there are cases of internally controlled sponsorships. Taking place in different cities around the world, the Adidas Streetball Challenge is a branded weekend event centred around local three-person basketball tournaments and featuring free-throw competitions, a street dance, graffiti events, and extreme sports demonstrations, all accompanied with live music from bands from the hip-hop and rap scenes. The Challenge was right in the sweet spot of target customers – a party. And it was connected to Adidas by its brand and supporting signage and Adidas-supplied caps and jackets. It revitalized Adidas at a critical time in its history. Owning a sponsorship means that the cost going forward is both controllable and predictable and even can evolve over time.

Endorsers

A brand may lack energy, but there are plenty of personalities who are contemporary, on-brand, energetic, and interesting. Football players such as Fernando Torres of Liverpool FC, Kaka of Real Madrid, and Messi of Barcelona lend their credibility as athletes and their energy and aura as winners to a range of brands including sportswear, watches, financial services, and charitable activities. Some sporting brands use their relationship with sports starts to name products after them, such as the Messi Adidas F50.9 football boot. Pepsi uses a number of the leading football players (Torres, Messi, Henry, Lampard, Fabregas, Kaka) from a variety of clubs and countries in its footvolley advertisement and in a supporting on-line footvolley game. Selecting and engaging an endorser is a critical first step in creating a strategic brand energizer. There are a host of considerations. An endorser target should have:

- An appealing image:
  - visible among the target audience (low visibility will limit the impact);
  - attractive, liked (simple liking can and does get transferred to the endorsed brand);
  - sincere (will there be a feeling that the endorser is doing it for money and lacks a sincere belief in the product?);
  - fresh, not overexposed (an endorser's impact can be diluted by overexposure as an endorser).
- On-brand associations:
  - matching the brand identity goals;
  - a natural match to the brand (does the link make sense?);
  - confidence that the positive associations can be leveraged and that the negative ones can be managed.
- Potential for a long-term relationship. How long will the endorser have the desired associations and how likely will it be that a compatible relationship will endure? A hot personality may not always be the one that will wear well. Tiger Woods has been associated with many of his brands for over 10 years.
- Potential to create programmes surrounding the endorser.
- Cost effectiveness and availability, which needs to take into account the cost of the programmes surrounding the endorser.

Branded Promotional Activities

Innocent smoothies have used branded vehicles as promotional devices. Most famous among these is their 'herd' of cow vans, painted in cow colours, each van coming with eyelashes and tails, and they can all moo. The company also operates dancing grass vans, which are grass-covered vans that dance when they are parked. They have windows on the side that allow drinks to be distributed directly from them. These vans generate a unique excitement about the brand while they go about their daily tasks of delivery and collection, and also when they turn up at events. Cow vans are branded individually, and the website features individually named vans (e.g. Pat) and identifies their variety (e.g. Lancashire shorthorn).

Memorable Branded Symbols

Brands that are blessed with strong relevant symbols, such as Ferrari's black stallion, Churchill Insurance's British bulldog (also called Churchill), or the Michelin man, can actively manage and use the symbols to become energizer brands. Such symbols can give a personality to even the blandest of brands. They can also suggest attributes.

Symbols can have a dramatic effect on a brand, particularly if that symbol has a humorous personality. Most competitors are serious about their offerings, and a business that takes itself lightly will often stand out. This is especially true in the insurance industry.

UK insurance company Comparethemarket.com was a late entrant into a mature market and was faced with the difficult task of trying to build traffic to its insurance comparison website. To achieve this objective, it introduced an entrepreneurial Russian meerkat, Aleksandr Orlov, as a brand symbol. Aleksandr wears a red velvet dressing gown and a cravat in advertising, where he owns a website, comparethemeerkat.com, and is frustrated in his attempts to redirect consumers to the comparethemarket.com website when they mistakenly visit his. In a TV ad, he explains how consumers continue to make the mistake and explains the obvious differences between the two. His closing catchphrase, 'Simples!', is fast becoming an iconic brand representation. Such has been the impact of the meerkat that competitors in the UK market have cited Alexandr as a challenge to their business and an explanation for their own falls in market share and profits.

It is important to understand the role of the symbol. Is it to create a personality? To suggest or reinforce associations? To be a vehicle to inject humour and likeability into an otherwise bland and uninteresting message? To create interest and visibility, like the duck has done for Aflac? With the role in mind, it is possible proactively to look for or develop the right one.

Branded Social Programmes

Branded social programmes can pay off by providing the foundation of a customer relationship based on trust and respect. However, it can also provide energy by generating interesting ideas and programmes and even passion, tangible results, and opportunities for customer involvement. Consider the energy created by the Avon Breast Cancer Crusade in the United States with its signature Avon Walk for Breast Cancer, a programme with substance (they have raised over US$ 550 million for the fight against breast cancer) and incredible involvement not only with the participants of the walks but also with the family members and sponsors as well. That interest and energy could never have been created by Avon products, however different they might be. And it is branded as Avon, which means that its track record is linked to Avon.

Creating branded social programmes can effectively be costless in that existing philanthropy dollars that are being spent without focus or impact can be diverted into branded social programmes. However, they are also extremely hard to generate; there are firms that would like to create and be involved in such programmes but simply cannot come up with one. Kellie McElhaney, the director of the Center for Responsible Business at the Haas School at UC Berkeley, has suggested several principles as a guide to action:[10]

- *Know thyself.* The goal is to create branded programmes that are authentic and effective. Ideally, they should support the business strategy, draw on firm assets and competences, and enhance the image of the brand. This means that the firm should address very basic questions as to what it is, its strengths and weaknesses, and what it wants to stand for.

- *Get a good fit.* Being authentic, being connected to the programme, and being effective will all be easier if there is a fit. Samsung donated its screen in Piccadilly Circus to the European Breast Cancer Campaign. The screen was used to feature younger women who had been diagnosed with breast cancer and to encourage traffic to the campaign website. Such activity hits on a key concern of Samsung's target market and reflects a relationship with its customers that goes beyond product. Danone, Areva, and Schneider Electric have cooperated to deliver a 'Diversity Day' to educate aspiring human resource managers about the value and importance of managing diversity. At the end of the day, students had the opportunity to make suggestions to the firms on how they could meet their own challenges of diversity.
- *Brand it.* If the programme has a strong visible brand, the people will be much more likely to learn and remember. Whirlpool is linked to the Habitat for Humanity programme of building homes for the less fortunate, a strong brand. Another challenge is to link the programme brand to the corporate brand. In the case of Proctor & Gamble, they have developed the P&G Live, Learn, and Thrive initiative, which has a single cause of improving the lives of children aged 0–13. This is achieved by contributing P&G resources and expertise to a number of initiatives. Most prominent among these is a commitment to provide 4 billion litres of clean drinking water to children in the developing world by 2012.
- *Create emotional connection.* An emotional connection in general communicates much more strongly than does a set of facts and logic. The message is punchier and simpler. Furthermore, an emotional connection will tend to enhance the relationship between the brand to which it is attached and the customer. The on-line films that supported the Dove Real Beauty campaign each featured the impact of the global industry on young girls and women, triggering a strong emotional response.
- *Communicate the programme.* There are a host of companies that are spending real money on programmes that are unknown to their customers and, often, even to their employees. To achieve its objectives of advancing a social cause, energizing the employees, and enhancing the reputation of a corporate brand, the programme needs to be communicated. That involves access to the right set of vehicles including the website, social technology, PR, and active employees. Beware of making it too complex, too detailed, and too quantitative. Simple with understandable symbols, taglines, and stories is what is needed. Metaphors can help – too much CO_2, for example, might be likened to a bath now half-full that will eventually overflow.
- *Involve the customers.* Involvement is the ultimate way to gain supporters and advocates. Method, a maker of environmentally safe cleaning products, has a brand ambassador programme where customers that sign on will get

products and T-shirts and information about why their friends should use the product. The Marks & Spencer Plan A programme provides customers with a range of actions that they could also take to make a contribution to environmental improvement.

Branded CEOs

Some firms have branded CEOs who can serve to capture and magnify the energy in the brand, or even create energy that can be transferred to the brand. Wee Cho Yaw, chairman of the United Overseas Bank Group, personifies the work ethic and growth ambitions of the company, as well as its commitment to the community. Michael O'Leary's robust statements and assertive personality have played a significant role in changing the airline industry in Europe and establishing Ryanair as the leading low-cost carrier. Terry Leahy, CEO of Tesco, personifies the Tesco brand with his commitment to meeting and understanding customers. Steve Jobs and Bill Gates have driven much of the energy of Apple and Microsoft with their visible thought leadership. The right CEO with the right message can often create news with credibility and has the advantage of being able to access media. To be an energizer, however, the CEO should have energy with respect to ideas, a distinctive personality, and be around for a long enough time period to become a recognized representative of the brand.

The Need for Energy

Relevance and differentiation have long been considered the basis of success for a brand. But recent studies involving the mammoth Y&R's Brand Asset Valuator (BAV) database – 70 brand metrics for each of 40 000 brands spread over 44 countries – have found that another component is needed – energy.[11] An analysis of the total database from 1993 to 2007 showed that brand equities, as measured by trustworthiness, esteem, perceived quality, and awareness, have been falling sharply over the years. For example, in the last 12 years, trustworthiness dropped nearly 50%, esteem fell by 12%, brand quality perceptions fell by 24%, and, remarkably, even awareness fell by 24%. Brands with energy remained healthy and retained their ability to drive financial return.

In fact, nearly all brands need energy, especially the traditional brands of the world such as Vodafone, Renault, Cadbury, Sunbeam Australia, Sony, and Nestlé, who are usually portrayed as being reliable, honest, dependable, assessable, and often innovative as well. But they often struggle with impressions that they are old-fashioned, out of touch, and boring, an impression that can affect their relevance for some segments. The remedy for this all too common profile is to inject energy and vitality. The need for energy for mature, respected brands is especially true for the key younger segment, the lifeblood of the future.

INCREASING THE USAGE OF EXISTING CUSTOMERS

Attempts to increase market share will very likely affect competitors directly and therefore precipitate competitor responses. An alternative, attempting to increase usage among current customers, is usually less threatening to competitors.

When developing programmes to increase usage, it is useful to begin by asking some fundamental questions about the user and the consumption system in which the product is embedded. Why isn't the product or service used more? What are the barriers to increased use? Who are the light users, and can they be influenced to use more? What about the heavy users?

Greater usage can be precipitated in two ways: by increasing either the frequency of use or the quantity used. In either case, there are several approaches that can be effective. All are based on becoming obsessed with what stimulates use and the use experience itself.

Motivate Heavy Users to Use More

Heavy users are usually the most fruitful target. It is often easier to get a holder of two football season tickets to buy four or six than it is to get an occasional attendee of games to buy two. It is helpful to look at the extra-heavy user subsegment – special treatment might solidify and expand usage by a substantial amount. Examples include the special services offered to British Airways Executive Club gold members, including lounge access even when not flying BA, complimentary upgrades for the members and a guest, and reservation assurance guaranteeing access to BA flights. Many firms own premium boxes at elite sporting and cultural venues such as Wembley, Santiago Bernabéu, and Sydney Opera House.

Make the Use Easier

Asking why customers do not use a product or service more often can lead to approaches that make the product easier to use. For example, disposable plates and cups or paper-towel dispensers encourage use by reducing the usage effort. Packages that can be placed directly in a microwave make usage more convenient. An on-line reservation service can help those who must select a hotel or similar service. Ready-to-cook foods, pizzas, salads, speciality breads, dips, pasta, soups, sauces, and prepared fruits all serve as examples of product modifications that increased consumption by making usage more convenient.

Provide Incentives

Incentives can be provided to increase consumption frequency. Promotions such as double-mileage trips offered by airlines with frequent-flyer plans can increase usage. A fast food restaurant might offer a large drink at a discounted price if it is purchased with a meal. A challenge is to structure the incentive so that usage is increased without creating a vehicle for debilitating price competition. Price incentives, such as two for the price of one, can be effective, but they may also stimulate price retaliation.

Remove or Reduce the Reasons Not to Buy

A business often reaches a ceiling because there are potential buyers who have a reason not to buy or to buy more. Denby Pottery's premium image in the tableware market, while competitive, also meant that the product was not used regularly and the long replacement cycle was retarding sales. Worse, buyers bought different brands for everyday use. To address this, Denby repositioned the product for everyday use. Advertisements and the firm's website showed Denby with the slogan 'love food, love Denby' and with the tableware being used with everyday foods such as chips. During the recession following the 2008 financial crisis, Hyundai addressed the problem of job insecurity with the breathtaking offer to buy back a car if the buyer lost his or her job.

Provide Reminder Communications

For some use contexts, awareness or recall of a brand is the driving force. People who know about a brand and its use may not think to use it on particular occasions without reminders.

Reminder communication may be necessary. Thedoghouse.co.uk offers customers the opportunity to be reminded of important dates, birthdays, and anniversaries, as well as the opportunity to buy gifts for the occasion. Other companies try to use communications to encourage use of products that are easily overlooked. For example, the Fresh Food Company is a UK-based organic foods provider that provides information on produce that is in season and a cookbook that supports the use of organic produce.

Position for Regular or Frequent Use

Provide a reason for more frequent use. On websites, what works is to have information that is frequently updated. People go to Timesofindia.indiatimes.com, BBC.co.uk, Guardian Unlimited, or elpais.es to see the latest headlines or catch up on their favourite football team, as often as every few minutes when important things are happening. Other incentives might include a new cartoon each day (the website of the *Daily Telegraph* drives traffic to its website each day by making its cartoons Alex and Matt available) or a best-practices bulletin board at a brand consulting site. The image of a product can change from that of occasional to frequent usage by a repositioning campaign. For example, Kellogg's Special K has used the Special K Challenge to increase the frequency of usage of its product. Similarly, Danone has

Strategy	Examples
Motivate heavy users to use more	Perks with more season tickets
Make the use easier	Microwaveable containers
Provide incentives	Frequent flyer miles
Remove or reduce reasons not to buy	Gentle shampoo for frequent use
Provide reminder communication	E-mail birthday reminder
Position for regular use	Floss after meals
Find new uses	Snowmobiles for delivery

Figure 10.4 Increasing Usage in Existing Product Markets

invited consumers to use its Activia yogurt daily for two weeks to reduce digestive discomfort. The use of programmes such as the MANGO Girls Book Club UK, CD clubs, Beer of the Month Club, DVD clubs, and flower-of-the-month or fruit-of-the-month delivery can turn infrequent purchasers into regular ones. Other ideas are included in Figure 10.4.

Find New Uses

The detection and exploitation of a new functional use for a brand can rejuvenate a business that has been considered a has-been for years. A classic story is that of Viagra, which was originally developed as a drug to deal with blood pressure and angina. Initial trials suggested that its maximum efficacy was in dealing with erectile dysfunction, rather than its intended use, and so a blockbuster drug with sales in its first two years in excess of US$ 1 billion was born. Another classic story is that of Arm & Hammer baking soda, which saw annual sales grow 10-fold by persuading people to use its product as a refrigerator deodorizer. An initial 14-month advertising campaign boosted its use as a deodorizer from 1 to 57%. The brand subsequently was extended into other deodorizer products, dentifrices, and laundry detergent. A chemical process used in oil fields to separate waste from oil found a new application when it was applied to water plants to eliminate unwanted oil. Kraft encouraged people to use cream cheese, stuck in the bagels-for-breakfast slot, with crackers or celery as a snack.

New uses can best be identified by conducting market research to determine exactly how customers use a brand. From the set of uses that emerge, several can be selected to pursue. Customer application tracking allowed the manufacturer of a heat rub to learn that much of its volume was going towards arthritis sufferers. The result was the development of a separate marketing strategy and a wave of growth. Another tactic is to look at the applications of competing products. Britvic has a long history as a brand leader and innovator in the mixers and juices sold in pubs. In response to a demand from consumers for healthy drinks and from publicans for premium juice brands, Britvic has launched a range of premium 100% juices, Britvic Squeezed Orange Juice and Britvic Pressed Apple Juice. In the confectionery market, one countertrend to health concerns has been for products that afford consumers the opportunity for indulgence products. In response, Nestlé has launched Aero Chocolate Truffle, and Mars offers its Galaxy range.

Sometimes, a large payoff will result for a firm that can provide applications not currently in general use. Thus, surveys of current applications may be inadequate. Technology firms, such as Alltech and Amersham, sponsor forums and conferences for scientists, to encourage them to develop new applications of their products in scientific research. For a product that can be used in many ways, such as stick-on labels, it might be worthwhile to conduct formal brainstorming sessions or other creative exercises.

If some application area is uncovered that could create substantial sales, it needs to be evaluated. Consideration needs to be given to the possibility that a competitor will take over an application area, whether through product improvement, heavy advertising, or engaging in price warfare. Can the brand achieve a sustainable advantage in its new application to justify building the business? Ocean Spray is associated with cranberries, which might protect its entry into a cranberry snack, but the firm's name will be less helpful in a processed application such as biscuits or cereals.

KEY LEARNINGS

- Energizing an existing business is a fruitful source of growth because it avoids the risks of venturing into new competitive arenas requiring new assets and competences.
- Improving the offering through innovation is always the best route to growth and profitability. However, innovations can represent short-lived advantages unless branded. A branded differentiator is an actively managed, branded feature, ingredient or technology, service, or programme that creates a meaningful, impactful point of differentiation for a branded offering over an extended time period.
- Sometimes innovation is not feasible, and then energizing the brand/marketing or creating a branded energizer is the best option. A branded energizer is a branded product, promotion, sponsorship, symbol, programme, or other entity that by association significantly enhances and energizes a target brand – the branded energizer and its association with the target brand are actively managed over an extended time period.
- Growth less vulnerable to competitive response can also come from increasing product usage by motivating heavy users to use more, making the use easier with reduced undesirable consequences, providing usage incentives, reminder communications, positioning for frequent use, and finding new use.

FOR DISCUSSION

1. Using the creative thinking guidelines, think about how you would increase the usage of products if you were the managers of:
   (a) Walkers Crisps;
   (b) Skoda cars;
   (c) Zara fashions.
2. Think of some highly differentiated brands. Do they have branded differentiators? If not, how did they achieve differentiation? Will it be lasting?
3. Think of some branded differentiators. How differentiated are they? Do the customers care? Are they impactful? Have they been managed well over time? Do they have legs?

4. Think of some brands that have high energy. What gives them that energy? Will that continue into the future?
5. Think of some brands that have branded energizers that made a difference. Evaluate them in terms of whether they are 'on-brand', energetic, and linked to the master brand.

NOTES

1. 'Do Ideas Cost Too Much', *Business Week*, 20 April 2009, pp. 46–47.
2. 'Vodafone: Embracing Open Source With Open Arms', *Business Week*, 9 April 2009.
3. Branded differentiators and branded energizers are introduced and discussed in more detail in David Aaker, *Brand Portfolio Strategy*, New York, NY, The Free Press, 2005.
4. Gregory S. Carpenter, Rashi Glazer, and Kent Nakamoto, 'Meaningful Brands from Meaningless Differentiation: the Dependence on Irrelevant Attributes', *Journal of Marketing Research*, August 1994, pp. 339–350.
5. 'ASDA Explains its Bold Attempt to Involve Customers in Decision-Making', *Marketing*, 6 October 2009, available at: http://www.marketingmagazine.co.uk/news/943449/ASDA-explains-its-bold-attempt-involve-customers-decision-making?DCMP=ILC-SEARCH (accessed 10 October 2009).
6. Naana Orleans-Amissah, Sophie Maunder-Allan, Paul Feldwick and Lousie Cook, 'The O2 – A Blueprint for 21st Century Sponsorship', Institute of Practitioners in Advertising, IPA Awards 2008. © 2009 Copyright and database rights owned by WARC.
7. 'Green Shoots, Green Scores! How E.ON got soccer fans to change their environmental footprint, WARC exclusive, June 2008 (accessed 10 October 2009). © 2009 Copyright and database rights owned by WARC.
8. James Crimmins and Martin Horn, 'Sponsorship: from Management Ego Trip to Marketing Success', *Journal of Advertising Research*, July—August 1996, pp. 11–21.
9. James Crimmins and Martin Horn, 'Sponsorship: from Management Ego Trip to Marketing Success', *Journal of Advertising Research*, July—August 1996, pp. 11–21.
10. Kellie A. McElhaney, *Just Good Business*, San Francisco, CA, Berriett-Koehler Publishers, 2008.
11. John Gerzema and Ed Lebar, *The Brand Bubble*, San Francisco, CA, Jossey-Bass, 2008, Chapters 1 and 2.

CHAPTER ELEVEN

Leveraging the Business

Results are gained by exploiting opportunities, not by solving problems.
—Peter Drucker

Always think outside the box and embrace opportunities that appear, wherever they might be.
—Lakshmi Mittal

The most dangerous moment comes with victory.
—Napoleon

Ultimately, growth avenues outside the existing business need to be explored. While it is risky to leave the comfort of the familiar and the tested, it also removes the ceiling on the firm's growth potential. There is virtually unlimited potential when you agree to extend the business.

The goal discussed in this chapter is to leverage the existing business into new product markets. The assets and competencies of the business, in particular, are potential sources of advantage in a new marketplace. The capabilities around marketing skills, distribution clout, developing and manufacturing products, R&D, and brand equities are among the potential bases for advantage for a new growth business. The idea is to build on the core business to create a synergy. The challenge, though, is to achieve real synergy with real impact on the customer value proposition, costs, or investments. Too often, apparent synergy is not realized.

The spectrum of available choices can be categorized generally in terms of how removed they are from the core business. Those that are close will represent less risk and have the greatest chance of leveraging business assets and competencies to achieve a real advantage. As more distance is allowed from the current business, opportunities become more plentiful but the risk increases as well. It can be difficult to gain the necessary knowledge and operational competence to run a business successfully that is far removed from one's core abilities. Of course, creating a new core business can have a huge upside, and taking the risk of moving far from the core business may pay off. But the risk should be visible and part of the analysis.

There are many ways to generate growth options that leverage the core business. Creative thinking processes, introduced in Chapter 10, can help. Good outcomes more often come from having good options on the table rather than making optimal decisions among mediocre ones. The creative thinking exercises can best be engaged around the following series of questions, which have proved to be a good source of options:

- Which assets and competencies can be leveraged?
- What brand extensions are possible?
- Can the scope of the offering be expanded?
- Do viable new markets exist?

After these questions have been discussed, some option evaluation issues will be addressed, and, finally, the critical concept of synergy will be analysed.

WHICH ASSETS AND COMPETENCIES CAN BE LEVERAGED?

A focus on assets and competencies starts by creating an inventory in order to identify the real strengths of the business. In doing so, the discussion in Chapter 3 around identifying and evaluating assets and competencies can be helpful. What are the key assets and competencies that are supporting the core business? What are their characteristics? How strong is each?

The second step is to find a business area where the assets and competencies can be applied to generate an advantage. A line of greetings cards sold through pharmacies might have an artistic capability and a distribution asset that could be leveraged. What other items are in pharmacies that might employ artistic talents? Are there items in the pharmacy that the retailers have difficulty sourcing, for whatever reason? A retailer problem might suggest an opportunity.

One fruitful exercise is to examine each asset for excess capacity. Are some assets underutilized? An accounting firm that considered this question took advantage of excess office space to offer legal services. A supermarket chain with obsolete sites went into the discount off-licence business. A bakery began making sandwiches. If a growth initiative can use excess capacity, a substantial, sustainable cost advantage could result.

The final step is to address implementation problems. Assets and competencies may require adaptations when applied to a different business. Further, new capabilities may have to be found or developed. Existing core businesses are sometimes best leveraged by making an acquisition, because developing the business internally may not be economic or even feasible. When acquisitions are involved, two organizations with different systems, people, and cultures will have to be merged. Many efforts at achieving synergy falter because of implementation difficulties.

As the partial list profiled in Chapter 3 suggests, there are a wide range of exportable assets and competencies. To give a flavour of the opportunities, consider the following: marketing skills, sales and distribution capacity, manufacturing skills, and R&D capabilities.

Marketing Skills

A firm will often either possess or lack strong marketing skills for a particular market. Thus, a frequent motive for expanding into new product markets is to export or import marketing skills. Procter & Gamble's (P&G's) acquisition of Gillette in 2005 was substantially about deploying and acquiring marketing skills. At a very basic level, P&G had great skills in marketing to women. Its brands include Olay, Camay, and Max Factor. On the other hand, Gillette, with its range of innovative razors and shaving products, had been regularly cited as the firm that understood the men's personal care market better than anyone else. Adding the two groups together widens the product mix in a logical way and provides avenues for market learning on both sides.

Applying marketing skills is not always as easy as it appears. Prada sought to take advantage of its exceptional marketing skills in the creation of high-fashion accessories, particularly handbags, with the acquisition of a variety of other labels including Fendi, Helmut Lang, and Jil Sander. The latter two were both sold in 2006 having failed to make a profit for Prada.

Capacity in Sales or Distribution

A firm with a strong distribution capability may add products or services that could exploit that capability. Thus, Tesco's store network and later its strength as an on-line store helped provide a boost to its financial services business. Post offices have strengths in distribution and security that provide them with an asset that can be exploited. In the United Kingdom, the Post Office uses these strengths to offer foreign exchange, insurance, and investments. Similarly, in Ireland the national postal service, An Post, offers money transmission and banking services. E-commerce firms such as Amazon often have operations that can add capacity just by adding a button to access another product group. The result can be additional sales and margins to offset the fixed costs of the operation.

Design and Manufacturing Skills

Design and manufacturing ability can be the basis for entry into a new business area. Cadbury's expertise in the manufacture of flake and in extrusion allowed them to create the TimeOut snack bar. The ability to integrate design, manufacturing, and store operations is central to Zara's leadership positioning in the fashion market. The ability to make small products has been a key for Sony as it has moved from product to product in consumer electronics.

R&D Skills

Expertise in a certain technology can lead to a new business based on that technology.

Nokia is often cited as a packaging firm that became a mobile phone manufacturer. While this is true, it masks the full story of its historical involvement in cable manufacture and then electronics and telephone exchange equipment. What is common among these areas and the driving force of Nokia's excellence is a commitment to R&D-driven innovation. The challenge is to be open to channelling R&D towards new business areas. Too often there is a tendency to focus exclusively on evolving the existing business. Dyson has been very successful at using R&D to drive new business, developing from the ballbarrow to the dual-cyclone vacuum cleaner to the two-drum washing machine to the Airblade hand dryer. In general, breakthroughs in a business area tend to come from technologies owned by other industries. Creativity, often in short supply, is needed to provide opportunities for basic technology and the R&D capability that supports it.

Achieving Economies of Scale

Product market expansion can sometimes provide economies of scale. Two smaller consumer products firms, for example, may not each be able to afford an effective sales force, new product development or testing programmes, or warehousing and logistics systems. However, the combination of these firms may be able to operate at an efficient level.

BRAND EXTENSIONS

One common exportable asset is a strong, established brand name – a name with visibility, associations, and loyalty among a customer group. The challenge is to take this brand asset and use it to enter new product markets. The name can make the task of establishing a new product more feasible and efficient, because it makes developing awareness, trust, interest, and action all easier.

In 2007, MTV exploited its global credentials for cool programming to launch MTV Arabia. Amul, the Indian dairy brand, has been able to use elements of its brand equity, including value for money, quality, wide availability, and commitment to the customer, to add a range of new product areas including pizzas, sports drinks, and ice cream. When the Chinese white goods giant, Haier, first entered the American market, it focused on two niche markets, minifridges and wine coolers, in order to build its brand in relatively uncontested spaces. Using the brand strength it developed there, it moved on to compete successfully with the major players.

Many firms have built large, diverse businesses around a strong brand, including Sony, HP, Mitsubishi, Siemens, Nestlé, Tata, Samsung, and Danone. More than 300 businesses carry the Virgin name, and all gain from the public-relations flair of Richard Branson, its owner. Tata has its name on many products and services, each of which contributes two benefits that are often underappreciated, name exposure and cumulative new-product vitality.

Disney, founded in 1923 as a cartoon company, with Mickey Mouse (made famous in the cartoon *Steamboat Willie*) as its initial asset, might be the most successful firm ever at leveraging its brand. In the 1950s, the company built Disneyland and launched a long-running TV show *The Wonder World of Disney*, dramatically changing the brand by making it much richer and deeper than before. Particularly after extending the theme parks to Florida, Paris, and Japan, and establishing its own retail stores, resorts, and a cruise line, Disney can deliver an experience that goes far beyond watching cartoons. As a result of this brand power, the Disney Channel has become a strong, differentiated TV network, an incredible achievement if you consider what others have put into that space.

It is instructive to see why Disney has done so well with an aggressive brand extension strategy. First, from the beginning the company has known what it stands for – magical family entertainment, executed with consistent excellence. Everything Disney does reinforces that brand identity; when it went into adult films, it did so under the name Touchstone rather than Disney. Second, Disney has a relentless, uncompromising drive for operational excellence that started with Walt Disney's fanatical concern for detail in the earliest cartoons and theme parks. The parks are run so well that Disney holds schools for other firms seeking to learn how to maintain energy and consistency. The cruise line was delayed, in spite of ballooning costs, until everything was judged perfect. Third, the organization actively manages a host of subbrands that have their own identities, including Mickey Mouse, Donald Duck, a mountain (the Matterhorn), a song ('It's a Small World'), film characters like Mary Poppins or the Lion King, and so on and so forth. Fourth, Disney understands synergy across products. *The Lion King* is not only a film but supports a video, the Disney store, and an exhaustive set of promotions at fast food chains and elsewhere.

It should be noted however, that in brand extensions the roads are always uneven. In 1992, when Disneyland first opened its theme park in Paris, attendance was disappointingly low. On the opening day, 500 000 guests were expected, but only a fraction of this number turned out, and the numbers fell further after the first three months. Additionally, the park failed to plan for certain cultural issues such as initially not offering wine in its restaurants and trying to offer more French food on its menus to visitors who were more interested in a distinctly American cuisine. High entrance fees were also blamed for the lack of visitors. Furthermore, the theme park faced protests by commentators who thought a Disney park in France would harm French culture with its American influence; some went as far as to call the project a 'cultural Chernobyl'.

More recently, Disneyland Paris was again under pressure, although its problems seemed to be less cultural and more marketing related. The Disneyland Paris theme park is generally full of guests and was the most popular tourist attraction in France in 2003. However, the opening of a second theme park, Walt Disney Studios, in 2002 coincided with a post-9/11 drop in visitors to France. In addition, one of the company's main sources of revenue, hotels, was affected by the opening of competing hotels. Also, the key driver of (particularly repeat) attendance at theme parks is the opening of new rides and attractions. In 2004 there had been no new rides at Disneyland Paris for some time. In late 2005 the company announced plans to manage the yield from its hotel business more aggressively, as well as its intentions to launch major new attractions.[1] The result was that in 2008 Disneyland Paris was the most visited tourist site in Europe.

In the early days of operation, Hong Kong Disneyland faced different problems with too many people turning up, with the consequence that the rides and dining facilities had long queues and the brand experience expected was not achieved.

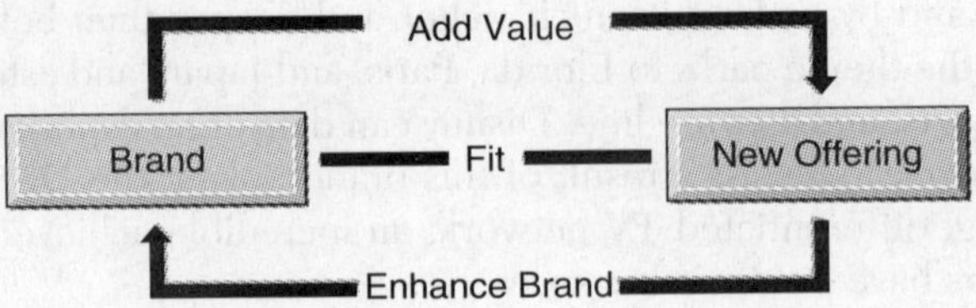

Figure 11.1 Brand Extension Logic

Brand extension options can be created by determining the current brand image and what products and services would fit these associations (see Figure 11.1). In what arenas would the brand be considered relevant? The evaluation of each extension alternative is based on three questions, each of which must be answered in the affirmative for the extension to be viable:

1. *Does the brand fit the new product context?* If the customer is uncomfortable and senses a lack of fit, acceptance will not come easily. The brand may not be seen as having the needed credibility or expertise, or it may have the wrong associations for the context. In general, successful extensions will have one or more bases of fit, such as:
   - a companion product – Bertolli extended from margarine into dressing, olive oil, and pasta sauce;
   - a common user – *The Economist*'s lifestyle magazine *Intelligent Life*, Gerber baby clothing;
   - a distinctive attribute/benefit – easyCar.com, Terry's Chocolate Orange bar;
   - an expertise – Disney English, located in Shanghai, uses Disney characters to teach English to Chinese children, building on its ability to deliver great service and its fun relationship with children and trusting relationships with parents;
   - a personality/self-expressive benefits – Kingfisher Airline took the personality of its founder, Vijay Mallya, and Kingfisher beer and extended them to the growing airline business in India.

   In general, a brand that has strong ties to a product class and attributes (for example, Airbus, Hyundai, or Petrobras) will have a more difficult time stretching than a brand that is associated with intangibles such as a brand personality (for example, Helmut Lang or Australia's Crown Entertainment brand). In a survey of brand extensions by TippingSprung, consumers were not enthused about Burger King men's clothing, Kellogg's hip-hop streetwear, Allstate Green insurance, and Playboy energy drinks, in part because of a fit problem.[2]

2. *Does the brand add value to the offering in the new product class?* A customer should be able to express why the brand would be preferred in its new context. In spite of the fact that cruise ships are difficult to tell apart, nearly anyone could verbalize rather clearly how a Disney cruise ship

would be different from others – it would have Disney characters aboard, contain more kids and families, and provide magical family entertainment. India's Kingfisher Airline is part of the United Breweries group, which also sells the well-known Kingfisher beer. Given the strength and financial importance of the drinks brand, it was imperative that the airline business add value. The firm's charismatic owner, Vijay Mallya, made this happen by buying brand-new aircraft, having in-flight entertainment in every seat, including economy, and delivering a unique cabin service. A recent move into international travel provided further enhancement of the brand and left customers in no doubt about why Kingfisher is different to other airlines.

If the brand name does not add value in the eyes of the customer, the extension will be vulnerable to competition. For example, easyJet is one of the best-known consumer brands in Europe today. It has recently extended its brand to a range of men's grooming products, easy4men. It is less obvious how the brand proposition of easyGroup might add value in this category. Sometimes a brand's value for extension can be reduced through overuse. At one point, Pierre Cardin was used on over 800 products. The Arm & Hammer name also spawned two failures – a spray underarm deodorant, for which the Arm & Hammer name may have had the wrong connotations, and a spray disinfectant.

A concept test can help determine what value is added by the brand. Prospective customers can be given only the brand name, then asked whether they would be attracted to the product and why. If they cannot articulate a specific reason why the offering would be attractive to them, it is unlikely that the brand name will add significant value.

3. *Will the extension enhance the brand name and image?* The ideal is to have extensions that will provide visibility, energy, and associations that support the brand. Monsoon's Accessorize supports its position as a concept fashion retailer. Disney's extension into theme parks in Europe and Asia, retail stores, and cruises all reinforced the brand. The extension of the original easyJet brand to on-line shopping (easyValue.com), job search (easyJobs.com), mobile phones (easyMobile.com), and on-line personal finance (easyMoney.com) and its ongoing move into other areas all provide an energy and momentum to the brand and help to attract new groups of customers to the brand and other offerings. Coach was a successful but slightly old-fashioned maker of leather bags until it hired a new designer and extended the brand to hats, shoes, sunglasses, coats, watches, and even straw beach hats, all with the signature 'C' in leather. The extensions provided energy to the brand and helped attract younger customers, who are vital to the firm's long-term future. The risk with extensions such as these is always whether or not they will deliver on their promise and thus enhance the basic brand values. Extensions must deliver the experience that will be expected or the brand will be at risk.

If an extension will damage the brand but represents a viable business opportunity, another brand option needs to be found. The fashion brand

Prada wished to have a presence in the larger but more price-conscious segment of the fashion market. To use the Prada brand to do this could potentially have undermined the parent brand. It thus entered this market with the Miu Miu brand. The use of subbrands and endorsed brands provides alternatives to creating a new brand, with all its costs and risks.

Subbrands and Endorsed Brands

Subbrands and endorsed brands become options when two unfortunate realities exist. First, the existing brands are judged to have the wrong associations or to have a risk of being damaged by the extension. Second, the organization does not have the size or resources to build a new brand, perhaps because the task is too difficult in a cluttered context or because the business does not justify the investment needed.

In such a situation, the answer may lie in the use of subbrands or endorsed brands. Sony has used subbrands effectively to enter a range of new markets such as gaming (Playstation), computers (Vaio), entertainment robots (AIBO), and television (Brava). Similarly, the Pentium Zeon subbrand allowed Intel to offer a high-end server microprocessor. A subbrand lets the offering separate itself somewhat from the parent brand, and it offers the parent brand some degree of insulation. For example, in 2006, Sony announced that the AIBO entertainment robots would be discontinued. This exit was achieved without casting any doubt on Sony's commitment to or achievements in the other areas of consumer entertainment in which it was active.

An endorsed brand offers even more separation. Tesco recognized the growth potential of two segments of the UK retail market. The first was the 'top-up' retail market, when consumers need a newspaper, milk, or a chocolate bar. In response, they launched the Tesco Express format, local stores, often located in petrol stations, to meet the demand. They also saw the potential for a wider retail format and launched a further endorsed brand, Tesco Extra, selling a wide range of goods such as homewares and electrical goods. These two are added to the existing endorsed brand of Tesco Express and the standard Tesco superstore. Leveraging a brand by using it to endorse other brands provides a trust umbrella.

EXPANDING THE SCOPE OF THE OFFERING

A firm may regard its in-depth knowledge of and access to a marketing segment as an underleveraged asset. Dometic, the Sweden-based international specialist refrigeration company, made absorption refrigerators characterized by silent operation, which were sold to hotels as minibars and for the wider mobile home, leisure vehicle, and marine industry.[3] This success led the company to add other products such as air conditioning, automated awnings, generators, and systems for cooking, sanitation, and water purification. The business was broadened from refrigeration to interior systems and enabled Dometic to create a direct-to-dealer distribution system that became an ongoing competitive advantage.

Considering the broader context in which the offering is used is a powerful idea. Thus, instead of being in the orange juice business, be in the breakfast business. Instead of selling only tennis rackets, consider making nets and courts. GE's Jack Welch was quoted as saying that dominant companies in slow-growing businesses should redefine their markets, looking at broader scope that will have more opportunities.

Slywotsky and Wise make a similar suggestion in their book *How to Grow When Markets Don't.*[4] They recommend identifying and serving the customer needs that emanate from the use of existing products. Cardinal Health, for example, moved beyond distributing drugs to pharmacies to managing drug dispensing and related record-keeping with hospitals and creating medical-supply kits for surgeons. A printing company went from cheque printing for banks to managing their customer relations, including running call centres and helping them come up with incentives to increase customer retention. *The Economist* offers a wide range of economic and business information via the Economist Intelligence Unit.

An analysis of the total set of tasks surrounding the customer use experience is a good way to begin determining whether there is a viable growth option in expanding the view of the offering. This task set could include buying, paying, transporting, storing, preparing for use, using, restoring, and disposal. It can be determined by walking through exactly what the customer needs to do in order to use the product or service. P&G, for example, has worked with Wal-Mart to provide a seamless integration of the two firms to determine what product is needed where and arrange the shipping so that administrative expenses, store outages, and inventory costs are all reduced. The net result is that P&G has an expanded scope beyond its products and a strong link to a customer.

The analysis of a consumption system may not result in an end-to-end solution. But even if two parts can be combined, replaced by an alternative, or made to work better, the result may have added value or a point of differentiation for the customer. A convenience food manufacturer created a meal kit whereby the sauce and noodles are combined into an easily microwaved dinner dish. In doing so, several steps for the cook were eliminated or combined, and the easy cook/serve features were appealing.

Another perspective on expanding the offering scope is simply to serve additional needs of customers. What other products or services do existing customers buy that could be provided by the firm's operations? Fast food chains have expanded their offering to attract customers in a time slot for which they have capacity. McDonald's has very successfully used gourmet coffee to build traffic and sales mid-morning and afternoon.

NEW MARKETS

A logical avenue of growth is to move existing products into new markets by duplicating the business operation, perhaps with minor adaptive changes. With market expansion, the same expertise and technology and sometimes even the same plant and operations facility can be used. Thus, there is potential for synergy and resulting reductions in investment and operating costs. Of course, market development is based on the premise that the business is operating successfully; there is no point in exporting failure or mediocrity.

Expanding Geographically

Geographic expansion may involve changing from a regional operation to a national operation, moving into another region, or expanding to another country. Yum! Brands, Tesco, Nestlé, IBM, and Visa have successfully exported their operations to other countries. Most of these companies and many others are counting on countries such as China, India, and Brazil to fuel much of their growth for the coming decades. Yum! Brands has invested in the Chinese market for more than 20 years, with the result that KFC is now the leader in the quick-service food market and Pizza Hut is the leader in the casual dining market in what is certainly the fastest-growing consumer market in the world. They realize that success will involve significant investment in logistics, distribution infrastructures, and organization building and adaptation. (Chapter 13 will elaborate.)

Moving from local to regional to national is another option. Often, however, this expansion is best implemented by connecting, through an alliance or merger, to a partner that already has the capability to market more broadly.

Expanding into New Market Segments

A firm can also grow by reaching into new market segments. If the target segments are well defined, there are always a host of other segments to consider that would provide growth directions. Consider, for example:

- *Distribution channel.* A firm can reach new segments by opening up a second or third channel of distribution. Many fashion retail brands offer the product through single-brand stores, other retailers, and through on-line stores. A direct marketer such as Oriflame could introduce its products into department stores, perhaps under another brand name.
- *Age.* Johnson & Johnson's baby shampoo was languishing until the company looked towards adults who wash their hair frequently.
- *Home versus office.* A supplier of office equipment to business might look to the home office market.

A key to detecting new markets is to consider a wide variety of segmentation variables. Sometimes looking at markets in a different way will uncover a useful segment. It is especially helpful to identify segments that are not being served well, such as the women's computer market or the fashion needs of older people. In general, segments should be sought for which the brand can provide value. Entering a new market without providing any incremental customer value is very risky.

EVALUATING BUSINESS LEVERAGING OPTIONS

There will be no shortage of ways to leverage the existing business. Ultimately, these need to be evaluated to see whether one or more should be pursued either immediately or within a planning horizon. This section poses several questions that represent important criteria to consider.

These criteria are all supported by a series of studies of initiatives to leverage existing businesses that were conducted by Chris Zook of Bain and Company, as reported in two books, *Profit from the Core* with James Allen and *Beyond the Core*.[5] In the first of these, case studies were created of 25 companies that had achieved sustainable growth performance over the decade from 1992 to 2002 far in excess of their peers. In the second study, twelve pairs of firms were examined, each within the same industry and with a similar starting point but with very different financial trajectories over a 10-year period; the resulting database contained 150 attempts to leverage a business. The third study focused on 180 attempts to leverage a core business, sourced from the United States and the United Kingdom. The focus of these studies was to attempt to determine what was associated with successful initiatives to leverage core businesses.

Is the Product Market Attractive?

Successful initiatives involve a foray into a market that has a robust profit pool going forward. Recall the five-factor Porter model introduced in Chapter 4. The most logical expansion will fail if there simply are no profits to be had because competitors control them or because the margins have been squeezed by overcapacity or the nature of the customer demand. The stampede of utility companies into telecommunications turned out to be a disaster because the profit pool was shrinking to the point where their ventures were uneconomic. In contrast, the controlled product expansion of Olam, the agribusiness commodity supply firm, was always into areas in which the margins were healthy. Projecting a market forwards, particularly a new one with potential new entrants, is difficult, but the risk of entering a hostile market can be significant. Recall the discussion of the risks of growth markets in Chapter 4.

Is the Core Business Successful?

There is no point in extending mediocrity. A weak business will seldom have either resources or assets and competencies to spin out to a growth initiative. The chances of success of leveraging a business has been estimated by the Zook studies to be around 25%,[6] which falls to well under 8% when the core business is weak.[7] Budget Rent A Car, for example, attempted a host of strategies without success to improve on their also-ran status, including efforts to enter the travel arena and the truck rental business.

Can the Core Business Be Transferred to the New Product Market? How Much of a Stretch Is It?

The ability of the business to adapt to a new product market and the chances of success increase the closer the leveraged business is to the core business. Tesco refined its retail offering by improving the checkout experience, parking, and the fresh foods. They grew in part by expanding into in-store pharmacies, optical product stations, petrol, kitchen products, and coffee shops. Each of these leverage efforts enhanced their core business. Such synergy is healthy not only because the core business benefits but because the new business is more likely to draw on the strengths of the core as well. In contrast to this disciplined expansion, their competitor Sainsbury, whose performance lagged behind Tesco, strayed further from its core, investing in a grocery chain in Egypt and two do-it-yourself chains in the United Kingdom. It is often said that France is the European country most resistant to American culture. However, one of America's most iconic brands, McDonald's, known in France as McDo, has been in France since 1979 and has more than 1000 restaurants around the country; France is its most profitable market in Europe. To achieve this, McDonald's has adapted its menu to meet French tastes, including offering French yoghurts, French coffee, and French soft drinks. The company has also promoted its commitment to French suppliers by advertising how many cows, chickens, lettuce, and tomatoes it buys in France each year.[8]

This effect has been quantified by the Zook studies, in which the new business initiative was separated from the core in terms of whether the involved customers, competitors, channels of distribution, cost structure, and assets and competencies were the same or different. The sum of differences could range from 0 to 5 (there could be a partial match on some dimensions). The success probability sank from over 25% to under 10% if the sum of differences was 2 or more.[9]

The task of adapting a business to a new market is easy to underestimate, as the experience of Wal-Mart when it entered the European market suggests. The first market it entered was Germany. It began with the acquisition first of Wertkauf and later of Interspar, which should have provided a smooth path. However, the reluctance of suppliers to participate in its centralized supply system, the challenge of introducing American managers to German business, and later regulatory problems with its low prices all caused problems for the retail giant. Its entry to the UK market via the acquisition of ASDA was smoothed as a result of this experience, as Wal-Mart gave local management a greater role and focused instead on offering them the benefits of its expertise in IT and included them in its global buying operations to reduce prices for ASDA customers.[10]

Will the New Business Be Successful and Become a Market Leader?

The first question, which is not trivial, is whether the new business can avoid failure because it simply lacks market acceptance for whatever reason. The acceptance of new products is low. Even for firms with high levels of competence in a market and with real synergy to buttress the new entry, failure rates are extremely high. And we know the primary reason. Dozens of studies in very different contexts and in different markets have concluded that the main reason for failure is that the new products lack a point of difference, a reason to succeed. Too often they are 'me too' products, at least as perceived by customers. There is in essence no reason to succeed, so they don't. There should be evidence that customers will value the product or service and that the offering can withstand the response of existing and potential competitors.

Even real advances may not be so perceived by customers. They may even read an advance as a reason not to buy. Clairol failed with Small Miracle hair conditioner, which could be used through several shampoos, in part because customers could not be convinced that the product would not build up on their hair if it were not washed off with each use. Even the use of an established brand cannot guarantee success. The concept of a colourless cola, Crystal Pepsi, did not achieve acceptance, and the appearance had a negative flavour connotation.

The goal, of course, should not be simply to survive but to become a market leader at least with an attractive submarket. Simply becoming the fourth or fifth or even third player creates the danger that it will be impossible to keep up with the ongoing investment needed. Without substantial market and financial success, needed resources from the firm may be hard to justify. There is always a competition for resources, even in 'wealthy' organizations.

Is the Leverage Strategy Repeatable?

There is great value in creating initiatives that are repeatable. Repeatability leads to learning curve effects, speed of execution, organizational simplicity, strategic clarity, and the ability to get the details right. In the Zook database, around two-thirds of the most successful, sustained growth companies had one or two repeatable formulas.[11] Nike, for example, has done much better over time than Reebok. While Reebok was buying a boat company, Nike was duplicating its success in basketball with a move into tennis, baseball, football, volleyball, hiking, soccer, and golf. In all these efforts, the strategy was very similar, starting with a prominent credible endorser, from Michael Jordan to Tiger Woods, and systematically moving from shoes to clothing to equipment.

THE MIRAGE OF SYNERGY

Synergy, as suggested in Chapter 7, is an important source of competitive advantage. However, synergy is often more mirage than real. Synergy is often assumed when in fact it does not exist, is unattainable, or is vastly overvalued.

Potential Synergy Does Not Exist

Strategists often manipulate semantics to delude themselves that a synergistic justification exists. In the pharmaceutical industry, mergers have been justified on the basis that global marketing and R&D muscle are required to drive drug development and success. Such a motive underlay the €24 billion merger of Glaxo Wellcome and SmithKline Beecham in 2000, but the benefits in terms of new blockbuster drugs were slow to emerge.

A school bus operator bought into the ambulance business only to find that it lacked the ability to operate a more complex and highly regulated medical business. Many supermarket chains have struggled to expand into other countries because of the lack of common suppliers and the difficulty of creating an information system, both of which prevent synergies from emerging.

THE ELUSIVE SEARCH FOR SYNERGY

The concept of a total integrated communications firm that comprises advertising, direct marketing, marketing research, public relations, design, sales promotions, and Internet communications has been a dream of many organizations for two decades. The concept has been that synergy will be created by providing clients with more consistent, coordinated communication efforts and by cross-selling services. Thus, Young & Rubicam had the 'whole egg' and Ogilvy & Mather talked about 'Ogilvy orchestrations'.

In spite of the compelling logic and considerable efforts, however, such synergy has been elusive. Because each communication discipline involved different people, paradigms, cultures, success measures, and processes, the disparate groups had difficulty not only in working together but even in doing simple things like sharing strategies and visuals. Their inclination was to view other disciplines as inferior competitors rather than partners. Furthermore, they were often reluctant to refer clients to sister units who were suspected of delivering inferior results, which created client-relation ownership issues.

The firms with at least some success stories to their credit, like Young & Rubicam, Denstu, and McCann Ericson, have a set of communication modalities such as direct marketing, public relations, Internet communications, and advertising in one organization, with shared locations and client-relation leadership. These firms make sure there is a strong, credible team leader with a dedicated space and a team-oriented performance measure. Even with such assets, sustained success is extremely rare. When a virtual team is formed with separate companies under one umbrella, even if they are within the same communication holding company, success is even rarer.

The lesson here is that synergy does not just happen, in spite of logic and motivation. It can require real innovation in implementation – not just trying harder.

Potential Synergy Exists But Is Unattainable

Sometimes there is real potential synergy, but implementation difficulties – usually far greater than expected – inhibit or block this synergy from being realized. When two organizations (perhaps within the same firm) have different cultures, strategies, and processes, there are significant issues to overcome. The synergies expected from the merger of Daimler-Benz and Chrysler never materialized, and they finally gave up and engaged in a costly separation. The efforts to create multiservice telecommunication companies and fully integrated entertainment companies in order to achieve synergies have struggled.

Even when progress occurs, the patience and resources may not last long enough to see success. And it can take a long time. The ultimate integration challenge is when a group of entities are integrated to provide a comprehensive customer solution. Morrisons is one of the United Kingdom's most successful retailers. Concentrating mainly on the north of England, it has a long history of sales and profit growth. In 2004 it moved to acquire the Safeway supermarket chain. The logic was unquestionable. Safeway's southern England concentration would complement the Northern bias of Morrisons. However, a number of problems quickly came to the fore. Morrisons maintained tight control over its stores, while Safeway had traditionally allowed its store managers more autonomy. Safeway had a much larger range of products than Morrisons. There were also difficulties in integrating the two companies' IT and finance systems, which added to costs and reduced the level of control senior management had over the business. Finally, there was a sense that Morrisons simply did not appreciate that the southern English customer was different to customers in the North. The result was that Morrisons posted its first ever loss in 2006. Following an aggressive restructuring and divestment of stores, the group returned to profitability and in 2009 had record profits before tax.

Potential Synergy Is Overvalued

One risk of buying a business in another area, even a related one, is that the potential synergy may seem more enticing than it really is. BMW bought the Rover car company in 1994 for about €1.1 billion with the objective of gaining access to the Land Rover brand as an entry point to the growing four-wheel-drive market, and to use BMW's upmarket engineering and marketing skills to push the Rover brand up the prestige ranks. BMW began by allowing existing management to continue to manage the business. It became apparent quite quickly both that this would not work and also that Rover was in a far worse condition than BMW had thought. These miscalculations meant that the integration of the two businesses and the resulting synergies were never realizable. When BMW disposed of Rover in 2000 (it kept the profitable Land Rover and Mini brands), the total losses were in excess of €1 billion, and it had to write off additional investments in the region of €3 billion.

The acquisition of The Learning Company – a popular children's software publisher with titles like *Reader Rabbit*, *Learn to Speak*, and *Oregon Trail* – seemed like a logical move by Mattel, the powerful toy company with Barbie among its properties. Yet less than a year and a half after paying $3.5 billion for it, Mattel basically gave The Learning Company away to escape from mounting losses.

One study of 75 people from 40 companies who were experienced at acquisition led to several conclusions. First, few companies do a rigorous risk analysis looking at the least and the most favourable outcomes. With optimistic vibes abounding, it is particularly wise to look at the downside – what can go wrong? Second, it is useful to set a price over which you will not pay. Avoid getting so exuberant about the synergistic potential that you ultimately pay more than you will ever be able to recoup.[12]

KEY LEARNINGS

- Leveraging assets and competencies involves identifying them and creatively determining to what business areas they might be able to contribute.
- Brand extensions should both help and be enhanced by the new offering, in addition to being perceived to have a fit with it.
- The business can be leveraged by introducing new products to the market or expanding the market for the existing products.

- Entering a new product market is risky, as the new offering might lack market acceptance or needed resources. Success likelihood goes up if the core business is healthy, if the new product market is attractive (competitors will be profitable), if the business model is repeatable, if market leadership is possible, and if the stretch from the core is small.
- Synergy can be a mirage. Too often it does not exist, or it exists but is unattainable or overvalued.

FOR DISCUSSION

1. Pick an industry and a product or service. Engage in a creative thinking process, as outlined in the Creative Thinking Methods insert in Chapter 10, to generate an improved offering. Do the same to create an entirely new offering that uses one or more of the assets and competencies of the firm.
2. Evaluate the following extension proposals:
    - *The Economist* operating a Business School;
    - HSBC going into home safes;
    - Lynx/Axe going into a chain of male grooming salons;
    - Ponsse (a Finnish logging equipment firm) going into cars;
    - Weight Watchers going into gyms.
3. Pick a branded offering such as Innocent smoothies. Come up with 20 products or services that are alternative extension options. Include some that would be a stretch. Then evaluate each using the three criteria provided in the chapter.
4. Consider the following mergers or acquisitions. What synergy was or would be logically possible? What would inhibit synergy? Consider operations, culture, and brand equities.
    (a) L'Oréal acquiring The Body Shop;
    (b) Cadbury acquiring Green & Black's organic chocolate;
    (c) Tata acquiring Jaguar.
5. Evaluate Starbucks' extension decisions: to put Starbucks on airlines, to open Starbucks in bookstores, to open Starbucks outlets in grocery chains, to license Starbucks ice cream, to offer oatmeal, and to sell soluble coffee in supermarkets.
6. Identify and evaluate a combination of businesses that have achieved synergy and another that has failed to do so.

NOTES

1. 'Trouble in le Royaume Magique', *The Economist*, 5 August 2004; Euro Disney SCA, Consolidated Financial Results, Fiscal Year 2005, Analysts Conference Call, 12 November 2005.
2. 'TippingSprung Publishes Results for Fifth Annual Brand-Extension Survey', *PRWeb*, 7 January 2009.
3. Chris Zook, 'Finding Your Next Core Business', *Harvard Business Review*, April 2007, p. 70.
4. Adrian Slywotsky and Richard Wise, *How to Grow When Markets Don't*, New York, NY, Warner Business Books, 2003.
5. Chris Zook and James Allen, *Profit from the Core*, Boston, MA, Harvard Business School Press, 2001; Chris Zook, *Beyond the Core*, Boston, MA, Harvard Business School Press, 2004.
6. Chris Zook, *Beyond the Core*, Boston, MA, Harvard Business School Press, 2004, p. 22.
7. Chris Zook, *Beyond the Core*, Boston, MA, Harvard Business School Press, 2004, p. 112.
8. 'Burger and Fries à la Française', *The Economist*, 15 April 2004.
9. Chris Zook, *Beyond the Core*, Boston, MA, Harvard Business School Press, 2004, pp. 87–88.
10. Wendy Zellner, Katherine Schmidt, Moon Ihlwan, and Heidi Dawley, 'How Well Does Wal-Mart Travel', *Business Week*, 3 September 2001.
11. Chris Zook, *Beyond the Core*, Boston, MA, Harvard Business School Press, 2004.
12. Robert G. Eccles, Kirsten L. Lanes, and Thomas C. Wilson, 'Are You Paying Too Much for That Acquisition?', *Harvard Business Review*, July–August 1999, pp. 136–143.

CHAPTER TWELVE

Creating New Businesses

The most effective way to cope with change is to help create it.
—*I. W. Lynett*

Only the paranoid survive.
—*Andrew Grove, Former CEO, Intel*

The devil doesn't need an advocate. The brave need supporters.
—*Seth Godin*

Enterprise Rent-A-Car, with operations in the United States, Canada, the United Kingdom, and Ireland, passed Hertz in sales during the 1990s, had sales of US$ 10.1 billion dollars in 2008, as opposed to Hertz's US$ 6.7 billion, and was much more profitable. Enterprise, formed in 1957 in St Louis, focused on the off-airport market, catering to leisure travellers and (more importantly) to insurance companies that needed to supply a car to customers whose car was being repaired, a market that Enterprise created and nurtured. With a signature 'We'll pick you up' offer, its inexpensive off-airport sites were run by entrepreneur managers motivated in part by a bonus system tied to customer satisfaction. Not until the late 1980s, when it was already nipping at the heels of Hertz, did Enterprise begin national advertising and get on the radar screen of its competitors, who were all after the prime market of business travellers who wanted a car at the airport.

Ryanair led the expansion of the air travel market in Europe. Through a policy of lowest fares, it made air travel available to a segment of the market that previously could not afford it. It achieved this by reducing and eliminating many of the features of standard airline travel, such as preassigned seating and free in-flight meals, drinks and newspapers. They also eliminated travel agents and their margins from the pricing equation and flew to secondary airports where charges per person were lower.

What they added to the equation was a point-to-point system that reduced the possibility of losing luggage, an enhanced safety record through having newer aircraft of a single type (allowing ground crews to specialize in servicing a single type), and, through on-line check-in and encouraging hand luggage, a reduction in the turnaround time at airports, and an increase in the number of flights that left and arrived on time. In 2009, Ryanair carried 59 million passengers, opened 223 new routes, and became the largest airline in Europe ahead of Air France, KLM, British Airways, and other historic leaders of the European airline market.

Grameen Bank is a microfinance bank that lends to people without collateral. Lending is mainly, but not exclusively, to women, and peer pressure is used to ensure that the money is not wasted but properly invested and repaid. The bank progressed to accepting deposits and to a range of other initiatives such as a partnership with Danone within which it produces and sells a high-nutrient-value yogurt. The business model for this is described as a non-loss, no-dividend basis one. The founder of Grameen Bank, Muhammad Yunus, was jointly awarded the Nobel Peace Prize along with the bank in 2006. Mosammat Taslima Begum accepted the award on behalf of the bank. In 1992, she had used a €16 loan to buy a goat. Her success with this found her in 2006 with a small mango orchard, a fish pond, a rickshaw, and elected to the board of the bank by the 7 million investor-borrower members. When asked to describe the impact of the bank, Yunus replied, 'If you multiply Taslima by 7 million you get a sense of the impact of Grameen Bank in Bangledesh'.[1]

Crocs are light, plastic clog-type footwear available in bright colours for children, women, and men. Using a type of plastic that moulds itself to the foot, the shoes are high on comfort. Easy to wear, they are also easy to put on and take off, making them very attractive as casual footwear for wearing around the home, at the beach, in the garden, and in the gym. Between 2002 and 2009, more than 100 million pairs of Crocs were sold. In 2009 the firm was seeking ways to consolidate the category it had created and establish relationships with other parts of the footwear market.

THE NEW BUSINESS

It is natural to look for growth by energizing the current business or by leveraging that business into new products or markets using the approaches described in the last two chapters. The organization understands the existing business and probably has programmes in place to improve margins, beat competition, enhance the customer experience, upgrade the products, and leverage their considerable assets and competencies.

There is another strategic route, though, that needs to be understood if not employed – to bypass established business arenas with their fixed boundaries and create a new business in which by definition there will be no direct competitors, at least initially. That route, as illustrated by Red Bull, Crocs, Ryanair, and Grameen Bank, involves changing what the customer is buying by creating a new market or submarket. It is usually based on a transformational innovation that transforms the market by introducing a qualitatively different business strategy to what came before.

Consider the new industries that have emerged through time, such as low-cost air travel, mobile phones, smartphones, servers, coffee shops, snowboards, video rentals, 24-hour news networks, multiplex cinemas, express package delivery, discount retail in various categories, 4 × 4 vehicles, low-carb foods, organic foods, and so on. Each of these innovations has supported high returns, sometimes for a lengthy period of time, for its participants. If a firm can develop or participate in such an emerging arena and do it successfully, growth and profits will follow.

Kim and Mauborgne suggest that such new businesses enter 'blue oceans', a space that contains all business arenas not in existence, an unknown market space.[2] In contrast, 'red oceans' are established markets where boundaries and operating parameters are established and accepted. When competing in a blue ocean, the challenge is to create demand where it does not exist and to make competition irrelevant. In red oceans, the goal is to beat competition, to improve market share. As the red ocean space gets crowded, overcapacity, commodization, and low margins are often seen.

Successful blue-ocean businesses are usually based upon significant innovations that create a new business model. The innovation is more often conceptual rather than technological, although a technological advance such as the steel minimills can be a driver. It can be based on an innovative idea such as exchange traded funds (ETFs), a new product form such as the blended wines of the new world, a new benefit such as that delivered by Skype, a new concept such as easyJet's city-to-city no-frills service, or a new channel such as Hindustan Lever's Shakti distribution model, which involves working with women to establish them as village distributors for household basics. The benefits for HUL are wider distribution, and the women receive additional income which often helps lift them from subsistence incomes.

The innovation often involves a qualitative leap in value. Innovations that may be dramatic but do not lead to a value jump are seldom drivers of a new business arena. The value achieved can have a cost component as well as delivering customer benefits. In fact, whereas in red-ocean strategies there is usually a trade-off between differentiation and cost, in blue-ocean strategy firms such as Red Bull and Crocs it is often possible to achieve both low cost and differentiation.

The concept of 'newness' is not black and white (or blue or red). There is a spectrum, from the creation to a new category to something less dramatic. A key indicator is the competitive climate – the length of time in which there is little or no competition, and the ability of competitors to become a factor when they do enter. A business that truly establishes a new category could still have very few competitors long after it has been launched, as was the case for Red Bull, Ryanair, and CNN, the first 24/7 news channel. Another indicator is how different the business strategy is from that seen before – the market served, the products or services offered, the value proposition, the assets and competencies employed, the service delivery, and the functional strategies. Many of the businesses discussed in the last chapter represented some degree of newness because some elements of the strategy were new and different, and the subcategories established had reduced or little competition.

In the case of Ryanair and Red Bull, the business could be described as radically different because it differed on so many dimensions of strategy from what came before and because the competition was subdued. In particular, new assets and competencies had to be developed.

There is evidence to suggest that blue-ocean businesses have attractive financial returns. In a study by Kim and Mauborgne of 150 strategic moves spanning a century, the 14% that were categorized as being blue ocean contributed 38% of the revenues and 61% of the profits of the group.[3]

Studies of the dynamics of companies provide supporting evidence. Of the S&P 500 in 1957, only 74 firms remained in 1997, and these firms performed 20% under the S&P average during that period – meaning that the newer firms performed at a higher level.[4] McKinsey has collected a database of over 1000 firms (all with sales of over 50% in one industry) from 15 industries over 40 years. One finding was that new entrants into the database (84% of the firms were new entrants at one point) achieved a higher shareholder return than their industry average for the first 10 years after entry.[5] That return premium was 13% in the first year, falling to 3% in the fifth year, and never rising above that level for the second five-year period. Furthermore, there was an extremely high correlation between industry newness (defined as the number of new firms entering minus the number of firms leaving during a seven-year period) and industry profitability. Thus, as new firms are more likely to bring new business models than existing businesses, the implication is that blue-ocean businesses will earn superior profits.

The fact is that firms with established businesses struggle to grow and thrive no matter how excellent their management is. An analysis of a database of some 1850 companies in seven countries followed for 10 years revealed that only 13% of companies were able to achieve modest growth (5.5% real growth) and profitability targets (exceeding the cost of capital) over a 10-year period.[6] If a firm has performed well for several years, the chances are high that it will falter soon.

There are several barriers to long-term success in existing product markets. First, competitors respond faster and more vigorously than ever. It is hard to turn a product advantage into a sustainable market position or point of differentiation. Second, incremental innovations are difficult to hide because of the 'flat world' phenomenon and information technology. A firm's strategy in established product markets is transparent. Third, the markets are so dynamic that it is easy to get behind and become less relevant. Fourth, overcapacity, which seems to emerge in all established industries as firms make capacity decisions based on growth objectives that collectively are unrealistic, results in price and margin pressures. Thus, in spite of their risk, new business models in the aggregate offer the best hope for sustainable growth and financial success.

THE INNOVATOR'S ADVANTAGE

A prime reason for new business innovators earning more than the average firm is the innovator's advantage. Innovation can create what is often termed a first-mover advantage based on several factors. First, competitors will often be inhibited from responding in a timely matter. They may believe that the new business will cannibalize their existing business. Thus, competitors to the original Dyson vacuum cleaner held back in responding to the new entrant because they wanted to protect their own revenues from vacuum cleaner bags. Furthermore, they could be worried about the impact on their brand. This is a clear explanation for the plight of flag-carrier airlines, which have either been pushed into bankruptcy or had their financial position irrevocably altered by low-cost airlines. They wished to protect what they saw as their key revenue driver – business-class travel. Because of these two concerns, firms are tempted to minimize the long-term impact of the innovation and make themselves believe that it is a passing fad.

Second, competitors are often simply not able to respond. They may be playing catch-up technologically, especially if the technology is evolving or if patents are involved. Sometimes there might be natural monopolies (an area might be able to support only one muliplex cinema, for example). More common are organizational constraints. Responding to an innovation might require changes in organizational culture, people, and systems, which can be all but impossible. Many new airlines have attempted to duplicate the low-cost model that has brought such success to Ryanair, easyJet, and Virgin Blue. Most have been unsuccessful because, although they could copy what the successful carriers did, they could not duplicate what the latter did as organizations.

Third, the innovator can create customer loyalty based on exposure to and experience with its product or service. If the concept and experience are satisfactory, there may be no incentive for a customer to risk trying something that is different. The innovator can also earn the valuable 'authentic' label. This was a factor facing competitors such as Kirin when they tried to duplicate Asahi Dry Beer's success in Japan. Customer-switching costs, perhaps involving long-term commitments, can create a distinct disadvantage for a follower. Or there could be network externalities. If a large community begins to use a service such as LinkedIn, it may be difficult for a competitor to create a competing community.

To capture a first-mover advantage, it is important to hit the market first and invest to build position. While high initial prices may be an attractive way to capture margin and recover development costs, a low-price strategy may serve to build share and thus increase the barrier to followers. Followers will have the benefit of seeing the innovation, but will often need to be significantly better to have a chance of dislodging the first mover among the user base. So it is helpful to make that user base as large as possible.

It turns out that true market pioneers often do not survive, perhaps because they entered before the technology was in place or because they were blown away by larger competitors.[7] Pioneers such as Korea's Saehan in the MP3 market, SixDegrees.com in the social networking market, Napster in music downloads, and Harvard Graphics in presentation software did not or could not capitalize on their first-mover status. In contrast, Tellis and Golder found that early market leaders, firms that assume market leadership during the early product growth phase, had a minimal failure rate and an average market share almost three times that of market pioneers, and a high rate of market leadership.[8] They noted that successful early market leaders tended to share certain traits:

- *Envisioning the mass market.* While pioneers such as Ampex in video recorders or Chux in disposable nappies charged high prices, the early market leaders (such as Sony and Matsushita in video recorders and P&G in nappies) priced the product at a mass-market level. Swatch in watches,

Kodak in film, Ryanair in air travel, Ford in cars, and Facebook all used a vision of a mass market to fuel their success.

- *Managerial persistence.* The technological advances of early market leaders often took years of investment. The first patent for Nestlé's Nespresso was filed in the mid-1970s. It took more than 10 years to launch the product into the consumer market, but today it is Nestlé's fastest-growing product. Similarly, it took two decades for the Sony and Matsushita firms to develop the video recorder.
- *Financial commitment.* The willingness and ability to invest are non-trivial when the payoff is in the future. For example, when Napster was launched in the late 1990s, it was the quintessential dot.com start-up, and without the financial strength and legal ingenuity required to negotiate the emergence of the digital music market. In contrast, Apple invested substantially in the iPod and iTunes in order to achieve and retain a dominant position.
- *Relentless innovation.* It is clear that long-term leadership requires continuous innovation. Gillette learned its lesson in the early 1960s when the UK firm Wilkinson Sword introduced a stainless steel razor blade that lasted three times longer than Gillette's carbon steel blade. After experiencing a sharp share drop, Gillette returned to its innovative heritage and developed a new series of products, from the Trac II to the Fusion.
- *Asset leverage.* Early market leaders also often hold dominant positions in a related category, allowing them to exploit distribution clout and a powerful brand name to achieve shared economies. Apple's brand strength and distribution experience were both assets that made its task in marketing the iPod, iTouch, and iPhone the great successes they are.

Being a first mover and owning an emerging submarket does more than provide competitive edge in that market. It also leads to a perception of being innovative. Gaining perceptions of innovativeness is a priority for nearly all businesses because it provides energy and credibility for new products. But few brands break out and reach that goal. Examine the top 15 brands on an innovativeness scale according to the 2007 BAV (Brand Asset Valuator from Y&R) database covering over 3000 brands that is shown in Figure 12.1.[9] Nearly all have created and/or owned a new submarket using transformation innovation.

1. Bluetooth	6. DreamWorks	11. Disney
2. Pixar	7. TiVo	12. Google
3. iPod	8. iMac	13. Swifter
4. IMAX	9. Discovery Channel	14. Wikipedia
5. Microsoft	10. Blackberry	15. Dyson

Figure 12.1 Perceived Innovativeness, 2007

MANAGING CATEGORY PERCEPTIONS

When new product categories or subcategories such as smartphones, netbooks, search engines, or hybrid cars emerge, the innovators need to be aware that their challenge is not only to create an offering and a brand but also to manage the perception of the new category or subcategory. A new business will change what people are buying. Instead of buying a car, some customers will be looking for a hybrid. As new entrants come in, there will be different types of hybrid. So Toyota, the early hybrid leader, has an opportunity to manage the perceptions of the category while simultaneously linking itself to the category as the leading brand, one with authenticity and ability to deliver. Equally, every search engine is measured against Google. For a business innovator, the focus is no longer just on what brand to buy (the preference question), but rather what product category or subcategory to buy (the relevance question).

PETER DRUCKER'S DOS AND DON'TS OF INNOVATION[10]

Do:

- Analyse the opportunities
- Go out and look, ask, and listen
- Keep it simple, keep it focused
- Start small – try to do one specific thing
- Aim at market leadership

Don't:

- Try to be clever
- Diversify, splinter, or do too many things at once
- Try to innovate for the future

In managing perceptions of a category, there are some guidelines. Incidentally, these guidelines apply whenever the category is new to the market, even if it is established elsewhere. For example, many categories of products (like people movers) are new to markets like China long after they have been established in the western world. First, there may be a need to focus on attributes and functional benefits at the outset to make sure that the category and its value proposition are communicated. The emotional and self-expressive benefits can have secondary status at the outset. Second, labels such as people mover, camcorder, 4 × 4, etc., help unless the first-mover brand such as Google or Xerox becomes the de facto subcategory label.

CREATING NEW BUSINESS ARENAS

The first step to innovation is to get ideas on the table and refine the best ones to obtain potential business concepts. Good ideas are more likely to happen if they are valued by the organization and if there is a process to stimulate them. Many firms have set a goal that each business should generate technology breakthrough ideas, concepts that could lead to a €50–100 million idea in the foreseeable future. As a result, time and resources are given to idea generation.

In the previous chapter, the starting point was the assets and competencies of the firm and how they could be leveraged. Here, the starting point is the customer in relation to offerings. In what way are the offerings disappointing? What are the unmet needs? What activities are the existing product or service a part of, and what are the goals?

New business ideas can come from anywhere. However, the history of blue-ocean ventures contains patterns and can suggest possibilities. Among them are technological innovation, going from components to systems, unmet needs, niche submarkets, customer trends, and creating a dramatically lower price point.

Technological Innovation

A new technology – such as disposable razors, notebook computers, a new fabric, or hybrid cars – can drive the perception of a submarket. By creating a subcategory of dry beer, Asahi Super Dry Beer made Kirin, the leading lager beer brand, irrelevant for a significant and growing segment in Japan. A minor player with less than 10% of the market in 1986, Asahi grew to gain market share leadership in the late 1990s, in large part by taking share from Kirin. Kirin finally mounted a comeback by taking leadership of the low-malt subcategory, *happoshu,* a beer brewed with ingredients that warranted a sharply lower tax, and another no-malt beer with an even lower tax, termed the third beer. Amazingly, in spite of all the new product introductions, around three per year, and marketing dollars spent in the Japanese beer market, three of the four changes in marketing share momentum were due to these three innovations, dry beer, happoshu, and the third beer.

Technological innovation can take many forms. Format innovation led to Kerry Group's Cheesestrings, which created a new market for children to eat cheese on its own. Software innovation created eBay's on-line auction category, where a host of imitators had difficulty matching both the operational performance and the critical mass of users established by eBay.

From Components to Systems

A classic way to change the market is to move from components to systems. The idea is to look at the system in which the product or service is embedded and to expand perceptions horizontally. Siebel, for example, changed what people bought by creating customer relationship management (CRM). CRM combined a host of software programs (such as call centre management, loyalty programs, direct mail, customer acquisition, customer service, sales force automation, and much more) into a single umbrella package. It was no longer enough to prove to be the best direct mail program, because firms were now buying something much broader and were simply not interested in stand-alone programs that would require idiosyncratic training and would not be linked to other complementary programs.

KLM Cargo's offering was providing space on its airplanes, a commodity that was becoming a low-margin business.[11] After studying the total system needs for customers who were shipping perishables, KLM determined that significant value could be added by providing not just cargo space but a transportation solution that would include end-to-end responsibility for the product. These customers, importers, and retailers were experiencing spoilage, and it was never clear who in the logistics chain was responsible. Under its Fresh Partners initiative, KLM provided an unbroken 'cool chain' from the producer to the point of delivery, with three levels of service: fresh regular, fresh cool, and fresh supercool (where products are guaranteed to have a specific temperature from lorry to warehouse to plane to warehouse to lorry to the retailer). Firms importing orchids from Thailand and salmon from Norway were among those using the service. This initiative allowed KLM to move from a commodity business to one that could capture attractive margins based on the value delivered to customers.

Unmet Needs

Unmet needs provide insight that, when translated into products or services, will be highly likely to be relevant to the customer and can lead to new business. The initial success of Napster was driven not just by the fact that it was free but also because it allowed users to choose the order in which they could listen to tracks, the tracks they had to store, and the ability to create individual mixes of music. Prezi, the dynamic presentation software tool, addressed the need for presenters to have more intuitive control over the progress of their presentations.

Cemex, the Mexican concrete company, realized that its customers had a lot of money riding on predictable delivery because concrete was highly perishable.[12] As a result, Cemex created capabilities of using digital systems that allowed drivers to adjust in real time to traffic patterns and changing customer timetables. It can now deliver product within minutes and process change orders on the fly. It addressed an unmet need, and the totally new business model that resulted has led to Cemex going from a regional player to being the third largest concrete company in the world, serving 30 countries.

Customers are not always a good source for some kinds of unmet need, especially those involving emotional and self-expressive benefits, and so insight from creative and knowledgeable people might be required. The attractiveness of a 4 × 4, for example, did not really result from its functional benefits. Furthermore, customers have a difficult time getting around the boundaries of the current offering and may not have been much help in going from a horse to a car to an airplane. So, in analysing the customer, it is important for the analysis to have both breadth and depth, and that is where ethnographic research excels.

Ethnographic (or anthropological) research, introduced in Chapter 2, is a good way to uncover and analyse unmet needs. Simply observing customers in their 'native habitat' can provide a fresh and insightful look at the problems customers are facing.

Niche Markets

The market can be broken into niches, with each niche having its own dominant brand. The energy drinks market ultimately fragmented into a variety of submarkets, including energy drinks (Red Bull, Lucozade Energy), sports drinks (Powerade, Lucozade Sport), and recovery drinks (Lucozade).

A niche can be defined by an application. Bayer helped define a new subcategory – taking baby aspirin regularly to ward off heart attacks – with its Bayer 81 mg. It attempted further to define the subcategory by introducing Enteric Safety Coating to reassure those who might be concerned about the effects of regular aspirin use on the stomach.

A niche can also be defined by a unique position that appeals to a distinct submarket. The superpremium vodka market, led by brands such as Grey Goose, Belvedere, and Ketel One, achieved great success by focusing on subtle taste differences and product quality. This is in contrast to the broad appeal in the vodka market, which emphasized the ease with which it could be consumed and its use as a mixer in cocktails. Superpremium vodkas created a different drinking experience that drove explosive growth and made other competitors irrelevant.

Customer Trends

A customer trend can be a driver of a submarket. The expression 'Find a parade and get in front of it' has some applicability. That was part of the strategy of Innocent with fruit smoothies and Apple's iPod with music-sharing.

It is even better if multiple trends can be accessed, because the competitors will be more diffuse. The dual trends towards wellness and the use of herbs and natural supplements have supported a new category, healthy refreshment beverages (HRBs). This arena now contains a host of subcategories, such as enhanced teas, fruit drinks, soy-based drinks, and waters. The pioneer and submarket leader is SoBe, which started in 1996 (with SoBe Black Tea 3G, containing ginseng, ginkgo, and guarana) and now has an extensive line of teas, juices, and energy drinks. The large beverage companies ignored this trend for too long and have been playing a frustrating and expensive game of catch-up.

Creating a Dramatically Lower Price Point

Many blue-ocean businesses occur when an offering appears that is simpler and cheaper than that of established firms. Clayton Christensen, a noted Harvard strategy researcher, has studied a wide variety of industries with a series of colleagues and developed two theories about disruptive innovations. His research is reported in three books: *The Innovator's Dilemma*, *The Innovator's Solution* (with Michael Raynor), and *Seeing What's Next* (with Scott Anthony and Erik Roth).[13]

The first theory is termed *low-end disruptive innovation*, where industries are altered by emerging products whose price appears dramatically low. In these industries, established firms target the best customers and attempt to sell them better products for more money. More features, services, and reliability are all aimed to capture a higher level of loyalty and margin. The firms that are successful develop structures, staffs, incentives, and skills designed to generate and implement a continuous flow of 'sustaining innovations' – the pursuit of which is considered a reliable route to profitable growth, and the absence of which risks loss of position. Incumbent organizations are not always the first to market with a sustaining innovation, but they usually win because of their resources and motivation. Financial institutions, for example, put a lot of investment into the wealthy clients. Packaged goods firms offer line extensions to provide variety and interest to loyal customers. Retailers and others invest in loyalty programmes.

This drive to service the most profitable customers provides an opening in the form of the low-end customer. These customers, often ignored or considered a nuisance by the established firms, are typically 'overserved' and would be happy with a simpler, cheaper product that delivered satisfactory performance. Capitalizing on this opportunity, firms (often new to the industry) engage in 'low-end disruptive innovation'. They introduce an entry that is easier to use and much less expensive. Typically, the entrant's product is so inferior that its appeal is to a limited number of applications and customers, which incumbent firms consider marginal anyway. But often these firms then improve their offering over time and become competitors in a broad section of the market. A study of stall points, where steady sales growth abruptly changes to prolonged decline, of some 500 firms over 50 years[14] showed that the leading cause, occurring in 23% of the cases, was low-end disruption innovation.

In the 1960s, steel minimills initially made low-quality steel, serving a market for rebar (reinforcing concrete) that did not require high quality and was a low-margin, unattractive business. Over the decades they improved their technology and products, however, and began to challenge the incumbents on a broad front. There are many similar examples. The Japanese car companies began their rise to leadership in the late 1960s and provided an option for buyers who did not need the features and self-expressive benefits of the larger cars that were popular at that time. The copier market in the 1970s was changed by Canon's low-end disruptive innovation strategy, which met the needs of small businesses that did not need the power of Xerox products.

The Christensen team also advanced a second theory, that of *new-market disruptive innovations* aimed at non-customers. In many markets, large groups of non-customers either do not buy because the products or services are considered too expensive or complex, or buy much less than they would like because the process is inconvenient. A more accessible offering that is priced right can open up the market. The Nintendo Wii attracted new users into the gaming market, and on-line retail stockbrokers enabled day traders to thrive. The mobile-phone camera provides a new market for photography, just as the Kodak Brownie did a century earlier. The simplicity and low charges of exchange traded funds (ETFs) attracted new buyers into the industry. The non-customers have typically been ignored by the established firms, which, again, tend to focus their efforts on the current 'heavy users', the most profitable customers.

An attractively priced option can appeal to both the low-end and non-customer segments simultaneously. India's Air Deccan targeted not only customers looking for a value airline but also people who could be lured from trains and other forms of transport, a segment that was ignored by the established airlines of the day. It also succeeded by serving the low end and attracting new users.

Evaluation – Real, Win, Worth It

The evaluation of a major or transformational innovation is difficult because it will stray from the comfort zone and knowledge base of a business. A structured, disciplined evaluation approach is helpful not only in providing a termination decision but also in identifying the roadblocks to success so that they can be addressed. The 'real, win, worth it' structure suggested by Wharton's George Day involves the following sets of questions:[15]

- Is the market real? Is there a need or desire for the product? Can and will the customer buy it? Is the market size adequate? Social network sites are popular around the world, but are users willing to pay, in fact or kind, for the service they provide?
- Is the product real? Is there a clear concept that will satisfy the market? Can the product be made? Putting nuclear energy plants in the ocean presented construction barriers.
- Can the product be competitive? Does it have a competitive advantage, one that is sustainable? If a competitor can copy or neutralize the new product, it may have only a short window to establish a loyal customer base.
- Can our company be competitive? Do we have superior assets and competences? Appropriate management? The success of the digital animation company Pixar depended on a unique blend of culture and people. It would not have worked in most film organizations.
- Will the product be profitable at an acceptable risk? Is the forecast ROI acceptable? Overoptimistic sales forecasts and unrealistic pricing expectations need to be considered.
- Does launching the product make strategy sense? Does it fit our overall strategy? Will top management support it? 3M launched a privacy computer screen that provided opened up markets for antiglare filters.

Keeping the Edge

The goal is to maintain dominance in the new submarket and the returns that go along with dominance. Not so easy when success breeds competitors. Those that have kept dominance have one or more characteristics. Some, like Logitech, keep innovating so that they are a moving target. Others, like Innocent and Crocs, are the 'authentic' choice. Yet others, like Red Bull, have created significant entry barriers in terms of competences and brand equity. And there are those like Ryanair and Kingfisher airlines that surround their innovation with a personality. The list goes on, but keeping the edge avoids a transformational innovation from becoming only a short-term win.

FROM IDEAS TO MARKET

The payoff for creating a successful new business is huge. Historically, most financially successful firms are based on the creation of a new business. Yet few firms can have a history of creating multiple new businesses. It turns out that it is not easy for an organization to be successful with an established business and still provide an environment that will foster new business ideas and allow them to flourish. That is exactly what is required, though, when markets become dynamic. The challenge is to create an organization that can excel in existing businesses and still allow a new business, especially a transformational business, to survive, if not thrive. In terms of Chapter 8, strategic adaptability needs to play a more prominent role, either in addition to or perhaps in place of strategic commitment or strategic opportunism.

Most organizations lack a healthy mix of transformational and incremental innovation. One study concluded that the proportion of major innovation in development portfolios dropped from 20.2% in 1990 to 11.5% in 2004.[16] And the proportion of total sales fell from 32.6% in the mid-1990s to 28% in 2004. Why should there be such a bias towards incremental 'little i' innovations? To answer that question, we will turn to a discussion of the several reasons why organizations fail to support transformational innovations at an optimal level.

Fatal Biases Inhibiting New Business Creation

Understanding the several biases that inhibit firms from innovating new business areas is a first step to dealing with them. These biases can be expressed in terms of six related 'curses': short-term pressures, product silos, success, incumbency, commitment, and size:

- *The short-term financial pressure curse.* When the organization is doing well, there is pressure to create short-term growth and margins, in part driven by the desire for stock return and in part driven by managers with short job tenures. Short-term results can best be obtained by diverting R&D funds to sustaining innovation and focusing effort on improving the business model, enhancing the value proposition, and improving efficiency and productivity. Creating a new business platform is risky and expensive and likely to result in short-term financial pain. A new firm, perhaps funded by venture capitalists, will have a time horizon to start making profits.
- *The silo curse.* The power of product silos within organizations often leads to a delegation of innovation and development from the corporation to the silo unit in part to gain accountability and funding ability. Silos by their nature have limited resources and are focused on a particular product line with its associated customer base, operations, assets, and competences. The natural goal is to respond to opportunities to improve the offering or to leverage the existing business. A transformational innovation will require more resources, will often need to operate between existing silos, and can be a threat to the existing profit stream.
- *The curse of success.* When times are good and the business is doing well, resources should be available to take risks and create new business areas. Curiously, however, complacency usually wins the day. Why change if the current business is generating growth and profits? Why not instead invest in a sure thing, to make the costs even lower and the profits even higher? It is much easier to change when there is a crisis than when things are going well, although in a crisis both resources and time may be in short supply.
- *The incumbent curse.* When a transformational innovation is aimed at the marginal customer or the non-customer, there is a tendency to ignore the

threat to the basic business. The natural strategy is to focus on the good, high-margin customers. If the new concepts steal marginal customers, so what? Those customers were more of a nuisance anyway. Furthermore, it does not seem wise to invest in an offering that will kill the golden goose. Why invest in an offering that may cannibalize your business?

- *The commitment curse.* Successful incumbent firms often have a tunnel focus on their strategic vision. In terms of Chapter 7, they engage in strategic commitment. They invest vigorously in incremental innovation to reduce costs, improve the offering, and satisfy their loyal customers. The people hired, the culture created, the systems developed, and the organizational structure employed are all tailored to the task of making the existing business better. In that context, it is difficult for any new business concepts to get resources or serious traction within the firm.
- *The size curse.* A new business by definition will start small. If a firm has been successful and grown to a meaningful size, it will look to business concepts that can make a difference to shareholders. McDonald's, for example, is inhibited from trying new restaurant concepts because even a successful concept aggressively expanded will have no impact on its financials; the core business is simply too huge. As a result, it became stuck in a model that was not supported by customer trends. Coke resisted marketing waters and other beverages in part because it was so unlikely for such business ventures materially to affect its shareholder value. A related problem is that a huge business will usually have built assets, processes, and organizations that are not adapted to run smaller businesses. One snack company once proclaimed that it was not capable of handling a business that was under $250 million. That inhibited it from participating in potential growth areas.

Making New Business Viable in Established Organizations

The basic problem is that a new business, particularly a transformational one, will require an organization that is very different from that of the core business. It will require people, a system, a culture, and a structure that must adapt quickly to an emerging market area, one that is almost by definition going to be very different from the core business.

One approach is to create a separate organization, either by acquiring the industry innovator and retaining its autonomy or by creating a stand-alone entity within the corporate framework. In either case, the separate organization will be free – indeed, encouraged – to create its own people, systems, culture, and structure. Of course, it can borrow elements of the core business, such as its accounting systems or perhaps marketing skills, but it needs to be committed to the strategic vision of the new organization while still being entrepreneurial and flexible. As the business matures, the link with the core business can become greater.

The other approach is to create a dual organization within the same firm. People who excel at 'start-up' adaptability and change, as well as those who have proven to be good at incremental innovation, will need to be developed side by side. A more diverse set of people will likely be the result. Entrepreneurial cultural values will need to be tolerated within the organization. Experimentation, trial and error, will need to be accepted if not encouraged. Different cost control systems and performance metrics will be needed. The new ventures will probably require a flatter organization.

Developing a dual organization is difficult and requires active management. However, it is possible and can result in providing new ventures with access to significant assets and competencies while also breathing energy into the core businesses.

In any case, an innovative new business cannot be starved of resources. The reason that most new businesses succeed as start-ups is because they have access to money from the stock market and from venture capitalists. Internally funded ventures are often at a disadvantage in obtaining needed resources. Too often, executives in large firms are said to have deep pockets but short arms.

To overcome resource shortfalls, top management has to make a commitment to grow through internal innovation and allocate resources towards that goal. Then a new venture will be able to compete for these resources with other new ventures and not from the existing business units. Google, with its programme of encouraging and supporting breakthrough initiatives, does just that. Another key to resource availability is the disciplined process to disinvest in businesses that are not going to be the future of the firm, so that they do not exert their priority over future resources. Chapter 14 discusses the disinvestment decision process.

FOR DISCUSSION

1. Why didn't Hertz or Avis start an off-airport business directed at insurance companies and holidaymakers? What advantages would they have had over Enterprise? Why didn't British Airways come up with the low-cost carrier model first? Why didn't Puma or Billabong think of Crocs?
2. Consider the transformational impact of Grameen Bank. What are the implications of this model for more traditional trading firms? What are the implications for those seeking to do business in the developing world? What are the implications for businesses of all kinds of the objectives of the bank and of its partnership with Danone?
3. Think of some transformational new businesses such as Ryanair, Crocs, and Grameen Bank.
   - **(a)** How was each different from what came before? What was similar? Scale them in terms of 'newness' from truly transformational to substantial (some elements common to what came before, but enough new to create a new subcategory).
   - **(b)** Was there an innovator advantage? How long did it last and why?
   - **(c)** Did the business originate from an established business? If not, why not?
   - **(d)** Where did the idea for the business come from? If you don't know, try to speculate.

4. Consider some new businesses that have managed category perceptions well. Consider others that have not.
5. What firms have changed from components to offering systems? Have they obtained an innovator's advantage?

NOTES

1. 'Yunus Unveils Vision to End Global Poverty', *The Daily Star*, 14 December 2009, **5**(903), p. 1.
2. W. Chan Kim and Renee Mauborgne, *Blue Ocean Strategy*, Boston, MA, HBS Press, 2005.
3. W. Chan Kim and Renee Mauborgne, *Blue Ocean Strategy*, Boston, MA, HBS Press, 2005, p. 7.
4. Richard Foster and Sarah Kaplan, *Creative Destruction*, New York, NY Doubleday, 2001, p. 8.
5. Richard Foster and Sarah Kaplan, *Creative Destruction*, New York, NY Doubleday, 2001, p. 47.
6. Chris Zook and James Allen, *Profit from the Core*, Boston. MA, HBS Press, 2001, p. 11.
7. Peter N. Golder and Gerard J. Tellis, 'Pioneer Advantage: Marketing Logic or Marketing Legend?', *Journal of Marketing Research*, May 1993, pp. 158–170.
8. Gerard J. Tellis and Peter N. Golder, 'First to Market, First to Fail? Real Causes of Enduring Market Leadership', *Sloan Management Review*, Winter 1996, pp. 65–75.
9. Susan Nelson, 'Who's Really Innovative', *Marketing Daily*, 2 September 2008.
10. James Daly interview with Peter Drucker, 'Sage Advice', *Business 2.0*, 22 August 2000, p. 139.
11. The example is recounted in James C. Anderson and James A. Narus, 'Selectively Pursuing More of Your Customer's Business', *MIT Sloan Management Review*, Spring 2003, pp. 43–49.
12. Rita Gunther McGrath and Ian C. MacMillan, 'Market Busting', *Harvard Business Review*, March 2005, pp. 81–89.
13. Clayton M. Christensen, *The Innovator's Dilemma: When New Technologies Cause Great Firms to Fail*, Boston, MA, Harvard Business School Press, 1997; Clayton M. Christensen and Michael E. Raynor, *The Innovator's Solution: Creating and Sustaining Successful Growth*, Boston, MA, Harvard Business School Press, 2003; Clayton M. Christensen, Scott D. Anthony, and Erik A. Roth, *Seeing What's Next: Using the Theories of Innovation to Predict Industry Change*, Boston, MA, Harvard Business School Press, 2004.
14. Matthew S. Olsen, Derek van Berer, and Seth Verry, 'When Growth Stalls', *Harvard Business Review*, March 2008, pp. 51–61.
15. George S. Day, 'Is It Real? Can We Win? Is it Worth Doing', *Harvard Business Review*, December 2007, pp. 110–120.
16. Robert G. Cooper, 'Your NPD Portfolio May Be Harmful to Your Business Health', *PDMA Visions*, April 2005.

CHAPTER THIRTEEN

Global Strategies

It has been said that arguing against globalization is like arguing against the laws of gravity.
—Kofi Annan

A powerful force drives the world toward a converging commonality, and that force is technology. ... The result is a new commercial reality – the emergence of global markets for standardized consumer products on a previously unimagined scale of magnitude.
—Theodore Levitt

My ventures are not in one bottom trusted, nor to one place.
—William Shakespeare, The Merchant of Venice

Many firms find it necessary to develop global strategies in order to compete effectively. A global strategy is different from a multidomestic or multinational strategy, in which separate strategies are developed for different countries and implemented autonomously. Thus, a retailer might develop different store groups, in several countries, that are not linked and that operate autonomously. A multidomestic operation is usually best managed as a portfolio of independent businesses, with separate investment decisions made for each country.

A global strategy, in contrast, represents a worldwide perspective in which the interrelationships between country markets are drawn on to create synergies, economies of scale, strategic flexibility, and opportunities to leverage insights, programmes, and production economies.

A global strategy can result in strategic advantage or neutralization of a competitor's advantage. For example, products or marketing programmes developed in one market might be used in another. Or a cost advantage may result from scale economies generated by the global market or from access to low-cost labour or materials. Operating in various countries can lead to enhanced flexibility as well as meaningful sustainable competitive advantages (SCAs). Investment and operations can be shifted to respond to trends and developments emerging throughout the world or to counter competitors that are similarly structured. Plants can be located to gain access to markets by bypassing trade barriers.

Even if a global strategy is not appropriate for a business, making the external analysis global may still be useful. A knowledge of competitors, markets, and trends from other countries may help a business identify important opportunities, threats, and strategic uncertainties. A global external analysis is more difficult, of course, because of the different cultures, political risks, and economic systems involved.

A global strategy requires a set of issues to be addressed, including the following:

1. What are the motivations (objectives) for a global strategy?
2. To what extent should products and service offerings be standardized across countries?
3. To what extent should the brand name and marketing activities (such as brand position, advertising, and pricing) be standardized across countries?
4. How can the global footprint be expanded successfully?
5. To what extent should strategic alliances be used to enter new countries?
6. How should the brand be managed globally?

Each of these issues will be explored in turn. The next section, in which the motivations for global strategies are presented, will be followed by discussions of how to select which countries to enter, standardization versus customization, global brand management, and the use of alliances in developing global strategies.

MOTIVATIONS UNDERLYING GLOBAL STRATEGIES

A global strategy can result from several motivations in addition to simply wanting to invest in attractive foreign markets. The diagram of these motivations (Figure 13.1) provides a summary of the scope and character of global strategies.

Obtaining Scale Economies

Scale economies can occur from product standardization. The Volkswagen global footprint, for example, allows product design, tooling, parts production, and product testing to be spread over a much larger sales base. Standardization of the development and execution of a marketing programme can also be an important source of scale economies. In the late 1990s, Samsung, the Korean global electronics brand, deleted a number of subbrands to focus on the single master brand of the company, with the intention of building a premium, global brand. In 2009 their investment and commitment resulted in them coming 19th in the Interbrand/Business Week Global Brand rankings, ahead of Sony.

Scale economies can also occur from standardization of marketing, operations, and manufacturing programmes. Brands that share advertising (even when it is adjusted for local markets) spread the production and creative effort over multiple

Figure 13.1 Global Strategy Motivations

countries and thus a larger sales base. Similarly, a firm benefits when fixed costs involving IT and production technologies can be distributed over countries.

Global Brand Associations

Being global generates the image of being global, which turns out to be a significant advantage. A study of associations made of global brands involved qualitative interviews with 1500 consumers over 41 countries, followed up with a quantitative study that included a preference scale of three leading brands in six product categories.[1] The result showed that associations with being global impacted upon preference. In fact, 44% of the variance in preference is caused by consumers believing that global brands have higher quality in part because they tend to have the latest innovations. Two other associations, the prestige of being global and social responsibility, also influence preference, but much less so (12 and 8% respectively) than the quality dimensions.

Global Innovation

Being global means that innovation around brand building, new product, and product improvements can be sourced anywhere. At P&G for example, the successful Pantene positioning ('For hair that shines') came from P&G Taiwan, and the mid-tier-priced feminine protection brand featuring the herbal ingredient chamomile, Naturella, came from P&G Mexico. GE sought to leverage its leadership in medical imaging in China by offering the same leading-edge technology there as it did around the world. However, high price and a lack of portability hampered its efforts. In

INDICATORS THAT STRATEGIES SHOULD BE GLOBAL

- Major competitors in important markets are not domestic and have a presence in several countries.
- Standardization of some elements of the product or marketing strategy provides opportunities for scale economies.
- Costs can be reduced and effectiveness increased by locating value-added activities in different countries.
- There is a potential to use the volume and profits from one market to subsidize gaining a position in another.
- Trade barriers inhibit access to worthwhile markets.
- A global name can be an advantage and the name is available worldwide.
- A brand position and its supporting advertising will work across countries and has not been pre-empted.
- Local markets do not require products or service for which a local operation would have an advantage.

response, it developed a low-price, highly portable ultrasound machine, which led tc exceptional sales growth in China. It also had strong sales in other western and inter- national markets as a portable device for use in emergency and other situations wher a quick response was more important than a perfect one.[2]

Access to Low-Cost Labour or Materials

Another motivation for a global strategy is the cost reduction that results from acces to the resources of many countries. Substantial cost differences can arise with respec to raw materials, R&D talent, assembly labour, and component supply. Thus, a com puter manufacturer may purchase components from South Korea and China, obtai raw materials from South America, and assemble in Mexico and five other countrie throughout the world in order to reduce labour and transportation costs. Access t low-cost labour and materials can be an SCA, especially when it is accompanied wit the skill and flexibility to change when one supply is threatened or a more attracti alternative emerges.

Access to National Investment Incentives

Another way to obtain a cost advantage is to access national investment incentiv that countries use to achieve economic objectives for target industries or depress areas. Unlike other means to achieve changes in trade, such as tariffs and quot incentives are much less visible and objectionable to trading partners. Thus, t

British government has offered Japanese car manufacturers a cash bonus to locate a plant in the United Kingdom. The governments of Ireland, Brazil, and a host of other countries offer cash, tax breaks, land, and buildings to entice companies to locate factories there.

Cross-Subsidization

A global presence allows a firm to cross-subsidize, to use the resources accumulated in one part of the world to fight a competitive battle in another.[3] Consider the following. One firm uses the cash flow generated in its home market to attack a domestically oriented competitor. For example, in the early 1970s, Michelin used its European home profit base to attack Goodyear's US market. The defensive competitor (i.e. Goodyear) can reduce prices or increase advertising in the United States to counter, but by doing so it will sacrifice margins in its largest markets. An alternative is to attack the aggressor in its home market, where it has the most to lose. Thus, Goodyear carried the fight to Europe to put a dent in Michelin's profit base.

The cross-subsidization concept implies that it is useful to maintain a presence in the country of a competitor. The presence should be large enough to make the threat of retaliation meaningful. If the share is only 2% or so, the competitor may be willing to ignore it.

Dodge Trade Barriers

Strategic location of component and assembly plants can help gain access to markets by penetrating trade barriers and fostering goodwill. Peugeot, for example, has plants in 26 countries, from Argentina to Zimbabwe. Locating final-assembly plants in a host country is a good way to achieve favourable trade treatment and goodwill because it provides a visible presence and generates savings in transportation and storage of the final product. Thus, Caterpillar operates assembly plants in each of its major markets, including Europe, Japan, Brazil, and Australia, in part to bypass trade barriers. An important element of the Toyota strategy is to source a significant portion of its car cost in the United States and Europe to deflect sentiment against foreign domination.

Access to Strategically Important Markets

Some markets are strategically important because of their market size or potential or because of their raw material supply, labour cost structure, or technology. It can be important to have a presence in these markets even if such a presence is not profitable. China and India have taken on such a status because of their enormous medium-term potential as consumer markets.

Sometimes a country is important because it is the locus of new trends and developments in an industry. A firm in the fashion industry may benefit from a presence in countries that have historically led the way in fashion. Or a high-tech firm may want to have operations in a country that is at the forefront of the relevant field. For example, a firm in the racing car market must have a presence in the United Kingdom's Motorsport Valley in order to keep abreast of technology developments and competitor strategies. Sometimes adequate information can be obtained by observers, but those with design and manufacturing groups on location will tend to have a more intimate knowledge of trends and events.

STANDARDIZATION VERSUS CUSTOMIZATION

Standardized products and brands gained widespread credence as a strategy because of Ted Levitt's classic 1983 *Harvard Business Review* article, 'The Globalization of Markets', which gave three reasons why they would succeed.[4] First, the forces of communication, transport, and travel were breaking down the insulation of markets, leading to a homogeneity of consumer tastes and wants. Second, the economics of simplicity and standardization – especially with respect to products and communication – represented compelling competitive advantages against those who held on to localized strategies. Third, customers would sacrifice preferences in order to obtain high quality at lower prices. The article provided an academic underpinning to the logical premise that standardization should be the goal of a global business.

Red Bull, HSBC, YouTube, Bang & Olufsen, The Body Shop, Vodafone, BP, BBC World, Samsung, Pantene, Danone, and Accenture are the envy of many because they seem to have generated global businesses with a high degree of similarity in terms of product, brand, position, advertising strategy, personality, packaging, and look and feel. Red Bull, for example, stands for energy, extreme sports, youth, vitality, 'fun', and energy drinks everywhere in the world. Furthermore, the Red Bull can, symbols, promotions, and advertising are almost the same globally. The Body Shop offers the same retail experience across all markets. Lynx/Axe offers the same brand promise to every young man in every market it operates in.

These 'standardized' products and brands are often not as identical worldwide as one might assume. McDonald's has disparate menus, advertising, and retail architectures in various countries. Pringles uses different flavours in different countries, and advertising executions are tailored to local culture. Heineken is the premium beer to enjoy with friends everywhere – except at home in the Netherlands, where it is more of a mainstream beer. Visa has even had different logos in some countries (such as Argentina), and Coke has a sweeter product in areas like southern Europe. Regardless of these variations, however, brands that have moved towards the global end of the local–global spectrum demonstrate some real advantages.

A standardized offering can achieve significant economies of scale. For example, when IBM decided to exchange some three dozen advertising agencies for one in order to create a single global campaign (even if it needed some adapting from market to market), one motivation was to achieve efficiencies. The task of developing packaging, a website, a promotion, or a sponsorship will also be more cost-effective when spread over multiple countries. Economies of scale across countries can be critical for sponsorships with global relevance, such as the World Cup or the Olympics.

Perhaps more important, though, is the enhanced effectiveness that results from better resources. When IBM replaced its roster of agencies with Ogilvy & Mather, it immediately became the proverbial elephant that can sit wherever it wants. As the most important O&M client, it gets the best agency talent from top to bottom. As a result, the chances of a well-executed breakout campaign are markedly improved.

Cross-market exposure produces further efficiencies. Media spillover, where it exists, allows the standardized brand to buy advertising more efficiently. Customers who travel can be exposed to the brand in different countries, again making the campaign work harder. Such exposure is particularly important for travel-related products such as credit cards, airlines, and hotels.

A standardized brand is also inherently easier to manage. The fundamental challenge of brand management is to develop a clear, well-articulated brand identity (what you want your brand to stand for) and to find ways to make that identity a driver of all brand-building activities. The absence of multiple strategies makes this task less formidable with a global brand. In addition, simpler organizational systems and structures can be employed. Vodafone's global 'Power of You' brand message is much easier to manage than dozens of country-specific strategies.

The key to a standardized brand is to find a position that will work in all markets. Zara is built on the same position globally – great design, value pricing, and a supply strategy that means the person next to you probably won't be wearing the same shirt. This is based on the observation that most people want to wear fashion that is affordable but has an element of uniqueness. Tsingtao beer has the same positioning globally, the world's number one Chinese beer.

Several generic positions seem to travel well. One is being the 'best', the upscale choice. High-end premium brands such as Mercedes, Montblanc, Heineken, and Tiffany's can cross geographic boundaries because the self-expressive benefits involved apply in most cultures. Another is the country position. Australia has regularly been placed at the top of the national country brand league table. The popularity of the Australian brand in the broadest sense enhances the appeal of brands from that country such as Billabong and Yellow Tail Wines and means that the Australian position will work everywhere (with the possible exception of Australia). A purely functional benefit such as Head and Shoulders' antidandruff feature can also be used in multiple markets. However, not all brands, even if they are high end, or have a strong functional benefit, can be global.

Standardization can come from a centralized decision to create a global product. Canon, for example, developed a copier that had a common design throughout the world in order to maximize production economies. Unfortunately, the copier could not use the standard paper size in Japan, resulting in substantial customer inconvenience. The risk inherent in a truly global standardization objective is that the result will be a compromise. A product and marketing programme that almost fits most markets may not be exactly right anywhere; such a result is a recipe for failure or mediocrity.

Another strategy is to identify a lead country, a country whose market is attractive because it is large or growing or because the brand has a natural advantage there. A product is tailored to maximize its chances of success in that country, then exported to other markets (perhaps with minor modification or refinements). A firm may have several lead countries, each with its own product. The result is a stable of global brands, with each brand based in its own home country. Nissan has long taken this approach, developing a corporate fleet car for the United Kingdom, for example, and then offering it to other countries. Lycra, a 35-year-old ingredient brand from DuPont, has lead countries for each of the product's several applications, all under the global tagline 'Nothing moves like Lycra'. Thus, the Brazilian brand manager is also the global lead for swimsuits, the French brand manager does the same for fashion, and so on.

Global Leadership, Not Standardized Brands[5]

The fact is that a standardized global brand is not always optimal or even feasible. Yet, attracted by the apparent success of other brands, many firms are tempted to globalize their own brand. Too often the underlying reason is really executive ego and a perception that a standardized brand is the choice of successful business leaders.

Such decisions are often implemented by a simple edict – that only standardized global programmes are to be used. The consolidation of all advertising into one agency and the development of a global advertising theme are typically cornerstones of the effort. Even when having a standardized brand is desirable, though, a blind stampede towards that goal can be the wrong course and even result in significant brand damage. There are three reasons.

First, economies of scale and scope may not actually exist. The promise of media spillover has long been exaggerated, and creating localized communication can sometimes be less costly and more effective than adapting 'imported' executions. Furthermore, even an excellent global agency or other communication partner may not be able to execute exceptionally well in all countries.

Second, the brand team may not be able to find a strategy to support a global brand, even assuming one exists. It might lack the people, the information, the creativity, or the executional skills and therefore end up settling for a mediocre approach. Finding a superior strategy in one country is challenging enough without imposing a constraint that the strategy be used throughout the world.

Third, a standardized brand simply may not be optimal or feasible when there are fundamental differences across markets. Consider the following contexts where a standardized global brand would make little sense:

- *Different market share positions.* Google is the market leader in most international markets in which it competes. But there are a few exceptions, one being Russia. The leader in that market is a local firm, Yandex. Initially, the problem was a greater ability of the Yandex search engine to cope with the inflection of the Russian language. This allowed Yandex to capture more than a 50% market share and establish its leadership. In the face of such competition, a standardized approach from Google would not yield leadership.
- *Different government contexts.* A ban on smoking in public places in Ireland significantly reduced the number of people going to pubs, with the consequent reduction in alcohol sales on-trade. An unintended consequence has been a significant growth in the consumption of alcohol at home. This change has had implications for packaging, distribution, and pricing, which has eroded the ability of brands to operate a standardized model.
- *Different brand images.* In Ireland and the United Kingdom, Guinness is a great traditional brand with values of quality, maleness, and patient satisfaction.

Growth has been driven by an updated image and an emphasis on take-home sales. In international markets, particularly in Africa, advertising Guinness as a source of strength and vitality has been the key to strong growth.

- *Different customer motivations*. P&G's Olay found that in India people wanted lighter-looking rather that younger-looking skin as in the case of western markets. Campbell Soups found little demand for ready-to-eat soups in soup-loving Russia and China but did better when they introduced 'starter soups'. According to a 2008 study, 78% of food consumers in China cited health benefits as important. In the United Kingdom and Argentina the number was less than half, and in Germany it was only 34%.[6]
- *Different distribution channels*. The distribution channel can affect the offering and the marketing strategy. In China, reaching rural areas can involve many levels of distribution, so that it is hard to control the brand using methods that would work in western economies, where the distribution channel tends to be shorter and clearer. In many countries in Europe and Asia, ice cream is sold on a stick or in a small cup as a portable snack. In the United States, ice cream is sold in bulk for use at home.
- *Different stages in customer trends.* A brand may not be at the same stage in all countries even though a common customer trend exists in each. The appreciation of wine varies from country to country. In China, it exists but is embryonic and affects the go-to-market strategy of wine brands. A commitment to organic and free-range food as well as an unwillingness to accept food that has been produced using GMOs or similar are further developed in Europe than in other countries.
- *Different social economic stage.* For some markets, such as in rural India or some parts of China and Africa, most products and brands sold in the West are simply irrelevant. When an area lacks electricity or when it is unreliable, the product profile and attribute preferences change dramatically. Or when the household budget is a small fraction of that in developed countries, constraints dictate buying habits.
- *Strong local heritage.* Nestlé and Unilever often retain an acquired local brand simply because there is significant customer loyalty based on the brand's heritage and connection to the local community that could not be transferred to a global brand. Relationships with local brands can be powerful, especially in contexts in which the incidence of advertising is low and the historical relationships therefore take on more weight.
- *Pre-empted positions.* A superior position for a chocolate bar is to own the associations with milk and the image of a glass of milk being poured into a bar. The problem is that different brands have pre-empted this position in different markets – for example, Cadbury in the United Kingdom and Milka in Germany.
- *Different customer responses to executions and symbols.* There are tactical concerns as well. A Johnnie Walker ad in which the hero attends the running of the bulls in Pamplona was effective in some markets, including

Spain, but seemed reckless in Germany and too Spanish in other countries. The attitude towards diet drinks and food also differs greatly between countries. In the United Kingdom and Ireland, the use of *diet*, particularly on soft drinks, is acceptable, but in many continental European countries the word *light* is used instead.

A global business strategy is often misdirected. The priority should not be to develop standardized brands (although such brands might result) but global brand *leadership,* strong brands in all markets. Effective, proactive global brand management should be directed at enhancing brands everywhere by allocating brand-building resources globally, creating global synergies, and coordinating and leveraging the strategies in individual countries.

EXPANDING THE GLOBAL FOOTPRINT

Motivation to be global naturally leads to global initiatives to expand a firm's market footprint, a task that can be messy and difficult. Strategy development gets much harder when the context is a different language, an unfamiliar culture, new competitors and channels, and a very different set of market trends and forces. There are many routes to failure. A study of some 150 international expansion initiatives during a five-year period ending in 2000 showed that less than half avoided failure. However, the examination of those that survived suggested that success was usually accompanied with four conditions:[7]

- *A strong core.* A strong home market provides resources and experience that can be leveraged in geographic expansion. It is a rare firm that finds success abroad without a successful home market.
- *A repeatable formula for expansion.* When the same model works in country after country, the risk of entry is reduced. The agricultural commodity firm Olam International uses a unique model of placing managers 'up country' close to farm producers. The success of this model has led to it being applied in many African countries.
- *Customer differentiation that travels.* When the same segments are targeted and the same product and position work across countries, there is no need to research the market and reinvent the offering every time a new country is entered. Quiksilver, Bang & Olufsen, and Heineken, for example, have been able to differentiate their respective brands the same way everywhere.
- *Industry economics.* It is important to recognize whether global share or local share will drive success. Some industries, like razors or computers, for example, provide cost advantages for global scale. Others, like beer, cement, and software, reward high local share.

To the extent that any of these conditions are missing, the task will be more difficult, but strategic considerations may still make it imperative to find a way to succeed.

What Country to Enter?

Once a firm has decided to become global, deciding what country or countries to enter – and in what sequence – is a key challenge. Entering any new market can be risky and take away resources that could be used to make strategic investments elsewhere. A frequently unforeseen consequence of global expansion is that healthy markets, especially the home market, are put at risk by this diversion of resources. It is thus important to select markets for which the likelihood of success will be high and the resource drain minimized.

Market selection starts with several basic dimensions:

- Is the market attractive in terms of size and growth? Are there favourable market trends? For many companies, China and India often appear attractive because of their sheer size and growth potential.
- Can the firm add value to the market? Will the products and business model provide a point of differentiation that represents a relevant customer benefit? Tesco has developed an Internet-based home delivery system for grocery retailers that adds value in many markets.[8]
- How intense is the competition? Are other firms well entrenched with a loyal following, and are they committed to defending their position? Aldi has found that its expansion in the UK market has been more challenging, in spite of a serious recession in 2008 and 2009, than it would have expected, mainly owing to the strong challenge presented by the low-price strategies of incumbent retailers.[9]
- Can the firm implement its business model in the country, or do operational or cultural barriers exist? How feasible is any adaptation that is required? Marks & Spencer attempted to export its products and the look and feel of stores to continental European countries, only to find that these offerings had little appeal. It did however, have great success in Ireland, the Far East, Southern and Eastern Europe, India, and the Middle East. In 2009, international sales were 10% of the company's total and growing at more than 25% per annum.
- Are there political uncertainties that will add risk? In addition to the obvious risks of political instability, there are more subtle issues. The Brazilian beef giant, JBS, has acquired beef and other processing facilities in a variety of international markets in order to overcome political uncertainty regarding its ability to export beef.
- Can a critical mass be achieved? It is usually fatal to enter countries lacking the sales potential needed to support the marketing and distribution effort required for success.

Nokia's withdrawal from the Japanese mobile phone market in 2008 is a good example of the challenges posed by the above forces. Although it had made a long-term commitment that was well supported financially, the brand failed to achieve the level of market share required to sustain the investment. The major problem appeared to be a cultural one, with Japanese consumers used to multifunctional phones made by Japanese firms. As the world's largest manufacturer of mobile phones, with about 38% of the market, its willingness to withdraw from the Japanese market is indicative of the problems presented in developing a truly global strategy. Significantly, given the advanced nature of the market, Nokia committed itself to maintaining a research presence in the market.

A strategy of entering countries sequentially has several advantages. It reduces the initial commitment, allows the product and marketing programme to be improved on the basis of experience in preceding countries, and provides for the gradual creation of a regional presence. Other factors, however, argue that global expansion should be done on as wide a front as possible. First, economies of scale, a key element of successful global strategies, will be more quickly realized and will be a more significant factor. Second, the ability of competitors to copy products and brand positions – a very real threat in most industries – will be inhibited because a first-mover advantage will occur in more markets. Third, standardization, a topic to which we now turn, is more feasible.

MARKETING IN CHINA

An Ad Age study by Normandy Madden, a student of developing markets, provided some warnings to those western firms that enter China:[10]

- China is not a single country. Rather, it is more like dozens of countries, each with its own points of difference in spending power, motivations, and channels. Looking at China as a single market is like believing Europe is a homogeneous entity.
- Western goods are popular and provide self-expressive benefits, but that does not mean that the Chinese people are not grounded in their Confucian traditions and culture.
- The Chinese consumer is price conscious, demanding, and knowledgeable, in part because of the rise of the Internet. Beware of talking down to them.
- Don't underestimate local brands. In many categories, local brands were bystanders at first, but rose to be market contenders if not leaders.
- Mass media in China have limitations –the audience will include many who are unable to buy some brands, and the programming is not compelling. The more effective route is often more focused marketing using events, sampling, promotions, or digital marketing.

STRATEGIC ALLIANCES

Strategic alliances play an important role in global strategies because it is common for a firm to lack a key success factor for a market. It may be distribution, a brand name, a sales organization, technology, R&D capability, or manufacturing capability. To remedy this deficiency internally might require excessive time and money. When the uncertainties of operating in other countries are considered, a strategic alliance is a natural alternative for reducing investment and the accompanying inflexibility and risk.

A strategic alliance is a collaboration leveraging the strengths of two or more organizations to achieve strategic goals. There is a long-term commitment involved.

It is not simply a tactical device to provide a short-term fix for a problem – to outsource a component for which a temporary manufacturing problem has surfaced, for example. Furthermore, it implies that the participating organizations will contribute and adapt needed assets or competencies to the collaboration and that these assets or competencies will be maintained over time. The results of the collaboration should have strategic value and contribute to a viable venture that can withstand competitive attack and environmental change.

A strategic alliance provides the potential for accomplishing a strategic objective or task – such as obtaining distribution in Italy – quickly, inexpensively, and with a relatively high prospect of success. This is possible because the involved firms can combine existing assets and competencies instead of having to create new assets and competencies internally.

A strategic alliance can take many forms, from a loose informal agreement to a formal joint venture. The most informal arrangement might be simply trying to work together (selling our products through your channel, for example) and allowing systems and organizational forms to emerge as the alliance develops. The more informal the arrangement, the faster it can be implemented and the more flexible it will be. As conditions and people change, the alliance can be adjusted. The problem is usually commitment. With low exit barriers and commitment, there may be a low level of strategic importance and a temptation to back away or to disengage when difficulties arise.

Motivations for Strategic Alliances

Strategic alliances can be motivated by a desire to achieve some of the benefits of a global strategy, as outlined in Figure 13.1. For example, a strategic alliance can:

- *Generate scale economies.* The fixed investment that Toyota made in designing a car and its production systems was spread over more units because of a joint venture with GM.
- *Gain access to strategic markets.* Nestlé and General Mills have a long-term alliance, Cereal Partners Worldwide, to sell breakfast cereal outside North America. This alliance reflects the strength of General Mills in cereals and Nestlé's global food expertise and distribution strength.
- *Overcome trade barriers.* One of the major challenges in marketing in India is the absence of a national retail structure. Retail remains one of the few industries in India with FDI controls; thus, many international retailers such as Tesco (with Tata Groups Trent Ltd) and Wal-Mart (with Bharti Group) have established partnerships with local retailers both to learn about the market and to develop a presence if and when government changes the rules.

Perhaps more commonly, a strategic alliance may be needed to compensate for the absence of or weakness in a needed asset or competency. Thus, a strategic alliance can:

- *Fill out a product line to serve market niches.* Ford has, for example, relied on alliances to provide key components of its product line. Ford's long-time relationship with Mazda has resulted in many Ford models, as well as access to some Far East markets. When Mazda decided not to build a minivan, Ford turned to Nissan for help. One firm simply cannot provide the breadth of models needed in a major market such as the United States.
- *Gain access to a needed technology.* Nestlé and General Mills, via Cereal Partners Worldwide, announced plans to build a cereal innovation centre in Switzerland in 2009 to accelerate their joint work in developing cereals with high nutritional value.
- *Use excess capacity.* A partnership may be established in order to deploy excess capacity of one firm and avoid capital investment in plant on the part of the other.
- *Gain access to low-cost manufacturing capabilities.* A host of companies, from Nokia to Apple, have alliances in China to source products and components.
- *Access a name or customer relationship.* COFCO Tunhe in China has a strategic relationship with Heinz to supply it with tomato paste for use in the Chinese market. There are clear long-term benefits on both sides of this relationship.
- *Reduce the investment required.* In some cases, a firm's contribution to a joint venture can be technology, with no financial resources required.

The Key: Maintaining Strategic Value for Collaborators

A major problem with strategic alliances occurs when the relative contribution of th partners becomes unbalanced over time and one partner no longer has any propri etary assets and competencies to contribute. This has happened in many of the earl partnerships involving international partners in consumer electronics, heavy machir ery, power-generation equipment, factory equipment, and office equipment.

The result, when one of the partners has become deskilled or hollowed out ar no longer participates fully in the venture, can be traced in part to the motivation the partners. Offshore firms are motivated to learn skills; they see the strategic ben fit in having a particular technology and they work to gain it. Often, the onshore firr are motivated to enhance profits by outsourcing elements of the value chain in ord to reduce costs. They start by outsourcing assembly and move on to components, value-added components, to product design, and finally to core technologies. Tl onshore partner is then left with just the distribution function, whereas the offsho firm retains the key business elements, such as product refinement, design, a production.

One approach to protecting assets and competencies is to structure the situation so that operating management is shared. Compare, for example, the joint Toyota/GM manufacturing facility, where GM is involved in the manufacturing process and its refinements, with Chrysler's effort to sell a Mitsubishi car designed and manufactured in Japan. In the latter case, Mitsubishi eventually developed its own name and dealer network and now sells its car directly. When the motivation for an alliance is to avoid investment and achieve attractive short-term returns instead of developing assets and competencies, the alliance will break down.

Another approach is to protect assets from a partner by controlling access. Many Japanese firms have a coordinated information transfer. Such a position avoids uncoordinated, inappropriate information flow. Other firms put clear conditions on access to a part of the product line or a part of the design. Motorola, for example, releases its microchip technology to its partner, Toshiba, only, as Toshiba delivers on its promise to increase Motorola's penetration in the Japanese market. Still others keep improving the assets involved so that the partner's dependence continues. Of course, the problem of protecting assets is most difficult when the asset can be communicated by a drawing. It is somewhat easier when a complex system is involved – when, for example, the asset is manufacturing excellence.

A second set of problems involves execution of the alliance. With strategic alliances, at least two sets of business systems, people, cultures, and structures need to be reconciled. In addition, the culture and environment of each country must be considered. The Japanese, for example, tend to use a consensus-building decision process that relies on small group activity for much of its energy; this approach is very different from that of Anglo-Saxon managers, but perhaps not so different from that in Scandinavia. Furthermore, the interests of each partner may not always seem to be in step. Many otherwise well-conceived alliances have failed because the partners simply had styles and objectives that were fundamentally incompatible.

When a joint venture is established as a separate organization, research has shown that the chances of success will be enhanced if:

- The joint venture is allowed to evolve with its own culture and values – the existing cultures of the partners will probably not work even if they are compatible with each other.
- The management and power structure from the two partners is balanced.
- Venture champions are on board to carry the ball during difficult times. Without people committed to making the venture happen, it will not happen.
- Methods are developed to resolve problems and to allow change over time. It is unrealistic to expect any strategy, organization, or implementation to exist without evolving and changing. Partners and the organizations thus need to be flexible enough to allow change to occur.

Alliances are a widespread part of business strategy (the top 500 global businesses have an average of 60 major alliances each) but need to be actively managed. One study of some 200 corporations found that the most successful at adding value through alliances employed staff who coordinated all alliance-related activity within the organization.[11] This function would draw on prior experiences to provide guidance to those creating and managing new alliances. One firm, for example, has 'thirty-five rules of thumb' to manage alliances from creation to termination. The dedicated alliance staff would also increase external visibility (an alliance announcement has been found to influence stock price), coordinate internal staffing and management of alliances, and help identify the need to change or terminate an alliance.

GLOBAL MARKETING MANAGEMENT

Managing a global marketing programme is difficult. The country or regions are often highly autonomous. Managers tend to think that they are different, and others, particularly those in 'central marketing', cannot understand the culture, customers, distribution, competitors, etc., of their country. As a result there tends to be little leveraging of successful programmes from country to country, and even little communication about common problems and programmes that are successful. Furthermore, the expertise around such areas as Internet communication, sponsorships, market research, etc., tends to be limited because of scale.

The challenge for global marketing teams is to change that – to create cooperation and communication where there has been competition and isolation. In Chapter 15 the problems that silo organizations present to marketing teams are further outlined, and practical ways to make marketing more effective in a silo world will be discussed.

KEY LEARNINGS

- A global strategy considers and exploits interdependencies between operations in different countries.
- Among the motivations driving globalization are obtaining scale economies, accessing low-cost labour or materials, taking advantage of national incentives to cross-subsidize, dodging trade barriers, accessing strategic markets, enhancing firm innovation, and creating global associations.
- A standardized brand is not always optimal. Economies of scale may not exist, the discovery of a global strategy (even assuming it exists) may be difficult, or the context (for example, different market share positions or brand images) may make such a brand impractical.
- Companies successful at expanding their global footprint usually have a strong core market, a repeatable expansion formula, customer differentiation that travels, and an understanding of local versus global scale. The selection of a country to enter should involve an analysis of the attractiveness of the market and the ability of the firm to succeed in that market.
- Strategic alliances (long-term collaboration leveraging the strengths of two or more organizations to achieve strategic goals) can enable an organization

to overcome a lack of a key success factor, such as distribution or manufacturing expertise. A key to the long-term success of strategic alliances is that each partner contributes assets and competencies over time and obtains strategic advantages.

- Global brand management needs to move the silo country business units from competition and isolation to cooperation and communication.

FOR DISCUSSION

1. Access the motivations for going global. What would be the most important for a food company?
2. What products are likely to be more standardized across countries? Why? What products are least likely?
3. Pick a product, like a car or food brand, or a service that is offered in only a limited number of countries. Assess the advantages of expanding to a more global presence.
4. For a particular product or service, how would you evaluate the countries that would represent the best prospects? Be specific. What information would you need, and how would you obtain it? Prioritize the criteria that would be useful in deciding which countries to enter.
5. For a firm such as HSBC, Danone, or COFCO, how would you go about creating blockbuster global brand-building programmes – for example, sponsorships, promotions, or advertising? How would you leverage those programmes?
6. Select a company. How would you advise it to find an alliance partner to gain distribution into China? What advice would you give regarding the management of that alliance?
7. What is the advantage of a global brand team? What are the problems of using a team to devise and run the global strategy?

NOTES

1. Douglas B. Holt, John A. Quelch, and Earl L. Taylor, 'How Global Brands Compete', *Harvard Business Review*, September 2004, pp. 68–75.
2. Jeffrey R. Immelt, Vijay Govindarajan, and Chris Timble, 'How GE is Disrupting Itself', *Harvard Business Review*, October 2009, pp. 56–65.
3. Gary Hamel and C.K. Prahalad, 'Do You Really Have a Global Strategy?', *Harvard Business Review*, July–August 1985, pp. 139–148.

4. Theodore Levitt, 'The Globalization of Markets', *Harvard Business Review*, May–June 1983, pp. 92–102.

5. The material in this section draws from Chapter 5 of the book *Spanning Silos* by David Aaker, Boston, MA, Harvard Publishing Company, 2008.

6. Karlene Lukovitz, 'Brands Lose Relevance in Food-Buying Decisions', *Marketing Daily*, 21 October 2008.

7. James Root and Josef Ming, 'Keys to Foreign Growth: Four Requisites for Expanding Across Borders', *Strategy and Leadership*, 2006, **34**(3), pp. 59–61.

8. Victoria Griffith, 'Welcome to Your Global Superstore', *Strategy ? Business*, 2002, **26**, p. 95.

9. 'Aldi', *Marketing*, 16 September 2009, p. 19.

10. Normandy Madden, 'Looking to Grow in China? Ad Age has 10 Surefire Tips', *Advertising Age*, 4 May 2009, pp. 3 and 30.

11. Jeffrey H. Dyer, Prashant Kale, and Harbir Singh, 'How to Make Strategic Alliances Work', *MIT Sloan Management Review*, Summer 2001, pp. 37–43.

CHAPTER FOURTEEN

Setting Priorities for Business and Brands – the Exit, Milk, and Consolidate Options

There is nothing so useless as doing efficiently that which should not be done at all.
—*Peter Drucker*

Obviously everyone wants to be successful, but I want to be looked back on as being very innovative, very trusted and ethical, and ultimately making a big difference in the world.
—*Sergey Brin*

Standing in the middle of the road is very dangerous; you get knocked down by traffic from both sides.
—*Margaret Thatcher*

All firms, from China's Sinochem Group to Nestlé to Australia's BHP Billiton to Reliance Industries, India's largest privately owned conglomerate, should view their business units as a portfolio. Some should receive investment because they are cash-generating stars in the present and will be into the future. The investment is needed to keep them healthy and to exploit growth opportunities. Others need investment because they are the future stars of the company, even though they now have more potential than sales and profits. Identifying the priority business units, the ones that merit financial and managerial resources, is a key to a successful strategy.

Equally important, perhaps more important, is to identify those business units that are not priorities. Some of them should assume the role of generating cash through a milking or harvesting strategy. These units, termed *cash cows*, should no longer absorb investments aimed at growing the business. Yet other units should be divested or closed or merged because they lack the potential to become either stars or cash cows – their profit prospects may be unsatisfactory, or they may lack a fit with the strategic thrust going forward. These decisions, which are strategically and organizationally difficult, are often crucial to organizational success and even survival.

A related issue is dealing with too many brands by eliminating or merging them. Brand strategy and business strategy are closely related because a brand will often represent a business. As a result, brand strategy is often a good vehicle to develop and clarify the business strategy. Too many brands, like too many business units, result in confusion and inefficiency. The firm can support only so many brands, and brand proliferation has often grown to the point of paralysing the organization. In the automobile field there are now over 300 brands, which has resulted in confusion, overlap, inefficiency, and, worse, an inability to fund promising brands.

We start with an overview of portfolio strategy and then discuss the divest and milk strategy options. We then turn to the problem from the perspective of brand strategy and explore how brand portfolios can be reduced so that more brand focus becomes possible and clarity can be enhanced in both the brand strategy and the accompanying business strategy.

THE BUSINESS PORTFOLIO

Portfolio analysis of business units dates from the mid-1960s with the growth-share matrix, which was pioneered and used extensively by the BCG consulting group. The concept was to position each business within a firm on the two-dimensional matrix shown in Figure 14.1. The market-share dimension (actually the ratio of share to that

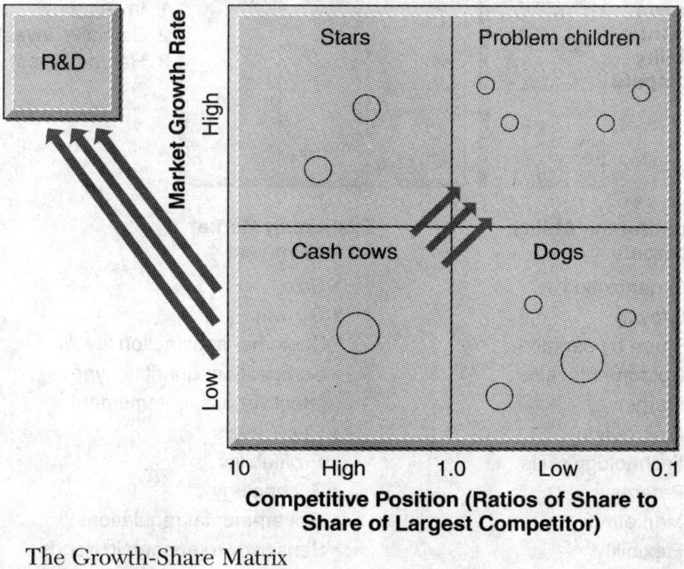

Figure 14.1 The Growth-Share Matrix

of the largest competitor) was a summary measure of firm strength and cost advantages resulting from scale economies and manufacturing experience. The growth dimension was defended as the best single indicator of market attractiveness.

The BCG growth-share matrix is associated with a colourful cast of characters representing strategy recommendations. According to the BCG logic, the stars, important to the business and deserving of any needed investment, resided in the high-share, high-growth quadrant, while the cash cows, the source of cash, occupied the high-share, low-growth quadrant. In addition, we have the dogs, potential cash traps and candidates for liquidation, in the low-growth, low-share quadrant and problem children, who have heavy cash needs but will eventually convert into stars, in the low-share, high-growth quadrant.

The BCG growth-share model, although naive and simplistic in its analysis and recommendations, was very influential in its day. Its lasting contribution was to make visible the issue of allocation across business units, that some businesses should generate cash that supports others. It also introduced the experience curve (discussed in Chapter 10) into strategy and showed that, under some conditions, market share could lead to experience-curve-based advantage.

A more realistic, richer portfolio model associated with GE and McKinsey also evaluates the business on two dimensions – market attractiveness and the business position. Each of these dimensions, as suggested by Figure 14.2, is richer and more

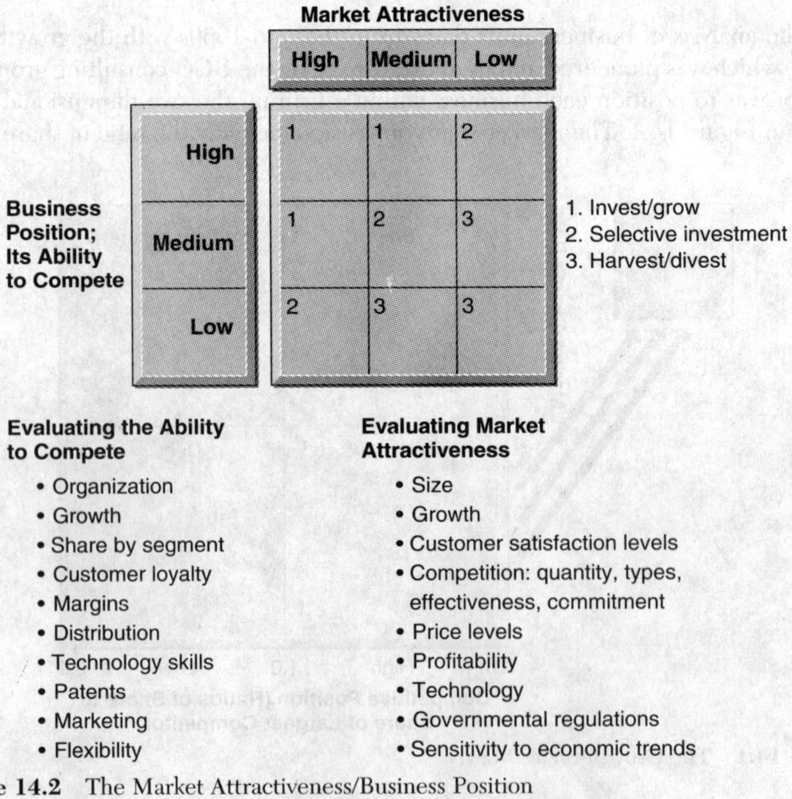

Figure 14.2 The Market Attractiveness/Business Position

robust than those used in the BCG model. The investment decision is again suggested by the position on a matrix. A business that is favourable on both dimensions should usually be a candidate to grow using the tools of the last four chapters.

When both market attractiveness and business position evaluations are unfavourable, the harvest or divest options should be raised. Of course, even in a hostile environment, routes to profitability can be found. Perhaps the business can turn to new markets, growth submarkets, superpremium offerings, new products, new applications, new technologies, or revitalized marketing. When the matrix position is neither unambiguously positive nor negative, the investment decision will require more detailed study.

DIVESTMENT OR LIQUIDATION

There are usually three drivers of a divestment decision besides the current and expected profit drain. The first is market demand. Perhaps demand estimates were overoptimistic in the first place, or perhaps the demand was there but deteriorated as the market matured and the excitement faded. The second is competitive intensity. New competitors could have emerged or the existing competitors may have been underestimated or could have enhanced their offering. The third is a change in strategic thrust of the organization, a change that affects the fit of the business. The firm may no longer be a synergistic asset, or the business may no longer be a link to the future. In fact, the business may be not only a resource drain but also a distraction to the internal culture and the external brand image.

These factors came into play when Philips decided to divest its semiconductor business in 2006. The decision was driven by two major forces: first, the need to reduce the volatility in earnings and revenue caused by the technology cycle in the semiconductor business – such fluctuations were considered incompatible with the high margin and stable sales cycles in other parts of the business; second, the desire of Philips to increase its focus on healthcare and wellness products. Following the divestment, the company deleted the term electronics from its corporate branding. Similarly, Danone wished to focus its business on health and wellness products. In 2003 it divested its involvement in the glass packaging business. In 2007 it sold its biscuit division to Kraft, and today it focuses on four businesses: fresh dairy, water, baby nutrition, and medical nutrition.

Being able to make and implement an exit decision can be healthy and invigorating. The opportunity cost of overinvesting in a business, and of hanging on to business ventures that are not performing and never will perform, can be damaging and even disastrous. Furthermore, this cost is often hidden from view because it is shielded by a non-decision. When a business that is not contributing to future profitability and growth absorbs resources in the firm – not only financial capital but also talent, the firm's most important currency – those businesses that do represent the future of the firm will suffer. Perhaps worse, some businesses with the potential to be important platforms for growth will be left on the sideline or starved, victims of false hopes and stubborn, misplaced loyalty.

One firm that has actively managed and developed specialization in divestment is Textron, a firm best known as a pioneer in the management of the diversified business model. One aspect of their business model is that businesses are often sold. Having developed a skill in divestment, the company is able quickly to identify buyers and to extract the best value from the deal for the firm. Between 2001 and 2008, 41 businesses were sold with a total value of US$ 4.4 billion. In the same time period, the average shareholder return was more than 6% higher than for other firms with similar business models.[1]

Such an active divestment programme can generate cash at a fair (as opposed to a forced-sale) price, liberate management talent, help reposition the firm to match its strategic vision, and add vitality. The divested businesses often benefit as well, as many will move into environments that are more supportive not only in terms of assets and competencies but also in terms of the commitment to succeed. It is healthy all-round to trim businesses. And there will always be business units to trim; one study by Bain & Company estimated that, of the major growth initiatives, only 20% are successful.[2] Many of the rest are ill-advised investments in businesses that should have been milked or divested.

As noted in Chapter 12, achieving sustained growth is rare, and when it appears it is often fuelled by new businesses. One theory advanced by James Brian Quin, a strategy theorist, and others on how to find and develop successful new businesses is to 'let a thousand flowers bloom', tend those that thrive, and let the rest wither. The venture capital industry lives by the mantra that, if you fund 10 ventures, two will be successful, and they will represent overall success. Achieving success requires the funding of many ventures. The key to the prescription that it takes many tries to find success is to have a process and the will to terminate business units that are not going to fuel growth in the future. Without that process, a thousand flowers will result in an overgrown garden where none is healthy.

Many firms avoid divestment decisions until they become obvious or are forced by external forces. In addition to wasted resources, delayed divestment decisions result in lower prices being obtained for the business. One study showed that the total return to shareholders from a divestment declines as the decision is delayed.[3] Another found that organizations that actively manage these decisions by systematically evaluating the strategic fit and future prospects of each business, and then regularly making divestment decisions or placing business units on a probationary status, are more profitable.[4]

When any of the following are present, an exit strategy should be considered:

- *Business position*:
  - The business position is weak – the assets and competencies are inadequate, the value proposition is losing relevance, or the market share is in third or fourth place and declining in the face of strong competition.
  - The business is now losing money, and future prospects are dim.
- *Market attractiveness*:
  - Demand within the category is declining at an accelerating rate, and no pockets of enduring demand are accessible to the business. It is unlikely that a resurgence of the category or a subcategory will occur.

  - The price pressures are expected to be extreme, caused by determined competitors with high exit barriers and by a lack of brand loyalty and product differentiation.
- *Strategic fit*:
  - The firm's strategic direction has changed, and the role of the business has become superfluous or even unwanted.
  - Firms' financial and management resources are being absorbed when they could be employed more effectively elsewhere.

Exit Barriers

Even when the decision seems clear, there may be exit barriers that need to be considered. Some involve termination costs. A business may support other businesses within the firm by providing part of a system, by supporting a distribution channel, or by using excess plant capacity. Long-term contracts with suppliers and with labour groups may be expensive to break. The business may have commitments to provide spare parts and service back-up to retailers and customers, and it may be difficult to arrange alternative acceptable suppliers.

An exit decision may affect the reputation and operation of other company businesses, especially if that business is visibly tied to the firm. At the extreme, closing a business could affect access to financial markets and influence the opinion of dealers, suppliers, and customers about the firm's other operations.

If there is any reason to believe the market may change, making the business more attractive, the exit decision could be delayed or changed to a milk or hold decision. Remaining in the business may be a contingency play. Nestlé acquired and supported the technology used for Nespresso in the early 1970s, but its exceptional success only began to materialize in the early 1990s. During that time, the company remained convinced that there was a market for superpremium instant coffee.

Biases Inhibiting the Exit Decision

There are well-documented psychological biases in analysing a business. One such bias is reluctance to give up. There may be an emotional attachment to a business that has been in the 'family' for many years, or that may even be the original business on which the rest of the firm was based. It is difficult to turn your back on such a valued friend, especially if it means laying off good people. Managerial pride also enters in. Professional managers often view themselves as problem-solvers and are reluctant to admit defeat. Several anecdotes describe firms that have had to send a series of executives to close down a subsidiary. Too frequently, the executive would become convinced that a turnaround was possible, only subsequently to fail at the effort.

Another obstacle is called confirmation bias.[5] People naturally seek out information that supports their position and discount disconfirming information, whatever the context. The audiences for partisan political observers do not represent a cross-section but, rather, involved people who seek out those who support their beliefs. Confirmation bias can be rampant in evaluating a business to which some have emotional and professional ties. Information that confirms that the business can be saved is more likely to be uncovered and valued than disconfirming information. Questions asked in market research may be slanted, perhaps inadvertently, towards providing an optimistic future for the business. When there is uncertainty, the bias can become large. When predicting future sales or projecting costs, for example, extreme numbers may be put forth as plausible. Such a tendency is seen in major governmental decisions, such as funding a fighter plane or building a bridge, as well as in forecasting sales.

Another bias to deal with is the escalation of commitment. Instead of regarding prior investments as sunk costs, there is a bias towards linking them to future decisions. Thus, a decision to invest €10 million more is framed as salvaging the prior €100 million investment.

All three biases were in view when Tenneco Oil Company made some decisions that helped lead to their demise.[6] Tenneco Oil was a healthy company, in the top 20 in the Fortune 500, but stole defeat from the jaws of victory, so to speak. They had a division, J.I. Case, a manufacturer of agricultural and construction equipment, that was doing badly, with weak products, weak distribution, high costs, and a 10% market share, facing a declining, low-profit industry with excess capacity and dominated by John Deere. Instead of facing reality, Tenneco instead made the same mistake twice by buying International Harvester, a competitor of Chase with 20% share and on the verge of bankruptcy. The market did not improve, synergies did not materialize in a timely fashion, and the losses of the combined equipment company were substantial, while the profit flow of the energy operations faltered as the price of oil fell. These events, coupled with high leverage, meant the end of Tenneco Oil – the company was basically sold off in pieces. A series of bad decisions were driven not by an objective analysis but, rather, by these biases coupled with the illusion that success and cash flow, largely dependent on external events, would continue.

Injecting Objectivity into Disinvest Decisions

To deal with these biases, the decision needs to be more objective in terms of both process and people. The process should be transparent and persuasive, thereby encouraging the discussion to be professional, centred on key issues, and discouraging emotional gut reactions. It helps if it is applied to a spectrum of business units instead of just the marginal ones. It is well known that the only way to close down a defence plant is to evaluate all of them and let the process identify which ones are no longer needed. When politicians are faced with such objective evidence and required to vote for or against, it becomes harder to fight for 'their base'.

It is also helpful to have people interjected into the analysis without a history that prevents them from being objective. Such people can be from within the firm, but sometimes an outside party from a consulting company or a new hire can be more objective. This can be done vicariously as well. There is the often repeated story of how Intel made the painful decision to turn its back on the memory business, which represented not only its heritage but the bulk of its sales. Intel's president, Andy Grove, at one point looked at CEO Gordon Moore and asked what a new outside CEO would do. The answer was clear – get out of memory. So the two men symbolically walked out of the door and walked back in, and then made the fateful decision to exit a business that had been destroyed by Asian competitors. Even after making the decision, it was difficult to cut out all R&D and close it down. Two people sent to close the business dragged their heels and continued to invest; finally, Grove himself had to step in. It turns out that the implementation of an exit decision is also difficult.

Peter Drucker recounted a story about a leader firm in a specialized industry that organized a group of people every three months to look critically at one segment of the company's offerings. This group was a cross-section of young managers and changed every quarter. They addressed the Andy Grove question – if we were not in this business now, would we go into it? If the answer was no, an exit strategy would be considered. If the answer was yes, then the next question was whether the existing business strategy would be used. A negative judgement would lead to proposed changes. One key to the firm's success was that this process led to the exit or modification of every single one of its businesses over a five-year period.

THE MILK STRATEGY

A milk or harvest strategy aims to generate cash flow by reducing investment and operating expenses to a minimum, even if that causes a reduction in sales and market share. The underlying assumptions are that the firm has better uses for the funds, that the involved business is not crucial to the firm either financially or synergistically, and that milking is feasible because sales will stabilize or decline in an orderly way without supporting investment. The milking strategy creates and supports a cash cow business.

There are variants of milking strategies. A fast milking strategy would be disciplined about minimizing the expenditures towards the brand and maximizing the short-term cash flow, accepting the risk of a fast exit. A slow milking strategy would sharply reduce long-term investment but continue to support operating areas such as marketing and service. A hold strategy would provide enough product development investment to hold a market position, as opposed to investing to grow or strengthen the position.

Conditions Favouring a Milking Strategy

A milking strategy would be selected over a growth strategy when the current market conditions make investments unlikely to improve a rather negative environment caused by competitor aggressiveness, consumer tastes, or whatever. Sometimes it is precipitated by a new entrant that turns a market hostile. In the mobile phone market the manufacture of handsets has become hostile, with fluctuating demands and falling average prices per handset. Nokia's response to this is to shift its business towards leadership in mobile solutions. This development fits well with its position as a leading handset manufacturer, with the latter providing the funds for the new business.

Several conditions support a milking strategy rather than an exit strategy:

- The business position is weak but there is enough customer loyalty, perhaps in a limited part of the market, to generate sales and profits in a milking mode. The risk of losing relative position with a milking strategy is low.

- The business is not central to the current strategic direction of the firm, but has relevance to it and leverages assets and competencies.
- The demand is stable or the decline rate is not excessively steep, and pockets of enduring demand ensure that the decline rate will not suddenly become precipitous.
- The price structure is stable at a level that is profitable for efficient firms.
- A milking strategy can be successfully managed.

One advantage of milking rather than divesting is that a milking strategy can often be reversed if it turns out to be based on incorrect premises regarding market prospects, competitor moves, cost projections, or other relevant factors. A resurgence in product classes that were seemingly dead or in terminal decline gives pause. Oatmeal, for example, has experienced a sharp increase in sales because of its low cost and associations with nutrition and health. Marketers in the product category helped by embracing the need for convenience and offering oatmeal in easy-to-prepare formats, an important missing factor resulting in the previous decline in sales.

Fountain pens, invented in 1884, were virtually killed off by the appearance in 1939 of the ballpoint. However, the combination of nostalgia and a desire for prestige has promoted a major comeback for the luxury fountain pen, particularly in Europe and China. Again, the marketers of fountain pens have driven this trend by producing more inexpensive pens, with fashionable design and in disposable formats. As a result, the industry now enjoys strong annual sales growth.

Implementation Problems

It can be organizationally difficult to assign business units to a cash cow role, because in a decentralized organization (and most firms pride themselves on their decentralized structure) it is natural for the managers of cash-generating businesses to control the available cash that funds investment opportunities. The culture is for each business to be required or encouraged to fund its own growth, and of course all business units have investment options with accompanying rationales. It requires a sometimes disruptive centralized decision to assign a large business unit a cash cow role. As a result, a fast-growing business with enormous potential but relatively low sales volume will often be starved of needed cash. The irony is that the largest businesses involving mature products may have inferior investment alternatives, but because cash flow is plentiful, their investments will still be funded. The net effect is that available cash is channelled to areas of low potential and withheld from the most attractive areas. A business portfolio analysis helps force the issue of which businesses should receive the available cash.

Another serious problem is the difficulty of placing and motivating a manager in a milking situation. Most business unit managers do not have the orientation, background, or skills to engage in a successful milking strategy. Adjusting performance measures and rewards appropriately can be difficult for both the organization and the managers involved. It might seem reasonable to use a manager who specializes in milking strategies, but that is often not feasible simply because such specialization is rare. Most firms rotate managers through different types of situation, and career paths simply are not geared to creating milking specialists.

There are also market risks associated with a milking strategy. If employees and customers suspect that a milking strategy is being employed, the resulting lack of trust may upset the whole strategy. As the line between a milking strategy and abandonment is sometimes very thin, customers may lose confidence in the firm's product and employee morale may suffer. Competitors may attack more vigorously. All these possibilities can create a sharper-than-anticipated decline. To minimize such effects, it is helpful to keep a milking strategy as inconspicuous as possible.

The Hold Strategy

A variant of the milking strategy is the hold strategy, in which growth-motivated investment is avoided, but an adequate level of investment is employed to maintain product quality, production facilities, and customer loyalty. A hold strategy will be superior to a milk strategy when the market prospects and/or the business position are not as grim. There may be more substantial and protected pockets of demand, better margins, a superior market position, a closer link to other business units in the firm, or the possibility of improved market prospects. A hold strategy would be preferable to an invest strategy when an industry lacks growth opportunities and a strategy of increasing share would risk triggering competitive retaliation. The hold strategy can be a long-term strategy to manage a cash cow, or an interim strategy employed until the uncertainties of an industry are resolved.

Sometimes, a hold strategy can result in a profitable 'last survivor' of a market that is declining more slowly than most assume. A strong survivor may be profitable, in part because there may be little competition and in part because the investment to maintain a leadership position might be relatively low. The cornerstone of this strategy is to encourage competitors to exit. Toward that end, a firm can be visible about its commitment to be the surviving leader in the industry by engaging in increased promotion or even introducing product improvements. It can encourage competitors to leave by pricing aggressively and by reducing their exit barriers by purchasing their assets, assuming their long-term obligations, or even by buying their business. Kunz, which made passbooks for financial institutions, was able to buy competitor assets so far under book value that the payback period was measured in months. As a result, Kunz had record years in a business area others had written off as all but dead decades earlier.

A problem with the hold strategy is that, if conditions change, reluctance or slowness to reinvest may result in lost market share. The two largest can manufacturers in the United States, American and Continental, failed to invest in the two-piece can process when it was developed because they were engaged in diversification efforts and were attempting to avoid investments in their cash cow. As a result, they lost substantial market share.

A hold strategy is particularly problematic if a disruptive innovation appears and the strategy prevents a firm from making necessary investments to remain relevant. As a result, firms may be slow to convert from film to digital, to reduce trans fats from packaged goods, or to adapt hybrid technology. The result could be a premature demise of a cash cow business.

PRIORITIZING AND TRIMMING THE BRAND PORTFOLIO

Brands are the face of a business strategy, and getting the brand strategy right is often a route to making the right business strategy decisions. One element of brand strategy is to set priorities within the brand portfolio, identifying the strong strategic brands, other brands playing worthwhile roles, brands that should receive no investment, and brands that should be deleted.[7]

One reason to prioritize brands and trim the brand portfolio is that the exercise provides a good way to prioritize the business portfolio because the brand will usually represent a business. When the brand perspective is used, the business prioritization analysis can sometimes be more objective and the resulting conclusion more transparent and obvious. The brand is usually a key asset of the business and represents its value proposition. Thus, a recognition that the brand has become weak can be a good signal that the business position is weak. Without prioritization of the brand portfolio, strategic brands will lose equity and market position because marginal brands are absorbing brand-building dollars and, worse, managerial talent. Managers simply follow an instinct to solve problems rather than exploiting opportunities, and too many marginal brands create a host of problems.

A second reason is that prioritizing and trimming the brand portfolio can correct the debilitating confusion associated with overbranding. Most firms simply have too many brands, subbrands, and endorsed brands, all part of complex structures. Some brands may reflect product types and others price value, and yet others customer types or applications. The branded offerings may even overlap. The totality often simply reflects a mess. Customers have a hard time understanding what is being offered and what to purchase; even employees may be confused. The business strategy therefore operates at a huge disadvantage.

A third reason is to address the strategic paralysis created by an overbranded, confused brand portfolio without priorities. It is all too common for a firm to be paralysed by an inability to commit to how a new offering or new business should be branded. To provide a brand to a new offering or business that will foster success, there needs to be a sense of what brands will be strategic going forward and what their role and image will be. Assigning a brand that lacks a strategic future or whose future is incompatible with that assignment can be a serious handicap to a business strategy.

One partial step to reducing overbranding is to be more disciplined about the introduction of new offerings, new businesses, and new brands. Of course, innovation requires that new directions be introduced, but this does not mean that ad hoc business expansion decisions should be made without a systematic justification process. In particular, any proposed new brand should represent a business that is substantial enough and has a long enough life to justify brand-building expenses, and it should have a unique ability to represent a business – that is, no other existing brands would work.

Controlling the introduction of new brands is only half the battle. There needs to be an objective process to phase out or redeploy marginal or redundant brands after they have outlived their usefulness. The strategic brand consolidation process,

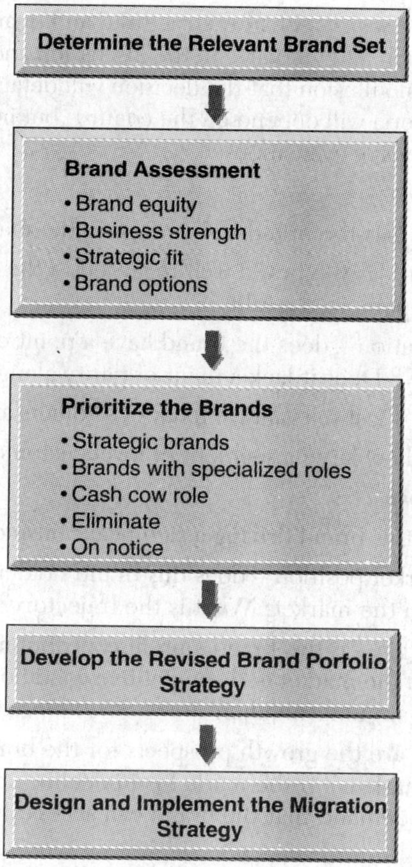

Figure 14.3 The Strategic Brand Consolidation Process

summarized in Figure 14.3, addresses that challenge. It involves five distinct steps: identifying the relevant brand set, assessing the brands, prioritizing brands, creating a revised brand portfolio strategy, and designing a transition strategy.

1. *Identify the relevant brand set.* The brand set will depend on the problem context. It can include all brands or subsets of the portfolio. For example, an analysis for Diesel might include Energie and G-Star. Or the Diesel brand might be analysed in its different contexts – clothing, footwear, intimate (underwear), bags, timewear (watches), jewellery, and shades (eyewear). Or it might include the brand set within a particular context, such as jeans brand, which might include Seven For All Mankind, True Religion, Nudie Jeans, Citizens of Humanity, and Tavertini So Jeans. When brands are involved that share similar roles, it becomes easier to evaluate the relative strength.
2. *Brand assessment.* If brand priorities are to be established, evaluation criteria need to be established. Furthermore, these criteria need to have metrics so

that brands can be scaled. A highly structured and quantified assessment provides stimulation and guidance to the discussion and the decision process. There should be no illusion that the decision will default to picking the higher number. The criteria will depend on the context, but in general there are four areas or dimensions of evaluations:

(a) *Brand equity*:
- Awareness – is the brand well known in the marketplace?
- Reputation – is the brand well regarded in the marketplace? Does it have high perceived quality?
- Differentiation – does the brand have a point of differentiation? A personality? Does it lack a point of parity along a key dimension?
- Relevance – is it relevant for today's customers and today's applications?
- Loyalty – how large a segment of loyal customers is there?

(b) *Business prospects*:
- Sales – is this brand driving a significant business?
- Share/market position – does this brand hold a dominant or leading position in the market? What is the trajectory?
- Profit margin – is this brand a profit contributor and likely to remain so? Or are the market and competitive conditions such that the margin prospects are unfavourable?
- Growth – are the growth prospects for the brand positive within its existing markets? If the market is in decline, are there pockets of enduring demand that the brand can access?

(c) *Strategic fit*:
- Extendability – does the brand have the potential to extend to other products as either a master brand or an endorser? Can it be a platform for growth?
- Business fit – does the brand drive a business that fits strategically with the direction of the firm? Does it support a product or market that is central to the future business strategy of the firm?

(d) *Branding options*:
- Brand equity transferability – could the brand equity be transferred to another brand in the portfolio by reducing the brand to a subbrand or by developing a descriptor?
- Merging with other brands – could the brand be aggregated with other brands in the portfolio to form one brand?

Brands need to be evaluated with respect to the criteria. The resulting scores can be combined by averaging, or by insisting on a minimal score on some key dimensions. For example, a low score on strategic fit may be enough to signal that the brand's role needs to be assessed. Or, if the brand is a significant cash drain, then it might be a candidate for review even if it is otherwise apparently healthy. In any case, the profile will be important, and judgement will need to be employed to make final assessments of the brand's current strength.

3. *Prioritizing brands.* The brands that are to live, be supported, and be actively managed need to be prioritized or tiered in some way. The number of tiers will depend on the context, but the logic is to categorize brands so that precious brand-building budgets are allocated wisely. The top tier will include the strategic power brands – those with existing or potential equity that are supporting a significant business or have the potential to do so in the future. A second tier could be those brands involving a smaller business, perhaps a niche or local business, or brands with a specialized role such as a flanker brand (a price brand that deters competitors from penetrating the market from below). A third tier would be the cash cow brands, which should be reduced with little or no brand-building resources invested into them.

   The remaining brands need to be assigned descriptor roles, eliminated, placed on notice, or restructured:

   - *Become descriptors.* Those brands that have no equity but serve to describe an offering could be assigned a descriptive role. This is a common strategy in the mobile phone market where manufacturers such as Nokia and HTC often use numbers to identify handsets, for example the Nokia N95 or the HTC P4350. These brands have little if any equity and thus are assigned a simple descriptive role.
   - *Eliminate.* If a brand is judged to be ill-suited to the portfolio because of weak or inappropriate brand equity, business prospects, strategic fit, or redundancy issues, a plan to eliminate the brand from the portfolio is needed. Selling it to another firm or simply killing it off become options.
   - *On notice.* A brand that is failing to meet its performance goals but has a plan to turn its prospects around might be put on an on-notice list. If the plan fails and prospects continue to look unfavourable, elimination should then be considered.
   - *Merged.* If a group of brands can be merged into a branded group, like MS Office, the goal of creating fewer, more focused brands will be advanced. Sony's 'make.believe' brand campaign is designed to bring each of its global brands (Sony Ericsson, Sony Pictures, Sony PlayStation, and Sony Music) under a single umbrella brand, reflecting the increasing convergence of these businesses and providing a focused response to consumer and competitive challenges.
   - *Transfer equity.* It is possible and practical to transfer the equity of a brand to be deleted to an existing brand.

Nestlé has long had in place a system of brand portfolio prioritization. Twelve global brands are the tier-1 brands on which they focus. Each of the global brands has a top executive that is designated as its brand champion. These executives make sure that all activities enhance the brand. They have final approval over any brand extensions and major brand-building efforts. The company has elevated six of these brands – Nescafé for coffee, Nestea for tea, Buitoni for pasta and sauces, Maggi for bouillon cubes, Purina for pet food, and Nestlé for ice cream and candy – as having priority within Nestlé. Nestlé has also identified 83 regional brands that receive management attention from the Swiss headquarters. In addition, there are hundreds of local brands that are either considered strategic, in which the headquarters is involved, or tactical, in which case they are managed by local teams.

4. *Develop the revised brand portfolio strategy.* With brand priorities set, the brand portfolio strategy will need to be revised. To that end, several brand portfolio structures should be created. They could include a lean structure with a single master brand, such as Lego, Durex, or BMW, or a 'house of brands' strategy like Mars, best known for its famous Mars Bar, but which also owns more than 50 major product brands in confectionery and petcare.

   The most promising options are likely to be in between. The idea is to create around two or three viable options, with perhaps two or three suboptions under each.

   The major brand portfolio structure options, together with suboptions, need to be evaluated with respect to whether they:

   - support the business strategy going forward;
   - provide suitable roles for the strong brands;
   - leverage the strong brands;
   - generate clarity both to customers and to the brand team.

THE CASE OF CENTURION

A large manufacturing firm, which is here labelled as Centurion Industries, went through a strategic brand consolidation process before selecting its portfolio strategy going forward. The process started when the CEO observed that the brand portfolio in a major division was too diffused and that future growth and market position were dependent on creating a simpler, more focused portfolio of powerful brands. The division had grown in part by acquisition and now had nine product brands, only three of which were endorsed by the corporate brand, Centurion. The nine brands served a variety of product markets that could be roughly clustered into two logical groupings. One, the green business group, included five brands. The other, the blue business group, involved four brands. Competitors with less brand fragmentation and more natural brand synergy had developed stronger brands and were enjoying share growth.

In the green business group, a brand assessment supported by customer research was conducted on all five brands. One, Larson, represented the largest business, had substantial credibility in that business, and had high awareness levels. Furthermore, it could be stretched to cover the other four areas, even though it had no current presence in any of those areas. It did have a visible quality problem, however, that was being addressed. The decision was made to migrate all of the green business brands to Larson and to make the quality issue at Larson a corporate priority. The first migration stage was to endorse three of the brands with Larson and replace the fourth brand, which drove a small business, with the Larson brand. The second stage, to occur within two years, was to convert all of the brands in the green business group to the Larson name and add an endorsement by the corporate brand.

In the blue business group, the brand Pacer emerged from the brand assessment stage as the strongest, especially in terms of awareness, image, and sales. Because Pacer was in a business area closely related to that of the other three brands, using the Pacer brand for the entire blue business group was feasible. However, one of the four brands in the blue group, Cruiser, was an extremely strong niche brand with a dominant position in a relatively small market and delivered significant self-expressive benefits to a hard-core customer base. Thus, it was decided that migrating the Cruiser brand to Pacer would be too risky, but that the balance of the blue group would operate under the Pacer brand. Again, both Pacer and Cruiser going forward would be endorsed by the corporate brand.

The end result was a brand architecture involving three brands rather than nine, with all three consistently endorsed by the corporate brand. The critical decision was making the tough call that in the long run the brand architecture would be stronger if niche brands were migrated into one of two broader brands. There were emotional, political, economic, and strategic forces and arguments against each move. The fact that one exception was allowed made the case more difficult to make and to implement. Critical to organizational acceptance was the use of an objective assessment template, which clearly identified the dimensions of the decision and facilitated the evaluation. It helped that much of each assessment was quantified from hard sales and market research data. Also critical was the strategic vision of the top management, because, at the end of the day, owners of some of the niche brands were not on board, and without a commitment from the top it would not have happened.

5. *Implement the strategy.* The final step is to implement the portfolio strategy, which usually means a transition for the existing strategy to a target strategy. That transition can be made abruptly or gradually.

The gradual strategy is the more common one, as it reduces the risk of alienating customers and other stakeholders. When Lenovo purchased IBM's PC business, it retained the rights to cobrand its machines with IBM for five years post-acquisition as a way of reassuring customers. Similarly, when Banco Santander acquired Abbey National in 2004, it did not immediately change the brand, only announcing that its UK banking business would be rebranded to Santander in 2009, with the project being completed by the end of 2010.

An abrupt transition can signal a change in the overall business and brand strategy; it becomes a one-time chance to provide visibility and credibility to a change affecting customers. An abrupt transition assumes that the business strategy is in place; if not, the effort will backfire.

The other option is to migrate customers from one brand to another gradually. This will be preferred when:

- there is no newsworthy reposition that will accompany the change;
- customers that may not have high involvement in the product class may need time to learn about and understand the change.

There is a risk of alienating existing customers by disrupting their brand relationship.

KEY LEARNINGS

- The exit decision, even though it is psychologically and professionally painful, can be healthy both for the firm, because it releases resources to be used elsewhere, and for the divested business, which might thrive in a different context.
- A milking or harvest strategy (generating cash flow by reducing investment and operation expenses) works when the involved business is not crucial to the firm financially or synergistically. For milking to be feasible, though, sales must decline in an orderly way.
- Proritizing and trimming the brand portfolio provides another perspective on prioritizing businesses, can clarify brand offerings, and can remove the paralysis of not being able to brand new offerings. A five-step prioritization process involves identifying the relevant brand set, assessing the brands, prioritizing brands, creating a revised brand portfolio strategy, and designing a transition strategy.

FOR DISCUSSION

1. In 2008, Ford sold the Jaguar brand to Tata Motors. For a number of years before this, Ford had been faced with large deficits. One contributor was the Jaguar line, which involved over US$ 12 billion in sunk costs, including a purchase price of around US$ 2.5 billion, with the rest coming from investments needed to upgrade the line and fix a quality problem. One of the strategic moves was to introduce a low-priced X car, which provided volume but seemed to affect the Jaguar image. What analyses should Ford have conducted before deciding to sell Jaguar? Would that have differed had the subject been another Ford brand, Volvo, which was profitable?
2. Consider a divestment strategy. Why is it hard to divest a business? Identify some cases of divestment. What are some of the motivations that led to these divestments?
3. Identify brands that are employing a milking strategy. What are the risks?

4. How would you determine if a firm had too many brands?
5. What in your judgement are the key problems or issues in the brand consolidation process?

NOTES

1. Michael C. Mankins, David Harding, and Rolf-Magnus Weddigen, 'How the Best Divest', *Harvard Business Review*, October 2008.
2. Chris Zook, *Beyond the Core*, Boston, MA, HBS Press, 2004.
3. Richard Foster and Sarah Kaplan, *Creative Destruction: Why Companies That Are Built to Last Underperform the Market – And How to Successfully Transform Them*, New York, NY, Currency, 2001.
4. Lee Dranikoff, Tim Koller, and Antoon Schneider, 'Divestiture: Strategy's Missing Link', *Harvard Business Review*, May 2002, pp. 75–83.
5. An excellent article that documents these biases and suggests solutions is John T. Horn, Dan P. Lovallo, and S. Patrick Viguerie, 'Learning to Let Go: Making Better Exit Decisions', *McKinsey Quarterly*, 2006, (2), pp. 65–76.
6. Dale E. Zand, 'Managing Enterprise Risk: Why a Giant Failed', *Strategy and Leadership*, 2009, **37**(1), pp. 12–19.
7. This material draws from David Aaker, *Brand Portfolio Strategy*, New York, NY, The Free Press, Chapter 10.

CHAPTER FIFTEEN

From Silos to Synergy – Harnessing the Organization[1]

If you are first you are first. If you are second you are nothing.
—Bill Shankly, Liverpool Football Club

Structure follows strategy.
—Alfred Chandler, Jr

The effective execution of a plan is what counts and not mere planning on paper; it is not what we put on our plate or even what we eat that provides nourishment and growth, but what we digest.
—J.R.D. Tata

In 1922, Alfred Sloan, a legend in management history, instituted a divisional structure at GM, with Chevrolet at the low end, Cadillac at the high end, and Pontiac, Oldsmobile, and Buick in between. The divisions had distinct offerings and no price overlap. His admonition at the time was that 'The responsibility of the CEOs of each operation should be in no way limited'. In no way limited!! The business world now had a method to deal with the emerging complexity of multiple product lines. Since that time, decentralization has refined and become the dominant organization form. Nearly every organization, from Nestlé to Microsoft to Toyota to Greenpeace, prides itself on being decentralized, with autonomous organizational groups termed silos, a metaphor for a self-contained entity.

There is good reason why silo units, usually defined by products or countries, are widely used – they have enormous inherent advantages. The managers are close to the market and can therefore understand customer needs. They are also intimate with the product or service and the underlying technology and operations, and thus can make informed offering and operational decisions. Being empowered to act quickly means no delays in making and implementing strategic decisions, an attribute that is vital in dynamic markets. Also, because distinct business units can be held accountable for investments and results, business performance will be known in a timelier and less ambiguous manner. The most impressive feature of decentralization, however, is that it fosters incredible energy and vitality. Managers are empowered and motivated to innovate, to gain competitive advantage by providing superior value propositions to the customers.

SILO-DRIVEN PROBLEMS – THE CASE OF MARKETING

Relying on an unfettered decentralized organization with highly autonomous silo units, even with all its attributes, is no longer competitively feasible (Figure 15.1). Looking at silos from the marketing perspective, six specific problems, or missed opportunities, can be associated with the silo structure. They provide a rationale not necessarily for eliminating silos but for finding ways to harness the silo energy so that both business and marketing strategies can emerge and succeed. It is important to understand these problems not only to motivate change but to provide a change target. The marketing set of problems may be the most severe, but there are serious problems, some virtually identical, that face other functions such as manufacturing, operations, or IT. Furthermore, the potential source of competitive advantage, synergy across silos, is put into jeopardy when the silos cannot be spanned.

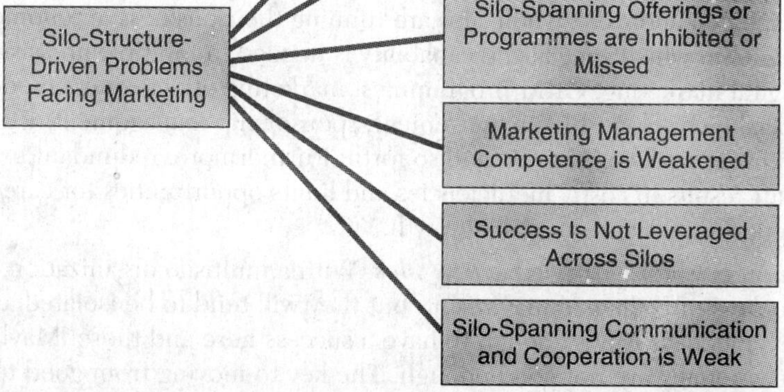

Figure 15.1 Silo-Structure-Driven Problems Facing Marketing.

- *Marketing resources are misallocated.* The silo structure nearly always leads to the misallocation of resources across product and country silo units, functional teams, brands, and marketing programmes, with smaller units being underfunded even when strategically important. Silo teams are organizationally and psychologically unable to make these cross-silo judgements. They only want more for themselves and view other silo units as competitors. Furthermore, such judgements require a hard-nosed, objective analysis of the potential of the business, using cross-silo data plus specialized frameworks and methods that will seldom be developed outside a central marketing unit.
- *Silo-spanning brands lack clarity and linkage.* Too often a master brand, perhaps even the corporate brand, is shared by many, sometimes all, silo groups. Each silo is motivated to maximize the power of the brand, without any concern for the brand's role in other business units. Especially when there is overlap in markets, inconsistent product and positioning strategies can damage the brand and result in debilitating marketplace confusion. Having a mixed brand message also makes it hard to convince the organization that the brand stands for something, and it is worthwhile having discipline in being true to that message.
- *Silo-spanning offerings and programmes are inhibited or missed.* Silo barriers often prevent marketing programmes from being shared. The result is that the most effective marketing programmes, requiring scale, such as the World Cup sponsorship and even a national advertising campaign, are not feasible. Furthermore, silo barriers can seriously inhibit the development of cross-silo offerings, in part because the cross-silo collaboration needed may not be in the DNA of the silos, and in part because autonomous silo units tend to look at the market with a narrow perspective and can often miss changes in the marketplace that are making their silo'd offering less relevant. Yet many customers are drawn to silo-spanning offers. The movement from products to systems solutions has become a tidal wave. Global customers are increasingly demanding global services and offerings.
- *Marketing management competences are weakened.* The quality of marketing talent, specialized support, and management sophistication tends to be dispersed and weak when silos are running their business autonomously at a time in which specialized capability is needed in multiple areas such as digital marketing, CRM programmes, marketing effectiveness modelling, social technology, blog management, sponsorship management, PR in an Internet world, and so on and so forth. Furthermore, redundant marketing staff results in costly inefficiencies and limits opportunities for career opportunities and specialty growth.
- *Success is not leveraged across silos.* With a multisilo organization, pockets of brilliance may result, but they will tend to be isolated and rarely leveraged. It is not enough to have a success here and there. Maybe and occasionally are not good enough. The key to moving from good to great is

to develop an organization that will identify marketing excellence within the silos and be nimble enough to leverage that excellence.

- *Cross-silo communication and cooperation is weak or non-existent.* The lack of communication and cooperation between silos is a basic problem that can directly impact upon organizational performance. When insights into customers, marketing trends, channels, or technologies that could impact upon strategy are not shared, an opportunity may be lost. When cooperation is not considered or is difficult to implement, successful synergistic programmes are unlikely to emerge. Furthermore, communication and cooperation failures are an underlying cause of many of the other silo-driven problems. Fixing them requires not only methods and processes but also changes to the inhibiting culture.

ADDRESSING THE SILO MARKETING ISSUES – CHALLENGES AND SOLUTIONS

Simply going to a centralized organizational form by getting rid of silos is not an option. First, managing a large complex multisilo organization centrally is not feasible. Second, as noted above, silos are there because they provide accountability, vitality, and intimacy with customers, technology, and products, so eliminating them would not generally be wise. The solution, rather, is to replace competition and isolation with cooperation and communication so that the overall business strategy will succeed and organization synergy will emerge. In the process, it is likely that some selective centralization of some activities and decisions will be useful – a tough assignment that is usually given to a new or revitalized CMO (chief marketing officer) slot.

Efforts by a CMO and his or her team to gain credibility, traction, and influence represents a formidable task in the face of silo indifference or, more likely, resistance. Succeeding and even surviving in this effort is at best uncertain. As result, the tenure of new CMOs is short – it was found to average 23 months.[2] The amazing short window reflects the difficulties of the new CMO's job, even when the assignment is labelled to be a strategic imperative.

In one study over 40 CMOs were asked what works in terms of addressing the silo problem. Three headlines from the study:

1. *Realize that non-threatening roles can be powerful change agents.* The CMO can take control of elements of strategy and tactics from silos, and that can be the right course in certain circumstances. However, there are other less threatening roles, with reduced risk of failure or even flame-out, that can have a significant influence on strategy and culture while building credibility and relationships. In particular, the CMO can assume the role of facilitator, consultant, or service provider. In a facilitator role, the CMO team can establish a common planning framework, foster communication, encourage and enable cooperation, create data and knowledge banks, and upgrade the level of marketing talent throughout the organization. In the

consultant role, the CMO would become an invited participant in the silo strategy development process. As a service provider, the silo business units would 'hire' the CMO team to provide marketing services such as marketing research, segmentation studies, and training, or marketing activities such as sponsorships and promotions.

2. *Aim at the silo-driven problems*. The all too common instinct of forcing centralization and standardization on the organization can be dysfunctional, even resulting in a flame-out of the CMO team. Reducing silo authority, making the organization more centralized, and moving towards more standardized offerings and marketing programmes is often warranted and useful. In fact, there is a strong trend in that direction, for good reason. However, these changes should not be goals in themselves but, rather, one of the routes to a set of goals. The goal should be to make progress against the silo-driven problems and therefore create stronger offerings and brands and effective synergistic effective marketing strategies and programmes.
3. *Use organizational levers: structure, systems, people, and culture.* Each of these involves powerful routes to change an organization. They are not only key to organizational change but also the basis for strategy implementation.

ORGANIZATIONAL LEVERS AND THEIR LINK TO STRATEGY

Organizations can be conceptualized as having four components – structure, systems, people, and culture. Their relationship to strategy and its implementation is summarized in Figure 15.2. The organizational components need to be informed by the strategy. For any business strategy to be successful, the right structure, systems, people, and culture need to be in place and functioning. Furthermore, the four components need to be congruent with each other. If one of the components is inconsistent with the rest or with the strategy, success will be a casualty, even if the strategy is brilliant and well timed.

When Mercedes Benz and Chrysler merged in 1998, the logic seemed impeccable. Mercedes was a luxury car maker seeking a foothold in the volume car market. Chrysler was a profitable volume car maker that could go further with fresh investment. The new DaimlerChrysler seemed a merger made in a US$36 billion heaven. However, Daimler management had failed to appreciate the challenges involved in implementing the merger strategy and realizing its goals. Although Chrysler was profitable, it had achieved this through early entry into the 1990s growth market of light trucks. The follow-up products were not as successful owing to pricing and quality problems and a much tougher and more competitive business environment. In addition, many Chrysler managers left post-merger, leaving the business without many of those who had led it to its success in the first place.[3] Finally, Daimler management waited for two years before they inserted their own management, as they feared that the Mercedes brand would be adversely affected by too close an association with Chrysler and also that the German and American management cultures

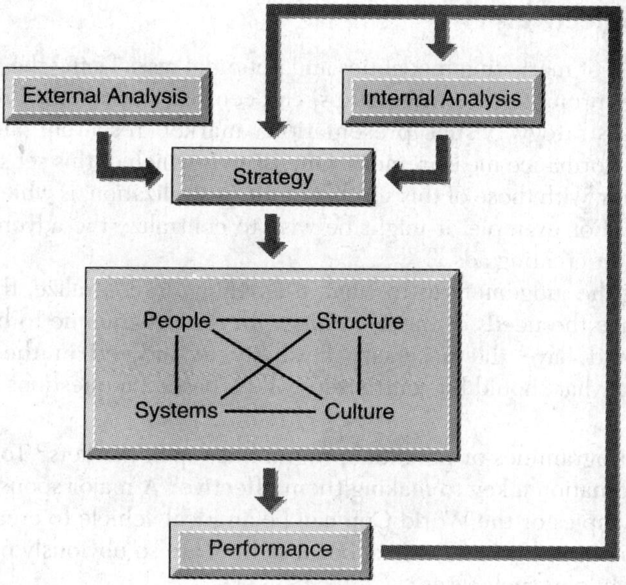

Figure 15.2 A Framework for Analysing Organizations.

might not mix well.[4] After a German CEO was appointed to Chrysler, a round of cost cutting, an emphasis on quality and new products led the firm to profitability in 2004 and 2005. However, by that time Mercedes was facing troubles of its own, primarily quality problems in its volume C- and E-class saloons, although there was optimism that a new CEO could turn the situation around. In mid-2006 the value of DaimlerChrysler was about half what it was at its most euphoric peak following the merger in 1999.[5]

The DaimlerChrysler story graphically illustrates the importance of making the organization internally congruent and capable of supporting the strategy. The assessment of any strategy should include a careful analysis of organizational risks and a judgement about the nature of any required organizational changes and their associated costs and feasibility.

Each of the four organizational components can be used to address any organizational problem. In the remainder of this chapter, we discuss how the organizational structure, systems, people, and culture can be employed to address the silo problem. In doing so, each of the four components will be elaborated and illustrated. The exercise will also illuminate the levers that an organizational designer can use to address other problems such as silo issues facing the IT group, how to cultivate innovation, or how to make the organization more customer centric. At the close of the chapter, an overview of strategic market management will be presented.

STRUCTURE

The structure of the organization, which includes the lines of authority and the way people and units are grouped, can encourage cooperation, sharing, and communication.

Centralize Selectively

There are a host of marketing modalities and potential tasks facing the CMO, including advertising, promotions, sponsorships, call centres, packaging, PR, digital marketing, brand strategy, visual presentation, market research, and marketing programme performance measurement. One issue is which of this set should be centralized. Another, with those of this set that merit centralization, is which parts should be centralized. For example, it might be wise to centralize the advertising strategy and not media or creating ads.

In making the judgement as to what, if anything, to centralize, the CMO must carefully balance the needs of the silo units with the programme to be centralized. The silos should have the necessary flexibility to succeed in the marketplace. Decisions as to what should be centralized will be based on questions like:

- What programmes or potential programmes span markets? To what extent is coordination a key to making them effective? A major sponsorship like the Olympics or the World Cup can be an ideal vehicle to create an acceptance of cross-business teams, because they are so obviously needed and worthwhile in such cases.
- Where is functional expertise best developed? Can redundancy be reduced? It is far better to have one group with a depth of competence in an area like advertising or sponsorships than many with shallow talent and capacity.
- What brands span markets? Does market adaptation compensate for a dilution of the central message? In India, McDonald's appears as it does in every other market, with burgers, fries, and soft drinks sold under the golden arches. The one difference is that none of the burgers is made with pork or beef.
- What truly requires local knowledge and management? Are there positions and programmes that work across products and markets? Pringles, for example, requires different flavours in different markets, but most of the social and functional benefits work everywhere.
- What deviations in budgets, reporting lines, and authority can be tolerated? What fights are worth winning? In the case of Visa, the integrity of the brand had the highest priority – the energy to fight battles was devoted to avoiding product offerings (such as charging for converting currency) that would compromise the brand promise.

Use Teams and Networks

The CMO should look towards employing some of the available organizational devices that will advance cross-functional understanding. HP's Customer Experience Council, IBM's Global Marketing Board, and P&G's Global Marketing Officer's Leadership team are powerful vehicles to create consistency and/or synergy. Perhaps more importantly, teams also provide a vehicle for cross-silo communication and relationships to develop.

Formal and informal networks, another key organizational tool, can be based on topics such as customer groups, market trends, customer experience contexts, and geographies, or functional areas like sponsorship and digital marketing. Nestlé, for example, has developed information networks around global customers such as Tesco or Wal-Mart and silo-spanning interest areas such as ethnic and niche markets. The network members are motivated to keep in contact with counterparts in other countries to learn of intelligence around the customer strategies and programmes that work in their stores. A formal network will have assigned membership, a leadership structure, and a supporting infrastructure such as knowledge banks.

Use Matrix Organizations

A matrix organization allows a person to have two or more reporting links. Several business units could share a sales force by having the salespeople report to a business unit as well as to the central sales manager. A silo advertising manager could also report to a central advertising or marketing group. An R&D group could have a research team that reports both to the business unit and to the R&D manager. As a result, the silo salespeople, advertising managers, and research team are each supported by a critical mass of employees and infrastructure that allows them to excel while still being a part of the business unit. The concept of dual reporting requires coordination and communication and often appears to be the ideal solution to a messy situation. However, matrix structures can be unstable and subject to political pressures. Thus, they can create a solution that is worse than the problem.

The Virtual Organization

The virtual corporation is a team of people and organizations specifically designed for a particular client or job. The people can be drawn from a variety of sources and might include contract workers who are hired only for the project at hand. Communication firms have used virtual teams to provide a integrated communication solution involving talent from different modalities. The chances of success are greater when the people are drawn from the same organization, such as a full service agency like Dentsu, Y&R, or McCann Erickson. When different companies are involved, success is more elusive.

WPP, the large communication holding company, founded a virtual company, Enfatico, to handle all the communication needs of Dell. The logic was that the new company would access the best talent throughout the WPP world, which included dozens of top communication and support firms of all modalities. This seemed like an ideal solution to a vexing problem. Just one year later, the entity was folded into Y&R, a major WPP agency. Enfatico had a difficult time delivering top creative work. Getting people from very different backgrounds to work as a team was always going to be challenging. Furthermore, it proved difficult to hire a CEO and top talent to a single client firm, with the associated risk involved. The Enfatico experience illustrates that asking people to leave a home discipline and firm and go with a new fragile organization without an established culture will be difficult.

SYSTEMS

Several management systems are strategically relevant. Among them are the information, measurement and reward, and planning systems.

Information System

Creating or refining a silo-spanning information system, a system that facilitates communication and stores knowledge, is the most basic and non-threatening element of the CMO's potential initiatives. The system can share market information regarding customer insights, trends, competitor actions, technology developments, and best practices, and well as internal information about processes and methods, new products and technologies, best internal practices, and strategies and programmes. Non-threatening though it may be, such a system can be complex, affected by organizational issues, and difficult to manage, so that the participation is widespread. There are a host of ways that communication can be fostered across silos, such as:

- *Knowledge-sharing sessions.* Formal and informal meetings not only result in information exchange but create channels of personal communication that can operate after the meetings. Personal links can result in someone feeling comfortable calling a colleague and opining that a proposed programme is crazy, or that a particular problem needs to be placed on the agenda. Such a conversation can stave off a disaster or encourage an initiative. Most companies have in-person meetings, which can vary from once a quarter to once every two years. These are often supplemented with telephone meetings. Many firms have their global product and functional teams have a conference call every two weeks. For example, such meetings are a big part of Dell and Honda's communication programme.
- *A common marketing education.* Following the merger of Grand Metropolitan and Guinness in 1998, the newly formed Diageo developed the Diageo Way of Brand Building, or DWBB. The objectives of the initiative were to drive organic growth through becoming a consumer-led organization. The process involved every person in the organization learning, practising, and using the same brand developments and management tools. For the two merging organizations, the opportunity was to create a common language and to use that to drive future growth. The system is still in operation and continues to drive efficiency and effectiveness in the firm.
- *A knowledge hub.* An organized repository of data, experience, case analyses, and insight can provide a sustainable asset by putting useful information at people's fingertips. It has the potential to make information handling and exchange productive, easy to use, and efficient. MasterCard, a firm that was early in its appointment of a 'knowledge-sharing facilitator' to identify and disseminate best brand practices, credited the programme with leveraging the very effective 'Priceless' advertising campaign across country silos.
- *A centre of excellence.* Within a central marketing team, this will have a group focusing on a particular issue that spans silos, such as a customer trend, an

emerging product subcategory, or a technology. The centre could be staffed by a single person or by a group of dozens. The charge would be to gain deep insights into the issue and to stay abreast of developments. The centre should actively reach out to the silo teams in order both to receive and to disperse information and thus provide a catalyst for communication and information flow. Sony Ericsson in recent times has centralized its marketing to improve alignment and effectiveness. The impact on the business is that marketing is available as horizontal global centres of excellence.

Measurement and Reward System

Measurement can drive behaviour and thus directly affect strategy implementation. The key to strategy is often the ability to introduce appropriate performance measures that are linked to the reward structure.

One concern is to motivate employees to cooperate, communicate, and create synergy. The reward system can operate at two levels. At the level of the individual performance review, the ability to be collaborative and to initiate and participate in cross-silo initiatives could be measured. In fact, the central marketing group at IBM evaluates people in silo groups in terms of how collaborative they are. At the organization level, rewards that are based too closely on a business unit's performance can work against this motivational goal. As a result, many companies deliberately base a portion of their bonuses or evaluations on the results of a larger unit. Prophet, a brand strategy consulting firm with seven offices, encourages cross-office support by making its bonuses conditional on firm-wide performance. Another business may focus on divisional performance because synergy across divisions is not realistic.

It is also helpful if the rewards are balanced with a long-term perspective as well as short-term financials. Thus, measures such as customer satisfaction, customer loyalty, quality indicators, new products brought to market, or training programme productivity may be useful to gauge the progress of strategic initiatives.

Planning System

A standardized brand and/or marketing programme, one that is virtually the same across country or product silos, is rarely optimal. What is optimal is to have both a business and marketing planning process, including templates and frameworks, and a supporting information system that are the same everywhere. Having a common planning process provides the basis for communication by creating a common vocabulary, measures, information, and decision structures. It also leads to a minimal level of professionalism throughout the silo units. Unless there is a clear, accepted planning process with understandable and actionable components, every unit will go its own way, and, inevitably, some will be mismanaged strategically and tactically as a result.

There should be a process that adapts brands to silo contexts. To prevent a silo-spanning brand from becoming confused and inconsistent, a best practice organization will have brands that are adapted to silo contexts while still maintaining consistency of the brand character. Mercedes Benz, for example, has a core brand identity that consists of values such as exclusivity, quality, heritage, and sophistication. In the German market the brand is sold on the basis of unquestionable quality. In the Chinese market the brand values of heritage and sophistication come to the fore. Other brands choose to interpret similar values in different ways in international markets. For example, a brand may have a value of family or community, which can mean different things in different markets. The result is greater ability to link with the silo customer.

PEOPLE

A key to overcoming silo issues is to have a strong CMO team that is staffed with quality talent. Any weak, visible link can be damaging. One CMO reported that an advertising manager who lacked competence set back the group a full year by interacting with silo organizations and making naive recommendations. Who is added and, even more importantly, who is asked to leave will be closely observed. Adding people who are respected can give the group a lift, while retaining people who do not fit the role can be debilitating.

The problem is that the qualifications needed by the central marketing group are extraordinary. Collectively, the group needs to be knowledgeable about marketing, branding, markets, products, and their organization. In addition, the group needs to have a strategic perspective and be collaborative, persuasive, a change agent, and, for a global firm, multicultural. Thus, people need to be sought that have as many of these characteristics as possible.

- *Knowledgeable.* An effective central marketing management team will need collectively to have a breadth of knowledge. Achieving that breadth can involve a mix of generalists with insight, specialists, and outside resources, but it needs to create competence in the following:
  (a) *marketing knowledge* – marketing strategy, communication tools (including new media), measurement, marketing programmes, and their management;
  (b) *brand knowledge* – brands, brand power, brand equity, brand roles, brand portfolio strategy, and brand-building programmes;
  (c) *market knowledge* – markets, country cultures, market trends, competitor dynamics, customer segmentation, and customer motivation;
  (d) *product knowledge* – product or service attributes and the underlying technology, plus the innovation flow that will define future products and services;
  (e) *organizational knowledge* – the organization, its culture, strategies, values, and formal and informal influence and communication structure.
- *Strategic perspective.* The CMO team needs to be able to strategize, to move beyond being proficient in a set of tactics to be involved in marketing strategy. Because they will be dealing with a dynamic marketplace, they will also need to be comfortable with adapting strategy to reflect that dynamics.

Without a strategic flare, they will not be capable of devising cross-silo marketing strategies, which should be a major goal, and will not be a candidate to sit at the strategy table.

- *Change agent.* The CMO team will need to be a change agent. This means that there needs to be the capability of generating the feeling and substance of being creative and innovative. There should be a sense of energy and purpose. Life will not go on as before. Change will happen. There is a fine line between being a loose cannon and being a positive catalyst for change; however, the change message should be surrounded by professionalism. To be a change agent, at least some members of the CMO team need to be persuaders, to have communication and leadership skills. Collaborative skills are also necessary, especially when the incentives are silo oriented.
- *Multicultural.* When the global overlay is added, the ability to work with different languages and cultures is added. Particularly in a culturally homogeneous country like Japan, the United Kingdom, or the United States, where few are proficient in other languages, it is necessary to build a team that is culturally sensitive with adequate language skills. One route, used by Alltech, the animal health company, is deliberately to staff the whole firm with nationals from around the world. The result is one of the few companies that can say they are truly multicultural. Another is to rotate people around the globe, as Nestlé and Sony do, creating the absence of country-specific people. Yet another is explicitly to train people in cultural knowledge, market insights, etc., so that their limitations can be reduced. But it will remain a challenge for the firm with global aspirations.

Sourcing: Insiders versus Outsiders

A basic decision is whether the CMO and his or her staff members should be outsiders or insiders. There is usually a sharp trade-off. The insider will be more likely to know the organization and its culture and systems, will have a network of colleagues to tap for help, and will know the actors behind the formal organization chart – who are the real keys to getting things done. The insider will thus be low risk. However, the insider may also lack the marketing skills and credibility to know what to do and how to do it. He or she may also be unwilling or unable to create the needed organizational change.

An outsider with the needed functional expertise, experience, and credibility can serve as a change agent in part because he or she is less tied to past decisions, relationships, and political pressures. The problem is that he or she will often lack a feel for the culture and an established network throughout the firm to draw on. This is the riskier route but one that might be more likely to make a difference when the organization is in need of change. The risk goes up when the outsider is changing industries (e.g. from packaged goods to B2B marketing) and facing new and different marketing challenges. Sometimes, team members from outside the firm can be more effective change agents than insiders.

The trade-offs between the inside and outside sources suggest staffing routes for the CMO slot. An insider with a proven record as a change agent and who has or could obtain credibility in marketing and brands may be available. Or an outsider who has demonstrated an ability to adapt to organizations may be a target. Sequencing the marketing manager is possible as well. An insider might get started and gain some momentum, providing an outsider with a platform for more rapid change. In other situations, an outsider who shakes up the organization would be followed by an insider to channel and broaden the momentum.

One way to reduce the tensions is to form a blended team of outsiders and insiders, as GE and others have done. An outsider playing a leadership role will be surrounded by insiders, and, when an insider is asked to lead change, he or she will be supported by whatever outside talent is needed. Another is to change the culture in order to make a new strategy viable and the task of a change agent more tractable.

Upgrading the Marketing Staff

A strong marketing team throughout the organization, not just in the central marketing group, is needed, for several reasons. First, a strong marketing presence in the silos will reduce the need to justify brand and marketing strategy. The conversation can be elevated. Second, whatever level of central control is achieved, silo organizations will still have a design and implementation role that will require talent. Dow Corning has a Global Marketing Excellence council that leads in building up the marketing capability of the firm. It detects capability gaps and develops initiatives to fill them by outside hiring, training initiatives, and mentoring programmes. They sponsored, for example, a 'lunch and learn' programme around lunch events. At GE, the CMO has a programme of identifying potential market talent through the firm and influencing their career paths.

Training and upgrading people is a key part of the equation. In general, they will need to be taught general marketing skills in functional areas of marketing, the process models and information system, the brand and marketing strategy, and the rationale for it. The first step is to understand the gaps of knowledge for each member of the marketing team. One role of several CMOs is to evaluate the marketing talent in the silo organizations and get involved in their career path, including guiding them into the right training programme.

STRATEGY AND PEOPLE DEVELOPMENT AT GE

Jack Welch, the legendary former GE CEO, created a system and culture to develop both strategy and people throughout his 20-year tenure. Five elements were involved:[6]

- Each January, the top 5000 GE executives gathered in Boca Raton to share best practices and set major business priorities. (In the past, priorities included e-commerce, globalization, and six-sigma quality.) Webcasts of the event were available to the whole organization.

- Each quarter, top executives met in two-day retreats facilitated by Welch and focused on initiatives related to the agenda set in Boca Raton. This was a key place for future leaders to emerge, earn respect, and demonstrate growth.
- Twice a year, Welch and others focused on personnel needs for each business, such as how to handle each unit's top 20% and bottom 10% of employees.
- In addition, biannual sessions (one in the spring and one in the autumn) looked at each business over a three-year horizon.

The entire effort was supported by the GE social architecture of informality, candour, substantive dialogue, boundaryless behaviour, emphasis on follow through, and making judgements on qualitative business dimensions.

CULTURE

The organizational culture drives behaviour and is the glue that holds everything together. It is hard to create a congruent organization that will make the strategy successful if there is not a strong, supportive culture. As suggested by Figure 15.3, an organizational culture involves three elements: a set of shared values that define priorities, a set of norms of behaviour, and symbols and symbolic activities.

Shared Values

Shared values or dominant beliefs underlie a culture by specifying what is important. In a strong culture the values will be widely accepted, and virtually everyone will be able to identify them and describe their rationale.

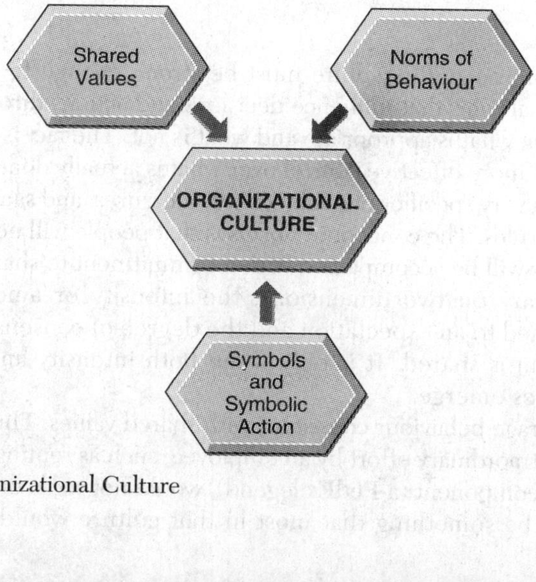

Figure 15.3 Organizational Culture

Shared values can have a variety of foci. They can involve, for example:

- *A key asset or competency that is the essence of a firm's competitive advantage.* HOK, a global firm of architects, is a leader in using green architecture and educating clients about the value of sustainable design.
- *An operational focus.* The success of small firms is most often built on a strong operational focus given the relatively small amount of funds they can dedicate to marketing or brand building.
- *An organizational output.* The World Economic Forum aims to be the foremost organization for building and energizing leading global communities. It achieves this through meetings, including that at Davos, where the world's leaders gather to discuss issues of global concern.
- *An emphasis on a functional area.* Volkswagen is seeking to become the world's leading car company by 2018 through building a portfolio of strong brands and exceptional advertising.
- *A management style.* This is an informal, flat organization that fosters communication and encourages unconventional thinking.
- *A belief in the importance of people as individuals.* Google has a legendary commitment to hiring the best people and treating them well on the basis that they will then provide the best solutions to problems.
- *A general objective, such as a belief in being the best or comparable with the best.* The Indian IT services firm Wipro has built a global position by focusing on high-growth niche business such as infrastructure support services.

For an organization to make progress on silo problems, cooperation and communication will need to become one of the shared values. This means that all employees and partners need both to know about the priority and to believe in it.

Norms

To make a real difference, the culture must be strong enough to develop norms of behaviour – informal rules that influence decisions and actions throughout an organization by suggesting what is appropriate and what is not. The fact is that strong norms can generate much more effective control over what is actually done or not done in an organization than a very specific set of objectives, measures, and sanctions. People can always get around rules. The concept of norms is that people will not attempt to avoid them because they will be accompanied with a commitment to shared values.

Norms can vary on two dimensions: the intensity or amount of approval/disapproval attached to an expectation and the degree of consensus or consistency with which a norm is shared. It is only when both intensity and consensus exist that strong cultures emerge.

Norms encourage behaviour consistent with shared values. Thus, in a quality service culture, an extraordinary effort by an employee, such as renting a helicopter to fix a communication component (a FedEx legend), would not seem out of line and risky; instead, it would be something that most in that culture would do under similar circumstances. Furthermore, sloppy work affecting quality would be informally policed by fellow workers, without reliance on a formal system. One production firm uses no quality-control inspectors or janitors. Each production-line person is responsible for the quality of his or her output and for keeping the work area clean. Such a policy would not work without support from a strong culture.

With a culture around cooperation and communication, people would instinctively reach out and communicate across silos. Teaming would become natural. Those abstaining would feel uncomfortable or worse.

Symbols and Symbolic Action

Corporate cultures are largely developed and maintained by the use of consistent, visible symbols and symbolic action. In fact, the more obvious methods of affecting behaviour, such as changing systems or structure, are often much less effective than seemingly trivial symbolic actions.

A host of symbols and symbolic actions are available. A few of the more useful are discussed next.

The Founder and Original Mission

A corporation's unique roots, including the personal style and experience of its founder, can provide extremely potent symbols. The concept of technology-driven solutions developed by Larry Page and Sergey Brin at Google, the laser focus on continuously reducing costs by Michael O'Leary from Ryanair, the commitment to philanthropy of the founders of the Mahindra Group, and the product traditions started by the founders of Guinness continue to influence the cultures of their firms generations later.

Modern Role Models

Modern heroes and role models help communicate, personalize, and legitimize values and norms. Jack Ma of Alibaba.com, one of the world's largest B2B on-line marketplaces, is a role model for entrepreneurs and managers everywhere, but particularly in China. The firm that he founded is highly competitive versus its international competitors such as eBay. The founders of Innocent Drinks, Richard Reed, Adam Balon, and Jon Wright, are role models for many, as they operate under a different view of business and how it should interact with society. The founders left their jobs as bankers to found a company that would provide people with a healthy habit each day, uses natural ingredients from local suppliers, and donates 10% of its profits to charity via the Innocent Foundation. These values were unusual in 1999, when Innocent was founded, but are more mainstream today. However, the firm remains at the forefront of encouraging entrepreneurs to follow a passion and for other managers to develop a more positive relationship with wider society.

Rituals

Rituals of work life, from hiring to eating lunch to retirement dinners, help define a culture. One prominent firm in the agribusiness sector is known for offering new employees a lower salary than that paid in their previous post. Thus, only those who really want to work for the firm apply or join.

The role of the CEO and other executives

The way that a CEO and other executives spend their time can be a symbolic action affecting the culture. A key element of the Diageo Way of Brand Building mentioned earlier was the commitment made by marketing leaders within the firm to running the DWBB workshops within the firm. This sent a strong signal to all within the organization regarding the importance of the initiative. Patterns of consistent reinforcement can represent another important symbolic activity. For example, a firm that regularly recognizes cross-silo activity accomplishments in a meaningful way, with the visible support of top management, can, over time, affect the culture. When a type of question is continually asked by top executives and made a central part of meeting agendas and report formats, it will eventually influence the shared values of an organization.

REPRESENTING CULTURE AND STRATEGY WITH STORIES, NOT BULLETS

Research has shown that stories are more likely than lists to be read and remembered. Nevertheless, most business strategists rely on bullet points to communicate both culture and strategy. 3M is one firm that has based its culture on classic stories – how initial failures of abrasive products led to product breakthroughs; how masking tape was invented; how a scientist conceived of Post-it notes when his bookmarks fell out of a hymnal, and how the Post-it Notes team, instead of giving up in the face of low initial sales, got people hooked on the product by flooding a city with samples. These stories communicate how innovation occurs at 3M and how its entrepreneurial culture operates.

At 3M, business strategy is also communicated via stories rather than the conventional bullets, which tend to be generic (the goal of increased market share applies to any business), skip over critical assumptions about how the business works (will increased market share fund new products or result from new products?), and leave causal relationship unspecified (if A is done, B becomes effective). A strategic story will involve several phases – setting the stage by describing the current situation, introducing the dramatic conflict in the form of challenges and critical issues, and reaching resolution with convincing stories about how the company can overcome obstacles and win. Presenting a narrative motivates the audience, adds richness and detail, and provides a glimpse into the logic of the strategist.[7]

Given that the CEO is crucial in culture development, how do you get the CEO on board with respect to enhancing cooperation and communication across silos? First, the problems need to become visible; too often they are ignored as part of the way it has always been done. If some of the inefficiencies and missed opportunities can be quantified, there will be a worthwhile problem for which cooperation and communication is part of the solution. Second, the CMO needs to become credible so that there is buy-in as to his/her role. One approach is to align the role of marketing with that of the CEO's priority agenda by focusing on growth objectives instead of brand extensions, efficiency and cost objectives instead of marketing synergy or scale, and building assets to support strategic initiatives instead of brand image campaigns. Third, get easy wins. These early successes often involve identifying organizational units that will support (or at least not oppose) change because they need help to address a meaningful problem or opportunity. They can also involve programmes that can be implemented 'under the radar'. For example, at Cigna, an estate agent who needed artwork for a building was persuaded to use brand visuals. The CEO of a major division saw the result and promptly decided to extend the idea to all buildings.

A RECAP OF STRATEGIC MARKET MANAGEMENT

Figure 15.4 provides a capstone summary of the issues raised in both strategic analysis and strategy development/refinement. It suggests a discussion agenda to help an organization ensure that the external and internal analysis has the necessary depth, breadth, and forward thinking, and that the strategy creation and refinement process yields winning, sustainable strategies.

CUSTOMER ANALYSIS

- Who are the major segments?
- What are their motivations and unmet needs?

COMPETITOR ANALYSIS

- Who are the existing and potential competitors? What strategic groups can be identified?
- What are their sales, share, and profits? What are the growth trends?
- What are their strengths, weaknesses, and strategies?

MARKET/SUBMARKET ANALYSIS

- How attractive is the market or industry and its submarkets? What are the forces reducing profitability in the market, entry and exit barriers, growth projections, cost structures, and profitability prospects?
- What are the alternative distribution channels and their relative strengths?
- What industry trends and emerging submarkets are significant to strategy?
- What are the current and future key success factors?

ENVIRONMENTAL ANALYSIS

- What environmental threats, opportunities, and trends exist?
- What are the major strategic uncertainties and information-need areas?
- What scenarios can be conceived?

Figure 15.4 Strategy Development: A Discussion Agenda (*Continued*)

INTERNAL ANALYSIS

- What are our strategy, performance, points of differentiation, strengths, weaknesses, strategic problems, and culture?
- What threats and opportunities exist?

STRATEGY DEVELOPMENT

- What are the target segments? What is the product scope?
- What value propositions will be the core of the offering? Among the choices are superior attribute or benefit, appealing design, systems solution, social programmes, customer relationship, niche specialist, quality, and value.
- What assets and competencies will provide the basis for an SCA? How can they be developed and maintained? How can they be leveraged?
- What are the alternative functional strategies?
- What strategies best fit our strengths, our objectives, and our organization?
- What alternative growth directions should be considered? How should they be pursued?
- What investment level is most appropriate for each product market—withdrawal, milking, maintaining, or growing?

Figure 15.4 (*Continued*)

KEY LEARNINGS

- Decentralization with powerful silo groups can inhibit synergy and efficiency. For marketing, it leads to misallocation of resources, confused brands, inhibited cross-silo offerings and programmes, weak marketing staff, the failure to leverage success, and inadequate cooperation and communication. In dealing with the problem, CMOs should consider non-threatening roles such as facilitator or consultant and should not have as an objective to centralize and standardize.
- The organizational levers are structure, systems, people, and culture. Each of these needs to be congruent and support the business strategy.
- The organizational structure lever provides the option to centralize selectivity, use teams and networks, use matrix reporting structures, and employ a virtual organization.
- Management systems include the information, measurement and reward, and planning systems, which can all promote cooperation and communication.
- People on the CMO team, who can be sourced internally or externally, need to be knowledgeable about marketing, brands, markets, products, and the organization, in addition to having the capability of buying strategy and being a change agent.
- Culture involves shared values, norms of behaviour, and symbols and symbolic action. The CEO is a key driver of strategy, and it is important to get him or her on board.

FOR DISCUSSION

1. What are the advantages of decentralization? Some people argue that more centralization is needed to develop and implement strategy in these dynamic times. Express your opinion, and illustrate it with examples. When would you recommend that the central team use a facilitative role, rather than impose its advice?
2. How could the problems with the DaimlerChrysler merger have been avoided? Was the problem one of strategy (overexpansion), or was it organizational? Why?
3. How would you go about changing the culture of an organization to improve the level of cooperation and communication?
4. If you were assigned to be the new CMO of a firm like Unilever with silo issues, what would you do in the first 100 days? Would this plan work as well in a technology firm such as Google or Facebook?
5. If you were the CMO of Nestlé with dozens of product units in over 100 countries, how would you make the decision as to what elements of advertising to centralize? Of brand strategy?
6. What do you believe would be the best way to get a finance-oriented CEO to support marketing and its efforts to get silos to work together on offerings, brands, and marketing programmes?

NOTES

1. This chapter draws on the material in David Aaker, *Spanning Silos: The New CMO Imperative*, Boston, MA, Harvard Business Press, 2008.
2. Greg Welch, 'CMO Tenure: Slowing Down the Revolving Door', Spenser Stuart Blue Paper, 2004.
3. 'Schrempp's Last Stand', *The Economist*, 1 March 2001.
4. 'The New European Order', *The Economist*, 2 September 2004.
5. 'In Tandem (At Last)', *The Economist*, 30 March 2006.
6. 'GE's Ten Step Talent Plan', *Fortune*, 17 April 2000, p. 232.
7. Gordon Shaw, Robert Brown, and Philip Bromiley, 'Strategic Stories: How 3M Is Rewriting Business Planning', *Harvard Business Review*, May–June 1998, pp. 41–50.

CASES FOR THE END OF PART II

Case 1

STRATEGIC POSITIONING. ALLTECH FEI WORLD EQUESTRIAN GAMES 2010[1]

Over a cup of coffee in 2006, Alltech's president, Dr Pearse Lyons, agreed that, for US$ 10 million, Alltech would be the title sponsor for the 2010 World Equestrian Games in Kentucky. His observation to Alltech's global marketing director, Catherine Keogh, was 'we are going to be like Rolex is to Wimbledon'. Irish born, but French domiciled, Keogh knew Lyons was already four years ahead, welcoming business partners to the first World Equestrian Games to be held outside Europe since its inception in 1990.

Lyons was an Irish national but had moved to Kentucky in 1980 to establish Alltech. Since then, Alltech had grown to be a world leader in the area of animal health. Although based in Lexington, Kentucky, Alltech was a global firm, active in more than 110 countries worldwide and with 23 production facilities around the world. With sales in the region of US$ 500 million and an average annual growth rate of 20%, Alltech was a company in a hurry. Since its inception, its growth ambition had been driven by long-term thinking. It had invested in science and the education of scientists, had pioneered in the area of natural animal health products, and had long been committed to the environment, to corporate social responsibility initiatives in Africa, and to AIDS treatment. It had a suite of global brands, including Bioplex, Bio-Mos, NuPro, Optigen, Sil-All, Yea-Sacc, and Allzyme SSF, and an exciting new brand for the equine market, Lifeforce. Perhaps the jewel in the crown was an organic selenium brand, Sel-Plex, which had had great success as an animal feed supplement but also had potential as a human food ingredient and a human supplement.

Keogh was inspired by the decision to sponsor the games. She understood that Lyons wanted to take Alltech closer to the customer with new products, leveraging their cutting-edge technologies into new markets and raising the company's profile to the status of a truly global brand. Her gut feeling was that this was an incredible branding opportunity. Although Alltech sales to the equine community accounted for only 3% of its turnover, potential existed to grow the value of this to 12–15% of current sales. More importantly, she saw the equine community as a portal to new markets – horses, pets, and perhaps eventually humans.

The Alltech FEI World Equestrian Games seemed to be the perfect vehicle for Alltech. The sport was linked with nature and offered an opportunity to build relationships on a lifestyle level. Moreover, as this was going to be the first time that the games had been held outside Europe, this represented an historic occasion, echoing

[1]Reproduced with kind permission of Alltech.

milestones in Alltech's own story. But Keogh faced a number of challenges: How to explain Alltech's involvement to its customers? How best to organize? How best to convince Alltech's stakeholders that this was money well spent? The Alltech way was to make things happen, with room only for excellence, but the company had never before engaged in the sponsorship of an international sporting event on such a scale. Some commentators might even have asked how any company could measure the benefits of investing US$ 10 million into acquiring the rights to sponsor a sporting event with which the sponsor shared little previous common history. So, Keogh wondered, how could Alltech best realize a return on its investment.

Passion, Excellence, and Performance

Alltech's first task had been to articulate the areas of synergy arising from the sponsorship and the messages to be conveyed, in other words defining the fit with the Alltech brand. In brainstorming with a sponsorship consultant, it was agreed by a group of Alltech directors that three common values stood out: passion, excellence, and performance. The distillation of a gut feeling into a meaningful set of common values would inform and facilitate the process of communicating the rationale and excitement about the deal with Alltech's various stakeholders. The directors strongly believed a credible alignment could be developed along these three themes, as clearly both the FEI Games and Alltech's activities were characterized by each of the values. As the governing body of equestrian sports, the FEI had a strong tradition in these values. Furthermore, the sense of fit was consolidated by the symbolism of equine sports – where man and animal cooperate for a higher goal. Crucially, this was the only championship sport where animals competed at the peak of their performance. As such, sponsoring an equestrian sporting event provided a bridge for Alltech from business-to-business marketing to the world of consumer marketing.

In that process, the directors set two strategic objectives: (a) to present Alltech as a major global brand and to articulate Alltech's core brand values – the sponsorship would provide a stage for this positioning as well as a platform for (b) developing business relationships in the sector. Involvement with the largest and most prestigious animal-related sporting event would underwrite the positioning statement, while core values would be demonstrated through this and a coordinated activation plan packaging the event as the Alltech Games. Following on from these two main goals, Keogh and the Director group laid out six specific business objectives related to return on investment:

1. Achieve 100% positive awareness among the equine community.
2. Increase sales and penetration in new geographic markets.
3. Increase equine sales to greater than US$ 10 million per annum.
4. Develop a number of key legacy partnerships – at least one in each major market.
5. Develop key relationships.
6. Foster internal pride about the 2010 Games.

In that regard, Dr Lyons and his directors wished to set a new standard in sponsorship and come to epitomize the spirit of the World Equestrian Games. In the vein of successful branding, he wanted people to think of the event as the Alltech Games.

A critical element of the message to reach the target audiences was that excellence and performance were delivered through the nutrition provided by Alltech products, technologies, and people.

Rising Star of Brand Communications

In spite of difficulties with measuring its effectiveness, globally, sponsorship was considered the rising star of brand communications. The total market for all sponsorship activity was estimated to have reached US$ 45 billion in 2009. The twenty-first century had witnessed the age of experiential marketing, where companies aimed to make their brand's values tangible and memorable for consumers. Up until mid-2008, investment in sponsorship, while slowing, was nevertheless growing faster than spending in either advertising or sales promotion. A number of factors were attributable to the preference of one tool over others.

Sponsorship permitted brands not only to be associated with an event but to involve people at an emotional level, in a positive and lasting way. Because of this, it tended to be more effective than advertising in achieving 'cut through', which was important in terms of brand communications. Generally speaking, sponsorship could be used for a number of goals, including raising a brand's profile in new markets and relationship-building in a more established market. Although advertising and sponsorship could be used to achieve similar ends, such as heightened brand awareness and brand preferences, advertising was explicitly concerned with selling a product, whereas sales were often a secondary goal of sponsorship.

The beneficial 'rub-off' effects of a successful sponsorship hinged on the notion of 'good fit', however. A qualitative concept, 'good fit' was the idea that the association made common sense, enjoying credibility and offering benefits to all parties concerned. Good fit depended not only on the initial matching of values but also on how the relationship was managed and nourished over time.

Sponsorship Issues for Alltech

The issues surrounding Alltech's decision to sponsor the games were somewhat complex at the time. The equine feed market was quite a specialist one that was concentrated in certain geographic regions around the world. Additionally, Alltech was faced with addressing two distinct target audiences: businesses and consumers. But the perception of horses as exclusive pets of the affluent was misconstrued. In the United States, for example, one in every three people owned or handled a horse, while the average income of horse owners was US$30 000, or only two-thirds of the average US salary. It was estimated that the US horse population was around 10 million animals in 2008. This profile could fit well with Alltech's core values, and the challenge appeared to be to convey this fit to other stakeholders.

While it represented a highly profitable niche and Alltech was confident it could increase its sales to the equine community, there were pertinent structural issues to consider, such as distribution, brand equity, and consumer behaviour. There was also the issue of leveraging brand equity in the sector to build a position of credibility among consumers. In any case it was felt that any marketing activities and equine-specific products would have to deliver real added value, improved animal performance, and value for money to achieve this fit. Conversely, being animal lovers, it was reasonable to assume many horse owners also owned pets such as cats or dogs, which represented another attractive market for Alltech's product technologies.

A second major issue for Alltech was that sponsorship theory usually dictated that a company determine its strategic objectives before approaching suitable events or properties with a commercial proposal. With the deal in place already, Keogh's priorities as a global director of marketing would have to be reconciled with the requirements of planning and communicating the vision for the Alltech FEI World Equestrian Games 2010.

In the first year after the deal was announced, Keogh's main goal was threefold. She had to develop a suitably comprehensive marketing plan, brand inside Alltech, and ensure the integration of the games into Alltech's corporate marketing activities. In relation to this, Keogh wondered whether Alltech's marketing department had the organizational structure, resources, and expertise subsequently to implement a sponsorship on such a scale, or whether a new department dedicated to activating the games was required. Dr Lyons was keen that the Alltech Games should fit in with the company's global marketing programme rather than as a stand-alone entity.

On the other hand, Alltech's ultimate aim had been to move closer to the individual consumer, and the games' audience figures were compelling. The estimated televized audience reach was in the order of 500 million viewers globally, while approximately 600 000 people were expected to attend the event over the course of the two weeks, a quarter of whom would come from overseas to visit Kentucky. As a benchmark, the Aachen Games in 2006 attracted approximately 570 000 visitors from 61 countries and 300 television broadcast hours reaching 450 million viewers. Economically, the Kentucky Games were expected to contribute US$150 million to the local economy alone.

However, being a title sponsor brought with it a raft of responsibilities and opportunities. Alltech's US$10 million fee represented a 25% premium on the total combined sponsorships of the Aachen Games in 2006, and the 2010 Games would be the first time the FEI had granted an exclusive title sponsorship to one company. The branding opportunity was enormous, but the challenge of getting a return on that investment was equally significant.

QUESTIONS

1. Evaluate Alltech's decision to become naming sponsor for the FEI World Equestrian Games.
2. Should Pearse Lyons have used a more extended process of decision-making in making the decision to act as sponsor?
3. How can Catherine Keogh best leverage the sponsorship of the Games to achieve the market development and sales growth objectives of Alltech?
4. How important is Alltech's global reach in securing commercial benefits from its sponsorship?
5. How would you measure those benefits at a tactical and strategic level?

Case 2

LEVERAGING A BRAND ASSET. INNOCENT DRINKS

Innocent Drinks was established in 1999 by three college friends who chose a jazz festival in London's Parsons Green to test their new product. They set up their stall at the festival with £500 worth of fresh fruit to be blended into a smoothie containing no sugar, water, or concentrates, and with two rubbish bins, marked with 'yes' and 'no', asking customers if they should give up their jobs to make the smoothies. If tasters thought they should, they put their empty cups in 'yes', and, if not, in 'no'. At the end of the festival the 'yes' bin was overflowing with cartons, and the next day they gave up their jobs. Innocent Drinks had been created. Since then, its total market share has increased to 71% of the smoothie market in 2009. The number of employees in the company has expanded from three in 1999 to 200 in 2009, and turnover in 2000 was Stg £1.8 million, increasing to Stg £141 million in 2009. It is the largest fruit buyer in Europe and the UK's leading smoothie manufacturer.

Innocent Drinks was established in recognition of a reduction in the popularity of traditional sugar-based soft drinks and the emerging healthier living trend. Innocent tapped into the emerging culture of health conscious, cash-rich, time-short consumers who were willing to pay a premium for products that are natural, convenient, and healthy. Consumers wanted healthy options not just in their supermarkets but also in their convenience stores where they could have easy access with minimal effort. Innocent was able to address this real customer demand by supplying its product to local convenience stores. But Innocent Drinks is not a passing fad, with the smoothie market just beginning to emerge and growing at a phenomenal rate. Innocent is growing at more than 25% per annum and is succeeding where many have failed by making fruit fun and being healthy easy. Innocent has managed to maintain its market position by listening to customers, monitoring and understanding customer trends, and innovating its product line to take advantage of these opportunities; for example, as the trend of healthy eating extends to parents' concerns over what their children are eating, Innocent launched a range for children.

The company takes pride in its products being natural, pure fruit juice and nothing else, with the selling proposition 'No sugar. No water. No concentrates'. But, as the fruit beverage market is already abundant with strong competitors in the United Kingdom, like The Feel Good Drinks Co. and PJ Smoothies, all promising pure, fresh, natural, healthy ingredients, what was it that provided Innocent with its strategic position? Innocent's phenomenal success is based on the strength of its brand and its marketing strategy. This involved developing a strong, clear brand proposition of 'makes sense, feels good' and a unique positioning strategy so that customers know what to expect when they buy an Innocent product and that it delivers consistent quality every time. It also involved developing a strong brand image as an asset by maintaining consistency across its communications, brand image, and identity throughout all aspects of the brand, from the language to the product, the packaging design, labelling, the website, its cow delivery vans and its delivery systems, the banana phone, and even its offices, known as 'Fruit Towers', and how it rewards staff. This enabled it to make a dramatic impact on the fruit beverage market and the competitive saturated beverage market where brands have to compete with the likes of

Coke. While the company has experienced dramatic growth in sales, it has managed to avoid the dangers associated with a fast-growing business by careful strategic planning. Developing the brand as an asset and building its image and reputation to a leadership position has allowed Innocent to develop the company by entering the market with a premium pricing strategy that customers are willing to pay, and with little money spent on advertising initially this meant that price premium revenues were pumped straight back into the company. This has enabled it to achieve a leadership position in the smoothie industry, with higher market share and volume growth as demand for the product increases. Its position as a brand leader in the smoothie market has also enabled it to achieve economies of scale that allows it to achieve lower costs.

At the centre of Innocent Drinks' success is the use of the words 'simple', 'honest', and 'fresh', which allow it to make a powerful statement about the unique nature of its products, the brand, and the company. Even the name itself is simple, honest, and easy to remember, leaving no doubt in the customers' mind about the product. Innocent focused on differentiating its brand as an asset by developing a fun, sense-of-humour brand personality that epitomizes feeling good.

While its competitors also used fun language in their own products to help sell their brand, Innocent took its fun brand personality a step further; for example, on the ingredients list on the side of an Innocent drink, hidden among the real product ingredients, 'a few small pebbles' is often included between the blueberries and strawberries, and then at the end of the list 'we lied about the pebbles'. Innocent represents feel-good consumerism. The packaging it uses is simple, plain-coloured, and straight to the point, with fun, witty, alternative labelling, not only telling customers to recycle the bottle but to go camping or bounce on a trampoline, on a small clear plastic bottle. It is an extremely clever representation of the brand and an effective brand differentiator when all the other brands on the shelf use brightly coloured opaque bottles. Buying the Innocent brand means that you are buying into the ideal of a healthier, happier, fun lifestyle. The simple, friendly, fun approach also extends to other areas of the business. The language and design that it uses on its website also adopts a simple but powerful approach, for example, a 'Bored?' section for the visitor. The website also has a unique feel to it, one of light-heartedness and fun where it pokes fun at itself and at customers, for example, 'we wanted people to think of Innocent as their one healthy habit; like going to the gym, but with the communal shower after', and on the company fact file sheet, along with basic information about the company, it includes Richard's shoe size and Adam's waist size (two of the original founders) to lighten the tone and show customers that the company does not really take itself seriously. The company has also published its own book called *Stay Healthy. Be Lazy*, which is consistent with the overall image and personality of the company, with an honest, simple, straightforward tone that also allows the reader to have fun. The company uses unique 'cow vans' to promote the brand sense of humour and raise brand awareness, as they are complete with fur, horns, eyelashes, udders, tails, and names.

Innocent has also developed a socially responsible brand image by working to do things that the founders believe are right by donating 10% of its profits to the Innocent Foundation which gives away drinks to the homeless, donates to the third world, recycles, and plants trees. If the company was to be called 'Innocent', the founders believed that they had a responsibility to be innocent, and they were promoting many of the current topical issues such as kids' health, ethical trading, and environmental issues long before other companies had even started. Moreover, staff are also treated exceptionally well – they are given money for the birth of a child, scholarships to realize dreams they have, and a free snowboarding trip each year. The environment in which the staff work is conducive to entrepreneurship – they are encouraged to try new things. Innocent recognizes that it is energetic brands with a human face that capture the public's interest.

In 2009, Innocent operated seven main product lines: smoothies, thickies, Smoothies for kids, orange juice, superfruit smoothies, vegpots, and pure fruit squeezies. Product innovations are continuous and are based on listening to customer trends and to what customers are saying and on what the company feels it is good at.

Some new products have been rejected on the grounds that they deviate from the strategic position of the company; for example, Innocent has decided against exploiting the current trend for adding vitamins, health, and medicinal ingredients to drinks, as this is not something that it is expert at. Instead, it prefers to focus on the enjoyment, fun, and taste of its products and sticking to what it is good at. Recipe innovations that are created in its 'Fruit Towers' London office are tested on people in the surrounding offices, the product ingredients are sourced from all around the world, and regular sampling is conducted to ensure that the best products with the best flavour are used in its smoothies.

The main problem Innocent encountered in production was the short shelf life of the product, as all of the ingredients were fresh and no preservatives or additives were added. Careful production and high-technology packaging were developed to give the product the longest possible shelf life but without interfering with the fresh, natural ingredients of the product. The company has continued to research ways in which its product life cycle can be expanded, and in 2004, with the introduction of its one litre take-home carton, there was an increase in life to four days once opened, as opposed to the previous two days.

Innocent has pursued a premium pricing strategy that targets health-conscious consumers who are willing to pay a premium price for the health benefits that its product contains. The price of an Innocent drink varies, with recommended retail prices of Stg £1.75–1.99 for smoothies and thickies, Stg £1.49–1.69 for really lovely juices, Stg £1.49–1.69 for Juicy Waters, Stg £3.29 for one litre cartons, and Stg £2.99 for four kids' drinks.

Until 2003, Innocent had not spent any money on advertising, with a low-cost, high-impact marketing strategy based on word of mouth. These communication techniques were very successful and they built brand awareness of 35% in three years on a budget of less than Stg £100 000. The company is proud that it was able to save money and still communicate with customers using unconventional channels. For example, in the summer of 2003, Innocent's summer marketing campaign featured a double-decker bus covered in astro turf grass and offering customers free smoothies and free rides around London. Word of mouth was key to its marketing campaign, the theory being that, if it made a good product, people would tell their friends, and the company felt that advertising might bring the perception of corporate dishonesty to a brand that was based on an image of honesty, simplicity, wholesomeness, and innocence. In fact, Innocent has always strived to distance its brand from the corporate image that success brings, and its alternative, simple, 'fruity', witty brand image is an effective marketing ploy in a world that has lost faith in the traditional corporate world.

It was only after six years of getting the product and distribution networks right that Innocent started using advertising campaigns to promote the brand, and the company was aware that any advertising that it did use needed to be consistent with its brand image and a true reflection of what the company really was. In March 2005, Innocent began advertising on television for the first time, and, to keep in line with the quirky, witty personality of the Innocent brand, the company shot the ad, which featured a talking carton in a sea of fresh fruit, itself over a weekend in a local park.

As a company, it also sees the social benefits that can be created as part of the marketing campaign. For example, it has developed social marketing activities making it possible to talk directly to the customer, such as the annual music festival called 'Fruitstock', to further promote the brand. This is a free music festival that Innocent hosts to say 'thank you' to its customers for using its brand. This festival holds good commercial value for the company, improves its customers' perceptions of the brand, and allows it to raise money for charity.

The founders' first venture into the market was very modest, with a local shop around the corner from where they worked agreeing to stock some of their drinks; Innocent supplied the shop with twenty bottles, all of which were sold out at the end of the first day. Over the first weekend that Innocent went on sale in 50 shops, it was an immediate success, with 45 shops wanting more. Initially, most of the sales came from delicatessens and sandwich shops, but Coffee Republic, which at the time was also a young growing business, agreed to stock Innocent's product in eight or nine shops. Since then, Innocent has developed its distribution to include supermarkets as well as smaller local convenience stores. In 2009 it supplied smoothies to over 6000 retailers, selling over two million smoothies per week.

But challenges still face this very successful, fast-growth company. These include how to continue using the brand as an asset to ensure that growth is maintained without stepping over the mark and undoing all that the brand has achieved. The company has opened other market fronts by adding product lines deviating from the original product that created so much success for the company, and many more product lines could be tested to see if they fit the company's brand image. For example, could the brand be extended to include baby food or alcoholic drinks? The only fear is that launching new product extensions might undermine the brand and dilute it rather than strengthen it. The company is also now in a position where, as demand increases, it is faced with the decision either to restrict the distribution of the brand and move it upmarket or to continue and get as many distribution outlets and sales as possible. But what implications will this have on the marketing strategy of the brand, its brand image, and its pricing strategy? While the brand image and personality are so easily understood and enjoyed in the United Kingdom, Innocent faces cultural and language challenges as it begins to expand internationally. With the aim to become 'Europe's favourite little juice company', how can it overcome these transferability challenges? While Innocent continues to research packaging technology that will enable it to achieve longer shelf lives, the short shelf life of the product also poses problems for Innocent as it looks to expand further into Europe. As distribution of its products increases, what steps can the company take to ensure that the natural nature of the product that made it so successful in the United Kingdom will not hinder its expansion into Europe?

In 2007, Innocent took a step to deal with some of these issues when it began to supply Innocent smoothies to McDonald's to be included with Happy Meals. This arrangement was abandoned after a trial period. However, in mid-2009 the company took a more definite step when it sold a minority stake in its business to Coca-Cola for Stg £30 million.

QUESTIONS

1. How was the Innocent strategic position conceived? How strong is its position?
2. How did the position that Innocent achieved drive sales growth for the company? How does Innocent maintain sustainability and relevance of its position in a fast-moving, developing market?
3. What impact will Coca-Cola's new role in Innocent have on the Innocent brand from a consumer perspective? From a growth perspective? From a Coca-Cola brand perspective?

Case 3

COMPETING AGAINST THE INDUSTRY GIANT. HTC – SOMETHING BEAUTIFUL IS COMING

Launched in 2009, the HTC Hero smartphone was the latest in a line of phones remarkable for their blend of design excellence and cutting-edge technology. Cher Wang, chairperson and founder of HTC, was being briefed on the success of her company's next-generation smartphones. Wang's vice president of HTC Europe, Florian Seiche, had just confirmed that Vodafone wanted to sell the HTC Touch Diamond with HTC's branding intact – a significant milestone and kudos for its marketing approach.

Of course, since its establishment in 1997 as a contract manufacturer, HTC had nurtured a reputation for high-tech expertise and great design; capabilities that helped it to win and retain valuable deals with handset brands and mobile phone networks around the world. But since 2006, when Wang and her CEO, Peter Chou, made the leap into marketing own-brand devices, HTC had struggled to sustain investor confidence as doubts surfaced as to whether the company had made the right choices in pursuing a branded strategy.[1] However, HTC's success was based on deeper strengths and a foresight stretching back to those early days of 1997. As a result, while Wang was relieved, she was also confident that HTC was well placed to capitalize on the expected boom in the global smartphone market of 2010.

The Global Smartphone Market

Smartphones were a relatively recent phenomenon in mobile communications markets. They were devices that blended typical mobile phone capabilities with aspects of computers such as wireless Internet access, multimedia functionality, email, and basic computing power. Annual sales figures had soared from about 30 million units in 2005 and were expected to hit about 375 million units per annum in 2011, surpassing PC sales at that stage. Worldwide, Apple's iPhone, several Nokia models, and the Blackberry from Research in Motion were the main brands in the market. Nokia's models together accounted for about 43% of all smartphone sales, while Apple and Blackberry each held around 15%. Meanwhile, HTC's share had grown to 8% in three years since it entered the sector under its own brand with the launch of the HTC Touch.

Company Background

In nominating HTC for Brand of the Year 2008, one blogger outlined his three reasons why HTC should be recognized: partnerships, product design, and goodwill.[2] These characteristics defined the company in its short history. HTC had nurtured

---

[1]Kathrin Hille, 'HTC Launches Its First Mass-Market Phone', *Financial Times*, 6 June 2007, available at: http://www.ft.com/cms/s/2/ac37c500-13ba-11dc-9866-000b5df10621.html (accessed 5 December 2009).

[2]'HTC Brand of the Year 2008', *1066 Blog, Observations from the Bazaar*, 13 December 2007, available at: http://marketing.blogs.com/marketing/2007/12/htc-brand-of-th.html (accessed 5 December 2009).

contracts into valuable business relationships, creating products that combined customer-oriented design with advanced technologies to cast a reputation for consistency and excellence that many in the industry valued and applauded.

Cher Wang, 52 years of age, was born into a business life. Her father founded and owned Formosa Plastics, Taiwan's second largest petrochemicals company. Wang herself had demonstrated a flair for business while still at University in California in the 1980s, buying hospital machinery for another of her father's business ventures in Taiwan and selling computers for her sister's start-up First International Computer. When she and her husband founded HTC in 1997, Wang wanted to manufacture personal digital assistants (PDAs) under contract for established brands. However, the company failed to convince buyers about PDAs and instead remained focused on contract manufacturer mobile phones according to its customers' strategic priorities and subject to their considerable power in negotiating prices.

Counter-intuitively, Wang's lack of engineering knowledge proved valuable to HTC's success. 'Cher approaches the business with the eyes of the consumer, because she is not an engineer', explained one executive at T-Mobile, who had worked with HTC.[3] Faced with increasing price pressures from her buyers, HTC sought to strengthen the firm's position in the value chain by persisting in the smartphone niche, winning PDA contracts with Compaq and Hewlett-Packard in 2000. After this, HTC began making customized smartphones running on the Windows operating system for mobile operators like Deutsche Telekom and Vodafone. This proved strategically shrewd, creating growth potential without having to rely on handset manufacturers who would have less incentive to reveal the identity of their device suppliers. Under this 'operator business model', sales exploded, growing 100% annually, with net profits rising some 300% per annum since 2003. Listed on the Taiwanese stock exchange, HTC soon became the darling of the market, with share prices soaring 1000% to a high of 1220 Taiwanese dollars in March 2006.

Taiwanese Branding

At the time, Taiwan's government had built a reputation in manufacturing, focused on high-quality, high-tech products at very competitive prices. Taiwanese companies had followed suit, placing emphasis on recruiting and developing the best engineers. Little emphasis was placed on marketing or branding; there was a strong belief that only technical advances could add value to the product. In fact, in 2009 not one of the world's top 100 brands by value was Taiwanese. 'Being a Taiwanese branded company means making the best products but cheaper than everybody else', commented Bonnie Tu, vice president of Giant bicycles, pinpointing the crux of the issue for the Taiwanese business community.

Even with HTC's strengths and capabilities, making the transition from contract manufacturing to branded handset marketing would be extremely challenging. Management had to invest significant resources in acquiring and developing the

---

[3]Kathrin Hille, 'Innovative Wang Becomes her Father's Daughter', *Financial Times*, 30 August 2009, available at: http://www.ft.com/cms/s/0/4e87ace2-9403-11de-9c57-00144feabdc0.html (accessed 5 December 2009).

know-how internally to cope with consumer-oriented marketing communications. Until that point, the company's marketing experience was exclusively at business-to-business level. As such, Peter Chou completed an MBA at Harvard to prepare himself for the role of CEO, while the company also began to invest millions in setting up a dedicated European sales, marketing, and distribution centre in England and recruiting Florian Seiche from the industry to manage the market entry. The date for announcing the launch of the first HTC smartphone was set as March 2006.

2006–2009 – Something Beautiful is Coming

In spite of the methodical preparation, investors reacted negatively and shares tumbled to one-third of its peak value.[4] Investors were unconvinced HTC could straddle two markets, producing its own branded handsets while continuing to manufacture under contract as well. Chou was quick to clarify HTC's stance: 'We will continue to prioritize the operator's demands. We will use our branded operations as a sluice gate that opens where the operators don't want to go'.[5] But the share price continued to tumble as investors scrutinized a proposal by HTC to purchase Dopod, a handset vendor also part owned by Cher Wang. Investors were not convinced of the move.[6] It was a potential PR crisis and an invaluable lesson in transparency and communications for the company. 'The recent changes are a good opportunity to start improving communication with investors', reasoned one analyst.[7]

It was clear, however, that, for HTC to survive in the consumer market, it would need to adopt a new tack and recover from these setbacks. In another interview, Chou seemed to place faith in the company's culture to achieve that goal: 'HTC is an innovative company. We innovate in the field of our business model.'[8] At the business level, HTC busied itself developing partnerships with Google to develop phones capable of running on Google Android in anticipation of the battle between Android and Windows-based systems that was expected by the industry.[9] But the company still needed to generate mass appeal. One of its first steps in achieving this was to devise

---

[4]Kathrin Hille, 'HTC Launches Its First Mass-Market Phone', *Financial Times*, 6 June 2007, available at: http://www.ft.com/cms/s/2/ac37c500-13ba-11dc-9866-000b5df10621.html (accessed 5 December 2009).

[5]Kathrin Hille, 'HTC Hopes to Allay Fears over Move to Own Brands', *Financial Times*, 22 June 2006, available at: http://www.ft.com/cms/s/0/a35e9cca-018b-11db-af16-0000779e2340.html (accessed 5 December 2009).

[6]Kathrin Hille, ' HTC Hopes to Allay Fears over Move to Own Brands', *Financial Times*, 22 June 2006, available at: http://www.ft.com/cms/s/0/a35e9cca-018b-11db-af16-0000779e2340.html (accessed 5 December 2009).

[7]Kathrin Hille, ' HTC Hopes to Allay Fears over Move to Own Brands', *Financial Times*, 22 June 2006, available at: http://www.ft.com/cms/s/0/a35e9cca-018b-11db-af16-0000779e2340.html (accessed 5 December 2009).

[8]Kathrin Hille, ' HTC Hopes to Allay Fears over Move to Own Brands', *Financial Times*, 22 June 2006, available at: http://www.ft.com/cms/s/0/a35e9cca-018b-11db-af16-0000779e2340.html (accessed 5 December 2009).

[9]Robin Kwong, 'HT Calls for More User-Friendly Smartphones', *Financial Times*, 16 February 2009, available at: http://www.ft.com/cms/s/0/bcea82c6-fc51-11dd-aed8-000077b07658.html (accessed 5 December 2009).

a customer-oriented positioning that communicated its strengths and tapped into the Zeitgeist of its target markets – tech-savvy trendy consumers interested in performance and design. From this, management devised the tagline 'HTC – Something Beautiful is Coming', combining anticipation with the design quality of its products.

Within a year of its near disastrous announcement, Chou announced the launch of the HTC Touch, its first mass-market smartphone. Small and stylish, the Touch featured a sensitive touchscreen interface that could be operated with one hand. Additionally, the user interface had been improved upon since earlier models, addressing the frustrating limitations of the Windows interface that made it difficult to answer a call while sending a text message, for example. With these issues ironed out, analysts believed HTC was on the verge of turning fortunes around if it could engage the market. Initial signs were promising, with T-Mobile in the United States agreeing to market it as part of its MDA series and the Orange network in Europe marketing the Touch under the HTC name. 'From the HTC Touch, you can clearly see our capability to differentiate ourselves', stated Chou in an interview around the time of the launch.[10]

Marketing HTC

By 2009 the company had a portfolio of 15 touchscreen smartphones, as well as five other type-pad and touchscreen devices. It had released a new phone every few months in the period since 2006, each time distancing itself from the niche of business devices. Over a decade of groundwork and preparation had positioned HTC as the star of a remarkable success story. Everything was in place to fulfil the brand identity to which HTC aspired.

Telling people about its products was the final and unfamiliar step, for which it adopted a double-pronged strategy. In addition to using established channels like PR and advertising, leveraging the Internet and viral marketing proved effective. Targeting younger consumers with ads featuring the phones being used in novel and highly contemporary situations in tandem with stylish product information videos helped to spread the word about the phones at a grassroots level quickly and cost effectively. Meanwhile, its sponsorship of the Columbia-HTC cycling team in the 2009 Tour de France ensured the message reached millions of viewers worldwide – with stage winners pointing to the HTC logo on their chests and miming a phone call as they crossed the finish line. Having won six stages in the race that year, the Columbia-HTC team was considered one of the best in the competition – a superb fit for a new brand entering the mass market.

However, the key to the strategy was its partnerships with networks. Vodafone, eager to eliminate the halo effect that its rival O2 had earned with its exclusive iPhone deal, provided HTC with an optimal partner for Europe. The deal guaranteed HTC a channel into the market, supported by marketing spend and a retail network that no money could buy. However, as HTC was consolidating its consumer-oriented position, the smartphone market was also expanding into the business device niche,

---

[10]Kathrin Hille, 'HTC Launches its First Mass-Market Phone', *Financial Times*, 6 June 2007, available at: http://www.ft.com/cms/s/2/ac37c500-13ba-11dc-9866-000b5df10621.html (accessed 5 December 2009).

with a proliferation of business applications being developed for the Apple iPhone and competitor devices following suit. What remained to be seen was whether HTC could sustain the engagement with the market and whether it could continue identifying emerging trends in the market for which it could build compelling new solutions.

QUESTIONS

1. What skills, resources, or competencies did HTC bring to the branded mobile phone market? If a board member, would you have supported HTC's initial move to sell branded phones? Why? Why not?
2. What is required of HTC in order to grow a significant position in the branded market? Would growth in this area damage the rest of its business?
3. What are the lessons for the many firms who have strong competencies as component suppliers but wish to enter a market under their own brand name? Consider this in a number of different industries such as food, televisions, gaming devices, and white goods.

BIBLIOGRAPHY

1. 'Smartphone Market Share Sees Rapid Worldwide Increase, Says Report', *Mobile Europe Online*, 24 March 2009, available at: http://www.mobileeurope.co.uk/news_wire/114697/Smartphone_market_share_sees_rapid_worldwide_increase%2C_says_report_.html (accessed 5 December 2009).
2. 'HTC Opens European Business', *Mobile Europe*, 14 December 2005, available at: http://www.mobileeurope.co.uk/news_analysis/111552/HTC_opens_European_business.html (accessed 5 December 2009).
3. 'European Telecom Operators to Sell HTC-Branded Handsets for a Change', *Unwired View Online*, 9 May 2008, available at: http://www.unwiredview.com/2008/05/09/european-telecom-operators-to-sell-htc-branded-handsets-for-a-change (accessed 5 December 2009).
4. 'HTC Brand Awareness Goes into Overdrive', *Cool Smartphone Online*, 24 April 2008, available at: http://www.coolsmartphone.com/news3992.html (accessed 5 Deember 2009).
5. Kathrin Hille, 'Taiwan's Top Companies Try to Break Brand Barrier', *Financial Times*, 20 August 2007, available at: http://www.ft.com/cms/s/0/d65e545e-4f45-11dc-b485-0000779fd2ac.html (accessed 5 December 2009).
6. Kathrin Hille, 'HTC Launches Its Mobile Brand in Europe', *Financial Times*, 16 June 2006, available at: http://www.ft.com/cms/s/2/0df4b372-fccc-11da-9599-0000779e2340.html (accessed 5 December 2009).

Case 4

CREATING A NEW BRAND FOR A NEW MARKET. TATA NANO – ESTIMATING THE TRUE COST OF THE CHEAPEST CAR IN THE WORLD

For Ratan Tata, 70-year-old chairman of the Tata Group, the unveiling of the Tata Nano in New Delhi in January 2009 was a landmark moment in his career.[1] Billed as the Indian people's car, the Nano was the cheapest production vehicle in the world, retailing at around 100 000 rupees (€1500) for the most basic model. Furthermore, it was the culmination of a four-year project, driven personally by Mr Tata, who claimed inspiration from seeing a traditional Indian family of four piled onto a motorcycle commuting through city traffic and believing such people had a right to greater comfort and safety at a price they could afford.[2]

With a population in excess of 1.2 billion, an economy growing at between 7 and 9% per annum, and an emerging middle class of some 200 million people, the market potential for an affordable small car was tremendous. Tata, a relative newcomer to the car industry, had confounded established opinion to deliver a vehicle laden with design innovation for half the price of its nearest rival, the Maruti 800. But the story of the Tata Nano was not all shiny paintwork and positive headlines. Serious questions about the impact of the Nano on the environment, Indian society, and government development policies were thrown up in the race to meet the backlog of pre-orders for the new car.

The Indian Car Market

Individual car ownership in India was rare. On average there was one car for every 143 people: a stark contrast with the United States and Japan, where the ratio was almost one car for every two people. But Indian car ownership was growing at a rate of about 10% in 2008. This was mainly attributable to the increasing prosperity of a vast swathe of aspiring middle-class consumers. While market penetration remained low, potential was high. A significant portion of India's estimated 50 million motorcycle and moped owners, many of whom used their vehicles to transport entire families over urban and rural routes, were expected to trade up to four wheels in the short term.

In 2007, about 7 million scooters and motorcycles were sold in India for prices between 30 000 and 70 000 rupees (€1000), not much less than a basic Nano. Expert opinion believed the Nano could expand the Indian car market by up to 65% given the shape of the income distribution curve for India and the low relative price of the Nano. But Tata was not alone in developing affordable small cars to meet the expected demand: Indian motorbike maker Bajaj Auto was also developing a 115 000 rupees car in conjunction with Renault and Nissan, the fuel efficiencies and carbon

---

[1]Randeep Ramesh, 'India Gears for Mass Motoring Revolution with £1260 Car', *The Guardian*, 11 January 2008, available at: http://www.guardian.co.uk/world/2008/jan/11/india.carbonemissions (accessed 5 December 2009).

[2]Randeep Ramesh, 'India Gears for Mass Motoring Revolution with £1260 Car', *The Guardian*, 11 January 2008, available at: http://www.guardian.co.uk/world/2008/jan/11/india.carbonemissions (accessed 5 December 2009).

dioxide emissions of which would beat the Nano's hands down. And other foreign-based car manufacturers were evaluating India as a base for affordable small car production also.

The Car

Physically, the Nano was a tiny jelly-bean-shaped vehicle that could seat five adults and perhaps a duffle bag. The car was designed and manufactured according to 'Gandhian principles' – deep frugality with a willingness to challenge conventional wisdom.[3] Items standard in western cars were stripped out, including air conditioning, power brakes, power steering, a radio, storage space, a second windscreen wiper and the passenger-side rear-view mirror. Yet the Nano was certified compliant with Indian safety regulations and furthermore offered fuel efficiency in excess of 20 kilometres to the litre (50 miles to the gallon approximately). The simplicity in design and the efficiency were attractive features because the car required less maintenance and less spending on petrol as a result. Additionally, carbon emissions were low; about 102 grams of carbon per kilometre travelled, which was a little over half the EU limit of 180 grams, a quality Tata emphasized in its public relations about the impact the Nano's revolutionary design would have on the car industry and the environment.

In total, the car featured 34 patent applications for design. The vehicle was oddly shaped to optimize internal capacity, making it 20% more spacious than the Maruti 800. The Nano had a high roof, its four wheels were positioned at the extreme corners of the car, the engine was located in the rear, and access to the storage space was by folding the rear seats forward. To save on weight and manufacturing costs, much of the Nano was made from pressed sheet steel and plastics, stitched together to save on industrial glue costs. Its 620 cc engine and several other parts were made from lighter and cheaper aluminium. But much of the true innovation in the development of the Nano was in the thinking behind it rather than in patents. Unlike the impenetrable 'black box model' design of modern western autos, featuring embedded computers and electronics, the Nano's beauty was its simplicity – a modular design that had more in common with the Model-T Ford than with its contemporaries.

This modular design was part of a deliberate strategy to deliver the 'people's car' to the market. Tata Motors' vision was that owners, mechanics, and entrepreneurs could participate in the Nano brand: owners could accessorize, mechanics could be sold tools and training to modify and even assemble the cars, and entrepreneurs could buy vehicle parts in bulk to set-up regional assembly lines. In this way, Tata was confident Nano sales would soon hit 1 million vehicles per year and secure the Tata Group's financial future.

The Company

While the car was designed with the market in mind, it also characterized the company that had made it. Tata was established in 1945 to build train locomotives but

[3] John Hagel and John Seely-Brown, 'Innovation on the Edge – Learning from Tata's Nano', *Business Week Online*, 27 February 2008, available at: http://www.businessweek.com/innovate/content/feb2008/id20080227_377233.htm (accessed 3 December 2009).

soon diversified into making buses, dump trucks, cement mixers, ambulances, and goods trucks. Its logo was ubiquitous and synonymous with Indian industry. Operating in a protected economy until the 1990s, Tata filed its first loss in 2000. Management was forced to refocus on costs and efficiencies on the back of an economic slump and new foreign-based competition entering the Indian market. Quickly, management teams began identifying areas for improvement, including processes and purchasing policies as well as revenue generators. In a bid to revitalize the corporate culture, this initiative trickled down to the shop floor, and the Japanese concept of *kaizen* or continuous improvement was introduced. It also secured contracts with Mercedes, Land Rover, and Jaguar for painting cars bound for the Indian market. The turnaround in profitability took three years, by which time Tata was producing two car models and had begun to sell internationally.

It was from the launch of the Tata Ace, a four-wheeled truck retailing for INR 235 000 (US$ 5100), in 2005 that critical marketing lessons were learned that would be applied in the case of the Nano four years later. The Ace was designed to fit the needs of the market – a sturdy, cheap truck with four wheels instead of three. A three-wheeled vehicle would have been cheaper, but market research indicated four wheels conferred status – a crucial value for Tata's target market: young male working men in rural India, eager to build a family and a future. The company sold 100 000 units in just 20 months. From this insight, Tata learned the value of understanding and meeting its target market's needs. Just like the Ace, the Nano was not merely a vehicle, but a portal to a new, improved, and upwardly mobile way of life for millions of Indians.

Government Developmental Policies

In one way the timing of the Nano's launch was problematic, and in another it was ideal. The initial fanfare around the announcement of the intention to create India's first people's car had turned sour very close to completion of the new INR 14 billion (US$ 300 million) assembly plant in West Bengal. At a very late stage in construction, Tata Motors pulled out of the project, opting to relocate manufacturing to a fresh site in Gujarat that would cost about INR 18 billion (US$ 390 million) to complete.

Thousands of farmers had been displaced to accommodate the new 1000 acre factory complex, and many were left in limbo as Tata's cancellation meant the loss of 10 000 jobs for the region, leaving local government to address the ensuing social unrest. The implication for the Nano project was that it fell behind schedule by 6 months. As a quick fix, production was shifted to an existing plant in northern India with a production capability of just 50 000 units per annum. Tata would no longer have the capacity to meet initial demand, but the company came up with an ingenious solution to resolve the problem. The first 100 000 cars would be allocated by lottery, with Tata accepting prebooking deposits worth 75% of the car's value, injecting a valuable INR 46.2 billion (US$ 1 billion) in cash into the business while it ramped up production.

On the other hand, the Nano arrived at a time of significant economic growth. Several years previously, the Indian government had announced a massive infrastructural development package worth almost INR 2310 billion (US$ 50 billion), allocated to extensive road building. The goal was to link by paved road every Indian village with a population of 1000 or more to the national road network by 2010. India's urban population amounted to about 290 million people, with some 45 million living in three cities alone – New Delhi, Mumbai, and Kolkata – but overall the subcontinent remained heavily rural. While Tata's marketing department touted the dream of Nanos driving from town to town, industry commentators were quick to point out that the Nano was designed for the city commute and was ill-equipped for longer often more dangerous rural journeys.

Environmental Issues

Following developments in the Tata Nano story from a western perspective was fraught with dangers, and the press was rife with accusations of eco-imperialism or double standards. One Australian newspaper, for example, had pointed out that, if market penetration were to approach US levels, it would double the total number of cars on the planet to 1.8 billion vehicles 'adding to global pollution'.[4] In fact, Tata's own production forecasts had been revised down significantly from 1 million vehicles per annum to 250 000. Furthermore, as was noted, the vehicle was designed for urban transport, meaning that, in spite of its fuel economy, most journeys would be quite short urban trips, perhaps replacing overloaded and underregulated motorcycles. Tata's own website claimed emissions for the Nano were below those of motorcycles and scooters, but India's carbon environmental and carbon emissions laws were lax compared with those of the EU. In spite of this prospect, many Indian cities were already severely congested and smog infested. The average traffic speed in New Delhi, for example, had fallen to 9 miles per hour by 2008, and air quality was a perpetual health hazard.

Conversely, the Nano symbolized a new era in mass-market private transportation, and it was the sheer scale of this that worried environmentalists. At the time of the Nano's launch, per capita carbon output in India was about 12% of the UK average,[5] but, as a country, India's consumption patterns were changing, with a growing middle class consuming more and more energy.[6] In a numbers game, the odds were stacked against the environment, as energy consumption levels in India were predicted to quadruple in response to economic and population growth over the long term to 2030, with the bulk of that energy being generated by fossil fuels instead of renewable sources. Against this forecast, Tata had made some gestures towards a more sustainable motorized future. Its partnership with a French firm to develop an engine that ran on compressed air as fuel (in competition for the US$ 10 million

---

[4]Brendan O'Neill, 'Nano and the Rise of Eco-imperialism', *The Guardian*, 24 March 2009, available at: http://www.guardian.co.uk/commentisfree/2009/mar/24/india-tata-peoples-car (accessed 3 December 2009).

[5]George Monbiot, 'Is the World's Cheapest Car on the Road to Ruin?', *The Guardian*, 23 March 2009, available at: http://www.guardian.co.uk/global/georgemonbiot/2009/mar/23/tata-nano-carbon-emissions-social-progress (accessed 3 December 2009).

[6]Brendan O'Neill, 'Nano and the Rise of Eco-imperialism', *The Guardian*, 24 March 2009, available at: http://www.guardian.co.uk/commentisfree/2009/mar/24/india-tata-peoples-car (accessed 3 December 2009).

Progressive Automotive X Prize) was considered a promising sign. The prize was to be awarded to the first company to build a mass-production vehicle that offered 42 kilometres per litre energy equivalence. Already, Nano's competitors Bajaj Auto had gained an edge, developing a 30 kilometre per litre petrol engine.

The True Cost

The world's cheapest car certainly carried with it more costs and benefits than its rock-bottom price tag indicated. At the heart of the issue, it was evident that the near-term environmental impact of an upwardly mobile Indian middle class would inevitably take its toll on the environment. Sheer numbers would prevail, and the sum total effect would be massive. The puzzle for stakeholders, however, was how to balance the needs and priorities of the community with the needs and priorities of the environment upon which it depended.

QUESTIONS

1. How would you explain the popularity of the Tata Nano? Why have other car companies not taken advantage of this opportunity?
2. How serious are the environmental concerns arising from the launch and sales of the Tata Nano? To whom are these of most concern? Are the environmental costs outweighed by the improvement in the quality of life of the Indian people who will buy it?
3. Why should other car companies be concerned by this development? How significant is the international market potential for the Nano?
4. How will this new initiative affect the Tata brand overall?

BIBLIOGRAPHY

1. 'The New People's Car', *The Economist* (print edition), 26 March 2009, available at: http://www.economist.com/businessfinance/displayStory.cfm?story_id=13381522&source=hptextfeature (accessed 5 December 2009).
2. 'Tata Nano May Expand Market by 65%: CRISIL', *Economic Times Online*, 12 January 2008, available at: http://economictimes.indiatimes.com/articleshow/2694186.cms (accessed 5 December 2009).
3. Rina Chandra, 'How Green is My Low-cost Car? India Revs Up Debate', *Reuters Online*, 18 June 2008, available at: http://www.reuters.com/article/businessNews/idUSBOM20393120080619?feedType=RSS&feedName=businessNews&rpc=23&sp=true (accessed 5 December 2009).
4. Robyn Meredith, 'The Next People's Car', *Forbes Online*, 16 April 2007, available at: http://www.forbes.com/forbes/2007/0416/070.html (accessed 5 December 2009).

5. Maura Judkis, '10 Things You Should Know about the Tata Nano', *US News Online*, 24 March 2009, available at: http://www.usnews.com/money/blogs/fresh-greens/ 2009/03/24/10-things-you-didnt-know-about-the-tata-nano.html (accessed 5 December 2009).
6. Andrew Buncombe, 'Environmental Concerns over Cheapest Car', *New Zealand Herald*, 12 January 2008, available at: http://www.nzherald.co.nz/business/news/article.cfm?c_id=3&objectid=10486377 (accessed 5 December 2009).

Case 5

TRANSFORMATIVE INNOVATION IN THE DEVELOPING WORLD

To many businesses, the billions of people living in the developing world represent a new frontier in strategic marketing. How can such businesses and their brands tap vast regional markets while meeting the needs of the people in those markets? To this end, established business models often offer only limited scope, because they rely on infrastructures, distribution networks, and income levels that may have no correlation to these new environments. Innovation in processes, technologies, applications, and thinking may be required to generate new business models that prosper and endure under such entirely new conditions. Furthermore, some developments are so profound that they may lead to innovation that is relevant to the rest of the world too – a sort of positive feedback loop. In this respect, there are multiple benefits from pursuing markets in the developing world.

Vodaphone M-Pesa – Mobile Banking in Kenya

Using mobile phones to transfer money electronically, M-PESA was a six-month pilot community project that quickly became a new banking service for millions of Kenyans. Launched in 2005 by Vodafone and its local partner Safaricom, initially it was designed to enable Safaricom customers to send cash safely and easily across large distances. M-PESA was functional effective branding: 'M' denoted mobile and 'PESA' was Swahili for 'money'. The process began with buying a code from a local approved Safaricom vendor. This code could then be sent by text message to a recipient for redemption of cash from another approved vendor in his/her vicinity. In this way, young men working in towns and cities, for example, could send money home to their families in remote villages. So clear were its benefits that very soon M-PESA was expanded to offer a wider range of financial services, including a system for the payment of school fees, with further innovation taking place in the way consumers began to use the service as a rainy-day savings mechanism as well. Soon other mobile phone companies and the international banking industry were taking note of how such a simple idea could transform the lives of the 'unbanked poor'. Within two years of launch, 7 million of Kenya's 18.3 million mobile phone owners were M-PESA customers.

The M-PESA system offered a number of advantages, allowing customers to deposit, transfer, and withdraw cash using their mobile phones and the Safaricom approved vendor network which included petrol stations and newsagent kiosks as well as Safaricom shops. It was a simple and secure service that did not require a banking licence, as no interest was charged on any transactions. In addition, upper limits of about €200 were set on each transaction to minimize the threat of money laundering. Furthermore, M-PESA offered an alternative traceable route for international remittances, which represented about 5% of Kenyan GDP, or just over €1 billion in 2008, much of which was carried into the country in hand luggage as people travelled home. But domestic circulation was also fuelling growth. Safaricom estimated that, by mid-2009, millions of transactions per month were taking place for values in the region of €5 and €15. One contemporaneous study mentioned in *The Economist* magazine in

2009 estimated that incomes of Kenyan households using M-PESA had increased by 5–30% since beginning to use the mobile banking system.

By 2009, Vodafone had launched versions of M-PESA in neighbouring Tanzania and Afghanistan, while in Uganda the local operator MTN was successfully test-marketing a similar system it hoped ultimately to launch across Africa. Mobile banking leapfrogged the barriers to a formal financial system, bypassing regulatory frameworks and typical market structures. M-PESA's success as a basic form of financial services was not met with universal acclaim, however, as many in the banking industry lobbied against the prospect of mobile phone companies entering their markets, citing security as a key issue if such systems became more widespread. But MTN's success in Uganda, in partnership with Standard Bank, demonstrated clearly the opportunities from cooperation made possible by thinking about money and markets in entirely new ways.

Learning to Learn – One Laptop Per Child Initiative

Nicholas Negroponte, professor of Media Arts and Sciences at MIT and cofounder of its highly progressive Media Laboratory, MediaLab, was a visionary with a mission. In 2004, observing how children in a remote Cambodian village learned and played with laptop computers he had provided them, he had an epiphany: What if every child in the world had access to a computer?[1] Some years later, when speaking publicly about his non-profit organization One Laptop Per Child, he would defend this bold intention, asking the audience to consider replacing the word 'laptop' with the word 'education' – did it still seem an imponderable he would then ask his listeners. Of course there would be many practical challenges to realizing his vision, perhaps chief among them being the design and manufacture of a functional laptop computer capable of withstanding a child's rigours and then bringing it to market at an affordable price. Furthermore, in believing that the widespread dissemination of computing power could help improve qualities of life around the world, Negroponte also faced challenges in swaying opinion and gaining buy-in from important stakeholders, especially the governments he hoped would become his customers.

The final production model, the XO1, was an impressive piece of engineering innovation, designed to fit precisely the needs of its users: children in all parts of the world. Four criteria were applied: children would own the laptops outright, and the laptops had to be rugged, require very little energy for use, and have wireless networking capability.[2] The laptops were distinctive, featuring a durable handle, a rotating screen that was visible even in direct sunlight, a reinforced plastic casing that was environmentally sealed for moisture protection, speakers, web-cam, a track pad that could be used for drawing and cursor pointing, and retractable aerials for Wi-Fi that also served to protect the laptop's USB ports. Additionally, the laptops contained no hard-drive, minimizing expensive parts that could be easily damaged. Instead, the computers ran on memory cards using specially designed open-source

[1]http://www.ted.com/talks/nicholas_negroponte_on_one_laptop_per_child_two_years_on.html (accessed 3 December 2009).

[2]www.olpc.org (accessed 3 December 2009).

software ensuring that new educational programs and games could be integrated seamlessly with existing systems. The computers and the materials were tested to western quality standards and were made to last at least five years. Rolling off the production line in 2007, Negroponte's XO1 was testament that cheap powerful computing was possible for a price tag of nearly €200 – unfortunately, nearly double the headline-grabbing price he had announced two years previously.

Negroponte was aiming for a €100 laptop that governments would buy in bulk, but that strategy faced significant challenges. Benefits in kind such as computers were considered more productive than offering governments cash, which could easily become misappropriated. There was, however, the trade-off issue whereby sums of €100–200 could also pay for a year's schooling for one student in some parts of the world, or even for much needed medicines in other parts, thus generating debate about the merits of investing in laptops. In response, OLPC's standard argument was that education had to work hand in hand with other development and relief efforts – children had the right to learn how to learn. In that respect, Negroponte was adamant computers were essential and that a non-profit business model was critical to his organization's success.

In addressing the renowned TED conference in 2007, he outlined his rationale: 'The clarity of purpose is there . . . I can see any head of state, any executive I want at any time, because I'm not selling laptops and . . . you can get the best people',[3] explaining that highly talented leaders and experts from the world of business were offering their services for free because they believed in OLPC's mission. As such, he was insistent that OLPC regarded children as its mission instead of a market. With a stated goal to produce 1 million laptops per month by 2009, Negroponte was aiming to produce 20% of the world's monthly laptop output. While this mission and Negroponte's attitude differentiated OLPC from the industry, his efforts had begun to attract attention from competitors eager to exploit the low-cost laptop market. Whether his mission would outpace their markets was a tantalizing question for the industry as the first commercial low-cost laptops launched onto the market in late 2009.

Merck – Making Life-Saving Drugs Accessible and Affordable

Extending back to 1958 with its Merck Medical Outreach Programme (MMOP), Merck, a leading global pharmaceutical manufacturer, had a long history of donating medicines and vaccines. But, with emerging markets in the developing world, it had adopted a different strategy. Preferring to minimize donations, Merck had opted instead for a more commercial approach featuring mechanisms like differential pricing, philanthropic policies, licensing, and resource-sharing. More recently, Merck's strategy had focused on middle-income countries in emerging markets including China, South Africa, India, and Brazil, requiring innovation in business models, practices, and corporate culture. Its goal for 2010 was to realize €1.4 billion in sales from emerging markets; by 2008 it had achieved €400 million, most of which came from

[3]http://www.ted.com/talks/nicholas_negroponte_on_one_laptop_per_child_two_years_on.html (accessed 3 December 2009).

one product, MECTIZAN, leaving analysts to ponder whether €1.4 billion was a realistic goal under the current strategy.[4]

In keeping with industry tradition, the company was firmly committed to the value of patents and copyrights as a source of competitive advantage. In December 2008, for example, Merck attracted media attention when it acted to enforce its rights by confiscating a shipment in the Netherlands of generic Losartan bound for Brazil – a country for which it did not have patent rights. Losartan was an active ingredient in COZAAR, a Merck antihypertension drug. The incident led Merck to reassess its policy on the role of generic medicines, announcing that it was committed to the role of generic medicines in the global healthcare system under certain conditions.[5]

In spite of this, the company had developed several critical factors that would help it achieve its €1.4 billion sales goal. First, Merck had a pedigree in researching 'neglected' tropical diseases prevalent in many developing countries. Second, it had implemented an initiative to reduce the time lag between launching a product in the developed and developing worlds. Historically, the delay was between 10 and 12 years, but Merck had virtually eliminated that gap with the almost simultaneous launch of the ROTATEQ® rotavirus vaccine in the United States and later in Nicaragua via a donation programme in 2006.[6] Third, it also began to disclose the company's product registration status for a range of products including its antiretroviral drugs used to treat HIV. Fourth, it was an active participant in several philanthropic initiatives and a founder of many others, including the Partnership for Disease Control Initiatives (PDCI), the Partnership for Quality Medical Donations (PQMD), and the GAVI Alliance – intended to improve access in the developing world and emerging markets. In tandem with this activity, Merck also worked with the World Health Organization to achieve prequalification for its products and increase the number of countries who purchased its products for their government access programmes.[7]

In respect of global pricing, Merck had adopted a tiered pricing strategy for its HIV medicines and had engaged in non-profit pricing for two vaccines: GARDASIL and ROTATEQ, believing that this would maximize access and ultimately prove sustainable for all stakeholders concerned. Meanwhile, licensing was used as a mechanism to extend market reach, granting royalty-free licences for antiretroviral drugs to generic manufacturers in South Africa, for example.

Nestlé – Creating Shared Value Through Business

In 2005, Nestlé issued the first in a series of biannual reports entitled 'Creating Shared Value'. The document featured a summary of the company's business activities according to principles of sustainability. Central to its definition of sustainability was the concept of generating value for all stakeholders in Nestlé: employees, shareholders,

[4]http://www.merck.com/corporate-responsibility/# (accessed 3 December 2009).

[5]http://www.merck.com/corporate-responsibility/# (accessed 3 December 2009).

[6]http://www.merck.com/corporate-responsibility/# (accessed 3 December 2009).

[7]http://www.merck.com/corporate-responsibility/# (accessed 3 December 2009).

suppliers, governments, and customers in the developed and developing worlds. After the introductory report, each subsequent document would focus on one of three strategic priorities deemed critical to Nestlé's long-term prosperity as part of the global food complex: nutrition, water, and rural development. Themed 'Nutrition', the 2007 report detailed, among other things, the Swiss giant's efforts to serve and support its customers in the developing world and to sustain its working relationships with its partners all along the food supply chain. Overall, its strategy could have been defined as one of corporate social responsibility blended with good business sense – emerging markets represented hundreds of millions of existing and potential customers, and Nestlé already sourced over two-thirds of its raw materials from such parts of the world. The innovative aspect of its strategy was in the implementation of a cohesive social plan: marketing products to fit local needs, fostering collaborative working relationships with suppliers, promoting learning, and improvements in the quality and traceability that benefited both Nestlé and its supply chain.

With its popularly positioned products (PPPs), Nestlé had assembled a range of products that could be packaged, priced, marketed, and distributed to fit the needs of customers in developing markets. Initiatives covered a variety of activities, including its Direct Store Delivery programme in Asia and Latin America, distributing products directly to small retailers with agents using motorcycles or small vans to access remoter rural locations. Similarly, Nestlé enhanced the nutrition content of products in the PPP range to address localized malnutrition issues like extra zinc in its Nido milk product, targeting Mexican children under 6 years of age, a third of whom suffered from anaemia.[8] Investment in research and development in using milk-based products as vehicles for enhanced nutrition totalled about 30 million Swiss francs annually.[9]

On the supply side of the equation, the company offered technical assistance, microfinance, and consultancy services to its farmer supply base, estimated at almost 600 000 individuals worldwide. In tandem with this, Nestlé had begun concentrating on optimizing its supply chain, upon which, it calculated, the livelihoods of 2.4 million people depended. Globally, many of its processing and production facilities were located near to agricultural suppliers, about half of them in the developing world, with Nestlé launching its social and environmental standards Supplier Code for all 165 000 suppliers. It had also invested in eliminating mycotoxins from grains and legumes in its supply chain, using a blend of farmer training and agronomics solutions that would directly benefit farmers receiving a higher price for toxin-free foods.

Supporting education as well as R&D into specific nutritional issues affecting low-income countries was key to many of Nestlé's advancements. Based in Lausanne, Switzerland, the Foundation for the Study of Problems of Nutrition in the World was established in 1966, marking the company's centenary. With activities taking place across more than 30 countries in Asia, Africa, and Latin America, programmes

[8] www.nestle.com Nestlé: Nutritional Needs and Quality Diets, Creating Shared Value Report 2008.

[9] www.nestle.com Nestlé: Nutritional Needs and Quality Diets, Creating Shared Value Report 2008.

addressed a diversity of subjects, from the best local food sources to treat malnutrition in Ugandan communities to supporting postgraduate studies in nutrition for local students in Senegal.

But it was the diffusion of Nestlé's Milk District Model as a means to promote the wealth, well-being, and quality standards in a milk-producing community that distinguished the company's developmental policies. Since its foundation, the Milk District Model had been deployed with measurable improvements in output and quality in markets as diverse as India and Pakistan, Colombia, Indonesia, and China. As a form of organizing high-quality milk production, the model featured district-level milk collection, technical advice and veterinary support, cash payment policies, and modern infrastructure for transporting, storing, weighing, and testing milk. In so doing, the Milk District Model benefited both supplier and buyer and epitomized the ethos of Nestlé's corporate social responsibility (CSV) strategy.

Selco – Solar-Powered Leds Paid for Using Microfinancing

Established in 1995 by 26-year-old engineering MIT postgraduate Harish Hande, the Solar Electric Lighting Company was slowly but surely revolutionizing rural Indian life. By 2009, it had only sold about 100 000 units to a market numbering 400 million, but Hande was unconcerned by this fact, or by SELCO's short history in profitability – breaking even in 2001 and falling in and out of the red in 2005–2007. Instead, he believed he was paving the way for other companies to follow: sustainable technologies marketed to poor people using affordable pricing structures, demonstrating that social ventures could be run successfully as commercial projects. As a social entrepreneur, Hande was selling a complicated product: need-based technology mixed with need-based financing.

After several years educating the market through personal sales calls the length and breadth of Gujarat and Karnataka states, in southern India, Hande gradually built up a successful business model incorporating custom design, installation and product training, microfinancing, customer service guaranteed within 24 hours, and twice-yearly check-ups. In 2009, with 170 staff in 25 service stations, he estimated that some 10% of turnover came from organizational buyers like hospitals and schools, but the primary target remained villages. Receiving a €1 million equity injection in that same year, he was planning to increase sales to an extra 200 000 homes by 2013.

To most customers living in the 'darkness' of rural India, where electricity supply was intermittent at best, the product benefits were clearly visible. Solar-powered electric lamps using long-life LED bulbs were far superior to burning toxic and expensive kerosene lamps that barely provided any light at all. Furthermore, well-lit villages allowed people to study, work, and play longer into the night, improving the general quality of life in the community. However, while economically more attractive in the long run, purchasing SELCO's products required a lump-sum upfront payment equivalent to a year's income that few villagers could afford. As such, his business model depended on gaining buy-in from local financial service providers to implement a microfinancing system. One byproduct of this relationship was that SELCO's own geographic expansion tended to follow the dispersion of sympathetic loan officers working in the region's banks.

Meanwhile, the company was facing its own challenges, too, as it sought to expand operations and consider its future. Early in its history, Hande had procured finance from a mixture of grants, loans, US venture capitalists, and investors. When the price of solar panels soared almost 50% in 2005, the investors began demanding staff lay-offs and other margin-saving measures to sustain their expected rates of return. It was an invaluable lesson for Hande, who, in the process of the deal, had only retained a 2.5% equity stake in his own company. Replacing profit-motivated investors with socially concerned backers gave him the latitude to steer SELCO back towards his vision of a social enterprise. Within two years he had returned the company to profitability, and by 2009, with an enhanced product range including water heaters and cooking stoves, Hande was evaluating SELCO's longer-term prospects. With no marketing budget, all money went in to after-sales services such as the biannual maintenance check-ups. Furthermore, SELCO's geographic expansion was still closely tied to the dispersion of banking loan officers in the region. Under these circumstances, Hande wondered if US$ 1.4 million was enough to reach his ambitious growth goal for 2013.

QUESTIONS

1. Evaluate each of these five initiatives for the benefits they offer to the recipients. Are they truly beneficial?
2. Explain your understanding of the benefits for each of the corporations involved.
3. Using the benefits you have identified, construct a presentation for shareholders, explaining why corporate resources were being invested in this way.
4. What lessons do these five examples have for those wishing to engage in similar initiatives?

BIBLIOGRAPHY

1. Rob Minto and Barney Jopson, 'Mobile Money Transfer Service Grows', *Financial Times*, 8 December 2008, available at: http://www.ft.com/cms/s/ 0/d8dfa00a-c557-11dd-b516-000077b07658.html (accessed 5 December 2009).
2. Ross Tieman, 'The Basics: Mobile Phone Operators Revolutionise Cash Transfers', *Financial Times*, 2 June 2008, available at: http://www.ft.com/cms/s/0/3c9fa2b4-2ece-11dd-ab55-000077b07658.html (accessed 5 December 2009).
3. 'The Power of Mobile Money', *The Economist* (print edition), 24 September 2009, available at: http://www.economist.com/opinion/displaystory.cfm?story_id= 14505519 (accessed 5 December 2009).
4. Amy Kazmin, 'Lighting the Way – Selco India', *Financial Times*, 20 March 2009, available at: http://www.ft.com/cms/s/0/cb0b871a-0f98-11de-a8ae-0000779fd2ac .html?nclick_check=1 (accessed 3 December 2009).

5. Amy Kazmin, 'A Bright Idea that Helped India's Poor', *Financial Times*, 25 February 2009, available at: http://www.ft.com/cms/s/0/be9c8a2c-02de-11de-b58b-000077b07658.html (accessed 3 December 2009).
6. Thomas Hazlett, 'Helping Young Minds Click', *Financial Times*, 29 November 2007, available at: http://www.ft.com/cms/s/0/fb56167c-9ead-11dc-b4e4-0000779fd2ac.html?nclick_check=1 (accessed 3 December 2009).
7. www.selco-india.com.
8. www.vodafone.com.
9. www.laptop.org.
10. www.ted.com.

APPENDIX

Planning Forms

A set of standard forms can be helpful in presenting strategy recommendations and supporting analyses. They can encourage a useful consistency of presentation over time and across businesses within an organization. They can also provide a checklist of areas to consider in strategy development and make communication easier. The following sample forms are intended to provide a point of departure in designing forms for a specific context. The external analysis in the example is drawn from the pet food industry. The forms are for illustration purposes only.

Planning forms need to be adapted to the context involved: the industry, the firm, and the planning context. They may well be different and shorter or longer given a particular context. Forms for use with other product types – an industrial product, for example – could be modified to include information such as current and potential applications or key existing or potential customers.

SECTION 1 – CUSTOMER ANALYSIS

A. Segments

Segments	Market (Billions US$)	Comments
Dog – dry	*7.1*	*Largest segment, segmented nutritional offerings, growing*
Dog – canned	*1.8*	*Made from real meat and byproducts, etc.*
Cat – dry	*3.1*	*Second largest segment, nutritional offerings, accelerating growth*
Cat – canned	*2.1*	*Made from real meat, high levels of flavour and textural variety, etc.*
Dog treats	*1.6*	*Del Monte dominates with Milk-Bone*
Pet Specialty (inc. Pet shops/Vet/Farm and Feed)	*5.6*	*Large players – Science Diet and Iams, uses vets and pet stores, about 70% dog food, mostly dry, growing at 5%*

B. Customer Motivations

Segment	Motivations
Dog – dry	*Nutrition, convenience, teeth cleaning, often better value than canned pet food*
Dog – canned	*For finicky dogs, taste and nutrition, variety*
Cat – dry	*Nutrition, convenience, complement to meal, teeth cleaning*
Cat – canned	*Taste, convenient sizes, easy to serve, for finicky cats, variety of textures and flavours*
Treats	*Complement to meal, reward, animal likes it, functional nutritional benefits (e.g. tartar control)*
Pet Specialty	*Health concern, scientific nutrition, perceived superior ingredients*

C. Unmet Needs

Information on pets
Further subneeds of segments (as defined by human nutrition, e.g., allergies)

SECTION 2 – COMPETITOR ANALYSIS

A. Competitor Identification

Most directly competitive: Nestlé Purina Petcare, Iams (P&G), Del Monte, Mars
Less directly competitive: Hill's Petfood (Colgate-Palmolive)

B. Strategic Groups

Strategic Group	Major Competitors	Dollar Share
(1) Mainstream brands from large consumer firms	*Nestlé Purina Petcare*	*33.8%*
	Mars	*11.7%*
	Del Monte	*10.3%*
	Iams (P&G)	*9.5%*
(2) High-end specialty brands	*Hill's (Colgate-Palmolive)*	*9.5%*
	Other	*9%*
(3) Private-label brands	*Other*	*9.7%*

Strategic Group	Characteristics/ Strategies	Strengths	Weaknesses
(1) Mainstream brands from large consumer firms	• *Mainstream products* • *Large portfolio of products* • *Wide range of price points to meet the needs of many* • *Sell to multiple channels* • *Heavy use of advertising* • *Emphasis on quality and variety*	• *Production scale economies* • *Huge presence in supermarkets and mass merchandisers where approx. 70% of industry volume is sold* • *Deep global financial resources and experience* • *Commitment to industry*	• *High-fixed cost commitment to capacity increases competitive pressure on all players to defend share through promotions, etc.* • *Perception as less nutritious than specialty brands* • *Private label share at Wal-Mart and elsewhere is increasing*
(2) High-end specialty pet food brands	• *Narrowly focused, super premium-priced product lines* • *High presence in non-supermarket channels, such as veterinary offices, pet breeders, and specialty stores*	• *Product line focus on health, natural ingredients, and nutrition, resulting in strong consumer demand; high-margin business* • *First-in advantage to high-end specialty segment, resulting in a perceptual edge that mainstream brands find difficult to overcome* • *Sell through alternative channels, which are growing faster and are less competitive and offer limited access to other brands, a barrier to entry*	• *Higher ingredient and production costs* • *Lack economies of scale* • *Ultra premium price points limit appeal*

Strategic Group	Characteristics/ Strategies	Strengths	Weaknesses
(3) Private-label pet foods	• *Sell through multiple supermarkets and mass merchandizers under house brand designation*	• *High volume and low unit costs* • *Profit margins are attractive to retailers* • *Power of Wal-Mart as number one retailer* • *Good-quality offerings with high perceived consumer value*	• *Little brand differentiation* • *Weak brand equity*

C. *Major Competitors*

Competitor	Characteristics/ Strategies	Strengths	Weaknesses
Nestlé Purina Petcare	• *Overall market leader, product line is broad and deep* • *Increasing more toward 'premiumization' with niche product lines and upgrade of products to premium status* • *Large, powerful brand names with high consumer loyalty* • *Heavy emphasis on innovative first-to-market new products* • *Massive advertising and promotional spending to grow share* • *High commitment to category* • *Deep financial resources* • *Company takes long-term view on brand-building efforts; high level of commitment to brands* • *Global commitment to building brands*	• *Economies of scale, low costs* • *Supply-chain efficiencies* • *Strong retailer relationships* • *Global expertise and R&D support*	• *Weak presence in specialty segment* • *Need to support multiple brands across multiple categories with finite resources*

Competitor	Characteristics/ Strategies	Strengths	Weaknesses
Del Monte	• *Emphasis on cat food and dog treats, but competes in all segments of market* • *Low-cost producer strategy* • *Migrating to a more consumer-centric model with recent acquisitions*	• *Focused on few brands and categories* • *Acquired strong brands in Milk Bone and Meow Mix*	• *Relatively weak in brand building* • *Milking strong brands, such as 9-Lives* • *Lack of product innovation in cat and dog food*
Mars	• *Leadership position outside the USA* • *Commitment to building brands* • *Upgrading supermarket brands for premium appeal*	• *Dog food expertise* • *Economies of scale, low costs with acquisition of the private-label supplier Doane* • *Deep financial resources* • *Private firm gives freedom from short-term pressures*	• *Lack of cat food expertise and market share in US*
Hill's Petfood	• *Leader in specialty and vet markets* • *Entry barriers in vet business for Science Diet brand*	• *Leading recipient of veterinary recommendation* • *Best niche-market product positioning in the industry*	• *No presence in supermarkets, where 35% of industry volume is sold*
Iams (P&G)	• *Traditionally a specialty market brand, with emphasis on specialty-store sales and referrals from pet breeders* • *Moved to grocery and mass merchandize channel, which stimulated growth*	• *Deep financial recourses* • *Strong brand equity*	• *Economies of scale* • *Limited market penetration* • *Limited portfolio variety*

D. Competitor Strength Grid

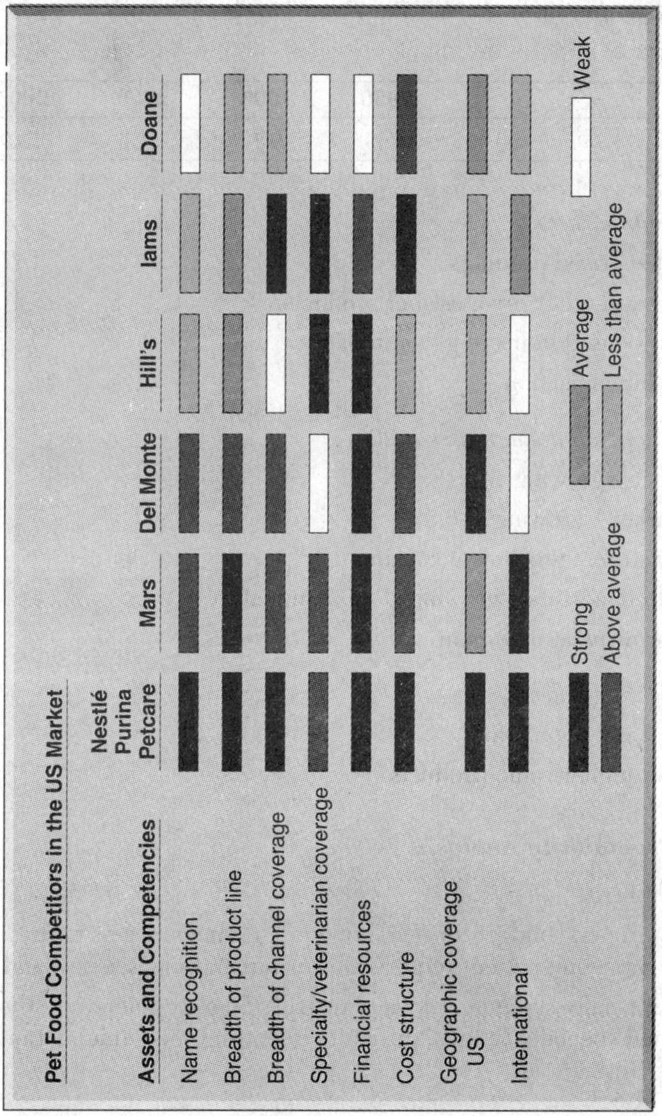

SECTION 3. MARKET ANALYSIS

A. Market Identification: the US Pet Food Market

B. Market Size

	1990	1995	2000	2005	2008
US industry sales ($ in billions)	*7.7*	*9.1*	*11.1*	*13.9*	*16.1*

Emerging Submarkets

- Special diet-based products
- Wal-Mart and other private-label products
- Wellness-focused items (e.g. Naturals)
- Product 'humanization'

Market Growth (in dollars, versus 2007)

- Overall pet – growing at 9.1%
- Supermarket – growing at 6.8%
- Specialty store – growing at 6% annually
- Mass merchandizers – growing at 14% annually
- Drug – growing at 9 percent

Factors Affecting Sales Levels

- Growth of pet population
- Growth of higher-value products

C. Market Profitability Analysis

Barriers to Entry

- Brand awareness, budget for marketing programmes, access to distribution channels, large investment required for manufacturing, science, and technology
- For pet specialty segment – loyalty to Hill's Science Diet and other entrenched specialty brands; difficulty in getting recommendations of vets and other influentials

Potential Entrants

- Other marketing giants, such as Unilever, might enter this industry if they feel it is attractive. However, the probability of new entrants is quite low because the pet food industry is already very competitive, with lots of incumbents, and the barriers to entry are high

Threats of Substitutes

- Human food leftovers
- Food cooked especially for pets

Bargaining Power of Suppliers

- Growing; raw materials shared with human food markets; consolidation of suppliers; quality of raw ingredients requirements growing

Bargaining Power of Customers

- Grocery stores, warehouse clubs have strong bargaining power over pet food suppliers
- Specialty stores, veterinarians might have moderate bargaining power
- Mass merchandizers (especially Wal-Mart, with around 24% of the volume in this category) have very strong bargaining power

D. Cost Structure

- Diversified firms have lower cost because of economies in advertising, manufacturing, promotion, and distribution
- Specialized firms have higher costs.

E. Distribution System

Major Channels

- Supermarkets are dominant in terms of quantity they deal with (35%)
- Mass merchandizers handle about 29% of the market and are growing
- Pet foods are effective traffic builders in supermarkets and mass merchandizers
- Farm-supply stores are generally located in suburbs
- Pet stores handle most premium brands and many 'mainstream' national brands
- Veterinarians handle only superpremium brands.

Observations/Major Trends

- Vets' sales are flat and have very high margins both for producers and for themselves
- Specialty stores' sales are growing at approximately 6%
- These two channels have captured high-involvement customers' needs to feed their pets healthier foods
- Warehouses have gained footholds in market-leader brands
- Innovations in packaging are begging to address unmet needs around convenience
- Product innovations are creating subcategories.

F. Market Trends and Developments

- Premium and superpremium brands have grown, and most producers are introducing new products in this area
- Large manufacturers are introducing new products continually

G. Key Success Factors

Present

- Brand recognition
- Product quality
- Access to major channels
- Gain market share in premium brands
- Introduction of new products
- Breadth of product line
- Marketing programme
- Cost reduction
- Awareness or recommendation by specialists
- Packaging
- Capitalizing on relevant human trends (naturals; shift to healthier, higher-quality ingredients)

Future

- Continue to capture the trends of consumers
- Packaging
- Follow the trends of distributors

SECTION 4. ENVIRONMENTAL ANALYSIS

A. Trends and Potential Events

Source	Description	Strategic Implication	Timeframe	Importance
Technological	*New product forms*	*Limited*		*Low*
Regulatory	*Impose standards of content*	*Limited*		*Low*
Economic	*Insensitive to economic changes*	*Very limited*		*Low*
Cultural	*Think of pets as members of families*	*Growth of superpremium brands*	*Since the mid-1980s*	*High*
	Demand for new, healthy products	*Introduction of healthy products*		
	Users' needs have diversified	*Multiple specialized segments*		
Demographic	*Household formation is slowing* *The number of cats is increasing more than dogs* *The baby boomer is ageing*	*Continued innovation of product and communications to keep brands relevant*	*Since the 1980s*	*Med–High*
Threats	*High dependence on animal proteins*	*Risk of animal-borne diseases (BSE) could severely impact on ingredient*	*Current*	*Med*
Opportunities	*Growing market for premium brands* *Expanding market for private labels*	*There is still room for growth in specialized segments*	*Since the mid-1980s*	*High*

B. Scenario Analysis

The two most likely are:

1. Little growth in specialty-store and superpremium segments.
2. High growth in both specialty-store and superpremium segments.

C. Key Strategic Uncertainties

- Will growth in demand for superpremium specialty products continue?
- What new subcategories will emerge as significant markets?

SECTION 5. INTERNAL ANALYSIS

A. *Performance Analysis*

Objective Area	Objective	Status and Comment
1. *Sales*		
2. *Profits*		
3. *Quality/service*		
4. *Cost*		
5. *New products*		
6. *Customer satisfaction*		
7. *People*		
8. *Other*		

B. *Summary of Past Strategy*

Problem	Possible Action

C. *Strategic Problems*

Problem	Possible Action

D. *Characteristics of Internal Organization*

Component*	Description – Fit with Current/Proposed Strategy

* Structure, systems, culture, and people.

E. *Portfolio Analysis*

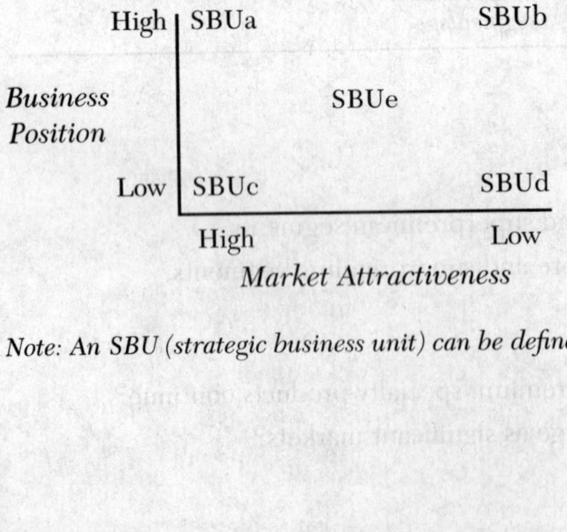

Note: An SBU (strategic business unit) can be defined by product or by segment

F. Analysis of Strengths and Weaknesses

Reference Strategic Group	Competencies/Competency Deficiencies, Assets/Liabilities, Strengths/Weaknesses with Respect to Strategic Groups

G. Financial Projections Based on Existing Strategy

	Past	*Present*	*Projected*
Operating Statement			
Market share			
Sales			
Cost of goods sold			
Gross margin			
R&D			
Selling/advertising			
Product G&A			
Div. and corp. G&A			
Operating profit			
Balance Sheet			
Cash/AR/inventory			
AP			
Net current assets			
Fixed assets at cost			
Accumulated depreciation			
Net fixed assets			
Total assets – book value			
Estimated market value of assets			
ROA (base – book value)			
ROA (base – market value)			
Uses of Funds			
Net current assets			
Fixed assets			
Operating profit			
Depreciation			
Other			
Resources Required			
....			
....			
....			
....			

Note: Resources required could be workers with particular skills or backgrounds, or certain physical facilities. A negative use of funds (i.e. profit) is a source of funds. Projected numbers could be for several relevant years.

SECTION 6. SUMMARY OF PROPOSED STRATEGY

A. Business Scope – Product Market Served

B. Strategy Description

		Product Market
• Investment Objective		
Withdraw	☐	
Milk	☐	
Maintain	☐	
Grow in market share	☐	
Market expansion	☐	
Product expansion	☐	
Vertical integration	☐	
• Value Proposition		Product Market
Quality	☐	
Value	☐	
Focus	☐	
Innovation	☐	
Global	☐	
Other	☐	
• Assets and Competencies Providing SCAs		
• Functional Strategies		

C. Key Strategy Initiatives

D. Financial Projections Based on Proposed Strategy

	Past	Present	Projected
Operating Statement			
Market share			
Sales			
Cost of goods sold			
Gross margin			
R&D			
Selling/advertising			
Product G&A			
Div. and corp. G&A			
Operating profit			
Balance Sheet			
Cash/AR/inventory			
AP			
Net current assets			
Fixed assets at cost			
Accumulated depreciation			
Net fixed assets			
Total assets – book value			
Estimated market value of assets			
ROA (base – book value)			
ROA (base – market value)			
Uses of Funds			
Net current assets			
Fixed assets			
Operating profit			
Depreciation			
Other			
Resources Required			
....			
....			
....			
....			

INDEX